The Cure
for Useless Dog Syndrome

Activities/Games/Learning
for Every Dog, Every Owner, Every Day

by
Ray & Emma Lincoln
Awesome Dog Professional Training

The Cure for Useless Dog Syndrome: Activities/Games and Learning for Every Dog, Every Owner, Every Day

By Ray & Emma Lincoln

Copyright 2009 by Ray & Emma Lincoln

Published by:
Awesome Book Publishing
P.O. Box 1157
Roseland, FL 32957

First Edition

Cover Photos & Interior Photos: Emma Lincoln; Ray Lincoln

ISBN: 978-0-9840538-2-7

Library of Congress Control Number: 2009911354

This book is lovingly dedicated to our Akita Casey,
our wise samurai.
You always were, and always will be, the best of us…

And to gentle little Coco, the Chow,
so that you'll always be remembered…

Table of Contents

Ch. 4- Mental Games & Activities (pg. 44)

"Working with your dog's intelligence improves his behavior, while neglecting it can cause serious problems."

Ch. 5- Indoor Games & Activities (pg. 64)

"There *are* alternatives- it doesn't have to be a "dirty little secret" if you can't exercise your dog outside in bad weather"

Ch. 6- Balance & Coordination Activities (pg. 87)

"Teach your dog these physical skills for control of his body and freedom from injury."

Ch. 7- Multi-Dog Games & Activities: (pg. 104)

"Lead your pack with positive activities and the inmates won't 'run the asylum'".

Ch. 8- Problem Dog Games (pg. 120)

"Specific positive activities can help solve emotional and behavioral problems."

Ch. 9- Therapeutic & Senior Dog Activities (pg. 137)

"Physical or emotional challenges no longer have to limit quality of life for dogs."

Ch. 10- Activities for High-Energy Dogs (pg. 170)
"Finding the right activity for high-energy dogs makes life a joy for owners with diverse needs."

Ch. 11- Water Activities (pg. 204)
"Water activities are diverse enough to help, and to entertain, almost any dog and owner."

Ch. 12- Useful Activities: (pg. 216)

"It's easy and vitally important to make your dog feel useful, because helping you was what he was bred for!"

Ch. 13- Family Activities: (pg. 255)

"Don't give up the American Dream of fun with your family dog."

Ch. 14- Activities for Owners with Limited Mobility (pg. 284)

"No matter your physical condition, simple changes can help you and your dog live and play together in harmony and joy!"

Ch. 15- Dangerous Games You Should Never Play (pg. 317) With Your Dog!

Ch. 1 -Introduction- No More Useless Dogs!

Is your dog a "useless dog"? Does he often interfere with your family's daily life so that you feel confused about what to do with him hour by hour and day by day? Has dealing with him become more of a chore than the pleasure you imagined it to be? Just like connecting with a dog positively can deepen your family's joy, never finding that connection can create a deep sense of emptiness and a constant feeling of something wrong in your home.

Or maybe you've just bought a new puppy. You want to do wonderful things with him and develop his best potential. Yet your family has run out of practical ideas for playing with him, training him, teaching him about the world and spending time with him. You quickly realize that "old standby" activities like throwing a ball do little to shape your dog's character, provide him a well-rounded purpose in life or engage your family to make them want to spend time with him. And environmental limitations like living in cities and suburbs, busier schedules and extremes of weather can make activities our grandparents might have enjoyed with dogs uncomfortable or impossible. But unfortunately, no one seems to have come up with alternatives.

We coined the term Useless Dog Syndrome to describe a modern malady that's common in suburban settings. A family falls in love with a certain breed of dog and they bring home a puppy, intending to provide him an extraordinary life. But, unfortunately, in a modern setting, they will never be able to provide the dog challenging work like he was originally bred to do. Instead, no matter how much the family may love their dog, it becomes

> Useless Dog Syndrome is a malady that affects many of our pet dogs today. The syndrome is a side effect of today's technological world, where almost all the jobs that used to be performed by working dogs are now completed by other means.
>
> This can leave a dog that was bred to do a demanding job with nothing to do in life other than to wait for his owners to return home.
>
> In time, this can lead to frustration and problem behaviors- because every living being needs to feel it's useful and has a reason to live.

a struggle to find anything for them to tell him to do rather than just lie around and be spoiled. Modern dog owners may also find they don't know how to communicate with their dog or to motivate him to work with them, play with them or take an interest in activities. Your dog looks up at you with bright inquiring eyes and, other than petting him, you have no idea what to do next. You sense that there should be something more to life.

Dogs react differently when they are not given enough to do. Some will simply act lackluster, never living up to their full potential and the owner may sense something is wrong and feel guilty for not doing enough or understanding enough. Meanwhile life with the dog just never seems to fulfill the family's high hopes. In other homes, dogs and puppies that are fundamentally bored will act out so severely that the family is forced to acknowledge something wrong.

For all those owners who feel frustrated and worried that there's no right way to live with their dogs, no matter how much they love their dogs, we urge you to once again imagine life with your dog as it should be! This in-depth book, unlike many "lightweight" game, trick or training books, details hundreds of activities designed to develop your dog's mind, his senses, his health, his athleticism and his behavior. Many of the activities are meant to take place indoors to work in cities and times when the weather interferes with outdoor activity. Other activities are designed to appeal specifically to children, seniors or dog owners with physical limitations. When owners are able to act proactively, and participate in activity with their dog, they can often channel his energy completely into the positive and this prevents behavior problems from ever beginning. It's even better if you can start positive activities with your dog from as early as eight weeks, to shape his future character and reactions to situations.

Extremely serious canine behavior problems like aggression or certain fears may have a medical or genetic cause, and require professional assessment and treatment. But most of the more common behavior problems are just symptoms of a deep sense of boredom- another manifestation of "Useless Dog Syndrome". This includes dogs that destroy owners' possessions, jump on all their guests or destroy their reputation by lunging at neighborhood dogs whenever the owner attempts a leashed walk.

As specialists in canine psychology and training, we're frequently called to customers' homes to treat dogs that literally bounce off walls. The dog may yank their owner down the street, relieve itself inside, destroy furniture and possessions and may even consume dangerous household items requiring surgery. And the costs of these behaviors easily run into the thousands.

Ironically and sadly, the owners likely bought or adopted the dog with high hopes. They probably imagined quiet times bonding and cuddling together with the dog or Saturday afternoons with their children and new dog happily playing together in the park. But when they are faced with unexpected problem behaviors, owners may experience helplessness and confusion. And this can lead to a vicious cycle. Because the owner feels they don't have adequate control of their dog, they start taking him out of the house even less. Then the dog or puppy misses out on critical exercise and socialization and the behavior problems worsen.

But what if you could solve 90% of your dog's problems by giving the dog something to do? Your reasons for welcoming a dog into your family would be vindicated if the activities were convenient, fun and varied enough to fit your lifestyle. And bringing dogs and owners together like this is the reason we wrote this book! The name of our business is Awesome Dog, and we define an awesome dog as, "a dog that carries himself with grace and pride that everyone can see". We believe that, just like each human needs a unique career and hobbies to bring him his personal fulfillment, each individual dog finds "inspiration" in slightly different activities.

In this book we introduce hundreds of easy and enjoyable games, activities and learning exercises that show you how to make the most of time with your dog. We offer alternatives for different breeds, different energy levels and stages in life from puppy to seniors, with enough variations for thousands of activities depending on the needs of your family and your dog. Rather than endless variations on impractical parlor tricks and strenuous "old standbys" that dog professionals so frequently suggest, we detail innovative alternatives that work for owners with limited space, time and physical fitness. As your fitness and your dog's fitness increases, the book also offers detailed suggestions for outdoor adventures and games and activities.

Not only will these activities exercise your dog's body, but some are designed to stimulate his mind, and even increase his intelligence. And many of the physical and mental activities we suggest lay the groundwork for balanced behavior in real-life situations. Just like the right games can make a child more alert clever and self-confident, the right activities can do the same for a dog. And the "games" we suggest are not meant for just an afternoon of fun in the park. Instead, you will be able to fill your dog's life with varied activities and stimuli for all the hours of all the days and all the environments in your life.

Dogs are an incredible source of joy and, for most of us in these modern times, they provide our only real link to the grandeur of nature. We believe that every family, not just the lucky few, should deeply enjoy the time they spend with their dog. And we believe that dogs also deserve the best in life, so that they can experience fulfillment to their highest potential. While it's instinctive for owners to feel awed by the beauty and grace when they witness show dogs in action, many have never experienced their own dog at his best. When you do see your dogs' true potential, you'll likely feel awed and, by writing this book, we hope to provide more owners this opportunity. Even if you start making changes when your dog is ten years old, you and he will quickly adjust to the new, more exciting and harmonious life together and you'll begin experiencing benefits right away.

Most owners hate to chase their dogs around the house constantly reprimanding, and this type of correction doesn't really work. A multi-faceted solution that introduces new ways to spend time with your dog feels easier and more natural than corrections or traditional military-style "training", and it best addresses the multi-level deficiency that exists in many households. When dogs and owners don't spend quality time or bond and function together well, the ailment feels almost spiritual. The owners sense that their families and their dogs should be interacting on a more satisfying level, but their best attempts to play with their dogs may only aggravate problem behaviors.

We wrote this book to give owners the answer they most crave. It feels frustrating when the majority of dog trainers and dog books repeatedly tell you what *not* to do with your dog, but never what *to* do. It's equally frustrating when a veterinarian's office suggestions are physically taxing and unrealistic for owners with limited time & energy. In contrast, *The Cure for Useless Dog Syndrome* gives you real solutions for what *to* do and the suggestions are made to fit *your* life and *your* dog.

Start with our suggestions for exercising your dog's mind and you'll be rewarded by a happier and more alert companion well into his senior years. Next try some of our safe and novel suggestions for exercising with your dog. Sharing the pleasure of moving together, you'll immediately feel stress melt away while keeping your dog in top shape for years of healthy bonding in future!

Use this book whenever you need it for the life of your dog as: a reference, a planner, a detailed step-by-step kitchen-counter resource for training dogs each activity, a rainy-day fun book for the kids, a conversation starter for friends, relatives, neighbors and office-mates, a manual for every season of your dog's life and a new source of inspiration for each dog you own.

How to Use This Book:

Read "*The Cure*" one game at a time and keep it handy for everyone in your family to use every day. Some sections including "New Learning Every Day" puppy and senior versions contain very many individual suggestions. **So you may wish to tab, flag or highlight your favorite sections and make notes. Then share those activities you enjoyed most with family, coworkers and your dog sitter or dog walker.**

Another way to use the book is to flip immediately to the section for your dog's life stage or his particular challenges. Or start with a warm-hearted laugh by first reading Chapter 2- *Games Dogs Play on Their Owners*. Every owner should also read *Ch. 15 Dangerous Games You Should Never Play with Your Dog* to make sure you're not choosing activities that create discomfort or bad behavior. The chapter offers healthy alternatives to popular misconceptions to improve your dog's behavior and your overall quality of life.

To read this book for your dog's life stages, new puppy owners can start with *Puppy Games and Activities*. Complementary chapters include *Mental Games and Activities* to build your puppy's mind (IQ increases with stimulation, and exposure to novel experiences and perceptions) and *Balance and Coordination Games & Activities,* which will build his body and his reflexes.

You can flip directly to *Multi-Dog Activities* if managing several dogs is your main concern. Or if you bought the book because of a problem dog, you can consult the *Problem Dog Activities* chapter first. Then follow up with *Therapeutic and Senior Dog Activities* if some of your dog's problems are emotional (for example, separation anxiety or storm fears.)

If your dog is a highly active breed, and you suspect physical boredom and frustration may be causing him to commit crimes around the house, try some of the *Activities for High-Energy Dogs.*

If your dog exists on the other end of the exercise spectrum- elderly, overweight or suffering physical problems that prohibit strenuous exercise, you can start with *Therapeutic and Senior Activities*. Many of the *Indoor Games and Activities* also work well for dogs with limited physical abilities.

Or perhaps you are the one who has limitations on performing strenuous physical exercise. If you're a senior, disabled or just out of shape, read some of the *Therapeutic and Senior Activities* and *Activities for Owners with Limited Mobility* that will keep you comfortable.

We're committed to helping dog lovers work around physical challenges to experience the highest quality of life while bonding with their dogs. You may not have thought of turning to your dog for help in many of the ways introduced in the *Useful Dog Activities* chapter. But give your dog the chance to help you and you may learn that he is courageous and generous and you will truly see him in a different light.

Yet another way to explore this book is by cross-referencing. At the beginning of each chapter there's a list of games from different chapters that also work with the particular life-stage, problem or situation. For example, a game listed as an indoor game can also be used for the whole family or a mental game can also be used for puppies or for problem dogs. You'll find over two-hundred and thirty individual activities detailed in the chapters. When you apply them as suggested in the cross-referencing, you and your dog will enjoy hundreds more variations.

Another obstacle that concerns many dog owners is weather- extreme summer sun and heat or winter snow and cold. Other dog owners live in apartments or condos with no yard or space to exercise their dogs. Unfortunately, many popular books on dog activities don't even mention bad weather and this concerns us. As specialists in home training, we often have to help customers that have made themselves and their dogs violently ill in the Florida heat trying to follow the exercise mandates of popular television dog trainers!

There are many days here in South Florida when even minutes of vigorous activity in the searing sun, extreme heat and choking humidity could easily put a person in the hospital. So, how about your poor dog? Rather than assuming dog owners are lazy, we offer creative alternatives for owners and their beloved dogs to exercise in cool air conditioning (or beside the comfy fireside). You can find these activities described in the *Indoor Games & Activities* chapter, the *Activities for Owners with Limited Mobility* chapter and throughout the book.

When the weather's fine and you want to enjoy the outdoors the *Water Activities* we describe can add a new dimension to your dog's life. So can many of the suggestions in *Activities for High-Energy Dogs*. They range from some that are adventurous; but most are simple and comfortable enough for the typical family. If you have kids, you may want to read *Family Activities* first, especially if you'd like to get your kids more interested in, and involved with, your dog.

You'll find veterinary cautions throughout the book where applicable and additional information in the Resources section on all activities and products mentioned.

Yet another way to explore this book is by cross-referencing. At the end of each chapter there's a list of games from different chapters that also work with the particular life-stage, problem or situation. For example, a game listed as an indoor game can also be used for the whole family or a mental game can also be used for puppies or for problem dogs. You'll find over two-hundred and thirty individual activities detailed in the chapters. When you apply them as suggested in the cross-referencing, you and your dog will enjoy hundreds more variations

.The Cure is a detailed adult book which addresses serious topics and warnings along with all the activities, so parents may wonder why we recommend it for interested children of all ages. The answer is that, when it comes to animals, children have great potential and they're capable of surprising maturity. Independently, both authors grew up training our German Shepherds and Shepherd mixes at grade school age, and both of us started researching veterinary medicine at that age as well. These days you'll observe expert junior handlers competing with their dogs at the most prestigious dog shows, showing the kind of passion that many adults may have forgotten.

We hope you'll make this book available to your kids no matter how young they are, and let them suggest activities they'd like to try. As long as no specific cautions are mentioned, many activities in the book are designed so your kids and dogs can practice together. Encourage the children to use the book as a jumping-off point for their own imaginations and your dog's particular talents and then let your kids and your dogs inspire you. We believe as long as we're kind to our dogs, the sky's the limit in how we can bring out their best potential- and how they can bring out ours!

Ch. 2- Games Dogs Play on Their Owners

Does Your Dog Play Games on You?

Catch Me If You Can

Try and Find Me

Find the Movement

Herding the Kids

Buried Treasure

Playmate

You're Killing Me!

See How High I Can Reach

Your Food's Better Than Mine

I'll Only Eat If

I Bark, You Bark, We All Bark

Make Mommy & Daddy Yell at Each Other

Entertaining Guests

Love for Sale

Does Your Dog Play Games on You?

As you read this chapter ask yourself if your dog attempts any of the behaviors in your home. Cute as some of these "games" may seem, they are all examples of dogs without adequate leadership trying to take control and/ or alleviate boredom. Rather than blaming your dog, try to view him as an intelligent animal that desperately craves something productive to do with his time. And then take control and channel his energy into positive activities with the hundreds of suggestions throughout this book.

We've drawn on our canine psychology and home training experience to compile the "games" in this chapter. Dogs play some of these "games" instinctually, and they learn to play others because the behaviors get them what they want from their owners. If the owner fails to recognize the intentional manipulation the first time, the dog may repeat the action more frequently. And then, whether you realize it or not, your clever dog has done a beautiful job of training you.

Rather than feeling bad, you can interpret this positively as evidence that you and your dog already communicate well. All you need do now is to channel this communication into positive activities and soon the bad games will be no more than memories and amusing stories to tell at parties!

Games Dogs Play on Their Owners:

Play Fun Games with your dog or he may play games on you to relieve his boredom. Here are just a few games bored dogs find fun to play on families. But the mischievous ways of dogs are endless!

Catch Me If You Can

Most of us have had our dogs play this game on us at one time or another. You call your dog to come in from the backyard and he stubbornly refuses, or you take your dog out for a walk and he slips his collar. Of course the most likely time for your dog to choose to play the game of "Catch Me if You Can" is when the weather's bad and you need to leave for work in the morning to make an important meeting. Instead of returning to you as you call for him with mounting frustration, your dog stands fifteen or twenty feet away, just looking at you. This is a dog that just wants to have a little "innocent" fun to spice up his day before you go to work, leaving him to a day of boredom. And most owners willingly take part in this game by trying to rush over and grab the dog. The dog then responds by jogging away a few steps, panting and seemingly "laughing", while staying just far away that you can't catch him. He'll then sit down and wait for you to get close again. Just as you think you have him, he's back on the run!

At about this time most owners get mad at their dog, raise their voice and start screaming, "Get over here right now!" Now your dog may look at you like you've scared him half to death and he may approach you gingerly. You grab for him again but at the very last second he dodges. Your dog repeats this process several times more.

And then, just when you're ready to give up, the dog surprises you by returning to the front door of your house to beg to be let in. As you follow behind him, out of breath, he may look back at you as if to say that it was his idea to come inside in the first place and he wonders what's taking you so long. As you plop down inside your house, too tired to even think of leaving for work right now, your dog may come to rest his head on your lap adoringly, as if to say, *"I love you, Mommy. I would have come to you if I knew you wanted me to. All you had to do was ask!"*

Try and Find Me

This is a scary game that small dogs love to play on their owners. First, the dog may do something impish, like stealing a piece of their owner's jewelry. Then, when the owner calls the little prankster to get the item back, the dog runs and hides in some of the smallest and weirdest places imaginable! Perhaps the dog knows his owner will never think to look under quilts in the bed or behind the refrigerator. One family couldn't find their Chihuahua for a full day after he disappeared inside their house. They finally found that he had somehow crawled up into the workings of the stove! (This family was left with a long term fear of ever cooking anything in the oven!)

Usually, when a dog plays this game, he will wait until his owners start to become hysterical searching for him. Then the dog jumps out of his hiding place with a little doggie grin on his face, as if to ask, *"Were you looking for me?"* At this point the owners don't know if they want to hug their dog or choke it to death. They were grief-stricken feeling like they lost their beloved baby, only to find he was just hiding all along!

Find the Movement

This unsavory game is not really played for fun. But dogs and puppies often learn to do it if their owners yell at them or hit them after they discover a bowel "accident" in the house. Dogs can't think like people, so your dog's not able to associate your anger with him *having* the accident hours earlier. But he *does* notice that you got tremendously angry when you *found* it, so he seeks for a solution. The solution is sometimes the game of "Hide the Movement". The dog knows you will yell at him if you find the bowel movements he's made in the house, so he starts getting creative, hiding all his accidents so he won't get in trouble when you get home.

We've heard of dogs that can make finding their movements as challenging as an Easter egg hunt. Then the dog "innocently" watches as you spend hours looking for the accident that you're sure you can smell somewhere in the house. And dogs seem to think it cutest when the owners try to use their noses to find the feces! After you step in the movement a day after your sense of smell failed you, your dog may appear to laugh at you, as though to say, "It's a good thing we don't have to depend on *your* nose!"

Herding the Kids

High Energy dogs that are allowed to get bored can cost you more than just money. We've seen dogs cause more family problems than any other source of stress. Know the dog breed you are bringing home and make sure your family can fulfill the dog's needs.

This is a game herding breeds in particular like to play, but we've seen many bored dogs do it just to keep occupied. The dog will wait until your children start moving around the house. And then he chases after them, nipping at their heels. In his mind, he is trying to "herd" the children to a certain place in the house or yard that he has determined safe for them. A dog that tries to "herd" children by nipping at their heels may even look for praise from the owner!

"Herding" kids, or even adult family members, is a dangerous practice and we've even been called to help customers whose heels were bitten bloody! If your dog ever bites at people's heels, the first step is to assess the situation to differentiate between herding- an instinctual behavior that sometimes comes out when a dog has nothing productive do with mental and physical energy- and biting for reasons of aggression.

In true cases of aggression, owners should immediately contact a professional, and never downplay the danger to their family. In other cases, if your dog is actually trying to "herd" your children, he's likely doing it because he loves them and feels anxious about keeping them safe. But, no matter the cause, nipping at heels can escalate, leading to serious injury or a dog being euthanized.

To change this behavior owners should first separate dog and kids sufficiently to prevent any further nipping while you obedience train your dog or puppy (see guidelines in "Obedience Minded" in Ch. 3, Puppy Games). Next, start giving your dog lots of physical activity daily, including several leashed walks. You must also exercise your dog's mind, challenge him and give him a purpose in life. You will find many, many helpful ideas throughout the book, especially in Chapter 10, Activities for High-Energy Dogs, Chapter 9, Therapeutic and Senior Dog Activities and Chapter 13, Family Activities.

If your dog's herding behavior is severe and does not stop right away with these interventions, consult a qualified animal behaviorist who can use gentle methods to extinguish the behavior. Herding may be instinctual, but it's a game that's not good for your dog or anyone in the household and the only way for a dog owner to win at this game is to stop it!

Buried Treasure

Buried treasure is a game that owners may find cute when it first starts. Your dog may learn that he can get your attention by taking something of yours, because every time he takes something you come over and try to get it away. The first few times your dog steals your socks and hides them in his bed, the owners may find it adorable. They may laugh when they see the little puppy struggling to bury his "treasure", give him an indulgent pet on the head and call him a little rascal as they retrieve their possession.

The tendency to bury treasured items is related to dogs' natural instinct to bury bones or meat for later when they cannot eat immediately. And it's reinforced by the fact that burying items belonging to the owner can often get the dog attention. You'll notice that bored, frustrated and under-exercised dogs most frequently play "Buried Treasure", so many of the games and activities in this book are healthy alternatives to the behavior.

In contrast, if you allow the behavior to continue when you're dog's a puppy, it will likely intensify as he matures. Your dog may start "lifting" items from your drawers, your purse or off countertops and hiding them outside, where you can't get them back as easily. If you don't catch your dog taking the items, you may just believe you're getting absent-minded until one day you find a stash of missing money and gold jewelry when you're doing yardwork. One owner even found their missing Rolex!

If you have a dog and you have missing items, you may be able to locate the "Lost and Found" box by observing where your dog goes to hide his own treasured items. There's a chance he may have buried *your* missing items in the same spot.

Playmate

This is a dangerous game played often in multi-dog families. It starts when owners who can't devote enough time to play with their high-energy dog notice that he's frustrated, and so they adopt another dog to occupy him. The problem can be even worse if the first dog is large and active, and the new dog is a toy!

At first the owners may think it's cute when they notice the dogs "playing" together constantly. But if they looked closer, they'd notice that the "play" is actually their bigger more frustrated dog bullying the newer smaller dog, hurting him and giving him no chance to rest. By the time the owners decide to break up the tussles the instigator of the "game" will likely resist- because now he's found a win/win scenario. By playing roughly with the little dog, he gets to release his frustration and he gets lots of attention from his owners when they try to break things up.

It's a myth that bringing home a new dog will solve problems for your existing dog. Instead, you should only consider adopting a new dog if your existing dog is happy and well balanced and if you have adequate time to work with two dogs. Before bringing the new dog home, you should first introduce the two dogs on neutral territory and observe how they get along. Usually dogs of the same sex tend to have more conflicts and paring large active breeds with small delicate breeds is often dangerous. There are notable exceptions to every rule however. If you desire lasting harmony in your home, you must do adequate research and introduce dogs carefully before making the final decision to adopt.

You're Killing Me!

This is a game certain dogs don't want owners to know about. This way they can play it whenever they're caught doing something bad and you try to force them to do what you want. You may catch your dog with his head in the refrigerator or garbage, and he'll ignore you completely when you tell him to stop. But then, if you so much as touch his collar he'll start to scream like you just branded him with a hot poker! Dog lovers will immediately drop the collar and start worriedly checking the dog from nose to tail to make sure their dog is okay. But just as you start lavishing him with kisses and apologies, the dog happily goes back to the same mischief he was doing before! You reach for him again and this time he screams before you can even touch him.

"You're Killing Me!" is a game that proves just how clever dogs can be. Even after your dog plays this game on you a hundred times and you know you're not really hurting him, just hearing him cry is enough to make a softhearted owner shrivel with guilt. Yes, you know your dog has found a way to get away with his sins, but you can't help but feel *you're* the one who sinned as you gaze into those accusing puppy-dog eyes.

See How High I Can Reach

This is the game where your dog steals items from high places in the house, including places you'd never think he could reach. In many homes, this game is played on Thanksgiving Day. The owners spend a long day cooking dinner for the family and ignoring the dog. So, when everyone is off setting the table, the dog sneaks into the kitchen, takes down the turkey and eats his Thanksgiving dinner before anyone else!

This game isn't always about food. We've heard of dogs that destroyed their owners' most beloved possessions that were placed on top of six-foot bookcases without breaking or moving anything on the lower shelves. And this wasn't a large breed like a Great Dane; it was a four-pound Yorkie.

Dogs love playing "See How High I Can Reach" when their owners hide their toys up on a refrigerator or cabinet. The owner will take the toy away from the dog with a smug expression, saying, "See, this is what happens when you play too rough!" Five minutes later the dog is playing with the same toy, looking at the owner with a twinkle in his eyes, as if to say, "I showed you!" The owner is left scratching their head, trying to figure out how the dog got to a shelf that even *they* had problems reaching.

Your Food's Better Than Mine

This game is played often these days. Owners start out feeding their puppy a high-quality dog food. Then the day comes when one of the children, or even the adults, notice the cute little pup looking up at them when they are eating dinner. Enraptured by those cute puppy-dog eyes, they offer the puppy a bite of food off their plate. The pup loves the food and gives the owner a big kiss.

Now the next time you sit down to eat, guess who's at your feet- an adorable puppy looking up at you with sad eyes, crying and begging for food. You have now created a dog that begs and won't leave you alone when you're eating. Some owners make the problem worse by continuing to indulge their dogs. Others start telling the dog to go away at mealtime and the begging behavior may stop.

But a few unlucky owners encounter another stage of the game of "Your Food Is Better than Mine". You sit down at the dinner table, you turn your back for a second and your hamburger is gone like magic. And you find your pup sitting back, acting like nothing happened while licking your hamburger off his lips. Now you can never turn you back on your dog again when food is around, even if it's on the counter. And your dog will no longer want to eat the dog food you paid good money for, because he now craves your food instead of his!

I'll Only Eat If…

This is a game savvy dogs have mastered many times over. In fact, we suspect they may even teach each other how to play this game!

The purpose of the game is to make the owner think the dog is starving so the dog can get his favorite foods. Dogs usually start playing "I'll Only Eat If…" after they've already acquired a taste for human food playing "Your Food's Better Than Mine" as described above. The owner may think they can get the upper hand by simply denying their dog human food.

But this only works until their dog goes on a hunger strike! The dog refuses to eat anything for days at a time, and may even appear weak or sick.

> *I'll Only Eat If! Never let your dog get in this habit. If you do, one day he may only eat if you hand feed him your food or he may even force you to stand outside the house before he eats.*

Now the owner feels the dog *has* to eat *something* because he's ill and needs his strength, so they add a little something extra to the dog's dry kibble to tempt his appetite- and suddenly the dog eats well.

Unfortunately, offering this first morsel of canned or human food sets the stage for some dogs to start playing "I'll Only Eat If…" Now every time you present the dog his regular dog food from this point on, he'll turn his nose up at it or look at you like he feels ill, waiting to see if you'll add something or change foods.

When you do, the dog will eat. You may suspect your dog doesn't like a particular brand of food anymore, so you change to a different brand, usually one that's a lot more expensive. The first few times you offer the new food, your dog gobbles it up like he hasn't eaten in days. And for a week or so he eats well on the new food. But then he goes on a new hunger strike.

The owner goes out and buys an even more expensive gourmet food and the same cycle repeats. Your dog eats the new food at first, but now only for one or two days.

The dog just keeps raising the stakes until he gets exactly the food he wants, under exactly the conditions he wants. (We even heard of one dog that would only eat if the owners cooked him a homemade meal, walked outside, rang the doorbell, stayed out for a while and then waited to reenter until he "gave them permission" by scratching at the door. The owners of this dog willingly performed this bizarre routine for over a year because they were so desperate to make sure the dog ate.)

The game of "I'll Only Eat If..." can be great fun for a dog, but it can cause loving owners a great deal of stress. The best solution is to feed your dog the right food, under the right conditions from the beginning. But assuming your dog is playing this game if he ever refuses to eat is *not* a safe solution. **Loss of appetite can be a symptom of many serious physical disorders. If your dog suddenly stops eating, you must have your veterinarian check the dog,** even if you suspect the dog is only acting finicky. If the vet clears your dog of any physical illness, there will be good news and bad news. The good news is that your finicky dog is healthy. The bad news is that he's playing "I'll Only Eat If..."

I Bark, You Bark, We All Bark

This is a game that small dogs (and some big dogs like German Shepherds) really seem to love. And most owners get suckered into this game by dogs every now or then. The game is learned when the dog starts barking and the owners yell to try to make him stop. The dog doesn't understand it this way. He thinks that he barked and the owner barked also. Most likely your dog will enjoy the fact his owner "joined in" and gave him attention.

> *Don't just stop the barking; find the cause of the barking. This is how you both stop the barking and have a happy dog!*

This is where the fun for the dog starts. You may be sitting at home relaxing on your day off when your dog comes over to get attention from you and instead you ask him to go lie down. Instead, your dog walks over to the nearest window and starts barking at some small thing he sees outside or barking at nothing at all.

After a few moments you yell, "Shut up!" But all the dog does is bark more and bark louder. You walk over to look out the window and, when you see nothing, you yell, "Shut Up!" even louder this time. This is how the game escalates, so you might as well not expect peace and quiet for a while.

All of us have probably yelled at dogs, trying to get them to stop barking, but there's a reason this doesn't work. When your dog barks and you yell at him to stop, he thinks you're barking also. If the dog barks at something that disturbs him, when you come over and yell, he thinks you're there to help him chase the scary thing away. And so he'll bark even more.

Alternatives include training your dog to bark and to stop barking on command, which you can easily accomplish with positive methods (see "Stop barking on command" in Chapter 8).

Make Mommy & Daddy Yell at Each Other

This is not only a game for clever dogs, but a favorite of children as well. If the lady of the house tries to correct the dog, or the child, or if she won't give them what they want, they immediately go to the man of the house for a "second opinion". A dog that looks especially pitiful can easily gain Daddy's sympathy, so Dad will give him what Mom refused. And some dogs (and kids) seem to relish watching the big uproar when a situation that initially began with their mischief turns to a heated argument about who's the better parent.

And if strictness in your home vacillates, with Mom crying one minute that Dad is too strict and the next minute Dad allowing the dog to break one of Mom's rules, a savvy dog will learn to go to one parent whenever he doesn't get his way with the other.

A simple solution for dog owners is for both spouses to stay completely consistent on the house rules. Dogs are bred to live by rules in their own wild packs, so they won't give much respect to a human "parent" who lets the rules of their home slide.

Entertaining Guests

A bored dog loves to have guests; they're the ultimate entertainment. Of course, we all know that poorly trained dogs can lose their manners entirely, acting painfully boisterous with guests. But some clever dogs take advantage of unsuspecting guests in a subtler fashion. First your family dog acts charming, lavishing tons affection on the guests. "Oh, your dog is so adorable!" the guests exclaim, completely smitten. And during their stay they'll constantly fuss over the dog.

The problem comes when the host's back is turned and the dog forces the guests to play whenever he demands, surrender the choicest morsels on their plates, fix makeup after sloppy doggie kisses, sleep at the foot of their bed so he can have the silk pillow and stay up half the night scratching his belly.

When the guest finally complains after they throw out their back lifting hundred-pound Teddy Bear into bed, the host explains that they never intended for the dog to be pampered like that. On the last day of their visit, the guest may stop spoiling the dog. But the dog doesn't mind. *He* knew the rules of the home all along- it was the guest's fault that they didn't. Now he just needs to be patient and await the next houseguests!

Love for Sale

A clever dog can easily spark a competition between his human "parents" over who will spoil him the most. Some adorable toy breeds are especially adept at this. The dog's human parents crave their dog's attention so much that they try to "buy" the dog, continually showering him with his favorite treats or privileges. And it never stops, as each parent tries to outdo the other, offering the next delicacy and then boasting, "See, he loves me more," when the dog cuddles up to them. And then the other parent simply raises the stakes. So how do you suppose a smart dog reacts to this once he sees what the "game" is about? The owners have created a dog that can force them to give him anything he wants!

"Your home is his castle!"

Ch. 3- Puppy Games & Activities

"What your puppy learns now, he'll do for the rest of his life."

Introduction

Follow the Leader

Find the Treat

Which Hand?

Find Mommy

Which Box Has the Fun In It?

Tunnel Crawl

Soccer

How Do I Get What's in There?

Let's Play Doctor

Shopping Spree

Walk This Way

Obedience-Minded

Soft Mouth

Puppy Grooming

New Learning Every Day (Puppy)

Also Try These Activities from Other Chapters for Puppies:

Mental Games & Activities (Ch. 4): Watch Me, The Shell Game, Wait, Move Slow

Indoor Games & Activities (Ch. 5): Hide & Seek, Get That Pose, A Room of His Own, Different Surfaces, Basketball

Balance & Coordination Activities (Ch. 6): Walk the Line, Stack, Teeter Totter, Double Hoops, Different Surfaces

Multi-Dog Games & Activities (Ch. 7): What's My Name, Under/Over

Problem Dog Games (Ch.8): Ring of Fire, Go to Your Place, Kisses, Stop Barking on command, In the Army Crawl, Drop It, Interactive Games, Different Surfaces

Therapeutic and Senior Dog Activities (Ch.9): Massage, Party in the Storm, Look in the Leaves, Doggie Stairs

Activities for High-Energy Dogs (Ch. 10): Weave Poles

Water Activities (Ch.11): Kiddie Pool, Chase the Hose

Useful Activities (Ch. 12): Bark for Help, Follow the Scent, Work with Livestock, Lap Dog

Family Activities (Ch. 13): Circle of Love, Diversity Training, Different Handlers, Junior Handlers, Junior Grooming Salon, Assess a Dog

Activities for Owners with Limited Mobility (Ch. 14): Long Lead, Playdate (Once inoculated, check with your vet), Fishing Pole, Service Dog, Bubbles, Balloons, Dog on the Table

Puppy Games & Activities- Introduction
"What your puppy learns now, he'll do for the rest of his life."

So you've got a puppy. And if your puppy is between the ages of seven to twelve weeks, he's at a very crucial point in life. Now is the time to teach your puppy all his crucial life skills and to introduce him to all the people, places and things that you plan for him to encounter later in life. This is also the period of your dog's development when he will learn many of his good and bad habits, whether you consciously teach them or not.

Using the puppy games in this chapter (and appropriate games from other chapters listed above) you can start teaching your pup good habits the day you bring him home. You don't need to wait until he's is six months old with bad behavior patterns already in place. In our belief, **by the time most owners feel it's time to bring their dog to obedience classes, the dog has lost much potential to be the great dog he or she could have been.** This is because formal obedience classes are only safe to start once your puppy has completed his shots and has full immunity. And group classes only teach your dog an hour a week, in a limited setting, with little personalization or room for feedback.

In contrast, by planning specific games and activities throughout your pup's day, and by consciously choosing how you relate to him in every situation, you can positively shape your puppy's behavior from the first day you bring him home. Just like children can actually become more intelligent if they are provided with a high level of stimuli and learning from a very young age, so can puppies.

Don't get us wrong, you *can* make a dog great at any age, so **never give up!** We've helped ten and fifteen year-old dogs that other trainers had given up on, and you can get good results with training and lifestyle changes at any age. But, unfortunately, a dog that you begin training at six months or a year may never be as good as the same dog that started learning at eight weeks. It's interesting to learn that the reason old-school dog professionals used to recommend waiting until six months to train puppies was because obedience classes utilized harsh physical corrections that could hurt younger dogs! This included choke and prong collar corrections and physically pushing puppies into position. We believe you get better results training with positive reinforcement, changes in lifestyle and an understanding of canine psychology.

Games in this chapter teach your puppy a wide variety of skills he'll need in life, including physical, mental, emotional and social skills. A game like "Follow the Leader" will teach your puppy how to stay out of trouble in the home and it will help with housebreaking without a crate, as your pup learns the best place to be is by his owner's side. "Walk This Way" can help teach your pup how to walk politely on a loose lead starting from the first day he comes into your home. This game also teaches the dog to start looking to you for information in life. "Find the Treat" sharpens your pup's senses and his mind, while "Tunnel Crawl" works on coordination and emotional confidence. "Soft Mouth" teaches a puppy not to bite humans and "Let's Play Doctor" is an essential game that makes your dog a better citizen at the vet.

Puppy games like these do more than just to prevent problem behavior patterns. If you stimulate your puppy's mind when he's young your puppy will become a more intelligent dog. A dog that practices decision-making early in life, through games, will learn to make better choices later in life in every situation, just like a child would. You can start with games like "Find the Treat" or "Which Hand?" They are great little brain teasers, and lots of fun for the puppy.

To burn off physical energy, try games like "Soccer" and "How Do I Get What's in There? The physical intensity of these games is increased by the mental component, and your pup will finish the games pleasantly tired, with a great sense of accomplishment.

We recommend that every new dog owner get this book before you get your new puppy, so you can teach your puppy from the first what *to* do. Teaching your dog ahead of time the specific things you want of him prevents you constantly getting stressed by having to tell him what *not* to do. And that kind of peace of mind is worth a lot!

Puppy Games & Activities:

Follow the Leader. If you plan to teach your dog to walk off leash in his life, you need to start this game the day you get your puppy home. If this game is done right your dog will never even need heeling lessons, for he will always know being at your side is the place to be.

Follow the Leader
- teaches your pup to like walking beside you; also prevents pulling & running away-

This is a good activity to practice when you first get your new puppy. First get the pup used to a harness and lead (see "Walk This Way", this chapter). Next, put the puppy on the lead and tie the lead to your belt. Now just walk around your house and praise the pup when he walks with you. If he starts to walk ahead of you, immediately stop. As soon as the pup gets the message and stops trying to pull, proceed walking. Following his owner around the house like this is easy for a young puppy, because dogs are genetically programmed to want to follow their "pack leader". This activity helps socialize your puppy and allows him freedom in the house while keeping him out of trouble. It also makes him feel natural sticking close to his owner's side.

Later on you should practice this same game without a lead. Most pups will follow you easily and naturally, but if your dog gets distracted, hold a treat by your leg to encourage him. Practice the game inside, outside, with distractions and with different family members and practice it frequently.

A benefit of "Follow the Leader" is that it also teaches your puppy how to go on neighborhood walks with you comfortably and without pulling. All you have to do is add the word "heel". If you've had dogs that have pulled on leash in the past, you may be surprised how quickly and easily your new pup will adjust to leash walking after he's played "Follow the Leader" indoors. The great part about the game is that it eliminates fighting with your dog, and pups find following their owners around the house great fun!

Find the Treat
- dogs never get bored with this simple scenting game -

"Find the Treat" is a good game to play with your puppy if you ever want to use him for scent work later in life. It's also an easy game that's good for every dog and owner- it's fun, entertaining and rewarding for both owner and dog and it's easy to learn. To start, sit on the floor with your pup and show him some treats, perhaps rewarding him for performing a few "sits" or "downs". Next, hide a treat behind your back when the pup's not looking, and then tell him, "Find the treat!" Sit back and let the pup sniff and look around.

At first you can cheer him on saying things like, "You're getting colder; now warmer..." When your pup finds the treat, praise him and tell him how smart he is. After he starts finding the treat easily, you will make it harder and harder for him to find. Just don't make it too difficult for a young puppy at first, though, because you want to keep him loving the game.

The game of "Find the Treat" can also help when you leave your dog alone in the house later. Rather than having your dog bored when you go out and possibly getting into trouble, you can hide some treats around the house and, before you leave, tell your dog to "Find the treat". But don't play this game *every* time you go out or your dog may think that when you go out he always has to look for treats, and he might get himself into the exact trouble you were trying to keep him out of!

Which Hand?
- great basic game to teach mental focus- anyone can do it -

This game makes a dog think, and this is always good for a puppy! The more your dog is made to think when he's a puppy, the smarter he'll be when he's grown up. And who doesn't want the smartest dog on the block? You can probably tell from the name of the game what the game is about. The owner shows their pup a treat and then puts it behind their back. You make a show of moving the treat from hand to hand behind your back, and then hold your closed hands out in front of the puppy and ask him, "Which hand?"

At first your puppy may use his nose to find out which hand the treat is in. Let the puppy pick a hand and, if it is the right one, praise and give him the treat. If the hand he chooses isn't right, just say, "Oh, oh, wrong hand. Try again."

After a little time you can make it harder for your puppy and not let him use his nose as much. If he tries to use his nose just laugh and say, "Oh, stop your cheating." If he looks at you and stops using his nose, then leave your hand out to continue play. If he keeps using his nose, just put your hands behind your back and put the game on hold for awhile. You will know that your puppy is playing using his mind when you notice him trying to predict patterns; for example, if you put the treat in the opposite hand after each trial, you'll notice him always looking in that hand. As soon as your pup masters one pattern, change to another. You can also make the game more challenging by having two people play and it's a fun and easy game for kids to play with puppies.

Find Mommy
- a joy to observe and a building block for making your dog more useful -

In "Find Mommy" you teach your dog to recognize the different names of the family members and how to go to a family member when you ask him. If your dog learns to go where he's needed as a puppy, he will then be able to confidently perform this helpful, even lifesaving, skill as an adult.

Teach this activity with two or more people. One person holds the dog while the other person walks a short distance away. The person holding the dog now commands, "Find Mommy" (or that person's name) while the second person whistles, makes noise or taps on their leg to get the puppy to come to them. When the puppy reaches them, they reward him with petting, praise and/or treats.

Once your pup reliably goes to the person on cue, start increasing the distance between the two people until he can find the person anywhere in house. You can even teach your dog to give one bark when he gets to the named person or to gently take the person's hand to lead the person back to you.

Which Box Has the Fun In It?
-uses cardboard boxes for mental and physical stimulation-

This is a good game to play with your puppy because the more you make him think when he is young, the smarter he'll be when he is older. And the habit of thinking things out, rather than immediately reacting, will help prevent the puppy developing fears and problem behaviors later in life. Your puppy will also use his nose in this game, refining his sense of smell and he'll use dexterity.

Start with three or more cardboard boxes of different sizes and shapes. Then show the puppy a treat and then put the treat in one of the boxes with the lid open. Put the boxes in the middle of the floor together, then just sit back and let the natural instincts of the puppy take over. He'll start looking in each of the boxes in order to try to find the treat. When he does find it, allow him to eat it and offer lots of praise and encouragement.

Next make it harder by closing the boxes, so the pup has to find a way into the box before he can get to the treat. You can also increase the challenge and make your dog have to think more by putting the boxes in different rooms around the house.

Remember to hide the treat in different boxes each time you play so your puppy won't think he has to look for just that one box to get a treat. And when the game is over, make a point of letting the puppy see you picking up the boxes. He needs to understand that the game is over and he needs to respect this; you don't want the pup looking for the boxes all day when we're not home!

If your puppy is like most dogs, he may start ripping the boxes up. If he does, there's not really any harm in this as long as he distinguishes between these boxes that you allow him to tear and other household items. Just make sure you pick up all the little pieces so he doesn't swallow the cardboard.

If your pup likes this game, you can also use it when you leave him alone. You may come home to a few torn-up cardboard boxes, but your sofa and table legs will stay in one piece because your dog won't be bored with all those boxes to tear up. All you have to do is clean up the cardboard and praise your dog for finding the treats. If the puppy didn't find the box with the treat, open the box now and give him the treat, and don't hide the box with the treat quite so well next time. You want the puppy to win most of the time so he's challenged but always motivated.

All you have to do next time you want to play is to hide treats in a different box and put the boxes down to start the game again. The game is pleasant for you, and exciting for puppy. But the best part is your house gets to stay in one piece while the boxes get all the ripping.

Tunnel Crawl
- builds a pup's courage and trust in his owners, along with his coordination -

This is another activity that will help your pup later on in life, because it helps teach him to trust you at times when he isn't sure of himself, and it teaches him not to fear strange objects and situations. Practicing the tunnel crawl also aids coordination and stimulates the senses and it's a must if you plan to enter your dog in agility competitions later in life.

To start the activity, bring home a tube that's wide enough for your puppy to run through so that he won't get stuck and use it either indoors, outdoors or both. Tunnels are available specifically designed for dog agility competition. Beginner's agility kits are available in catalogs (see Resources). Some pet stores carry agility equipment (call to make sure) or you can buy a tunnel made for children or for cats at some department stores if the size is right for your dog.

To teach your puppy to enter the tunnel the first time, start with a shortened tube. Have a helper hold the puppy at one end of the tube while you kneel at the other end. Call your pup to you, offering a treat as your helper simultaneously releases him. As your pup steps into the tunnel, encourage and entice him. When he gets to you, offer praise and treats and then repeat the process with your pup running through the tunnel in the other direction.

If you want to make the tunnel crawl more challenging, you can make the circumference smaller so the dog has to crawl through the tube. The additional challenge of crawling through the tunnel may appeal more to breeds that were used in the past for hunting game in tunnels underground. Dachshunds will naturally love the tunnel game; so will many terrier breeds and some herding dogs.

Dogs of other breeds might be more naturally skittish around the tunnel (for example, dogs of the larger working breeds or dogs with naturally high-strung temperament). As long as there are no physical prohibitions, either walking or crawling through the tunnel (as tolerated) can be good for these dogs as well, as it steadies them and helps them become bolder. But make sure your dog first practices crawling though a short tube before you make the tube longer. The worst thing to happen at the first practice session is if the dog gets stuck, since then he'll feel reluctant to enter the tunnel again.

Once your dog is comfortable, you can expand the length of the tube. To further increase the challenge, make some bends in a long tunnel. Or introduce the "chute" type tunnel used in agility competitions. This tunnel starts rigid, but the far end is a fabric sleeve that the dog has to lift as he crawls through. When first training your puppy to master the "chute" type tunnel, you should hold the far end open so that he can see you. If you're not sure whether your dog will take to this style tunnel, or you are not prepared to purchase one yet, start with your existing tunnel and then drape a sheet loosely over the far end, holding it up the first few times so that your puppy can see you. As soon as he masters this challenge, drop the sheet down and be prepared to smile as you watch your pup moving under it. Call and praise him energetically and, as soon as he reaches you, reward him with treats and praise.

Soccer
- a fun way to burn off excess energy; pups can even play alone -

This activity helps your puppy learn body/eye coordination-he learns to watch the ball as you kick it around and then he runs with it, pushing it with his nose or his feet as he attempts to grab it. Soccer is a great bonding game where you learn to work as a team with your puppy while having fun. This game is easy to learn for both you and your dog, it comes naturally for people to enjoy kicking a ball around and most puppies love to chase anything that moves.

The only equipment you'll need to play is an old soccer ball, blown up tight so your dog can't get a good bite on it. Or buy a soccer ball from a pet store that's made of hard plastic meant for dogs, so it can last forever. When you first play this game, just kick the ball around the yard and see if your puppy wants to join in on the fun. If he shows interest, gently kick the ball over his way. The worst thing a person can do to spoil all the fun for a puppy the first time they play is to kick the ball so hard it hits the puppy in the face and he falls over and whimpers. This puppy may never want to go near that ball again!

When you first start there's usually no need to even kick the ball very close to the puppy. If it looks like you're having fun, your puppy will probably come over and chase the ball, trying to get it from you. When he does this, allow him to steal the ball, run around the yard a little and have some fun. Now you can come over and try to steal the ball from the puppy, play with it awhile and then let him get it again.

Some dogs will eventually learn to push the ball over your way or "invite" you to take it just to continue the fun and now your kids have a soccer partner who will happily knock the ball back and forth with them for hours. Just follow a few safety precautions.

Make sure your dog can always take breaks and that he has water available. (But don't allow him to drink large amounts of water immediately after exercise as this could cause life-threatening bloat.) Also, if your pup is a large or giant breed you should prevent him from jumping and running around too vigorously until he is fully grown, to prevent future hip problems. This doesn't mean you can't play with your large puppy; you just have to prevent the puppy from stressing his growing bones too much by leaping and coming down too hard.

The great thing about teaching your puppy to play soccer is that he can also learn to play on his own. Your dog can get a lot of great exercise this way without you having to exhaust yourself. Your dog will happily play with the soccer ball, chasing it all by himself while you relax in your chaise lounge or finish up an outdoor project. But don't forget about your puppy! You should always keep an eye on him to keep him out of trouble and to let him know you love him and want to be outside spending time with him. Even if your dog often plays on his own, you'll still want to play soccer with him at family picnics or as a fun way to release stress when you return home from work.

How Do I Get What's In There?
- keeps your pup occupied while teaching him to problem solve -

This activity helps mischievous puppies stay out of trouble. And it also teaches your puppy to think whenever he encounters a new situation.

Set the game up by placing a safe toy or treats in a cardboard box. Tape the box closed, but not tightly, and poke some holes in the box so your pup can sniff the goodies inside. At first your puppy will probably try to push at the box, hit it with his paw or try to push his face in the box top. The object is for the puppy to figure out how to get inside the box, and watching your pup's attempts will likely provide the family with some enjoyable entertainment. This is much more fun than chasing the puppy around to keep him out of mischief.

Make sure that when you play this game with your puppy there aren't a lot of breakable items around, because your pup may try to throw the box in the air or push the box up against walls to get leverage, trying to get the box open. Provide several different boxes and this game can keep a puppy or adult dog busy for hours as he works on opening box tops and shaking treats out. Your pup may even get as skilled at this as the octopus that is famous for getting his tentacles into closed containers!

Some dogs learn that they can get into the boxes more quickly by just ripping them up. If this happens, you can make it harder by changing what you put the treats in. You can use any safe container as long as you supervise carefully. (For example, some people use plastic milk jugs with the openings partially blocked.)

We also recommend interactive toys like the "Tug-a-Jug" or the "Buster Cube" that are designed to occupy smarter dogs (see Resources). These products are made for dogs that make short work of most games. The Buster Cube has a maze inside, and the dog must manipulate the toy to get dry treats out. With the Tug-a-Jug, your dog has to pull a rope on one end to get the treats out of a bottle-shaped toy. These activities will make your puppy work for his treats; he won't get bored, and your furniture will stay undamaged.

Let's Play Doctor
- an essential for health & safety- start young!

"Let's Play Doctor" is an activity that can save your puppy's life one day. Have you ever taken a 90 pound dog to the veterinary clinic, only to have him flail around in panic when the vet looks into his mouth or touches his paws? Perhaps your dog even growls at, or nips at the vet. If this happens during a routine physical exam, imagine the risk to your veterinarian and his assistants if your dog is injured or has a face full of painful porcupine quills! The veterinarian could get bitten, or he may even tell you he can't help your dog because the dog gets too upset and bites during exams. Some veterinarians have to handle aggressive dogs by tranquilizing them. But not all vets will do this and, medically, it's a risky way to treat a sick dog.

As an alternative, you can make life easier for yourself, your veterinarian and your dog if you get your dog used to people touching him all over his body when he is a puppy. Most puppies under 16-weeks old naturally like to be near their owners all the time, and this is also the best age to teach your puppy to get used to human touch. Practice by "playing doctor" with your pup.

The process is easy. Have you ever watched your vet give your dog a good looking over? He looks into the ears, mouth and eyes and he also runs his hands all over the dog's body to see if he can feel anything abnormal. A trained professional can tell a lot about an animal's health just running their hands along the animal's body. He might notice a lump that he needs to keep an eye on, or a bone that the dog injured when he fell going down the steps.

> *You can make life easier for yourself, your veterinarian and your dog if you get your dog used to people touching him all over his body when he's a puppy.*

Just like your veterinarian examines your dog and looks for small inconsistencies that may be the first signs of illness, you will also learn to notice such important signs when you get into the regular habit of examining your dog. This keeps your dog healthier between scheduled vet exams, since you notice possible problems before they become serious.

When you first teach "Let's Play Doctor", **never call your dog to you.** Instead, pick your puppy up and place him on your lap, or kneel down by your pup if he is too large to pick up. Have some special treats in your pocket. You will use these if your pup presents resistance when you try to touch certain spots and you can also give him some treats at the conclusion of the exam.

Start at the ears. Pet your pup on one of his cheeks and then move up to his ears. Touch the ears in a smooth gentle way that the puppy likes and speak to him encouragingly. As the puppy calms down more, lift each ear and look in like the vet does. Praise your puppy for allowing you to do this. Next move your hands gently over his body.

If your puppy ever flinches when you touch a particular spot, first check the area carefully to make sure that there is no injury, swelling or broken skin. If you rule out these problems, it's likely that you've stumbled across one of the common sensitive areas on a dog's body. You can now desensitize your puppy by praising and treating him as you gently work your way closer to touching the sensitive area. Practice this when your dog is a puppy and you can avoid common problems with touch when he's an adult.

Some spots you may initially have problems handling are the mouth, ears, tail and feet. It's important not to let these problems persist. Practice until your puppy becomes comfortable with touch in these areas, since continued sensitivity could cause flare-ups when people touch him as an adult. Children often grab dog's tails and you don't want your pup to reflexively turn and bite a child. Your dog must also allow his feet to be handled, so the groomer can clip his nails. And, of course, you want to be able to safely approach your dog's mouth in every situation. If your dog lets you open his mouth without a fuss, he'll allow you take away dangerous items that he picks up on the floor. And you can also start brushing his teeth, another healthy necessity.

If you gently touch your puppy all over his body when he's tiny, you probably won't have any problems when he matures; he'll completely enjoy human touch. Unfortunately some owners may buy or adopt their puppies after the pups have already developed an aversion to human handling. This often happens in overcrowded "puppy mills" where the young puppies aren't adequately socialized. If the new owners suspect their dog comes from a puppy mill it helps to understand the root of the problem and understand that it can be overcome with frequent, positive training and lots of patience.

Never get angry at your puppy for acting fearful when you touch him, and never take it personally. If your pup seems to hate touch, the worst thing you can do is to give up and stop handling him. This will definitely make the problem worse. Even skittish dogs that are fully grown can be helped with careful practice (plus the help of an animal behaviorist, if the problem is serious). If your pup is still relatively young and he acts nippy or skittish when you touch him in certain areas, correcting the problem at home is simply a matter of patient practice and the right reinforcement.

Note any places on your pup's body where he seems to show a resistance to being touched. If your pup is highly protective of a certain area, hold an especially tasty treat in front of him when you approach that area. As he eats the treat, touch him gently on the sensitive spot. Practice repeatedly, never pushing him beyond his comfort zone, and eventually your pup will associate your touching him with the pleasant stimulus of receiving treats. Couple this with lots of baby talk and affection, and eventually your puppy will learn to love "playing doctor".

Shopping Spree
- read this *before* taking your pup out shopping or socializing -

One modern invention that provides great opportunities to exercise and socialize your dog is chain pet stores that welcome well-behaved pets! (Florida examples include Petco, Petsmart and our personal favorite, Pet Supermarket). Excursions to such stores can be used as a stimulating Mental Game, a Problem Dog Game (to practice socialization) or a Family

Activity if you include the children. Owners can also use trips to the pet superstores as a way to get their dogs out of the house and stimulate the dogs' senses a bit during bad weather.

A trip to a chain pet store is obviously good for multi-tasking, since busy owners can take care of their pet-care shopping while simultaneously bonding with their dogs. It also saves owners of new puppies some money, since your dog can pick out the toys he likes best and is most likely to play with. If your dog turns away from a toy in the store, it's likely he wouldn't have liked it at home either. Choice-making stimulates his mind, so it's a good idea to let him make his own (safe) selections.

The pet store is also a good place for your dog, or fully inoculated puppy, to practice his training exercises in a real-life situation with lots of distractions as long as you don't interfere with other shoppers. Teach your puppy to show restraint, sitting and/or staying willingly when you command him, without leaping around. You can also practice "drop it" if you want your puppy to drop a toy or treat that's not appropriate- or one that you can't afford! Once your dog has behaved appropriately on the shopping trip, you can buy him one toy he's picked out as his reward!

You can bring your puppy to the pet store as soon as he's safely vaccinated, and with your vet's okay. After this, have your puppy visit the store frequently, increasing the time and socialization with each subsequent visit.

On your pup's first visits to the store, you should start with him looking at people and dogs, but not yet having physical contact. Approach near store employees and shoppers so your pup can look at them, and feed him treats and/or pet or praise him as long as he remains calm. If he acts wild or agitated walk away and then try again at whatever distance is necessary for him to remain calm around the people.

After your young puppy acts appropriate on a few shopping trips where he does no more than look at people, you can initiate his first actual meeting with a stranger.

This first person your puppy touches can be a friendly store employee or even an agreeable fellow shopper. Make sure the stranger approaches your puppy gently, offering a (safe) treat rather than immediately attempting to pet or grab. Allow the puppy to initiate physical contact at his own speed. If your puppy initiates contact, and if he seems completely comfortable and happy, it's okay for the stranger to gently pet him and or hold him. Even people who are dog lovers may not know that leaning over a dog, hugging a dog or petting directly on the head can be interpreted as signs of dominance, so advise anyone who pets your puppy to approach in a low-key manner.

After a successful first meeting with a stranger, your puppy can meet a few more people on the next trip. But never allow too many people to handle your puppy on one outing- two strangers in one trip is plenty. You may have to turn admirers away from petting the puppy, but this is okay, especially if you notice him acting tired or burnt out. (It's a good idea to bring a soft-sided ventilated carrier your pup can rest in if things ever get too intense or provide a stroller with mesh that he can retreat to.)

It is also your social and legal obligation never to impose your puppy on strangers unless the encounter is consensual for everyone, and you should be especially careful when introducing your pup to children. It's important that your pup learn to like children during his critical socialization period. But since kids sometimes handle tiny dogs roughly, you must carefully supervise.

You must also protect the kids. Get parental permission and make sure your puppy doesn't jump on or nip children. It's your responsibility to make sure your puppy is not aggressive and will not bite, so always use caution.

As your puppy is practicing meeting people in the store, you should begin to let him look at dogs and cats from a distance. To be completely safe around strange animals, your dog should have full immunity before the first physical contact, so we recommend starting physical meetings with people at a much younger age than physical meetings with dogs. But when your puppy is younger than 16 weeks, you should start accustoming him to the *sight* of dogs of different breeds, ages and sizes. As long as your puppy stays calm, offer him treats and praise for proper behavior and practice frequently.

After your puppy has full immunity, at some point another shopper will probably want to let their pet sniff yours. Make a careful judgment call because there's a chance a stranger's pet might not be vaccinated, or might carry parasites. The dog might bite your puppy even if the animal acts friendly at first and there's also a possibility that *your* pet could bite. Owners should use their own judgment, erring on the side of caution, before agreeing to a meet and greet session. Clarify with the other shopper what kind of socializing you'd like to see and agree to immediately separate the dogs if anything seems inappropriate. An owner who is not patient enough to negotiate this also will not act responsibly if their dog is aggressive to yours, so feel free to walk away!

Remember, you don't *have* to let your pup physically greet other dogs in pet stores if you don't want to, or if you sense he's uncomfortable. You can always let him socialize in a more controlled situation on another day. If your puppy acts shy around intense stimuli, try visiting the store when it's quietest. Never start out with weekend visits to busy stores. The idea is to slowly introduce increasingly intense meetings to build to an ideal situation where your dog will be completely comfortable for years of enjoying his favorite store.

Walk This Way
- start out leash walking right and it will always be easy -

What is it about a long leisurely walk with your dog that feels so elemental? For dogs, the answer is easy. Walking is the activity through which wild dogs (or wolves) bond with each other all day, every day. Wolf packs are known to travel thirty miles a day or more through challenging terrain, seeking prey, water or safer hunting grounds. And how cleverly and effectively the alpha wolf (or dog) leads his pack represents life or death for the other animals. Likewise, the obedience of the other animals is necessary so they can travel and hunt effectively as a group. Since wolves can't talk as they travel, they communicate primarily through body language in order to move seamlessly.

It's genetic destiny that your dog naturally enjoys following his owner on walks and encountering the world together. He'll learn from you how you want him to respond to stimuli you meet along the way, such as people or other dogs. And he will savor glancing at you to read your intentions and blending his pace to perfectly match yours, in order to help you in any way you want him to.

Perhaps this does not sound like dogs you've had in the past, and your previous dogs may have made walking stressful for you. The good news is, if you're reading this section, you probably have a new puppy. If you ever had previous problems walking a dog, or if you know friends who complain about such problems endlessly, now is the time to make a difference. And we could easily fill an entire book with warnings about how important it is to teach your dog to walk correctly with you *now*, when he is young, to avoid the next fifteen years filled with disappointment, frustration and stress.

One of the most common problems people call us for help with is getting their dogs to walk properly on a leash. But often part of the problem is dogs that are a year and a half old and have hardly been outside of their owners' yards! The owners complain that they *can't* walk the dog- he simply pulls too much. Then the dog spends even more time without walking on a leash, and the vicious cycle continues.

The extremely good news is that an eight or ten week-old puppy cannot pull you off your feet, no matter what his breed, so you can easily lay the groundwork for walking him correctly now. You should be gentle with your very young pup. Start by making him comfortable and matter-of-fact about the collar and leash. Choose an appropriately sized harness for your young pup. Or you can use a regular nylon or buckle collar, but you must never pull hard on the collar to correct the puppy.

You should never train a puppy under six months using force, "correction" or "compulsion" methods. In fact, it's debatable whether dogs of any age should be trained by these methods. But owners should be aware that compulsion used to be widely accepted and is still taught in many classes. If you hire a trainer for your puppy, ask him about his methods, and look out for mention of "leash corrections" or "training collars". And then observe. The trainer should use positive methods, luring your puppy with treats and handling him like the delicate little treasure he is. If the trainer jerks or shoves your young puppy or uses any harsh leash corrections, this is unacceptable.

Never use a choke or a prong collar on a puppy under six months and never let a trainer use one! Choke collars (made of chain and also euphemistically called "training collars" or "slip collars" to cover up what they really are) and prong collars (also known as "pinch collars" and resembling metal torture devices with bent nails sticking into your dog's neck) can cause serious injury to puppies with undeveloped musculature. (We personally don't recommend prong or choke collars for any age dog. There is a school of thought amongst trainers that justifies their careful use, but if you train your pup to walk nicely on the leash when young, there's no reason to ever have to use choke or prong collars in future, even if your dog is of a "strong" breed.)

The first step in training proper leash walking is to accustom your puppy to collar and leash. Start by leaving the items lying around with some treats on them and your pup will take the treats and then sniff around collar and leash. Reward him again.

Many puppies will stay calm enough that they will allow you to simply put the collar around their neck. They may act a bit nervous and try to twist around to bite at the collar. If the puppy doesn't seem deeply distressed, distract him with treats and play and soon he'll seem to forget he's wearing the collar. But take it off and then put it on again, treating and encouraging him each time he wears it. Soon he should be wearing it full time. Just make sure the collar is properly fitted. Puppies grow fast, so you will have to keep replacing collars!

If your puppy is extremely wiggly, and/or frightened, you can enlist the aid of a helper who will distract him with toys or treats when you first put on his collar. You can also start by simply laying the collar over his neck at first so he will feel more comfortable with it.

While your puppy is getting comfortable with his collar for a few days, you should also be making him comfortable with walking at your side. First, call him to you on and off throughout the day, encouraging him with kissing sounds, running backward or clapping your hands. Puppies under sixteen weeks are hard-wired to desperately want to follow their "parent" and they will *want* to come to you. *Capitalize on this tendency now.* Each time your pup comes, lavishly reward with praise and/or treats.

Next, start calling the pup to you as you walk. Make him follow, luring with treats if necessary. Praise and encourage with loads of excited baby talk! Next, approximate heeling by having your pup walk alongside you off leash. Some trainers stick a treat onto the end of a small dowel or stick to lure the dog. Or you can hold a treat or toy in your hand, hung down at your left side. Make your dog stay by your left side, walking near you for as long as possible, and practice this type of walking together in the house whenever you get a chance. Wind around obstacles, speed up and slow down and make staying by your side a challenge. Take the game into your enclosed yard if you wish, and have different family members try it.

This is a great way to "play" with your puppy, and it can replace many of the "Dangerous Games" in chapter 15. When practicing with puppies, it's best to keep all individual training sessions short. Just do short five or ten minute sessions frequently through the day. As the dog becomes older, sessions can last longer. *You should continue playing this "game" for the life of your dog at least a few times a week.* "Heel" off the leash like this everywhere in your house and yard. Your dog should want to stay so close to your side that you'll hardly be able to shake him!

As your puppy learns to walk with you in a heel off leash, you should also be accustoming him to the leash. Introduce the leash along with the collar. Hook it on and offer treats. Allow him to drag the leash around under your supervision, just so he learns to treat it as an everyday item and it doesn't overexcite him. The first place to use the leash is in the house. Call your pup to you as you lightly hold the leash. Then practice "Follow the Leader" (described in this chapter) using the umbilical cord technique, where you keep the leash looped around your wrist or connected to a belt loop.

You can walk your puppy around the house with you on and off all day. He'll come to feel perfectly natural walking at your side, watching you as you complete your daily tasks and matching his pace to yours. His species are genetically destined to feel comfortable matching their walking to their pack leader's, and working and walking properly with the pack leader gives dogs a sense of purpose. Your puppy will graduate to walking delightedly beside you as an adult and you will avoid many of the boredom-caused behavior problems many of your neighbors may suffer with their dogs.

The first formal leash walking your puppy should experience is when he goes outside each time he urinates or defecates. At first, you shouldn't put your puppy out in the yard on his own, or it will be extremely difficult to housebreak him. Instead, you should be with him to supervise when he "does his business". Each time you take him out, clip on the leash. If he's in the middle of a bowel or bladder accident, carry him out rapidly, but then place him down on leash.

Because of undeveloped immunity it's safest to take your puppy for walks in the backyard or another private area at this age, rather than out on a public street. If you do take him in public areas you must be hyper-vigilant until your puppy has had his final vaccinations. (This is usually around 16 weeks, but check with your veterinarian.) *Do not expose your young puppy to the droppings of other dogs. Doing so might expose him to deadly infection. And don't expose him to high levels of stress at this age either.*

You've probably heard that you should socialize your puppy and socialization before twelve weeks is important. Exposure to varied stimuli, such as the sight of pedestrians and the sound of traffic, helps your puppy build confidence and learn that the world is safe. On the flip side, too much exposure to frightening stimuli (like unfriendly dogs) may backfire. There is also risk because of your puppy's weak immune system. The best course of action is a moderate one. You can walk your young puppy a little bit on leash in public areas, but wherever you walk him should be safe and relatively calm and uncrowded. The temperature should also be in an ideal range at the time of the walk.

On these first walks a young puppy (8, 10 or 12 weeks old) is not likely to wander far, or pull on the leash hard enough to injure himself. If he tries to pull, distract him first. Lure him with treats, sounds or running backwards. (A harness may also be more appropriate for some young puppies than a buckle collar if you need to pull on him to get him moving or correct him from pulling forward or going after dangerous items. But never pull too hard on your young puppy, even if he is wearing a harness, since injury is possible.)

The art of walking is learning how to make your dog follow you. At his young age, you won't be teaching the puppy the command "heel" yet. He'll simply learn to walk with you softly on the leash. **If he's not paying attention to you, quickly change direction and he'll follow. Increase pace if he slows, but slow your pace if he tries to walk too fast. Teach him the "Watch" command** (see Chapter 8- Problem Dog Games) **and use it to make him focus on you at times as you walk. Do not use any harsh leash corrections on a young puppy.** Books with instructions on making your dog heel better abound but, if you read these books, ignore any instructions that involve jerking or pulling your puppy. **Turns, stopping, speeding up and body language are better alternatives.**

Your young puppy should respond beautifully to walking with you on a loose leash. You should also teach him to heel, right up by your side, dog-show style, even if you don't think now that you'll need the command. When your dog's older, you'll want him perfectly controlled in the face of distractions, and teaching him to "heel" when he's tiny will help immeasurably and possibly change your entire future together for the better. If your puppy is not progressing well with heeling and loose leash walking and you've already read many books, the next step is to try a DVD to see gentle techniques in practice. You can also consult a professional trainer for advice and to demonstrate gentle techniques so you can start practicing perfectly with your puppy.

Safety note: Do not copy everything you see on television! Taken out of context, and practiced at home, forceful leash training methods demonstrated by certain of the most popular television trainers with adult dogs can seriously injure young puppies! These methods are not intended for puppies under six months or for any dog that is physically compromised or for some dogs with serious emotional disorders. Even with mature and physically sound dogs, we recommend trying the softest methods first.

Obedience-minded
-not just what you already know, but some important facts you probably *don't* know about obedience-

Training your dog obedience is not a form of drudgery, nor is meant to be harsh or domineering. If you love your puppy, you'll want to train him obedience because failing to do so would be like not training your children to talk, read or write. Obedience is the language through which dogs and their owners learn to communicate with each other and, as such, it is miraculous. There is a moment when your dog first "gets" that a certain verbal command brings reward that feels as beautiful as the sun peeking through the clouds on a cloudy day. That instant is nothing short of transcendent and we are privileged as in-home dog trainers to experience it on a regular basis. When an owner first experiences their puppy responding to them their face lights up. This is truly owner and dog relating to each other at their finest!

> *The best time to start obedience is the moment you meet your puppy. Believe it or not you are teaching your puppy how to behave from the moment you meet him.*
>
> *Puppies learn from every interaction they have in life with humans or dogs.*
>
> *Do you want your puppy to learn good or bad behaviors? It's up to you!*

The time to start teaching your puppy "obedience" is from the moment you bring him home. If you do not teach him desired behaviors, you'll be reinforcing undesired ones with every interaction. For example, if you pet your dog each time he jumps on you, even if he hurts you, he'll want to jump on all your guests as well. And he won't understand if you simply shriek and squeal. You'll have to teach him an alternative. The classic obedience commands are "sit", "down", "stay", "heel" and "come". And these commands can be combined with standardized hand signals as well as given verbally to accommodate most needs.

The reason these commands have been around so long is that they work. "Sit" is usually the easiest command to teach and it comes in handy as an alternative to many undesired behaviors. Commands like "watch me", "stand", "leave it" and "drop it" and "go to your place" are also useful. In addition to formal practice sessions, you and your family should practice your dog's obedience commands throughout the day in real-life situations. All family members should know the dog's obedience commands and you should practice obedience with your dog, in small real-life increments, *every day for the rest of his life.*

There is no best way to teach your puppy obedience- *as long as you use gentle methods, gentle equipment and always use a patient and loving attitude.* (Please see all the cautions in the "Walk This Way" section above.) **In most cases, with healthy emotionally stable pups, we recommend researching and reading up on obedience training and training your dog yourself.** You can also consult DVD's, watch trainers on television, attend group classes and/or hire a home trainer (see cautions in the sections above.)

A home trainer may be most costly but they can demonstrate methods in your home in a manner that best "clicks" with your family and your lifestyle. In the unregulated dog training industry, trainers that advertise as "professional" range from highly educated dog lovers who have devoted their whole lives to the study of animals, to well-meaning young people whose education is limited to a single two-week technical class to individuals who use rough methods and/or misrepresent the fair cost of training. Screening for a dog trainer's education or certifications can be helpful. But, there's no standard license or qualifications required for dog trainers, so even these methods of screening fall short and much depends on the trainer's personality and bond with your pet.

Another way to start your search is by looking for personal references or a recommendation from a veterinarian. But these methods aren't foolproof either. (Everyone has friends, and some in the dog community truly believe that painful training methods are best!) Another good way to start your search is by having long conversations with several trainers and grilling them about all their methods in specific situations. But, unfortunately, some trainers are very comfortable promoting themselves, but they might not put as much energy into your dog. To be safe, we recommend owners use *all* the methods mentioned to narrow down the field when screening dog trainers, but you should also go one step farther. The best way to decide on a good home dog trainer is to observe them with your dog and your family.

Make sure that the person who does your evaluation will also be the person training your dog. (Some franchise companies actually send out salespeople on the first visit, so it's best to ask.) A true professional will ask you a lot of questions as well, and they will demand to know that your dog is healthy before training him. They will also be able to give you a detailed assessment of your dog's needs and how they will be training each command.

Obedience training is exhausting, both mentally and physically (it's like learning a new sport) and, at the end of the session, don't be surprised if both you and your puppy feel completely bushed. (This is a *good* thing. Even the *trainer* may feel a little tired.) But an ethical trainer will not exhaust your puppy in hot sun, or train to the point where the puppy feels ill. Don't expect a professional trainer to spoil or fuss over dogs any more than a teacher or coach would their students, since this might defeat the aims of training. But you should get an underlying feeling that your trainer feels warmth towards your puppy and truly enjoys educating him.

Even though training is tough, just like a day at school, your puppy should also indicate that, generally, he enjoys it. Good signs are if the pup "smiles" at, wags at or "kisses" the trainer and if he greets the trainer happily the next time the trainer comes for a session. *Note: some dogs with serious fears or aggression problems or undersocialized dogs may not greet anybody at the door, ever. And it's realistic for a professional trainer who specializes in these cases not to expect any affection to be shown until many sessions later.*

But, if a trainer is working with a normal young puppy with no existing fears, we'd be concerned if the puppy did not cuddle up to them a bit on the second session. And if a trainer ever used force, yelled at our puppy or made our puppy scream or squeal in pain, we would immediately stop the training. **Unfortunately, some of the dogs we're called to treat suffer from severe life-destroying fears that started in popular group training classes when trainers pushed them!** Rough training methods can sometimes intimidate a dog enough to make him obey in the short run- but they don't teach him to want to obey you- and often all these methods produce in your dog is fearfulness and aggression.

Most puppies start out balanced. But genetics or early upbringing can make some young puppies emotionally compromised to the point where the owner may have difficulty shaping them with regular obedience training. In these cases, and if anything feels "off" about your pup, we recommend you seek the help of a true animal behaviorist with an advanced degree. Whether you do it on your own, or with expert assistance, **the most powerful thing you can do to get your dog to behave the way you want him to as an adult is to teach him right as a puppy!**

Soft Mouth
- do this rather than letting your pup grow up to bite you -

Everybody wants a dog that won't nip at their hands, their body or their family members when the dog plays or feels excited. There are many ways people think they can prevent this, but most of these "methods" will do more harm than good, and some even make your dog bite more.

> *Pushing roughly at a dog's mouth or sticking your hands in a dog's mouth in any context, including play, will only teach him to bite.*

The first step in dealing with the problem is to teach your puppy to stop biting you. One way we teach owners to get their pups to stop biting them is the way the pups' littermates would. Right from the start, if your puppy ever puts his mouth on your skin, yelp sharply like a puppy in the litter would, "Yipe!" Your puppy will most likely stop what he's doing and look up at you with a shocked expression on his face. As soon as he does, praise him and put your hand back in front of him. If he tries to nip again, yelp and then walk away from the puppy for a few moments to deprive him of your company. This teaches your puppy that, if he bites, you'll leave the room and take your treasured attention away from him.

Now that your puppy has learned to stop biting at your hands or any other part of your body, you can proceed to teaching him how to have a "soft mouth" and to use his mouth on you properly. Teach the technique by holding a treat in your hand with a very small piece showing out the edge of your fingers. If the dog tries to take the treat too fast or too hard, turn your hand so the dog can't get the treat. Show the treat again and say the word, "Gentle." Only give the dog the treat when he'll take it gently. The point is to teach your dog that he will be rewarded for using his mouth gently when he interacts with you.

(A popular method of teaching a dog to take treat gently that can backfire is offering the treat on the end of a metal spoon. The problem with this technique is that if the dog does bite too hard, he may break his teeth., so it's best not to try it.)

Some people unfortunately think that you can break a dog of biting by holding him down by the back of the neck and shaking and yelling at him. This will only serve to make your dog afraid of you, and it will not teach him to use a soft mouth. An even worse response that a good number of people resort to is responding to a pup that nips by punching him in the face or shoving their fist down his throat. Despite the fact that it strikes us as horrible, many people do it. Unfortunately, hurting the pup like this when he's nipping in play will never make your dog gentle. It will make him fear or distrust humans and it will likely incite him pup to bite more and harder next time.

Pushing roughly at a dog's mouth or sticking your hands in a dog's mouth in any context, including play, will only teach him to bite. (See "Bite Me" in Ch. 15). If someone treated us humans this way, we'd probably want to bite, too. Remember that if we want our dogs to be gentle, we can only do this by showing gentleness to set an example of what we want.

Puppy Grooming
- a highly recommended daily activity to build the dog/owner bond -

Why would you want to groom your 8 week-old puppy if he really doesn't need it? Because gently brushing your puppy, or grooming him in some fashion every single day is one of the best things you can do to create the kind of temperament that you want in your adult dog.

As home dog trainers specializing in severe canine emotional problems, we often encounter dogs and puppies who do not like to tolerate their owners' touch! These dogs' reactions range from showing stress and discomfort, to shying or jerking away, to growling at, snapping at or even biting whenever their owner tries to pet them! Not every dog will show severe reactions like this, and these reactions could stem from complex problems that require professional assessment. But there is a strong correlation between proper handling during a pup's developmental stages and how the dog will react to human touch throughout its life. Unfortunately, once a dog starts resisting activities like grooming, the owner may give in and avoid the activity, creating a vicious cycle.

Proper grooming is important to dogs' health and well-being and it's also one of the cornerstone activities for developing a healthy dog/owner bond. Not every breed of dog requires the same amount of attention to their coat. Some short-haired breeds do not physically need to be brushed every day, while some of the popular small breeds with lush coats must have proper trimming and brushing to avoid illness. But every dog requires time to experience his owners' gentle touch every day, and grooming time is the perfect opportunity.

Canines naturally groom each other in the wild as part of their bonding ritual, and puppies should understand that their owner grooms them out of caring. Thus the process should feel good. Start by brushing your puppy with the softest brush you can find- the equivalent of a human baby brush. Or wipe your pup down with a pleasantly warm damp towel. If the pup resists at first, you can simply hold him close and wait for him to calm down, or you could hold a treat out for him to nibble on. This is not, however, a time for you to set your pup down, even if he wiggles and tries to get free. He should learn that the grooming process is overall pleasant and nothing to fear; but he should also learn that his owner knows best and that he must tolerate the owner manipulating his body, whenever required.

The best way to create a healthy mindset in your puppy is to start young and practice every day. Make daily brushing a pleasant experience and also introduce your pup to tooth brushing, nail clipping (or touching nails), ear cleaning and bathing at a young age. Family members should alternate brushing the puppy, so that the pup will come to enjoy and respect everyone's touch. And parents can use this time to teach even young children how to handle dogs with a calm and gentle touch, so that the tiny puppy will fall asleep happily in their arms. Rather than playing too rough with the puppy, children can learn a steadier and calmer manner of interacting through practice.

Adults should supervise grooming sessions at first, to make sure the children handle the puppy correctly. And parents must also confirm that the puppy reacts appropriately and does not attempt to snap at the children. Unfortunately, a good number of adult dogs and even some puppies that come from unknown backgrounds may not have been socialized properly prior to coming to your home. Notable examples are pups bred and raised in "puppy mills" or pups that have suffered abuse. Dogs and pups that are highly sensitive to human touch may bite severely during grooming, so young children should not be put in charge of grooming on their own. An adult should carefully supervise until you are certain of the dog's temperament. Start young with your puppy, offer occasional treats and lots of praise and soon grooming will become a highly relaxing daily ritual that feels completely natural to everyone. And even your pup will happily anticipate grooming time!

New Learning Every Day (Puppy)
- if you're not doing this, your pup can't achieve his full potential -

Scientists still haven't come up with a definitive answer to how smart dogs are, but each study seems to indicate dogs (and other canines) are much smarter than we previously thought. Watch a video of wolves hunting and then imagine the skill it takes to hunt together successfully as a pack without using any words to communicate!

Of course, dog lovers like the authors don't need science to tell us how intelligent our dogs are- just looking into our Akita Casey's contemplative eyes was enough to tell us he was a sentient being. And then there was Casey's Oriental pride- this dog understood exactly what we said about him, and he took deep offense if we ever laughed inappropriately!

You may have your own stories to tell about your dog's intelligence. And hearing about the life-saving accomplishments of service, rescue and working police dogs should be enough to convince anyone how smart dogs are. So, if people know this, why do many of us leave our dogs alone all day with nothing at all to do?

Some owners come home from work after hours of leaving their dog with nothing to engage his mind and they immediately usher him out into a blank yard to spend his evening alone until bedtime with nothing to stimulate his senses other than some sandy turf and a privacy fence. These owners forget that, depending upon what their dog was bred for, years ago he might have spent his time flushing small game out of tunnels, protecting a tax collector on his rounds, herding sheep or cattle, rescuing lost hikers, saving drowning swimmers or even hunting bear!

Knowing the intensity of activity dogs were bred for, is it any wonder that when we give them absolutely nothing to do, they develop behavior problems including destructiveness, anxiety or depression? Worse yet, if an owner doesn't provide their dog's life with meaning the fire may go out of the dog's eyes and he may have difficulty understanding or caring about what they want of him. The dog may start acting up simply out of frustration and boredom and he'll never fulfill the great inner potential his owner may have never even been aware of.

So that this never happens to you, now, when your dog is still a puppy, is the ideal time to learn about his unique potential. Start by reading up on the history of his breed and you may be amazed!

If you own a young puppy, we challenge you now to help his full potential bloom to set the stage for an ideal life with him for years to come. The best way to do this is with learning, learning and more learning. **We recommend new learning every single day for dogs, and we also recommend it for people!** Vow right now to present your puppy with at least one new learning experience every day. Take the quality time to be with him and help him learn something new.

The first type of learning everyone thinks of is obedience training. And, while it is important to practice obedience, the real challenge comes in working the tasks into everyday life. Some good examples of **using obedience in real life** include teaching your dog to sit while allowing his owner to enter and exit doors first, or practicing a "stay" with ever increasing distractions. Other useful commands include "Watch Me" (see Chapter 8- Problem Dog Games) and "go to your place". Take time to practice these commands with your dog, and you'll be rewarded with a more comfortable lifestyle.

Socializing your dog to interact properly with humans and animals in diverse situations is also a form of learning. (See "Shopping Spree," this chapter and "Diversity Training", Chapter 13). Teaching your dog to distinguish and track down different family members is also an important skill (See "Find Mommy" in this chapter and "Find the Missing Person" in Chapter 12, Useful Games). If your dog masters this skill, he may one day save somebody's life!

Teaching your dog proper house manners (for example, to stop barking or not to jump on furniture) is also a positive learning experience for your dog. Believe it or not, if your dog could talk, he would thank you for expressing your desires to him, for it gives him a sense of structure.

Taking a dog for long, bonding walks with you also serves as a form of learning, especially if you experience new terrain and new stimuli. Try a different route, walk in snow, sand or leaves, weave through obstacles or jump over small hurdles together. Play outdoor games like "Frisbee" and "Fetch" (described in Chapter 10, High Energy Activities). Play or swim in the water together (described in Chapter 11, Water Activities). All these are great activities for healthy dogs and puppies with no physical limitations.

This book also includes imaginative choices for owners- and dogs- with less mobility (chapters 9 & 14). And whatever method you use to get fit and healthy together, your dog will experience a primal feeling of bonding with you.

Exercise options can also be formalized, of course. Join an obedience club, show your dog in the AKC ring or join a Rally, Agility or Flyball club with your dog. Or just set up your own mini agility course in your back yard. Each time your dog masters a new obstacle, that's new learning. Also learn to enjoy activities like dancing, meditation, stretching or yoga with your dog- these are all forms of learning as well, and activities like this that fit your lifestyle can also be enjoyable to your dog. All these activities are described in detail in this book.

Other games described in this book (including walking over different surfaces, searching for a hidden treat in cardboard boxes in your living room, distinguishing different color balls, barking yes or no, performing tricks- even jumping rope or dancing with you) may seem a bit silly, but they're actually great fun. Teaching your puppy these activities makes everyone smile, and the kids will happily join in for some high-quality, stress-free family time.

Throughout your dog's life, you will have the opportunity to introduce him to literally thousands of new learning experiences- at least one new concept or opportunity a day. This book alone contains hundreds of different ideas and we will be delighted if you use some of these as jumping-off points. The only thing necessary is planning and commitment. You must actively set aside time every day to work with your dog. We recommend you put it on paper, writing down the new activity you wish to practice with your dog each day and how you will teach it. Two lines in your appointment book is preferable to letting all your other commitments crowd out healthy fulfilling time with your dog.

And get your family involved as well, including your children. Let them think up new games that might be fun to play with your dog, and let them take the responsibility for setting things up. Planning ahead what you want to accomplish with your dog will also keep you from playing bad or destructive games with your dog (see Ch. 15- Dangerous Games). Some of these bad games have been old standbys of puppy husbandry for Americans for many years. The problem is that these activities tend to bring out bad behaviors later on in your dog's life. Instead, **write a wish list of all the different things you'd love your dog to accomplish. And then, over the course of his lifetime, spend time with him and make the wishes come true.**

New learning is something you should be doing every single day of your dog's lifetime, but there are some types of learning especially suited to young puppies. These include teaching your puppy to snuggle gently in your arms, to handle you gently with his teeth

("Soft Mouth") or to happily tolerate a veterinary exam ("Let's Play Doctor"). Another important game for a puppy is learning to love to come to you ("Circle of Love"). There is no age too early to teach your puppy that coming to you is fun.

You can also work on his senses now, with Balance and Coordination Activities (see Chapter 6), fine-tune his sense of smell (see "The Shell Game", Chapter 4), or his mental acuity ("Which Hand?") and attention span ("Watch Me"). **Start teaching your young puppy the proper manner of greeting guests, how to potty outside, how to love to walk beside you on a leash, even how to ask you for attention by doing something you want him to do, rather than pestering you.** All of these things are learning and, when you view it that way, you will see that one new task a day is really not much- your dog has the capacity to learn many, many new things each day.

Randi- "Teachers Pet!"

And what does your dog do if you don't consciously teach him the things you *want* him to learn? He learns things you'd *never* want him to learn, like the surest route to climb up onto your countertop, to bark when he demands attention or to open your refrigerator door. One of the things many of our customers find hard to understand at first is that your dog is wired to be a pack animal and to learn from each and every interaction with your family. Each time he repeats a negative behavior and it isn't extinguished, it only becomes more ingrained. But the solution doesn't have to be to punishment. A much easier solution to fill those empty hours is teach your dog to *want* to be the dog you want him to be, and you will both lead a happier life!

Ch. 4 Mental Games & Activities

"Working with your dog's intelligence improves his behavior, while neglecting his mind can cause serious problems."

Also Try These Ideas From Other Chapters For Mental Activities:

Puppy Games & Activities: Follow the Leader, Find the Treat, Which Hand?, How Do I Get What Is In There?, Obedience-minded, Which Box Has the Fun In It?, Shopping Spree, New Learning Every Day, Find Mommy

Indoor Games & Activities: Yes or No, Hide & Go Seek, Freestyle

Balance and Coordination Activities: Play the Seal, Walk the Line, Stack, Catch the Frisbee, Basketball, Different Surfaces

Multi-Dog Games & Activities: Simon Says, What's My Name, The Long Long Stay, Under/Over, Agility Competition at Home, Obedience Competition at Home

Problem Dog Games: Interactive Toys, When I Move, You Move, Stop barking on command,

Therapeutic and Senior Dog Activities: Meditation, Look in the Leaves, More Learning Every Day

Activities for High-Energy Dogs: Tracking Competition, Agility, Flyball

Water Activities: Net Pull, Submarine

Useful Activities : Follow The Scent, Personal Bodyguard, Service Dog, Find My Keys, Carry My Purse, Help Your Special Needs Family Member, Check On Grandma, Bark for Help, Check the Perimeter, Work With Livestock, Watch Your Children, Real Dog Careers, Movie Star, Lifesaver

Family Activities: Diversity Training, Petstar at Home, Demonstrate Tricks, Junior Handlers, Different Handlers, Jump Rope

Activities for Owners with Limited Mobility: Service Dog, Obedience/Agility Clubs, Balloons, Be Creative

Mental Games & Activities- Introduction
"Working with your dog's intelligence improves his behavior, neglecting his mind can cause serious problems."

Many people are surprised when we tell them that, in order to thrive, dogs need mental games in addition to physical games and exercise. And many people who should know better still believe that dogs are menial animals without complex thought processes. But scientific studies have shown that dogs (and other canines) are capable of highly advanced thinking and incredible memory. There's also evidence that dogs possess the ability to count and solve complex mathematical problems.

> _In order to thrive, dogs need mental games in addition to physical games and exercise._

Dogs also excel in their ability to understand what humans are thinking and they're able to read and mimic our facial expressions almost as well as chimpanzees, the primates known to be most sophisticated at this. Many owners have experienced our dogs mimicking our smiles or frowns, and part of the reason we love dogs so much is because they seem to always understand and empathize with what we feel. Have you ever frowned and rubbed your forehead in frustration while paying the household bills and your dog immediately noticed your worry and hurried over to give you a gentle kiss? Have you ever smiled, and your dog "smiled" back?

You've probably heard that dogs only live in the present, and this is the opinion of most experts, but dogs' understanding of reality is much more complex than most people give them credit for. Dogs may not understand the concept of time in the same way people do, but dogs _can_ remember. If dogs had no memory, they wouldn't be able to learn from past mistakes and they might die from those same mistakes if they made them again. Observe dogs and wolves and you'll also notice they learn from actions they see hurt other canines.

The real reason punishing dogs after-the-fact doesn't tend to work has more to do with dogs' emotional state of living in the present then their memory. In other words, your dog does have capacity to remember past actions and consequences. What he cannot understand is why a loving owner would be angry at a given moment because of something that happened hours ago and has no current impact.

If, on the other hand, the dog's action has immediate negative consequences, he can display what's called "single event learning". For example, one of our customers' pups teased a horse until the horse nipped her. "Single event learning" means she will likely act cautious around horses for the rest of her life, without ever having to repeat the bad experience. Dogs also possess an intelligent ability to generalize. So if this puppy encounters a cow in later life, she'll likely easily generalize from what happened with the horse.

As another evidence of dogs' mental abilities, many of us have firsthand experience of dogs that understand what we are talking about. You ask your dog, "Do you want to go to the park?" and he replies with whining and a furiously wagging tail. If you're a skeptic, you may argue that this reaction only has to do with the fact that you seem excited and you may believe that human feelings also affect your dog if he overhears you mention a trip to the veterinarian and he cringes. But it's harder for skeptics to explain away the intelligence of dogs that learn to identify every one of their toys and every family member by name, and seeing-eye and assistance dogs that learn hundreds of tasks and make lifesaving judgments.

The fact is, dogs are definitely intelligent. Humans may find them less so because we have difficulty understanding their motivators or their tendency toward stoicism and living in the moment. We also have difficulty understanding mental powers that are different than our own. And current methods of research may not be equal to dogs' varied ability and scope, including their keen intuition and accuracy reading energy. But in future, as observation methods become more sophisticated, more holistic and more imaginative, perhaps science will reveal much more of what dogs are really capable of.

Working dogs already perform challenging jobs including search and rescue and helping disabled owners with a wide variety of tasks. And many loving dog owners have their own individual stories to tell of their dogs' remarkable accomplishments. Dogs are not exactly like us, and their brains may not be wired exactly like ours. Nor can their responses be quantified like ours. So perhaps, when future studies are done on dogs' intelligence, there will be no further need for laboratories, electrodes or cages. The best place to learn the truth of dogs' abilities is in the real world.

Once a dog owner gets a glimpse of the true complexity of a dog's mind, they also have a better idea of why it's so dangerous to let that mind atrophy, without proper stimulation. A tragic example is puppies brought up in a "puppy mill" environment, denied any proper positive socialization between 7-20 weeks. Studies have shown that puppies completely deprived of socialization during this developmental period grow up to show a severe aversion to contact or interaction with humans. They also suffer from lifelong difficulties learning-similar to symptoms of autism in children.

Proper mental stimulation is necessary for development of a dog's senses and his emotional balance. Often, dogs left long-term in a blank environment with nothing to engage them start showing symptoms of anxieties or depression including listlessness, loss of appetite, fears, phobias and self-mutilation.

Insufficient stimulation and engagement can also hurt your dog later in life. If your older dog's life was full with activity when he was young but he suddenly becomes disabled and loses his daily work, he can suffer like some retirees suddenly faced with nothing to do. To keep your dog vital and active, you must always give him something to occupy his mind. If your senior dog loses sources of mental stimulation, this will likely show up in a downward spiral in his physical health, as well as a greater susceptibility to deterioration of his mind, similar to senile dementia in humans. Providing more mental activities can sometimes help this serious disorder.

Dogs whose minds are given lots of interesting puzzles and games actually get smarter. And dogs that master one challenging activity can more happily and effortlessly learn others. For example, a surprising number of champion show dogs also work full-time at complex activities ranging from shepherd to therapy dog and many also compete in obedience and agility. The more you teach a dog, the more they seem able to learn. And dogs whose days are full of demanding "career" activities also seem to be the best behaved.

One of the most important aspects of your dog performing mental activities is that it teaches him to use judgment in all things. In other words, not every dog reacts, or *overreacts*, similarly when faced with new situations and some dogs consistently react with better judgment than others. No owner can practice for every new stimulus or situation their dog may encounter in life, and we all know those dogs that seem to react to new things wildly, immediately going out of control. On the other hand, **a dog that regularly practices mental activities will tend to think before he acts in new situations**. In turn, this makes the situation more manageable and positive and leads to further confidence, self-esteem and presence of mind in the dog.

Some owners may experience decades of disappointment with dogs that act reactive to everything. And they may have never experienced the pleasure of a life companion who acts like a centered and sentient being. If you meet a friend or neighbor's dog that displays the quality of careful judgment, you may envy the person, wondering where they bought such a unique animal or what they had to pay. But the quality of sound judgment and mental reflection was more likely something they taught their dog than something inborn. Ask this person to describe in detail what their dog's days are like, and you will likely find that he regularly exercises his mind and has been doing so since he was a puppy.

Don't ever hesitate to give your dog activities to engage his mind- the more the better. Boredom is toxic for a dog, and extreme boredom can actually send susceptible dogs' nervous systems off kilter. Some dogs become depressed or listless. But some react in the other extreme, acting out with constant problem behaviors like jumping on people, soiling the house or destroying possessions. Meanwhile, improving the dog's behavior may literally be as simple as offering him the right type of toys to engage his mind!

Taking time to plan some interesting mental games for your dog can help save your sanity and your possessions. When a dog becomes bored or frustrated, their inborn reactions start to resemble those of a caged wolf including: chewing on things, pacing nonstop, digging holes and barking incessantly. These behaviors come naturally to canines, and they tend to relieve boredom, just as an addiction or compulsive habit might offer solace to a human being. So it's up to us to offer the dogs an alternative.

People should also remember that every dog breed was created to do a specific job. But most of those jobs don't fit in today's world. So now our world is filled with dogs bred for tasks that demanded tremendous energy and thought, with most of those challenging tasks taken away. Instead, many of these dogs now live isolated in homes (or locked in crates) all day long with nothing to do with their minds. Dogs like this seem to spend this time either planning how to drive their owners crazy with bad behavior or manipulate their owners to give them what they want.

A dog in this situation is not actually planning to act malicious. But when he's finally let out of a crate after eight hours he may focus all his mental power on immediately getting what he needs to make himself feel better. The dog may act wild or disrespectful or, in extreme cases, fearful or even aggressive. This can lead to the owners becoming frustrated and putting him back in the crate for even less attention. The vicious cycle may end with a dog placed in the pound, or even euthanized, when the right daily activities could have prevented the problem. Of course, every case is different and fear and aggression can have many causes, including genetic. But, sometimes, simply engaging with your dog and refocusing his mind can have remarkable effects.

Start mental games and activities immediately when your dog is a puppy and watch your dog bloom as he matures. He'll bond with you better, listen more to your commands and make you proud in ways you might not even have anticipated. But if your dog is already an adult that won't listen to you or drives you crazy with bad behavior, simply try some of the mental games in this chapter and the mental games from other chapters throughout the book. Then get creative. The more mental demands you make on your dog, the happier he'll be. You'll have a better behaved dog, a dog with a stronger bond with your family and a dog that you'll be proud to bring out into the world to show off to others. Now *your* neighbors may be the ones asking you where you found such a wonderful dog!

Mental Games:

Movie Star
- you'll never regret making movies of your dog, but you'll regret it if you don't -

You can train your dog like they do for the movies! Of course, everybody likes to videotape their dogs, but why not take it a bit more seriously? First decide which activities you'd like to film your dog performing. Obedience? Tricks? Sports? Two your dogs interacting together? Or your dog just looking cute and affectionate? Prepare ahead, and then practice short takes in front of the camera. You can indicate to your dog that filming is starting with a word like, "Action", and then release him with a word like "Okay" when the film has stopped rolling.

Some intelligent/inquisitive dogs seem to be natural hams in front of a camera. While they have no way of envisioning the finished product, they seem to understand that when they perform in front of the camera, they make their owners happy. And some dogs particularly savor being the center of attention. Filming is a good way to give these dogs the attention they crave in a highly focused manner.

Making a movie also focuses the human owners and provides a welcome challenge. Rather than feeling bored on a lazy afternoon, you can accomplish something while bonding with your dog and creating a permanent record of what you love about him. Your teens or preteens may especially enjoy tackling the movie project and showing their creativity, and filming is a good way to interact with your dog when bad weather keeps you inside.

Just be cautious about too much moviemaking with your dog if he's not comfortable with it! Some dogs have a great sense of humor, great control and they are big "hams" who love every minute of filming. But others can get stressed if they don't understand what's wanted of them and the owner keeps correcting while "chasing" them with the camera. So, always keep sessions short and upbeat and fun!

Note that if your dog appears truly fearful of the camera, it's possible his fear could be a phobia. Cameras have been implicated in phobic reactions in some dogs and the symptom is more likely in dogs that suffer other phobias. You may be able to get your dog past a fear of cameras by slow desensitization; for example, providing treats as he approaches the camera at closer and closer distances. (See the book *Help for the Fearful Dog* in Resources for more information on desensitization.) Never force the camera on your dog during his training or push him past his comfort zone; simply keep cameras away from him until he can be calm around them. If your attempts at desensitization don't work and the problem with cameras concerns you, consult a professional animal behaviorist, just as you would with any other serious fear.

An easier solution, if the distaste for the camera is an isolated fear, is to simply find other activities as alternatives to using a camera with your dog.

Watch Me
-when your dog looks in your eyes, you know he's listening; not making trouble-

When you teach your dog to watch you, you're teaching him to concentrate on you completely. This focus keeps your dog from running after every distraction and it also makes it easier for him to care for you, anticipate your needs and follow your instructions. Teaching the command is extremely easy and it's an extremely powerful tool to increase bonding. Just imagine a person staring deeply into your eyes and how you felt connected.

The "watch me" command, which you may also wish to teach as "look" or "look at me", is suitable for dogs ranging from young puppies to seniors. It helps with problem dogs including shy and hyperactive dogs and you can use it regardless of any physical limitations on the part of owner or dog. This is truly an all purpose command with no downside, and sometimes it's the best command to initially get the attention of a dog that won't focus or won't keep his body still. When done properly, a dog practicing "watch me" or "look at me" will look very much like a show dog staring up at its handler.

You first teach the command by holding a treat in your hand near the dog's nose, and then bring the treat up to your own nose, calling attention to your face. The second the dog makes contact with your eyes say, "Good watch me," and immediately reward him with the treat. Impeccable timing is essential. You must mark the eye contact with immediate praise and offer the treat quickly. Never wait until your dog glances away!

Practice at least five or six times, or more if necessary, until your dog is making the connection that he gets the reward for looking at you. Next hide the treats in a pocket, put your empty hand with no treat in it near the dog's nose and then bring it up to your eyes, while commanding, "Watch me". The moment your dog meets your eyes, praise and reward. Repeat as many times as necessary until your dog masters the command at this level.

Next make the challenge more complex by waving around a treat held out in one extended hand, while you hold your other hand near your nose to draw attention to your face. If your dog is distracted and keeps staring at the hand with the treat instead of your eyes when you command, "Watch me", withhold reward. Instead, quit for a moment, walk around a few steps and then try the command again. The second your dog's eyes do meet yours, immediately praise and reward.

Practice many times a day at unexpected moments. As your dog becomes more proficient, only offer food rewards for the quickest and best performances. You should also practice frequently without the hand gesture so your dog will watch you with just the voice command.

Next practice "watch me" outside and introduce distractions. Start with a helper running around and making noise. When your dog gets good at ignoring this, you can gradually build up to making him watch you as dogs, cats, squirrels and kids on skateboards go by.

Before you know it all you'll have to do is say, "Watch me," and your dog will look up at you from anywhere. This becomes a valuable tool to use when your dog is distracted when outside on a walk. The stronger your control of your dog with this command, the less you will have to fight his instincts, even in the most challenging situations.

(Note: Don't confuse the "watch me" command with the "Watch him!" command used in protection training. Most average owners and dogs will never encounter situations where you'll want to command your dog to attack an intruder. However, if you don't know your dog's history and there's a chance he may have been protection trained, or if you wish to protection train him in future, make sure not to confuse him. Simply choose the wording "Look" or "Look at me" when you command him to look into your eyes.)

Wait
- basic command to teach self-control -

This is a good game to make your dog think more and learn greater self-control. It can help stop your dog from running away and can be used any time you just need your dog to be calm and wait for you. For example, you may be familiar with days when you are trying to leave for work in the morning and your dog runs out the door for a daily run that you didn't plan for! You may be late for work or have to take the day off as you travel the town frantically looking for him.

Dogs also seem to run out the door just as their owners return home from a tiring day at work, anticipating a nice dinner. Instead, by the time you find the dog, your dinner is stone cold and no longer the great meal you had planned. Just remembering such incidents is stressful.

The good news is that it's easy to change this behavior, starting with the knowledge that it's in the deepest nature of dogs not to want to rush past their owner in a doorway *if*, and only if, that owner shows complete confidence.

To first teach the command, call the dog to the door and ask him to sit. Then say, "Wait," and open the door just a little. If your dog breaks from sit, just close the door, repeat, "Wait," and try again. If the dog waits this time, go ahead and step out the door. If he remains waiting, you can now tell him, "Okay," and let him out the door. You will now practice this exercise as frequently as necessary until your dog will wait for your command to step out the door.

The "Wait" command is versatile. You can use it during walks, and if you want your dog to hesitate during play. Use this great command anytime you need your dog to hesitate at a doorway, including in public places and when you are allowing him to get out of your vehicle.

Another way to use the "Wait" cue is to stop your dog from running up and jumping on your visitors whenever they step through the door. Teach your dog that when a guest enters your home he can only approach them when you release him with "Okay". This way you can control when and how your dog greets guests.

The best way to practice proper greetings is with the help of somebody the dog sees frequently, but still rushes to meet. Have them knock on the door, and wait. You walk to the door and, if the dog attempts to follow tell him, "Wait." While he's waiting, open the door and let the person in. If your dog attempts to come forward to greet the person coming in, immediately have the person step back out the door again. Command your dog again to wait, open the door and let the person in again.

You may have to repeat the exercise quite a few times. When your dog does wait, you can release the dog with the "Okay" command. Your guest should then call your dog to them, and ask the dog to sit. Now they can pet your dog, and/or offer him a treat and your dog rewarded for all of his patience.

Hold That Position
- more challenging; helps hyperkinetic dogs have fun while gaining control -

This game can be a joy not only for owners whose dogs easily take to the "Stay" command, but also for those of you whose dogs won't voluntarily stay still for one second.

To teach the game to a dog who seems like he wouldn't stay if his life depended on it, start out with lots of patience and love, a handful of treats and your dog on a leash. First put your dog into a sit, and then tell him to "Stay" while holding up your hand in front of him as though directing traffic to stop. (If your dog is at your side you can sweep your hand towards your dog, open palm facing him, as a signal to block him.) Take one step away from your dog and then step back. (If your dog has never successfully stayed before it sometimes helps to hold the leash with very slight pressure over his head.) When your dog stays in place long enough for you to walk away and return to him, praise and give him a treat.

Next repeat the process, but stay away a few more seconds. The better your dog gets at staying, the more you can increase the time. And practice having your dog "Stay" in the "Down" and "Stand" positions as well.

If your dog ever breaks and tries to move around before you release him from the "Stay", just laugh it off. Tell the dog he was silly to move, and withhold reward. For the next attempt after this failure, go back to the point where your dog last succeeded. In other words, if he was successfully staying for three minutes at a time, but failed to hold the "Stay" the first time you attempted four minutes, go back to three minutes for a few successful trials before once again attempting four.

With a little practice, the dog you thought could never stay still will now be staying patiently for longer periods of time and around all kinds of distractions. Remember though, that patience is the key for the owner as well. If you get impatient and act angry while training your dog to stay, it will likely backfire. Your dog will feel confused and alarmed and may lose focus completely.

Once your dog has perfected doing "Stays" under normal circumstances, you can now introduce "Hold that position", a challenging command that will make your dog have to pay attention to you at all times and always think. With this command, you can get your dog to stay still in any position- not just sitting our lying down. All you will do is to give the hand signal your dog already knows for "Stay" and add the verbal command, "Hold that position" or "Hold it".

Start out with dog sitting or standing and then practice with more challenging positions. For example, you can ask your dog to roll over, or put his paws on a family member in a particularly cute position and ask him to "Hold that position" long enough for you to grab a camera. You can also have your dog freeze in a compromising pose!

Some owners have even enlisted this command to help them break their dog's otherwise incorrigible bad habits. Imagine if you catch your dog with his paws up on the kitchen counter and a sandwich in his mouth. You can command "Hold that position" and quickly call everyone in the family as "Witnesses". Your dog will experience a moment of shame when your family members laugh and shake their heads. By the time you release him from the mortifying pose with the "Okay" command a few seconds later and call him to you to you for petting, he will likely not wish to repeat the counter-surfing. And you won't even have to get mad at your dog to solve the problem.

But make sure the command itself holds more positive associations than potentially negative ones. You should use the challenging game of "Hold that position" primarily for fun. You don't want your dog thinking you only use the cue when he is bad or when you want to laugh at him or he won't want to play the game anymore. And we wouldn't blame him; we want things to be fun when we are with our pets.

Never make your dog hold a position that could feel scary or physically uncomfortable. But choose varied enough positions to make the game challenging and fun. The more your dog enjoys this challenge the better. Frequent practice helps keep your dog on his toes at all times, and keeps him thinking to prevent boredom.

And this cue might even become a lifesaver if you needed to stop your dog from running at an animal, person or out into traffic. If your dog is accustomed to obeying you each and every time you command "Hold that position", he will likely stop immediately in these critical situations as well, just out of habit. A dog that practices "Hold that position" frequently will show more restraint and focus more on their owner. He'll also be less likely to run off impulsively on his personal business when he thinks at any moment his owner might just appear and command "Hold that position!"

Listen
- engages your dog by working his refined sense of hearing -

This is an activity that will make your dog better distinguish different sounds and pick up on smaller and smaller sounds. Not only does the practice stimulate the mind, but it will also help your dog to watch your house for intruders.

Since the game makes hearing more alert, you won't want to play "Listen" with a problem barker, or he may start barking at every sound. But, on the other hand, if you have a (physically healthy) dog that consistently acts too shy to bark or that seems listless and bored by life, teaching "Listen" may put some life in him.

To start, first call your dog to you and ask him to sit. Then have a human helper go to another part of the home and snap his or her fingers and then whistle, starting and then restarting the sounds. When your dog's ears first perk up, say, "Good Listen," immediately give the dog a treat.

The next time the person makes a sound, say your dog's name and say, "Listen!" As soon as the dog looks in the direction of the noise, immediately tell him he's good and offer a treat.

You can also teach your dog to bark on cue, if you'd like him to bark when someone is at the door or outside. First ask your dog to listen when an unknown stranger that you enlist makes noise outside the house. If your dog immediately runs accurately to the location nearest the source of the noise, command him "Bark". As soon as he barks, offer a treat. After several occasions you will no longer have to command, "Bark". Simply instruct your dog to "Listen," and offer reward and praise only after he runs toward the source of the noise and barks.

Some owners don't want their dogs to bark or to defend their house at all; they simply want to teach "Listen" as mental stimulation and diversion for their dog or puppy. For this purpose, you could teach your pup to focus on birdsong or the sounds of a rushing stream. And focusing on sounds like this also helps keep senior dogs' senses keen and their minds fresh. If you want to train your dog to listen like this, when your dog shows he hears the sound, reward him for perked up ears and a tilted head, but never reward barking.

Move Slow
- if you don't believe your dog can slow down, he needs this game -

This is a game for people whose dogs act like tornados in the home, running at visitors as they come in the door and knocking them off their feet. One pit mix Emma knew growing up ran around the house so fast the dog literally left the ground and pushed off the walls! If you know a dog like this, you definitely need this game.

Do you enjoy watching nature shows about wolves? It's amazing how wolves can deliberately move so slowly that you almost can't tell they are getting closer to their prey, and then they spring forward with a tremendous burst of speed to catch the animal. Unfortunately, if these wolves just ran out into a field

> *The game of "Move slow" is a way to slow those overexcited pups down.*

like some of the hyperactive dogs we encounter in society today, the species would quickly go extinct because the prey would always know they were coming!

The game of "Move Slow" is a way to slow those overexcited pups down. First leash your dog or puppy and ask him to sit. Then tell the dog, "Slow," and take a step forward. If the dog moves along slowly next to you, allow him to continue moving with you. But if your dog shoots out of the sit like a rocket, just bring him back to your side. Repeat the cue,

"Slow," and give the dog another try. Practice with your dog on leash, until he exhibits perfect control.

Once your dog performs the cue well with the leash hooked, you can move up to practicing off leash. The rules of the game are the same off leash as on, and you can hold a treat at first to encourage your dog to walk along close to your side. If your dog makes a mistake, and lunges ahead too fast, just bring him back to where he started. Give the cue again and when your dog gets it right offer a treat and lots of praise. (You will eventually phase out food rewards for all but the most stellar performances.)

The next step is to practice with a helper to teach your dog to "Move slow" rather than running at guests. Use the same methods, starting on leash. And practice first with a guest your dog is already relatively comfortable and relaxed with. (If he usually acts like a kamikaze pilot around unfamiliar guests, introducing one at his first practice session would certainly set the dog up for failure.) Once he learns "move slow" in the presence of the first helper, practice with additional guests. Depending on your dog's progress and your degree of control, **and assuming your dog is always friendly to strangers**, you can eventually practice with your dog off leash, even when unexpected guests arrive.

It's obvious how teaching your dog to "Move slow" will improve your dog's behavior, but it also works as a great mental game because it hones concentration. Many owners struggle to provide their dogs adequate aerobic exercise, never knowing how adding *mental* exercise can increase intensity and reduce frustration. It is natural for dogs to want to run, but learning to control their bodies adds a whole new dimension. Try the "Move slow" exercise frequently at all times of day, including during play and during walks, and you'll soon notice your dog acting more balanced and happy.

Doggie Einstein
- teach your dog a useful working vocabulary & let him impress you -

Dogs vary in intelligence, between breeds and between individuals, and dogs vary in the way they express their intelligence. (For example, some dogs may be better at scenting and others at herding.) Some owners marvel at their dogs' intelligence and constantly love to tell stories about it. For example, have you met people who have to spell out words like "Walk" because their dog knows exactly what they are talking about? Their next problem comes when their dogs learn to spell! Of course, these owners never stop boasting how brilliant their dogs are.

More common are owners who underestimate their dog's intelligence. Many owners we work with finally get their dog to heel perfectly for the first time and then they walk with him in complete silence! Dogs in the wild do rely mostly on non-verbal communication, and proper body language is essential to communicating with your dog- but **your dog can also learn a little of our language as well. In fact, a dog can easily learn hundreds of distinct**

words during his lifetime. If you fail to teach him a full practical vocabulary, you are needlessly limiting daily communication.

Start by ceasing to use "No" as an all-purpose command. (You may notice that it doesn't work very well anyway.) Instead, introduce distinct commands like "off" for each specific behavior you want to change and never use contradictory commands. For example, never tell your dog to, "Sit down". Use one or the other. And, although, you can train dogs any word in any language, we recommend using the standard terms for "sit", "down", "heel", "stay" and "come". Teaching your dog standardized words for these particular commands will help when your dog works with people like his veterinarian or groomer or if you ever want him to compete in obedience or receive a Canine Good Citizen certification.

Most dogs learn these standard commands very easily, and they still have capacity to learn very many more terms for real items and activities. Introduce your dog to standard terms for everyday items and activities like "house", "car" or "go for a walk". Teach him every family member's name, so in case anyone ever gets lost he can now help you track them (see "Go to a Person by Name", in this chapter, "Find Mommy", in Chapter 3, Puppy Games & Activities and "Find the Missing Person, in Chapter 12, Useful Activities).

Next, work on putting together sentences your dog can understand. For example, you can first teach the standard command, "Go to your place", and then expand it to "Go to your bed" or "Go to the car".

Not all dogs do equally well with learning a vast vocabulary. So get the basic commands down first. Then reward your dog each time he learns and demonstrates consistent proficiency with a new term. You can even list each new word he learns and have the list on hand for dog sitters and friends you want to boast to. Use all the words regularly to keep them fresh and don't teach your dog too many terms that might upset him if he overhears the family talking!

Teaching words to dogs differs from teaching to humans in that you must always enunciate words properly and *never* use two terms to mean the same thing. Unlike humans dogs *cannot* understand ambiguity, so two different terms used to mean the same thing will completely confuse them.

The more you teach your dog, the better the two of you can communicate. Believe it or not, dogs are great at learning different languages. We've seen dogs that can do commands in three different languages without making mistakes. So never doubt what your dog can learn. Teach him something new every day. You never know- you may have the next canine Einstein.

Discern Objects by Name
- builds intelligence and gives your dog a way to talk to you -

Perhaps you've seen friends show off with this one to entertain party guests. They told their dog, "Go get your red ball," and their dog ran and did exactly that. Next they told the dog, "Now go get your Frisbee," or, "Go get your Beanie Baby," and they repeated the process with the dog retrieving ten highly diverse items, each referred to by its own exact name.

Is an accomplishment like this a parlor trick? Does the dog possess supernatural powers? Neither. Dogs are highly intelligent and certain breeds have been carefully bred for hundreds of years to be more work-oriented and verbally responsive than others, so they excel at the ability. Ray grew up with two K-9 trained German Shepherds who had no problem discerning everyday objects around the house and could help him with almost any practical task. This is no surprise at all. Had they been working with the police as they were trained for, they could have just as precisely pointed out drugs or contraband on command.

Emma's first dog, a Collie-Shepherd prodigy, learned more than three hundred discreet words in her lifetime and could also understand some words combined into complex thoughts. Again, this ability is not so surprising when you consider the intelligence, judgment and communication a herding dog must possess to effectively do its job.

Some owners teach dogs names of different toys just for fun and your dog will certainly enjoy the challenge and the praise of family and friends. But may we suggest instead that you teach your dog real, practical terms and allow him to help you out around the house a little? For example, your dog can learn to bring you his food bowl on command or retrieve your purse or keys (See Chapter 12, Useful Activities.)

Learning to discern between different objects also gives your dog a way to "talk" to you. For example, when you take him to Petsmart you can actually ask him if he wants a "ball" or a "stuffed toy" and you won't waste money on a toy he won't play with. Or ask him whether he'd rather go to "Pestmart" or "the park" or if he just wants to "go for a ride". Your smart dog can let you know his preference when you mention the item he is interested in by barking or body language.

To teach your dog the names of things, state the name whenever your dog touches the object, comes to the location or performs the activity in question. You can also use a reward each time he distinguishes correctly between two objects. Even if you're not interested in investing the time to train your dog to distinguish objects' names right now, just for the fun of it, why not test your dog to see what he already knows? Mention the names of a few objects central to his life, for example "treats" or "leash" or "car", and see if he immediately goes to those items. You may be surprised to find that, even without you formally training him, your dog has already learned some of the names!

<u>Ring Toss</u>
- simple, cheap, mild exercise and just enough difficulty to hold your dog's concentration -

As a tiny baby, Emma particularly enjoyed this game that involved carefully slipping plastic donut-shaped rings of various sizes and colors onto a short wooden pole, one on top of another. And dogs can play this game as well, with proper equipment and human supervision. Not only can your dog be taught to carefully place the rings over the pole or dowel one by one, he can also carefully remove them one by one. To add incentive, you can provide the dog with a treat as a reward each time he successfully works a ring onto or off of the pole.

Once your dog masters one ring at a time, gradually reduce reinforcement, so that he only gets a food reward after successfully completing all the rings. After he masters this game of concentration and coordination on its basic level, you can advance to much more complex versions. For example, several dogs in your household can take turns putting rings onto one pole, or each dog can be given his own setup and the one with the fastest time wins the food reward.

You can make this game very much harder by teaching your dog the names of different color rings. When he gets the correct color ring onto the post, he gets a reward. There is some debate about what colors dogs are actually able to see. It is possible that he will be able to distinguish certain rings only by shade or by size rather than color. If he's successful at the task, this is fine. But if he repeatedly has trouble with only one color, try replacing that ring with a new one of a completely different color.

Dogs that advance to this level will truly be exercising their minds. But every dog that plays "ring toss" will greatly improve their ability to focus and accomplish a task, as well as learning more patience and self control.

Working and herding breeds will have lots of fun with this game. Retrievers and hunting dogs will also enjoy another variation: toss all the rings out far and wide to different positions in the yard and the dog must run out, find a ring, hurry back with it to the post, and then slow down to carefully lower the ring over the post. Then he rushes out to find the next.

You can increase the difficultly of this exercise tremendously by timing it and taking the post away if your dog doesn't return quickly enough with the last of the rings. Another variation can make this game easier for puppies. Rather than having a challengingly long post like you would want to do with adult dogs, start out with a really short post and rings with larger spaces in their centers. This makes lowering them easier for a puppy with shaky coordination. A nice alternative to plastic donut-style rings could also be simply using a few nylon-style dog Frisbees or nylon dog toys in ring shapes. Using these can make the game possible for the tiniest toy dogs or puppies. Just make sure to always supervise carefully and/or use sturdy rings that your dog or puppy can't tear apart.

The Shell Game
- one of the favorite mental games for dogs and owners, and one of the easiest -

This game is modeled after the "shell game" where street hustlers ask passersby to bet on whether they can find an object under one of three shells that the huckster shuffles around. It's a gambling game and tourists to New York City are known to lose at the game. But the version of the game played with your dog will depend only on the power of his nose, not on his luck.

You can use three upended flowerpots, three sturdy plastic disposable bowls with small holes punched in the bottoms, or the classic equipment- three large shells. Just make sure the shells are wavy enough to allow just a little room for the scent of the treat to waft out. First show your dog the treat, then place it under one of the "shells" and move them around a bit until he's not sure where the treat is hidden.

Now say something along the lines of, "Where's the treat, Lucky? Where's the treat?" Then allow your curious dog to move forward and sniff around until he finds the shell that he believes hides the treat. Some dogs will push at their choice with their nose, while others will yap or touch the shell with their paw.

If your dog makes the right choice, lift the shell and allow your dog the reward of eating the treat. If he makes the wrong choice, shake your head and say something along the lines of, "Sorry, wrong choice. Let's try again!" The words you use are not vitally important, just as long as your dog understands the rules of the game. It is not a difficult game to master and it will help dogs increase their focus.

If you want to advance to more difficult versions of the game, you can add a second dog and allow him to take his turn. This helps dogs to learn patience and to play fair with each other while deferring to your judgment as "pack leader". But, of course, keep it fun and never attempt this version of the game if either dog is food aggressive!

Another way to make the game harder is if you notice that your dog doesn't seem to be using his nose at all. He may prefer fine tuning his observations, and choosing shells based on his observations, rather than his nose. Or he may actually enjoy the feeling of letting luck and fate determine if he gets a treat. For dogs that prefer to play the game by thinking, rather than sniffing, why not eliminate the nose holes entirely? Or you can substitute a non-smelly token like a small toy or a poker chip for the food treats (just *don't* let your dog eat these small items that could be choking hazards!) At first you can reward the dog with a food treat every time he finds a token. As he becomes more adept you can add challenge by only providing a food treat each time he had amassed a set number of tokens (say three, or even five).

Your kids will enjoy playing the shell game with your dogs, and you can add it to the agenda on games night. Adults have fun with the game as well, as long as you don't mind if your dog's skill beats yours occasionally!

Go To a Person by Name
- a fun skill to practice that every family with children should teach their dog -

Maybe your dog already knows this game. If he doesn't, you should definitely teach it. Knowing your family members' names has different useful functions.

It can be simply utilitarian. For example, if "Daddy" is downstairs and already dressed, and yet Fido is upstairs in the bedroom pestering mommy for a walk, she can simply tell him, "Go to Daddy, Fido", and buy herself an extra hour's sleep on Sunday morning.

Your kids will feel delighted if your dog knows their names and you can make teaching the skill a fun game. For example, start with your son and command your dog, "Go to Brandon" or, "Where's Brandon?". When your dog or puppy goes to your son, Brandon will give him a treat. Repeat until your dog seems to recognize your son's name. Next, introduce your daughter's name. Tell your dog, "Go to Ashley" or, "Where's Ashley?" Then have your daughter offer a treat when your dog comes to her. Next start alternating names; cheer your dog on and practice until he's accurate. Introduce additional names as necessary using the same process.

> *Every dog should know their family members' names. It is fun, practical and, in extreme situations, it might help save a life.*

Knowledge of the family's names can be fun and practical. And, in extreme situations it might possibly help save a life. For example, if one of your children wanders off momentarily you may be able to ask your dog for the assistance of his nose. (See "Find the Missing Person" in Chapter 12, Useful Games). Or if you're not feeling well, you can ask your dog to carry a note outside to your husband. Obviously, additional training is necessary for your dog to perform consistently in these situations. But knowing each family member's name is simple, basic knowledge that every dog should start with.

Make Any Game a Mental Game
**-   vitally important; the more you practice, the calmer
& better behaved your dog will be -**

The first few times it happened we were surprised. While working with customers in their homes, we mentioned that, in addition to exercising their dogs physically, the families should also give their dogs mental exercise and play mental games. We noticed that whenever we said this we got painfully blank looks, followed by the inevitable question, "What is a mental game?"

Perhaps the fact that owners find this so hard to conceptualize contributes to the problem- dogs with antsy bodies and minds that are used to reacting impulsively and explosively without taking that one second to first consider their actions. Even when these dogs' owners notice the animal is frustrated, they may only think of giving him additional physical activity- a game of Fetch or Tug-of-War, or a long jog around the neighborhood, for example. But something is still missing.

A mental game is anything that makes a dog stop and think. For example, it may require several steps for the dog to get his desired reward or the dog must recognize and act on a symbol before receiving the reward. Common elements of mental games include 1) decision making, 2) symbols and/or 3) delayed gratification.

A good example of a mental game is teaching a dog to retrieve the one of three identical dumbbells that has the handler's scent on it. Obviously, picking up a metal dumbbell is not an instinctive action, nor is it rewarding in itself. The dog must also recognize the command to select only the dumbbell with the human scent. And then he must carry the item back to his handler before he receives his reward (praise or a treat).

This is the way the task is accomplished in advanced obedience competitions and some dogs become very skilled at it. But let's say a handler wanted to challenge their dog's mind even more. One way they could do this is decide to suddenly change the rules of the game, so that they would only reward the dog when he retrieved the dumbbells without the human scent. This would take a while to learn if the dog already knew the standard rules of obedience. But an intelligent dog would eventually make the connection that the "rules" had changed when he noticed that the only times he was getting a reward was when he made a "mistake". You would probably notice a clear change in the dog's facial expression as he strained to make the new connection and eventually figured it out.

You could then add another step to the task to make it even harder. For example, not only would your dog have to pick out the item with the scent, but he'd also have to place it inside an open "evidence bag". When he finished, he could then be taught to bark. In fact, most cute movie stunts involve complex chains of actions like these. The key to creating a great mental game is to make the task hard enough to challenge your dog with rewards just attainable enough that he won't feel like giving up.

Even teaching your dog to ring a bell next to the front door when he has to relieve himself is an example of a mental task. In this case, the bell is symbolic. But it gets your dog a real reward- the chance to relieve bowels and bladder. And even most little puppies are able to make this symbolic connection.

Dogs need physical exercise, but they need mental exercise as well. And adding a mental component to games and activities is often what's needed to finally take the edge off a dog's boredom or frustration. You can try a simple experiment by adding a mental component to a familiar game. For example, your dog may enjoy vigorous games of Fetch, but you may notice that it's impossible to fully tire him out and he still returns home edgy and wired. So, test your dog. On one day, play regular Fetch with him for the amount of time you usually do, perhaps a half hour. On the next day, start out with regular Fetch for the initial fifteen minutes, but then change the game for the remainder of the time.

Have a helper hold your dog while you make a big show of walking to several different locations and hiding his ball in one of them, although you don't clearly let him see which one. Then when you release him, your dog has to recall the locations you went to and rush to each, using his nose to ferret out where you hid the ball. Most dogs love this game and your dog will likely return home more tired and more emotionally centered and gratified than if he had used those last fifteen minutes in the much more vigorous activity of running back and forth for regular Fetch.

Brynne & Max-
Play the Shell Game

If you own a highly intelligent dog, you may notice that your dog immediately takes to mental games, even complex ones, and seems to actively beg for more. But, if your dog is a charming goofball, not noted for his mental acuity, it's equally important to frequently challenge him with mental games. A dog's mind can develop with use just as it can "atrophy" with disuse. Teach your "clueless" dog to use skills of mental discernment to get what he wants, and you may actually boost his mental powers!

Ch. 5- Indoor Games & Activities

"There *are* alternatives- it doesn't have to be a "dirty secret" if you can't exercise your dog outside in bad weather"

Introduction

Hide & Seek

Yes or No

Agility Inside

A Room of His Own

Put Away Toys

Dancing Dog

Get That Pose

Doggie Gymnasium

Basketball

Doggie Treadmill (Indoors)

Also Try These Ideas From Other Chapters Indoors:

Puppy Games & Activities: Follow the Leader, Find the Treat, Which Hand?, Find Mommy, Which Box Has the Fun In It?, Tunnel Crawl, How Do I Get What's In There?, Let's Play Doctor, New Learning Every Day, Walk This Way, Obedience-Minded

Mental Games & Activities: Movie Star, Watch Me, Wait, Hold That Position, Listen, Move Slow, Doggie Einstein, Ring Toss, Shell Game, Discern Objects By Name

Balance and Coordination Activities: Will the Real Dog Stand?, Play the Seal, Walk the Line, Walk Like a Man, Be a Parrot, Stack, Double Hoops, Different Surfaces

Multi Dog Games & Activities: Limbo, Duck, Duck, Goose; Simon Says, Sit on a Bench, Dancing Dogs, What's My Name; Long, Long Stay; Obedience Competition at Home

Problem Dog Games: Ring of Fire, Go to Your Place, Take a Bow, Up and Down, Stop barking on command, In the Army Crawl, When I Move, You Move; Drop It, Jump Over, Interactive Toys

Therapeutic and Senior Dog Activities: Message, Meditation, Stretching, Party In the Storm, Talking Toys, Kong Time, Doggie TV, Bring Me the Puppy, Doggie Stairs, Help His Comrades

High Energy Dog Activities: Doggie Treadmill, Picture Windows

Useful Activities: Find My Keys, Get My Shoes, Check On the Baby, Check On Grandma, Help Your Special Needs Family Member, Bark for Help, Watch Your Children, Personal Bodyguard, Lap Dog,, Ring a Doorbell

Family Activities: Circle of Love, Jump Rope, Different Handlers, Junior Handlers, Junior Grooming Salon, Doggie Bakery, Assess a Dog; Demonstrate Tricks, "Petstar" at Home

Activities for Owners with Limited Mobility:
Continuous Pool, Playdate, Cat Toy, Balloons, Bubbles, Games On the Floor, Dog Stairs, Doggie Daycare, Service Dog, Rehab Together, Be Creative, Upstairs/Downstairs, Chaise Lounge Training, Dog On the Table

Indoor Games & Activities - Introduction
"There _are_ alternatives- it's no longer a "dirty secret" if you can't exercise your dog outside in inclement weather"

Which do you think hurts you and your dog more- vigorous exercise in extreme hot weather or exercise in extreme cold? The truth is that both can be uncomfortable and sometimes dangerous. Yet we frequently meet home training customers who have gone to these extremes in the name of their dog's health until they literally couldn't take it anymore! It's ironic that the same exercise that's a health necessity in mild weather can become dangerous, or even deadly, in weather extremes. And exercise in extreme weather is a health threat not only for dogs, but for owners as well.

Southeast Florida, where we live, is notorious as one of the country's hottest climates. The authors are dedicated nature lovers and we live for outdoor time, but we've learned to make peace with this climate by carefully choosing when and how we exert. We showed the same courtesy for our beloved and very furry Akita Casey. Well-behaved Casey accompanied us to more parks, rivers, beaches and attractions than most humans ever see and he also enjoyed leisurely neighborhood walks at regular times each day. Yet all his real exercise was timed for when the weather was cooler and/or there was plenty of shade.

While we provided adequate exercise for our Akita Casey, who possessed the sensibility of a wise old Samurai, we never exerted with him in the hot summer sun. The most vigorous exertion our dog ever did on ninety-five degree days was a lot of deep and intense thinking and a lot of interaction with his owners. "No pain, no gain" was not our philosophy, nor did we use it with our hundred and fifteen pound dog. Instead, we found alternate activities to do inside while the heat shimmered outdoors.

On summer days Casey enjoyed early morning and late-night walks on our street. But we drove him a distance to take him for his noon walk in the coolest spot in the county- a unique park with well shaded pathways, cooled by a strong river breeze. After walking, Casey would spend more shady time relaxing watching the sailboats. And then the hottest part of the day was spent shopping at nicely air-conditioned pet stores and boutiques.

Unfortunately, not every owner and dog enjoy such pleasant summer days. Dog "professionals" are telling many well-meaning owners that they must vigorously work their dogs out in full sunshine on searing days like this! We've seen them running alongside the expressways- owners sheened with sweat, dogs with tongues lolling, while we turn up the air conditioning in our vehicle another notch just to be able to breathe the stagnant air and sadly shake our heads.

One South Florida customer told us she had been hiring dog walkers _on rollerblades_ to jog her giant St. Bernard for miles in full sunshine each summer afternoon! This treatment of a long-haired dog bred for the snowy Swiss Alps borders on animal cruelty, and it was completely unnecessary for that dog's exercise needs or his health. Rather than risking heat exhaustion for the dog, the walkers simply could have briefly let the dog out to relieve himself when the sun was blazing and then returned after sunset for the jog. Or they could have walked the dog mellowly, and in the shade.

Many owners in South Florida feel they don't have adequate space to exercise their dogs on their small properties, so they spend a lot of money sending the dogs to cage-free facilities that claim to be like fun "day camps" for dogs. The problem is that in extreme summer heat dogs risk serious illness if they run madly for hours as a pack, overexcited by the other dogs, in yards with no shade (see "Dangerous Daycare" in Chapter 15).

South Florida weather is tropical. From May to October we rarely see daytime temperatures less than 88-92 degrees. It's always humid and almost always sunny, with summer heat indices of over 100 degrees common. Many South Florida cities are also vast islands of suburban sprawl, paved over with concrete. Walk from your air-conditioned vehicle to the supermarket at noontime and you narrowly escape feeling that you will pass out! The searing sun hurts your body and starts to fry your mind if you stay out in it too long. (Some may point to South Floridians' aggressive driving, suggestive dressing and risky financial speculation as evidence of this.)

Summer evenings around here can be a godsend for taking dogs on longer walks. But sometimes even at night temperatures remain in the eighties and any vigorous movement triggers an immediate sweat unless you find a strong beach or river breeze. Sometimes even then the humidity is so thick that you question if you'll be able to draw your next breath. And then there are the mosquitoes, the sand flies, etc.

If you're a Northern person, you may assume that you don't find many long-haired dog breeds in South Florida. However, if you know South Florida, you know you find *everything* here- big black furry Newfoundlands, puffy and push-nosed Pekinese, Huskies, Malamutes and St. Bernards. The real problem happens when you see sweaty owners in Speedos and bikinis out jogging with these dogs. These owners know that they must exercise their dogs to keep the dogs' cardiovascular systems healthy, so they make the mistake of taking heat-intolerant breeds out for hours of extreme exercise at noontime in the summer, trying to do right.

Before you resent such people for exposing their dogs to heat illness (which can cause long-term, life-threatening organ damage to a dog even after symptoms subside), you must realize that they are exposing themselves as well. Every day, new customers of ours who are overweight, elderly or who suffer chronic illness tell us of their heroic efforts to exercise their dogs in the hot summer sun and humidity. The fact that these people have lived to call us is amazing and so is the fact that their dogs have survived. Yet most of them come to us ashamed that the weather got too much for them and they could not fulfill their dogs' exercise needs, so they gave up.

Of course, our readers know the flip side of a dog without exercise. In addition to the risks to the animal's health, frustrated dogs are prone to behavior problems. Dogs without exercise are likely to damage the home in every way from marking to barking to chewing furniture, to literally "bouncing off walls" and landing on the owners' heads!

You may follow television dog trainers like Cesar Millan, *The Dog Whisperer,* who tells all his clients that they should leash-walk their dog two times a day for forty-five minutes each walk. In theory, Cesar is right. Walking together as a pack *is* indeed important for dog/owner bonding and for the dog's emotional balance and soundness of mind and temperament. But most people who are not from Southern California don't realize that the climate there is relatively cool. Emma can vouch for this, because when she lived in a beach community there she happily walked everywhere, every day and almost forgot she owned a car!

Unfortunately it would be dangerous and foolhardy to attempt those same walks in summer in Florida. And summer in Coastal Georgia, where we've also lived, is even hotter and more humid. The same is true for much of the Deep South and the Mid-Atlantic during the summer months, especially if you live in a city. And then there are the desert states. And in much of the country during the winter snow, storms and extremely low temperatures often make exercising dogs outside difficult or impossible.

> *People seem to have problems talking about the terrible barrier of weather and dog ownership and many hide the problem like they would some dark family secret.*

Owners who crave to be "good" seem ashamed to admit that it hurts them to exercise their dog in extreme summer or winter weather. Or they may be completely confused because they know exercise is necessary, yet they sense that exercise in extreme weather could hurt their dog.

We also find it interesting that no shelter or rescue society where we live seems to adequately address the problem. Potential adopters may sign a form promising they'll exercise the dog, yet it's June and already ninety-three degrees out when they bring their dog home! Perhaps the shelter/breeder, etc. doesn't want to talk about the truth. In the summer months in Florida, if you vigorously run your extremely high-energy dog long enough to fulfill his exercise needs (many hours) you'll also make him sick with heat illness. Unless potential adopters know indoor fitness alternatives (which we describe in this chapter) they might get so discouraged about the weather that they'd hesitate to adopt a dog.

We focus on summer heat because it's such an extreme example but, in many areas of the country extreme cold and snowstorms are common. If you're a working person living in the North, the likelihood is that in wintertime when you get home from work ready to walk your dog, it's already dark. Ice-slick streets and blizzard conditions often make it impossible to get in good exercise. And weather problems can be even more challenging if you live in a city or if you have any physical limitations. Some breeds of dogs are also particularly vulnerable to cold.

So now the truth is out. Many of you have been hiding it because you felt ashamed, but **the truth is, much of the year you simply cannot exercise your dog outside.** Even leaving your dog out in your yard can hurt him under some weather conditions, and if you leave him out alone during the "dog days" of summer, he's more likely to lie by your back door panting than he is to move around enough to get any healthy exercise.

One of the main reasons we wrote this book was to provide indoor exercise alternatives for bad weather. Just like other dog trainers, we think activities like organized agility competitions are great for healthy dogs, healthy owners and good weather. But we diverge from other many other trainers' philosophies in that we seek out difficult questions and issues rather than avoiding them and we seek to help real people.

We want to show owners how to cooperate with their dogs so life can be a glory every minute they share together *without changing the essence of their lifestyle.* Your dog should make your life better; **nothing you do with your dog should cause you discomfort, nor discomfort your dog. But giving up is not an alternative.**

Exercise is necessary and, at its best, also engages your dog's mind and his spirit. Exercise also improves humans' emotional and spiritual health. Every single day, every family member and their dog should engage together in moments of physical exercise, emotional bonding and spiritual centeredness. It's especially important for children to engage in healthy times like this also. And having moments of fun, activity and bonding with your dog are not as hard as it may seem if you don't have to be daunted by weather. All you have to do is be willing to think "outside of the box". Take your exercise routine inside whenever the weather's bad outside, be willing to innovate and don't mind if anyone calls you weird!

Start by trying the indoor games and activities in this chapter, and add some of the activities from the other chapters geared to different needs and lifestyles. For example, imagine playing "Limbo" as a high-energy family game with your dogs and kids. Ideas from other chapters include hosting obedience or "Petstar" competitions in your home, or setting up a "Doggie Bakery" or "Junior Grooming Salon". This occupies the kids and the dogs, it saves you money and you can even invite the neighbors.

Many of the indoor activities we describe also build valuable skills for puppies. "Hide and Go Seek" makes a puppy want to go to his people. "Tunnel Crawl" builds physical coordination while teaching the puppy not to be afraid of unfamiliar things and "New Learning Every Day" becomes a cornerstone for your puppy's education and lifestyle.

A new twist on a traditional activity is to practice agility inside. Your neighbors (or even some dog trainers) might tell you that there is no way you could practice canine agility anywhere but outdoors, but sneak a little teeter totter, a tunnel or some weave poles into a corner of the family room and see how much fun you, your kids and your dogs can have in climate controlled comfort! (This is especially true for high-energy small dogs.)

If you're embarrassed working your dog on agility equipment inside, you might also feel embarrassed using a cat toy! But cat toys on sticks are a great way for owners who have difficulty bending down to interact with their small dogs. Teaching your dog or dogs to dance to music with you (Freestyle) might also seem embarrassing at first, but it's good for physical exercise and mental focus and fun for owners, once you release your inner child.

Indoor activities for your dog should include not only physical challenges, but mental as well. For example, every dog should practice obedience in the home every day for the rest of his life. This shouldn't be show ring obedience. Instead, challenge your family to be spontaneous and give relevant real-life commands as a surprise to the dog at different times during the day. Teaching your dog to "Stack", as he would in a dog show, is another valuable command because of the mental focus and self control necessary. And when it's time for some Zen-like moments, make a practice of "Massage" and "Meditation" with your dog.

Sometimes, it's the simplest things that people most fail to see just because they are simple. **Owning a dog should never be a pain.** And the weather need not rule out owning the breed you love. Yes, we are outdoor people, and we mourn the loss of simpler times. But, the world of global warming and rampant suburbia is upon us and we have to face facts that it's not always possible to exercise outside for long periods every day.

Just because you live in this challenging era doesn't make you a bad pet owner. You can focus instead on the health, confidence and love you want to give your dog and then figure out what activities make that happen, rather than trying to force traditional exercise that may be a struggle. If you have lots of land and lots of good weather, healthy dogs will enjoy all the outdoor exercise you give them. But if much of your dog's vigorous exercise has to take place inside when the weather is bad, it still counts as exercise. You can then take a little time outside just for fresh air, leisurely leashed walking and dog-owner bonding. The payoff for a little flexibility and a lot of exercise and games in the house will likely be a happier dog and a happier, easier life.

Indoor Games & Activities:

Hide & Seek
- customer favorite; inspires even adult dogs and owners to get up & play -

This is a classic indoor game that both you and your dog can enjoy. First tell the dog, "Let's play hide and go seek." Next, hide somewhere in your house and see if your dog can find you. At first make it easy. Just hide around a corner and call the dog. When he finds you, give him lots of praise and maybe even a treat.

Later you can make it harder and harder for your dog to find you. Ask a human helper to hold the dog when you go to hide, or you could put him in a stay and then release him from a distance. (This will also improve your dog's stays and recalls.)

Next your dog gets to have the hiding fun! First you will teach your dog to hide. Have an object near that you would like the dog to hide behind and tell him to, "Go hide." Walk the dog behind the object so he can hide and tell him to stay. Allow him to hide for just a moment at first. Then show up and enthusiastically say, "I found you!" and offer a treat.

Family favorite game!

Once your dog gets the idea of the game, he might find some spots you never even thought a dog could hide in. (Have him trained well in the recall in case he ever takes the game too seriously and you really can't find him!)

After your dog knows the rules of "Hide and go seek", you can have kids play the game with him. Have the dog search the house, finding each of the kids in turn and have each child give him a treat when found. If your kids want to "seek" out the dog, advise them to play nice and gentle. You want your dog to always enjoy playing the game. Keep it playful. If children act too loud or rough while searching for the dog, he may not want to play anymore.

Yes or No
- truly impressive & most dogs can learn to do it -

This is an adorably cute skill that you can easily teach your dog. (Some dogs can even learn to use this skill for real-life communication.) The object is to teach your dog to shake his head "yes" and "no". Start by holding a treat in your hand and moving it up and down. If the dog follows it with his head say, "Good say yes," and give the dog the treat. Repeat this a few times, moving your hand up and down and saying, "Say, yes".

71

Some dogs will catch on quickly and, after a few times they will learn to shake their head up and down when you say, "Say, yes" without using the treat to lure them. Once your dog has achieved this you can start the same teaching process for, "Say no", but this time you move your hand side to side rather than up and down.

After your dog has learned to do both yes and no, you can start asking him to answer some easy question like, "Do you want to go out?" When starting out, it's okay to cheat and help your dog when he needs it. You can lead him with a treat if he seems stumped answering a particular question, or teach him to watch you subtly nod or shake your head, and then follow. When your dog gets good at this game, he will be the life of the party. Ask him if he wants a steak and when he nods his head "yes" your guests will respond with surprised laughter. Everyone will be amazed and ask how the dog knew how to do that, but that will be your secret!

Agility Inside
- highly recommended for exercise inside; just adapt it to your needs -

This idea may not be something you want to boast about to your friends, especially if you're concerned about appearing eccentric. But, before you write it off as too bizarre, you may want to wait until the next weeklong hundred-degree heat spell to consider. Then, take your dog outside for as much of a walk as the two of you can comfortably bear. (Five minutes perhaps? Just long enough for little Peppy to mark the fire hydrant?) As you reenter the sanctuary of your home, sucking in air-conditioned air with force enough to shake your body down to your toes, contemplate the facts about dogs' exercise needs. The first fact is that your exhausting five minute-morning walk in hundred degree heat just got your dog's day of required exercise off to its start.

Now, if your little Peppy happens to be an active breed (a Dalmatian or a Jack Russell Terrier for example) all he will require to fulfill his needs for the day is an additional twenty-five to fifty-five minutes of vigorous exercise! That's right, many of the most popular breeds require one half to one full hour of exercise equivalent to full-tilt running each day. Some extremely high-energy breeds require twice that!

Now that we've got you thinking, consider the next question. Do you have one room in your house that has rather large floor space, either with no furniture or furniture that can be moved, and can you and your dog spend a half-hour to an hour in that room? Most likely, pondering this was a lot less disturbing than considering that hour-long run under the summer sun. If you do have the space, all you need to do is to use that space several times a week (or every day) to set up agility equipment for your dog.

Obviously, the idea works best for relatively small breeds. But it can theoretically be used with dogs of any size. If you possess a gigantic room or open floor plan under heat and air, with no valuable antiques, lamps or glass figurines delicately balanced, you might be able to steal enough space to fit in a whole agility mini-course, with all the obstacles of a real course. If you require the room for other functions, you'll have to disassemble the obstacles when your dog's exercise session is done. But agility obstacles are made to be broken down easily. (See Resources.)

Agility inside is not for every dog or every owner. If all you have available is a furnished area, only try working agility if your dog is light on his feet and you already know that he can safely dodge furniture while running. In all fairness, agility gets quite vigorous and dogs sometimes slip, so be sure that all the furniture is pushed far enough out of the way to give your dog plenty of room to maneuver. And only try this game with dogs that are well-behaved and able to control themselves inside. (For example, don't teach this game to a dog that is a compulsive jumper!)

If you're lucky and have an empty room with no purpose, or an empty basement or bonus room, you could keep your little agility course set up all the time rather than having to break it down. (The room can also serve as a multi-purpose space for your dog. See the "A Room of His Own" section in this chapter.) But even if your space is limited (for example, in an apartment or condo) you can still do some agility inside. First, observe some agility competitions, read books or watch videos (see Resources) to familiarize yourself with the different obstacles. Then consider which obstacles your dog would like best and which would fit best in your space for the least expense.

Imagine how much fun your small dog might have navigating a tunnel, for example. And these are easily collapsible. You don't necessarily have to buy jumps. Research the correct height for your dog and then improvise jumps with a broomstick balanced lightly over two low tables. If a tire is too heavy to hang from your ceiling beams you could use an inner tube, an inflatable pool float with a large hole or a hula hoop for the tire jump. And weave poles are great for your dog's concentration and coordination and they only take up a few inches of

space. You can buy these ready made, build your own out of PVC or even improvise with traffic cones.

Your dog will come to cherish the fun agility sessions he shares with you inside your home and *he* won't know that your human peers may consider the activity a little strange. If you choose to buy regulation equipment to use inside your home, you can also transfer it outside when the season changes and the weather improves.

Max, waiting for his next cue

A Room of His Own
- not just a utopian solution; many homeowners have the space to try this or variations -

One of the biggest problems that plague the owners we help is how they can possibly exercise their dogs enough, especially with busy schedules and extreme weather constraints. Here in South Florida heat is more of a problem than cold- and heat makes it impossible to safely exercise your dog outside on quite a few days. But letting your animal's exercise needs slide is not a solution.

It's also ironic when we meet dog owners living in "McMansions". Their homes offer expansive square footage, yet they're usually filled with so much pricey furniture, electronics and delicate ornaments that there is literally no space for a dog to safely run around without damaging something. We see the same problem with owners who live in reasonably-sized suburban homes. On the outside their homes look big- certainly big enough for a medium sized dog. But between room-size sectional sofas, looming entertainment centers, kids' play areas littered with toys and backyards largely filled by screened-off swimming pools there is, literally, not five feet of contiguous space where the dog can jump around without damaging something!

Owners who fail to exercise their dogs due to time and weather often face the frustrated dog's unruly and damaging behavior. So they often resort to a cruel solution that is advocated by much of the dog industry. Because their dog is bouncing off walls and can't be trusted not to stay calm in the house, they lock him up for eighteen hours a day in a crate! We feel crating can be damaging (see "Dog in the Box" in Ch. 15). And crating dogs for behavior problems is only a stopgap solution, since it only makes the unexercised dog even more frustrated, and makes his bad house manners even worse during the brief period he is let out each day.

Most of our customers agree that they'd rather not crate their dog. And yet they often try to train their puppies never to run around or play in the house because there simply isn't any safe area where the dog *can* run around. In fact, the vast majority of customers who consult us about their dogs' behavior problems do not have any adequate space for their dog to jump around, even in generous-sized homes.

So, here is a novel solution that we've never seen in other training or activity books. Why not give your dog a room of his own? Not a crate, but a good-sized room. You or your kids can play or exercise in here also if you like, but just don't put any valuables in the room, or anything that could topple and hit anybody. The best flooring is simple, washable flooring like vinyl and you can use expendable non-slip rugs on portions of the floor for additional cushioning (as long as your dog won't chew a rug.) A nice dog bed can occupy one corner. In the other, provide a toy-box. Your dog can even be taught to "Put Away Toys" (see Chapter 12, Useful Games).

The design of your dog's room is only limited by your imagination. You can build custom shelves and stations for feeding or bathing your dog and add a custom closet or wall of storage for organizing pet paraphernalia. Or you can install a bench that you and the kids can rest on if you get tired during play and this can double as more storage. Some owners may include a doggie door with access to the backyard in their dog room. And it's a good idea to locate the room near a side entrance to your home (not one of your frequently used entrances.) This way you can use the room to leash your dog or dogs on the way out for walks and clean them up when they come inside without disrupting activities in the living room or kitchen.

Paint the walls of your dog room with non-toxic paint that cleans up easily, and expect to someday redo these walls since they may get dinged and dented by claws or bouncing balls. Allow no hanging cords, cover all outlets and remove any chemicals or electrical equipment. **There are only two necessities in this room- it should be heated and, most essentially air conditioned and it should have adequate floor space for a little running.** The more floor space you can spare, the better. Nice windows or sliding French doors for a view are good for well-behaved dogs. Dogs love the stimuli of watching the neighborhood and the mental activity is good for them. But safely *cover* any windows if your dog's a problem barker so he won't disturb the neighborhood (and next get him some positive training). And never use low windows or French doors if there's any chance you think your dog might break the glass! (This dog needs positive training as well!)

Leave the doggie playroom door open and train your dog to wander in to play or to take some private time whenever he wants to. Include a water dish and whatever toys and bedding are appropriate and the "doggie playroom" can be a safe and hazard free area to contain a young puppy during housetraining when you are away- with enough space and stimuli to keep his mind and body occupied.

If you have guests and your dog's acting too boisterous, you can easily train him the command, "Go to your room" and he can easily hang out in the playroom, jumping around with his toys and leaving you and the guests to private conversation. You can also *briefly* contain your dog or dogs in the playroom for a little "chill time" to work off some hyped-up energy. The same is true if your dogs are jumping around when you are attempting something delicate-working from home, completing a work of art or cuddling the baby.

Just make sure your dogs always associate the playroom with comfort and fun. It shouldn't be used as a place for "time-out" for specific behavioral correction; use other spaces in the house for corrective time-outs if necessary. Teach your dog that whenever fun playtime happens in the house, it happens in the playroom and soon he'll seek out the "doggie playroom" on his own, rather than playing wildly underfoot.

We recommend making decisions about a "doggie playroom" before you buy a home, if possible, or before you bring home a new dog. Families may worry about the expense of maintaining a big "unused" room. But this expense pales next to expenses you might incur in trainers, veterinary bills, ruined furniture and the immeasurable expense in lost quality of life.

Also consider that on extremely hot, cold and rainy days, you can play with, bond with and exercise with your dog indoors, rather than having to go out and pant, shiver, suffer and perhaps become ill. You won't have to resent the kids playing with the dogs in this unbreakable room, and it's a great area to get in your daily obedience practice.

If you literally *cannot* earmark a room for your dogs to play in due to expense or limited space (although this probably does *not* apply to the average suburban home) you *can* adapt some of your current space to multitask as a place your dog can run. You can make major changes like replacing flooring or breaking down a half wall if you own your home. If you rent, or don't want to make a major commitment, you can rearrange furniture or buy furniture on wheels to push to the sides of the walls to create a play space. If the room serves a dual purpose, and some furniture remains, just make sure to train your dog which areas are off-limits.

Even if the only spare space in your home is a guest room, you can install an easily cleaned flooring surface, slide the bed out temporarily and move other furnishings out or against walls whenever guests aren't staying. A bare guest room used for a dog may not fully complement your décor- but the sight of your dog enjoying the room whenever your guests aren't will likely make you smile. It's a great way to add space without adding cost!

Put Away Toys
- just easy enough, yet challenging enough to teach most dogs; great for small breeds -

Does your dog like to remove his toys from his toybox one-by-one, very methodically, but then leave them scattered around the floor for you to pick up? Wouldn't it be great if instead you could train him to always put away his own toys after each play session? And putting away toys can feel more satisfying for your dog than just playing with them. The challenge of putting away the toys one by one gives your dog a task to focus on mentally; it makes playtime feel more demanding and gives your dog a chance to feel a sense of accomplishment.

You can train the process any way you wish. The first way is if your dog happens to drop a toy into the toybox on his own- this is considered "capturing" the behavior. As he drops the toy into the box, you should quickly say the command you've chosen, for example "In the toybox!" and then immediately reward and/or praise.

If your dog doesn't do the task on his own, another method would be to hold the toybbox under his mouth while he's holding a toy and then let gravity take over, or gently lead him to the toybox when he's got a toy

Anna, "Put Away Your Toy"

in his mouth that he looks about ready to drop. As soon as he drops the toy, you'd say the command and then praise/reward. Allow, or instruct him to go get another toy (see "Fetch", Chapter 10) and repeat the process. It will take patience, but if you persist, using perfect timing, your dog will get the idea.

Another way to accelerate the process is to train using a method called "chaining". This is a way to train multi-step commands, starting by training the last segment of the desired outcome first. As above, you would lead your dog to his toybox, then gently remove the toy from his mouth and drop it in, while giving the command, "in the toybox." Praise and reward immediately and repeat until the dog is successfully dropping toys in on his own.

Next, put your dog on a leash when he is holding a toy and back up a few steps. Then gently lead the dog to the toybox, while giving the command, "In the toybox". Praise if he successfully approaches and drops the toy in. Repeat, until you no longer need to guide with the leash and your dog is successfully walking a distance with the toy and dropping it in the box whenever you give the command.

Next, help your dog to lift the toy from the floor while commanding, "In the toy box". After he takes the toy in his mouth, lead him or lure him towards the toybox, starting from a short distance away. Reward him after he drops the toy in. Now extend the distance, and try giving minimal help with lifting the toy. Next, only reward your dog when he lifts the toy on his own, carries it to the box and drops it in.

Now, you can point with your finger as you give the command. First, working with only one toy, point at the toy as you give the command, "in the toybox". When your dog successfully goes to the toy you've pointed at, lifts it and drops it into the toybox, reward and praise him and practice this several times. Now place down a second toy and point at that one. Soon, you will reward your dog only after he retrieves the particular toy that you've pointed at and places it in the toybox.

Next build up the number of toys he has to place in the box before getting a reward. First two, then three. Eventually, he'll only receive a reward once he's put all the toys away. Now you'll start weaning him off treats. Intersperse praise and petting with food rewards so he's not getting a food reward every time and try to save the food rewards for the best performances. An example would be the first time your dog takes the initiative and puts the toys away on his own. When he first does this, you will want to give him a handful of treats!

Although putting away toys is an involved task, most dogs enjoy the challenge.

Other dogs find it quite easy, and they'll start putting away toys on their own as a habit. Even if your dog becomes conscientious like this, don't take a great behavior for granted. Always remember to praise your dog for the accomplishment and give the occasional food reward.

If you want to really challenge your high-achiever dog, you can add another wrinkle by teaching your dog to distinguish each of his toys by name (see "Discern Objects by Name" in Chapter 4, Mental Games.) You can actually advise your dog the exact sequence of toys he should place in the toy box. For example, start with, "Max, red ball, in the toybox!, and next

"Max, yellow bone, in the toybox!" and continue with a few more toys. Be patient .ching this highly complex task, and be ready to accept compliments with lots of nen your dog shows everyone what he can do. Not only is this quite the parlor trick, it also iearly attests to the amazing intelligence and ability of dogs.

Dancing Dog (Freestyle)
- ranging from mild to wild; builds fun, bonding & self-expression- a customer favorite -

Freestyle dancing is absolutely one of the best indoor activities for you and your dog for bonding and physical and mental exercise. Depending on the intensity, dancing can work for dogs of all sizes, shapes ages and fitness levels. But even though this activity is so intense, so much fun and so versatile, many owners still haven't heard of it.

If you're lucky enough to have witnessed dogs and owners moving together in coordinated dance-style movements set to music on television or in person, you already know that Freestyle dancing is highly entertaining. And even though it's more fun for some of us than formal agility practice and requires no equipment, Freestyle yields similar exercise and obedience benefits.

Watching dog and owner move together in graceful choreography is enough to make Freestyle spectators "ooh" and "aah". Yet the fact that a dog can learn to carry out complicated movements alongside its owner is not surprising. Dogs are descended from wolves and, every day, wolves carry out complicated choreography with each other in order to surround their prey for a successful hunt. A talent for coordinated movement is thus hardwired into dogs' genetics, although not all dogs are equally interested or talented.

How do you know if your dog would be a good candidate for Freestyle? First you should train your dog the obedience basics. You can start puppies on simple gentle obedience as soon as they come home. But give puppies a bit of time to grow their attention span before you start training Freestyle. You could start at six months old with a mature-minded puppy. But don't push your sessions too long or teach highly demanding moves until your pup is over one year, or the pup may feel stressed and learn to dislike dancing.

Owners should also understand that not all dogs are equally suited to learn complex series of commands, and you never want to push a dog to dance with you if it causes him more stress than pleasure. If your dog understands basic obedience, but seems distressed trying to understand dance moves, you still have a good dog that respects you and you may want to find an activity or sport other than Freestyle. (This book gives many suggestions!)

But if your dog is an unusually quick learner, and sometimes seems to cock his head at you as if to ask, "Isn't there more?" whenever you complete the same old obedience lessons, he's likely a good candidate for learning Freestyle routines. Herding breeds known to excel at agility and Flyball also make good dancers. And Golden Retrievers, known for excellence in obedience, are often champions. However, Freestyle is all about free interpretation. Thus, any dog can dance with you if he wants to if you are performing the activity simply for fun. Your dog does not necessarily have to be an athlete. Any breed or any age dog can participate. Simply adapt the movements in your routine to your dog's body type and physical capabilities.

Check with your veterinarian, of course, if your dog has any serious disabilities that might limit his movements or if he's being treated for any medical condition. And common sense should prevail. If your dog is ten years old and quite overweight, moving back and forth in simple dance steps with you will benefit his health, but don't attempt lengthy routines or those where he has to jump. Giant dogs (and puppies) should never jump high or stand on hind legs because of strain on their joints, but they will benefit from other steps and routines.

If your dog is vigorously healthy, full of energy and has no physical limitations, then you can build his athleticism with much more challenging dance routines and you may want to perform Freestyle routines competitively. Some routines include dogs jumping on, and then balancing on, their owners' back or shoulders (see "Be a Parrot", Ch. 7) or leaping into their owners' arms from a distance! Other routines, set to faster music, are incredibly quick moving and are challenging not only for athletic dogs, but also for physically fit owners. See the Resources section for more information on Freestyle, and you will be able to go as far as you like with the sport!

If you and your dog tend to be couch potatoes, competition Freestyle may not be for you. But dancing at home, with no spying eyes, is a great way for both of you to limber up, stretch

Guys especially may worry about male friends, neighbors or fishing buddies laughing if they see them dancing in public or outdoors with dogs. So until these onlookers become more enlightened, you can always dance in private. Your dogs will enjoy the routines and they will never laugh at you!

out and have a few laughs together. Dancing in private may also be more comfortable for shy teens or husbands! To start out each Freestyle session, tell your dog in an upbeat fashion, "It's time to dance now" or "Dance time!" or simply, "Freestyle!" Then play some music that's a good fit for your fitness levels and the mood and energy of the moment. We suggest starting with music that's somewhat upbeat. Freestyle pros will tell you that different dogs do better with different songs or musical styles, so have fun experimenting.

Begin with some gentle stretches for you and your dog to warm up (see "Stretching", Ch. 9) and you can keep your dog on a leash the first few times you practice. Go through a few basic obedience commands like "sit", then "come", then "down" and set these moves to music to see how your dog adapts to this activity. You can also incorporate a trick like "roll over" if your dog knows it. (If not, instructions are included later in this section.)

If your dog does well the first day, you can continue on to the next stage. However, if picking up the pace and practicing the obedience commands to music seems to challenge him, just practice at this level for the first session and reward lavishly afterwards. The next step, to try the first day or later depending on your dog's proficiency, is to add slightly more difficult movements to the routine.

Teaching your dog to move backwards in step with you is featured in many Freestyle routines and the command also comes in handy in other situations, so it's one of the first dance moves to teach. Start with your dog leashed facing you and take a few steps forward. Your dog will likely naturally step back. As he does, say the word "Back" and reward him. If he doesn't step back as you first move, you can gently step up into him. He'll feel off balance and, if he considers you pack leader, he'll naturally move back when you step up. (Just don't step on you dog!)

Practice until your dog will back up reliably on command. Phase out the food rewards to no more than occasional, while continuing to reward lavishly with praise, petting and an upbeat tone of voice. Eventually, your dog may be performing complicated ten-minute Freestyle routines with no break, so we suggest you get away from food treats for training these routines as your dog progresses. A quick pet or saying, "Good dog" may be more appropriate rewards if spectators are watching your routine; then the dog can have his treats once the routine is over.

Once you've taught your dog to back up on command, try some more moves. Walk forward and back with your dog on leash, perfectly on time with the beat as though you are dancing. Or stand in front of him. When you step up, he steps back, when you step back, he steps up. Or command your dog, on his own, to step forward and back. Keep giving verbal praise. You should also teach your dog to step to the side along with you in time with the music, one of the more popular Freestyle moves. This is a bit trickier to learn than back and forth movement, so start slowly and don't trip at first. Eventually the moves will become second-nature for both of you and, in the process, you will both gain added muscle tone and coordination.

Simple dance moves are great indoor exercise for both you and your dog, and many owners may find it satisfactory to stop at this stage. Just turn on the music and enjoy a fun little workout. If you ever want to add moves, the possibilities are endless. Just teach your dog one new move a day, and practice a few sessions after that with the new move added to the old ones before going for more.

If you don't already have your dog trained to roll over, you could train him to now. You can shorten the command to one word (for example, "roll"). Next you can train him to roll repeatedly. Let him achieve two rolls in sequence before going for more several days later. You will never master Freestyle entirely, since only imagination will limit the routines you and your dog can perform. This is an activity to build on in daily practice over your dog's entire lifetime. And there's no timetable for how quickly you need to master routines, since just practicing Freestyle is highly rewarding.

When your dog has mastered some of the other moves, and if his physical condition allows it, you will likely want to teach him the command, "Jump". Start by training the dog to clear an obstacle, like a small hurdle. Then you can teach him to jump over your arm or to jump through a hoop (see "Jump Over" and "Ring of Fire", Chapter 8). You can add props like scarves or ribbons and train your dog to work with these to give the dance a mesmerizing look. If you advance to this point, you can also enlist a helper with a video camera. Or you can practice in front of a floor-to-ceiling mirror.

When it's time to start learning more complicated dance movements, you can start using "targeting" to lure your dog with a treat on the end of a stick, or a treat or peanut butter offered on the end of an attractive baton, which you may also use during performances. The idea is for the dog to follow the end of the stick with his eyes and his body movements, so that he'll chase the target in any manner you want. You can get your dog to "target" on the stick to move in circles around you, to move his head up and down as though bowing before you, to move in figure-eights or to jump. You might even encourage your dog to stand up on his hind legs, to spin in circles or to crawl. Eventually, you can phase out the stick and have the dog target on subtle movements of your finger so that your audience will think he's being guided by magic! And at this point you may want to teach your dog hand signals to use interchangeably with your voice commands.

Some owners with multiple dogs will now take the opportunity to add their second dog or third dog to the dance performance. Just practice the moves first with each dog individually so they will understand what you want of them. And then the sky is the limit. Additional family members can act as helpers, or a dedicated and patient child or teen could be the family member to train the dogs the routines.

One word of advice, however, is to never *force* your dog to dance with you! Dancing like this together should be sheer joy and you, your dog and any spectators should all leave each session with a great big "smile". Not all dogs will take to Freestyle equally, so consider your dog's temperament and personal preferences and choose this as your sport only if your dog seems to love it.

Another interesting fact to note is that you can certainly practice Freestyle outdoors, like other more popular dog sports. But try it indoors frequently! It's so incredibly hard to find challenging and vigorous exercise activities that can be performed inside, and Freestyle is one of the best. So we suggest you use this aerobic activity whenever weather keeps you inside. While your neighbors' dogs are fretting away inside, chewing up the couches because their bodies are aching with unspent energy, you and your dogs will be dancing away the cold winter days!

Get That Pose
- teaches self-control; your dog might amaze you so snap plenty of photos!

This is an activity for aspiring photographers or those of you who'd like your dog to be a dog model. It's also a fun way to practice teaching your dog self control. In "Get That Pose" you teach your dog to remain in any position that you put him. Now you can practice your photography, and most dogs enjoy the attention.

Depending on your dog's level of training and physical condition, the pose can range from something as easy as a "sit" or a "down" to having him stand on his hind legs with a treat on his nose. But always show patience with your dog and keep it fun. People sometimes get mad at their dogs because they ask the dog to accomplish some Herculean feat they saw on television without realizing their dog doesn't have the training or physical stamina to do what's asked. Each dog has his own talents. Your friend's dog may be a Border Collie, bred for activities like jumping high in the air and catching Frisbees. If your dog is a two-hundred pound mastiff made for guarding, he'll be more comfortable with more dignified activities and poses.

Whatever pose you want your dog to hold, take time and be patient. The only way for your dog to get better is to work from success. So, if the dog can hold a pose for ten seconds but you want him to hold it for five minutes, praise him for the time he stayed for ten seconds. Next time try for eleven or fifteen seconds, then praise. Before you know it, your dog will be holding the pose for the whole five minutes as long as you aren't asking for the impossible.

The possibilities are endless for any breed of dog. You just have to be patient and spend time working with your dog. You may be familiar with the famous photographer William Wegman who achieved fame taking photos of his pet Wiemeraners with cute props. For serious pet photography like this, invest in a fast camera and use some toys that your dog absolutely loves to focus his attention. Animals don't like to stay still for long periods of time and these are two ways to guarantee the perfect shot.

Lulu, "Always ready to strike a pose."

If you want your dog to be a pet model or you want to sell your pet photos, we'll advise you from the point of view of professional photographers that you should aim for shots of your dog that make him stand out in the crowd. One way to make your pet stand out is to take the photo from the pet's point of view and catch the emotion in the animal's eyes. Professional dog models tend to make a large range of people feel an emotion. People who see them are compelled to try to figure out what the dog is thinking because they can't miss the look of thoughtfulness in the dog's eyes. And, after all, that look that makes your particular dog so unique is the reason you love him.

Doggie Gymnasium
-   a truly ambitious utopian idea, but your family or group
may have resources to try it -

Since this chapter is about indoor exercise for dogs, we need to mention one of the best, and the most ambitious, ideas for indoor fitness. The idea is to build a "doggie gymnasium" in your own backyard. This idea may not be practical for every owner, but every dog owner should probably think about it before completely ruling it out. Even if you cannot do it right now, it may be a possibility in the future, or several neighbors or the residents of a gated community may choose to do it as a group endeavor.

First, decide whether you wish to build from scratch or convert an existing outbuilding. Next, check with your local zoning and building departments to find out what types of structures are code-compliant and check with realtors to determine how a new structure would affect resale values. Then decide what type of structure will best suit your needs. You might decide to convert an existing barn or an unused two or three-car garage. You could use a metal outbuilding (of the type available in farm catalogs) if permitted. Or you could start from scratch and build your own concrete shell. You can even build a large, open gym area as an addition to your home and make the design as simple or complex as you like. There are only two absolute prerequisites for your doggie gymnasium. **You must have enough uninterrupted square footage that your dogs can actually run in the building. And the building must be air-conditioned and, preferably, heated.**

The need for air conditioning is important enough that we could repeat it a hundred times. Excessive heat is the biggest obstacle we have seen to owners exercising their dogs intensely while still keeping safe. We constantly hear complaints from owners that they simply cannot exercise their dogs adequately because of heat. Other trainers might label these complaints as copouts. But when you follow heat indices in our area in Southeastern Florida, you'll notice we sometimes have thirty days in a row when the heat index never goes lower than the nineties, even at nighttime.

We cannot, in good conscience, recommend that owners run their dogs vigorously at any hour of these days when it could prove deadly! This doesn't mean they shouldn't be exercising the dogs, but the possibility for vigorous exercise indoors becomes a necessary alternative. Yes, exercise in nature is best and cannot be replaced. But our dogs of today live in the same harsh world where their human owners often must retreat from "heat island" city climates, dangerous, polluted streets and lack of green space to get their vigorous workouts at indoor gyms.

When we first tell people that we are dog trainers they often have a lot of misconceptions. One is that most of our work takes place outside. That's because many of us have grown up watching videos of trainers vigorously working dogs in obedience- always out in a sunny field. Unfortunately, certain climates are more conducive to that kind of training than others and very few places in the country boast comfortable enough climate to practice like that year-round.

Most dogs cannot endure vigorous workouts in sunny fields for hours at a time in the summer and remain healthy. And neither can many owners. This book and this chapter in particular are aimed at "real" people, not athletes who have built up a great endurance to exercise in heat and cold. We'd like real people to learn to love working with their dogs in such a way that dog and owner become healthier and fitter together without a lot of stress and strain. **If your climate is harsh, with extremes of heat or cold (or both) and if you're lucky enough to own a spacious property and have some cash on hand, why not be the first in your community to build a "dog gymnasium"?**

You don't necessarily have to take all of the expense yourself. You could make it a family project. The family member with the land and/or outbuilding would have the gymnasium on their property. Other family members could buy agility equipment, treadmills, toys or easily cleaned non-slip flooring material or they could devote their time to setting things up or to practicing with the dogs.

Maybe you live in a subdivision that tends to be "dog friendly". And many subdivisions also have unused common buildings. Perhaps you could get a bunch of your neighbors together and convince management to let you use it in a novel way- as a dog exercise facility. (A selling point is that this would be a good way to occupy kids as well!) Your club, your veterans group or your church group may also be able to pool resources to set up an exercise facility for dogs. It could be a permanent building or just somewhere you could use once a week, seasonally.

Hosting dogs at this facility could be a fun activity and even a fundraiser. We're not necessarily suggesting that if you build a nicely heated and cooled "gymnasium" on your property you have to charge people to use it. But, providing it's legal in your area, why not? This applies to pet sitters and owners of doggie day care facilities as well. We believe a large outdoor yard is a must for a day care facility. But for full-out running, why not provide somewhere indoors as well?

Yes, this is one idea that's truly not cheap, and it will be beyond some owners' budgets. If you have read through this section and you feel bad because you'd like to build the indoor gym, but don't have the space or the cash, there are some other things you can do for your dogs' well being. In the meantime during times of extreme heat, don't stop exercising your dog. Instead, use our ideas for indoor exercise during the peak of day and bring your dogs outside to exercise during off-peak hours with low heat indices. Nighttime may still be hot or humid, but you can avoid the sun, which greatly intensifies danger of heat illness. You can exercise at twilight when you still have a little light (use mosquito repellent and heartworm preventative for your dog.) If you still want to keep going after dark, avoid the dangers of poison toads, snakes and predators by keeping your dog on a long lead, lighting up every corner of the exercise/play space as bright as daylight and keeping a vigilant eye. (Note that, even with these precautions it is just too risky to allow tiny breeds off leash in a darkened yard.)

Most breeds tolerate mildly cold weather better than heat, but split up your sessions in winter into small chunks, even if it means going out repeated times. Also seek out venues shielded from extreme wind or hide behind a building when you work.

You could also inquire of local doggie daycare facilities if they happen to have a large empty room where you could exercise your dog(s) privately. Yes, it might cost a bit, but perhaps you can strike a deal if the room is empty certain hours. It just may be the most exercise fun you've ever had without breaking a sweat!

Basketball
- good for families and indoor exercise; more challenging than Fetch -

This game is good for dogs of any age or physical fitness level and you can simply adjust the size of the equipment based on the size of the dog. You can play indoors or outdoors (even at picnics or on the beach), the equipment is inexpensive and your kids will enjoy teaching this game to dogs.

Start by purchasing (or building) a miniature basketball hoop on a stand that is the perfect height for your dog. Then choose a dog-friendly ball (you can buy one that looks like a basketball) and teach your dog to lift it in his mouth and drop it through the hoop. Reward him with tons of praise, and perhaps a treat or two, the first few times he makes a basket, until he learns to love the game solely for the challenge.

There are several different ways to teach your dog to place the basketball into the hoop. Some highly alert dogs will mimic your actions if you demonstrate how you put the ball through the hoop and associate the action with a command like, "Make a basket!" But this method is challenging, and the average dog may not learn this way. Another way to train is by "shaping". This means your dog doesn't need to be perfect the first time to get a reward. He just has to get a little closer to the final behavior on each attempt; for example, first simply lifting the ball to get a reward. Next he will carry the ball near the hoop; then he'll drop the ball near the hoop, etc.

Another way you could teach the trick is if your dog already knows the command, "Drop it". Just tell him "drop it" after leading him to hold the ball over the hoop. If he doesn't know the command "drop it", you can quickly teach him. Have him hold the ball over the hoop. Then unexpectedly provide a very yummy treat. Say the word, "Make a basket" as he's relinquishing the ball. (Or you could teach the command as "Drop it" if you wish for him to generalize the useful command of dropping other items. You can always teach the basket command later.)

Having your dog make baskets is a great party game, and a more pleasant way to first introduce your dog to guests than having him jump up on them with muddy paws. And most dogs really enjoy this coordination-building game. You can teach your dog to run up to the basket from a distance if you want to increase his abilities and give him more exercise. And you and the kids can join in the game with him.

Soon your dog will be making baskets not just for treats, but for fun. You may even catch him "shooting hoops" when you're not home. (Just leave the equipment somewhere where there's plenty of room and no fragile breakables if you do leave him alone to play ball.) And, if you thought the game couldn't get more challenging, how about trying it with multiple dogs? It will definitely test your skill training dogs. But imagine the exhilaration when you get your whole pack of dogs playing basketball!

Doggie Treadmill (Indoors)
- mentioned in 3 chapters, this is the best exercise solution for many dogs, but requires caution -

Provided your dog is healthy (and cleared by a vet) and he has no fears that would prevent it, you may be able to include a treadmill as a mainstay of his exercise routines. See the "Doggie Treadmill" sections in Chapters 10 and 14 for cautions and full instructions on how to get your dog started. Most dogs can safely run on treadmills made for humans, but you can also buy treadmills made specially for dogs. (See Resources.)

Ch. 6- Balance & Coordination Activities

"Teach your dog these physical skills for control of his body and freedom from injury."

Also Try These Ideas from Other Chapters for Balance & Coordination:

Puppy Games & Activities: Tunnel Crawl, Soccer, Which Box Has the Fun In It?

Mental Games & Activities: Hold That Position, Move Slow, Ring Toss

Indoor Games & Activities: Limbo, Agility Inside, Dancing Dog (Freestyle), Get That Pose; Basketball

Multi Dog Games & Activities: Simon Says, Sit on a Bench, Under/Over

Problem Dog Games: Catch, Ring of Fire, In the Army Crawl, When I Move You Move, Jump Over

Therapeutic and Senior Dog Activities: Stretching, Doggie Wheelchair, Doggie Stairs

Activities for High-Energy Dogs: Fetch, Frisbee, All Terrain Run, Hiking, Backpacking, Snow Games, Spin Circles, Weave Poles, Hurdles, Track & Field, Flyball, Ocean Swim, Sand Run, Run in Snow

Water Activities: Chase the Hose, Hydrotherapy, Pool Float, Net Pull

Useful Activities: Find My Keys, Wagon Pull, Pack Animal, Sled Dog, Carry My Purse,

Family Activities: Jump Rope, Playground Built With Dog Games

Activities for Owners with Limited Mobility: Doggie Treadmill, Balloons, Bubbles, Upstairs/Downstairs, Dog on the Table

Balance & Coordination Activities - Introduction
"Teach your dog these physical skills for control of his body and freedom from injury."

This chapter can be used to help new puppies as young as eight weeks or older dogs that haven't had this aspect of mind and body stimulated correctly. Dogs recovering from injury or serious illness like stroke may also need additional help. And, just like children must be taught good balance and coordination through practice, so should your puppy. Proper practice during early months will create an adult dog with stronger balance, sharper reflexes and better body coordination. It will also make your dog more confident and resistant to injury.

This chapter will also help owners who want their dogs to participate or compete in activities like Freestyle dance, Agility, or Skyhoundz (Frisbee competition). These dogs need to be masters at coordinating their bodies while catching flying items or making fast turns. Dogs also must control their balance masterfully in sports like agility. During agility competition (or agility practiced for fun in your backyard) your dog jumps hurdles, crawls through tunnels and sails through obstacles like hanging tires at the fastest speed possible. Agility is a highly satisfying sport for healthy dogs of active breeds. It provides intense exercise and prevents frustration, but agility is physically demanding. Owners who intend for their dogs to be active in agility or other high-intensity sports or exercise should set an early groundwork for a confident injury-resistant dog.

Choose which balance and coordination activities to start with based on what you most want your dog to be doing later in life. All the activities in the chapter keep dogs busy and engaged, and each also provides a good source of exercise in itself. If your priority is to keep your dog from getting bored, select a well-rounded schedule of activities, including ones that include physical exertion and challenge.

Different ideas in this chapter are also intended to appeal to different human personalities in your household. Fun party tricks like "Play the Seal" and "Will the Real Dog Stand?" will help your dog do better with his balance and prepare him for all the professional dog sports out there. They are also fun for the kids in the household to teach the dog. "Walk the Plank" and "Teeter Totter" help with agility in particular and they also improve confidence and strengthen the dog/owner bond in nervous or skittish dogs. "Catch the Frisbee" is a good way to exercise your dog and to prepare him for Skyhoundz competitions, and it's also something your active family members will want to do for fun. "Walk Like a Man" and "Double Hoops" can build your dog's body coordination for Canine Freestyle and these are also activities that appeal especially to kids.

We also include activities for their specific health and rehabilitation benefits like "Walk the Line" and "Stack" for those dogs that are just recovering from surgery or illness and starting to learn to use their bodies again. Both these activities also build your dog's self-control, which will help him with every aspect of living with people later in life.

Proper balance and coordination is very important to every dog; it can help your dog avoid injuries in every phase of life and can bring a dog that is recovering from illness back to his former great self. So why not go out in the backyard, observe where your dog could use a little help with balance and coordination- and then try some of these activities and make him the best he can be?

Balance & Coordination Activities:

Different Surfaces
- prevents fears, builds mental stability & trust for owners; Emma's favorite -

If you have a free moment, make it productive for your dog or pup by introducing a new surface. There are many creative ways to do this even if you stay at home.

This is a great learning activity for dogs of every age, every stage (including puppies and geriatrics) and every physical condition. It's easy to do, even in an apartment or on the road; it's fun and interesting for the family and it works equally well for canine rehabilitation as it works for stimulation. Whenever you find yourself with only a few minutes you can do something productive for your dog by introducing him to a new surface. And see "New Learning Every Day (Puppy)" in Chapter 3, Puppy Games & Activities for more details on introducing new surfaces as part of a healthy introduction to the wide world for puppies.

Introduction to novel surfaces stimulates and engages your puppy's senses, and builds balance and coordination at the time when muscles and nerves are undergoing critical development. Just like all the other new tasks a conscientious owner undertakes with their puppy when he is young, pushing your dog to develop in this area will make him a healthier and stronger adult. Learning to keep his body balanced on different surfaces when he's still a wobbly pup can create a more coordinated athlete when your dog matures, and reduce his vulnerability to later injuries.

Meeting new challenges also builds character and courage, and the best time to start is when your dog is young. As a puppy, your dog possesses an open and inquisitive mind.

When you introduce him to new things in positive fashion early, he'll accept those same things properly and without stress if he encounters them in the "real world" in later life.

As trainers specializing in the treatment of dogs with severe emotional problems, we often see adult dogs that are terrified of surfaces including: grass, brush, stairs, water, tiled floors, sand, decking, stone, surfaces that tip, moving cars and raised surfaces like grooming tables. We must then work with the owners to carefully undo these fears through painstaking desensitization combined with other therapies, and it's regrettable when we find out that some of the fears could have been easily prevented if the owners had just taken the time to introduce their puppy to all the novel stimuli when he was young.

The benefit of introducing your puppy to different surfaces also extends to other new stimuli for all his senses, ranging as far as your imagination. Introduce him to sounds, smells and textures in different lighting conditions. For example; teach him to boldly walk through billowing sheets on a clothesline; crawl through a nylon tunnel (the type used for canine agility or at a kids' playground) or mince through crinkly newspapers or wrapping papers on your living room floor. You, and your family members are only limited by your imagination and those stimuli that you feel your pup should learn about for his future in your particular locale. (Thus a Florida puppy will not have to encounter snow, but getting him used to water could be more important.)

Even if you are not able to transport your pup to a lot of different outdoor venues (for example if you are elderly or don't own a car) you can still recreate many novel experiences and textures in your home, using readily available supplies. There are literally thousands of different possibilities, but always select things that you and your pup will find enjoyable, interesting and pertinent.

The only other caution is that you *must* make sure your puppy stays safe and never gets terrified when trying a new surface or this experience will totally defeat the purpose of empowering your dog! Physically, for example, if you want your puppy to confidently step on a wobbly surface, you must make sure that he will not slip and hurt himself. If you are introducing him for water for the first time, the top step of your family pool will be more appropriate than cold water and high waves in the ocean. Pups also go through "fear periods" at certain phases in their emotional development. At these times a puppy will naturally act more timid, and you should not push him farther than he is comfortable going. A caring and careful owner will take their cues from their puppy. The idea is to present strong leadership, while urging him past hesitation and timidity and helping him conquer the new stimuli or the new surface.

It's okay to urge the dog past hesitation and worries, because this will actually help him learn to trust you in future situations. But don't attempt to push a pup (or dog of any age) past flat-out panic or terror. Don't give up the day's attempts entirely- but calmly direct your puppy back to a less challenging activity that you already know he can master confidently, end with a positive attempt and then revisit the tougher surface or stimulus on another day or even a little later in his development. (If a problem persists beyond your reasonable efforts or resembles a phobia, you may want some professional advice.)

You will always want to start out with a competent adult owner introducing the pup to new things or supervise your children if they are attempting it, just in case the puppy does get overly afraid or ever tries to snap or bite. Nine times out of ten, however, introducing your puppy to new surfaces and stimuli is great fun for everyone. You'll probably find yourself proud of your own resourcefulness and your kids will enjoy thinking up new challenges, once you are sure of your dog's temperament.

And, of course, this is not just a puppy activity. Let introducing a new surface be a go-to activity whenever it's raining outside and your adult dog is looking up at you forlornly when he is bored. Or use this activity during other times of change in your dog's life- sometime when you're not around to give as much attention as usual or when he's laid up after surgery and needs something to do around the house rather than his usual run. Also introduce novel surfaces as a low-stress, low-impact activity for your senior dog to keep his mind engaged and his body active and to remind him that his family loves him.

(**Safety Note**: **Slowly** introducing new surfaces is also something you will have to **carefully** include as part of the education for any new dog you bring into the home, including shelter and rescue dogs whose backgrounds are unknown. But in these cases, for safety's sake, only adults should attempt this. **Proceed carefully and never push a dog that seems like he might bite to do something he doesn't want to do. It's always a good idea to enlist the help of a high-level behavioral expert with scientific background to ease the transition for any rescue dog whose background you are uncertain of.** A reputable professional will never sell you services you don't actually need, and a consultation is well worth the cost for peace of mind. Most dogs will easily get over past fears and abuse as soon as a kind owner shows them that new stimuli are benign. **Unfortunately certain rescue or shelter dogs may have violent triggers from previous abuse that the new owner may not know about, so be especially careful about introducing these dogs to any new stimuli.** Watching your dog's demeanor and not pushing past any extreme reaction will usually be enough to keep everyone safe, but consult with a professional if you are not sure…)

Will The Real Dog Stand?
- standing on hind legs on command builds muscles & prevents problem jumping -

Do you own dogs that love standing on their hind legs to reach up to get things on high shelves or to look out the windows? Many dogs naturally love to stand on their hind legs trying to glimpse interesting things that they wouldn't be able to observe as well if they remained on all fours.

But, as endearing as this behavior sometimes seem, many dogs get hurt trying to stand on their hind legs. Because of their weight and a tendency toward weakness in their hips, some large breeds are most at risk, but smaller dogs can get injured as well. (In one case a Boston Terrier stood on his hind legs looking up at a squirrel for so long that when he tried to walk away his legs collapsed under him!) Teaching your dog to stand on his hind legs properly, on command, will serve to build his muscles. It can also teach him that this behavior is not something he should do on his own, without your command. All of this will protect him from future injury from improperly standing on his legs later in life.

And, of course, the game is great fun for most dogs. But, like all physical activities, before starting this one, owners should use caution based on their own dogs' health and physical limitations. If your dog or puppy is a large or giant breed; if he is ill or injured or if you suspect for any reason that standing on his hind legs might physically hurt him, please check with your veterinarian to see if he sets any limitations on the activity.

An easy way to teach your dog to stand on his hind legs is to hold a treat over the dog's head and, when he goes up on his hind legs to reach the treat tell him, "Good stand," and praise while giving the treat. Do this a few times and your dog will start to stand on his hind legs by you just asking him to stand even without a treat as long as you continue to lavish him with great praise. You can also use this game to gain control over your dogs if you own more than one dog. First you have to teach each dog to stand by his name because they will need to do this in order to play the game.

When playing "Will the Real Dog Stand" with multiple dogs, start with all your dogs sitting in front of you. One by one, ask the dogs to stand by name. If the correct dog stands, immediately give him a treat. But if one of the other dogs stands on its hind legs praise only the one that you asked to stand. Tell the other dog that he was silly; and then only give him a treat when you call him to stand and he does it. As the dogs get better at the task you can ask more than one to stand at a time. In addition to the challenge, the fun and the fact that your guests will be amazed, the best part about practicing a game like this is the control you have over your multi-dog household!

Play the Seal
- this classic trick makes people smile, while building reflexes, concentration & muscle tone -

Have you ever enjoyed the seal show at Sea World? The first time Ray attended as a child he was amazed to see the seal balance the ball on his nose at the trainer's instructions. Six-year old Ray did not have much success duplicating the feat himself, but he did find that his dogs could willingly and easily do the trick! Not only is "Playing the Seal" lots of fun for your family and guests to observe but, when your dog balances a ball on his nose, it can help build focus, concentration, reflexes and muscle tone. Just remember that you cannot, and should not, force your dog to do any game or trick that he doesn't want to try and, while some dogs will love this particular game, others may not.

If your dog is a fun-loving good sport and a little of a showman, this is probably a great trick for him to learn, so why not give it a try? First put your dog in a "sit" and show him the ball you are planning on using. Next bring the ball over his head so that, as he watches it, his nose points up in the air. While his nose is pointed in the air, place the ball on his nose, and ask him to, "Hold it."

The first few times you practice, reward the dog with a treat even if he holds the ball on his nose for a just a second. Now build up to asking him to hold the ball on his nose for a little longer each time you repeat the game. If your dog ever fails and lets the ball fall off his nose, just go back to where he did well and try again until he succeeds and earns a treat. Dogs tend to learn this game with surprising ease because, unlike humans, they have an incredible natural sense of balance.

To make the game easier, start out with a large ball because large balls are not as likely to overexcite and distract highly "prey-driven" dogs. (Some prey-driven dogs may act too intent on grabbing and chewing a tennis-size ball, rather than balancing it on their noses. For safety in this and any game you never want to risk using a ball that is small enough for your dog to swallow, because he could get the ball caught in his throat and literally choke to death.)

As your dog advances in skill in the game of "Play the Seal", you can really amaze your party guests. Try an advanced variation and teach your dog to balance a treat on the end of his nose and then toss it up in the air, catch and eat it on your command. Good luck and have lots of fun!

Walk the Line
- improves dogs' balance; also slows dogs that pull -

Have you ever actually tried to walk a straight line? Until you've done it, the task seems a lot easier than it really is (and maybe this is why the police have people walk a straight line to see if they have been drinking). As long as you don't think about walking it's easy. But if you start to concentrate on walking as straight as possible, it can feel like you are thirty feet in the air, balanced on a piece of string and about to fall! Once you learn to walk on a line more confidently, without straining to think about it so much, your balance will improve. And practicing this activity with your dog aids your dog's balance in similar fashion.

Having to walk a line without stepping off is also great for those dogs and puppies that act wild and have trouble controlling their bodies and their overexuberance. It also slows down dogs that pull their owners down the street, because frequent practice teaches your dog to think about each step he takes.

"Walk the Line" will take time a little time to teach your dog. First put your dog on a leash then and lay a long strip of white tape down on a floor (you can also place a string or an extra long lead down in a straight line). Start your dog at one end of the tape and now ask the dog to "Walk the Line". As the dog starts to walk with you standing in front of him and coaxing him forward, watch that he stays on the line. If he steps off the line bring him back to the beginning, shaking your head like you were disappointed and try again. If your dog stays on the line tell him, "Good walk the line," and praise and encourage.

As the dog gets better at staying on the line start walking at his side rather than walking in front as you ask him to walk the line. Your dog will not only learn to walk with more focus but the exercise will also help him to become more coordinated and have better balance. You can also see this game work as a real life skill by teaching the dog to balance on a small log in the woods or you can support a piece of wood a few inches off the ground for your dog to walk on. But never make your dog balance on anything that makes him nervous or is very high off the ground. You don't want your dog to ever fall off and get hurt or to acquire a fear of heights. So always use caution, be sensitive to your pet and use every activity to the best advantage.

Walk Like a Man
- for healthy dogs only- builds muscle, balance & coordination -

We humans feel we're the most advanced animals on the planet. And one of the things we take pride in is the fact that we are able to walk upright on two legs. But maybe man should rethink that we are superior just because we walk on two legs. Most animals can also walk on two legs for short distances- but they find their own advantages in walking on four. Animals are faster and stronger than humans because of moving on four legs and they only use two legs when it has distinct advantages. (One example was an unstoppable dog featured in a popular magazine. After having both front legs amputated following an accident he learned to walk on only his hind legs and still play ball with other dogs!)

Occasionally standing and walking on hind legs can benefit dogs' balance and coordination as long as the animal does not suffer from certain medical conditions (which you should clear with your veterinarian). And walking on the hind legs is not an easy activity for all dogs. It will challenge your dog and make him very tired at first because he may not understand exactly what's wanted of him. He may even lose balance or fall over at times as he learns to control and strengthen his muscles and properly adjust himself, but this can help him build his muscles and avoid future injury.

Some breeds have a much easier time with this activity (Poodles of all sizes are one example.) But for some giant dogs (notably Mastiff breeds) any time at all spent walking on the hind legs can be dangerous because of the weight they carry and pressure on delicate hip joints. Owners should ask their veterinarian about his or her recommendations for their dog's hips before attempting this exercise.

In the case of most breeds, intentionally practicing walking on the hind legs occasionally can be beneficial because it strengthens your dog's body and builds control, while dogs with no experience holding this position may hurt themselves if they jump overexcitedly on their own. Walking on hind legs occasionally can also build the strength in your dog's back legs and improve his balance so he won't be as prone to injury during dog sports that include running and jumping.

The game of "Walk like a Man" is fun for dogs, fun for humans to teach and it's one of the building-block move for some other physical activities like dancing (Freestyle). The best idea is to use walking on hind legs judiciously based on your veterinarian's advice, your dog's breed and his individual needs and physical condition.

As long as your dog's hips are sound and you don't push him to do too much, it should be easy to teach him to walk on his hind legs. Start by holding a treat over the dogs' head and when he stands move the treat away from him. Encourage him to move forward for the treat and reward and praise even if he just leans forward to get it. Each time you try, ask your dog to go just a little further. See if you can get the dog to take one step the next time you work on the trick. Say," Good walk," and reward with a treat, then ask for a few more steps. Soon you will see your dog walking on his hind legs just like a human!

Be a Parrot
- classic showstopping move for adventurous and physically fit owners and dogs-

This activity is for the all the really physically fit and adventurous dog owners out there. Have you ever watched the shows on Animal Planet early Sunday morning featuring all the different dog sports? One Ray always loved is the show where owners and dogs compete as a team in creative ways to play Frisbee. At the grand finale, sometimes a dog will jump on the owner's back or shoulders standing on his hind legs looking like a parrot!

You can learn to do this with your dogs as long as you are willing to follow a few safety precautions. First, never teach this activity to a dog that has problem jumping on people unless you really want your dog jumping on your back every time you walk in your door! He might even hurt a guest doing a trick that you taught him. So teach this only with a well-mannered dog that you're sure will attempt the stunt only when asked. And next, please refrain from trying this with your dog that weighs over 100 pounds, or any puppy that is expected to one day grow to that size, or you'll be spending lots of time in your bed, with a hurt back.

Also, this is one activity that is suitable only for dogs and owners that are already strong, highly physically fit and healthy. This trick is not recommended for the average dog, so you should first clear with your veterinarian that your dog is physically capable of doing it and would suffer no ill effects as long as you practice the activity safely.

Balancing on his owner's back is not very hard to teach your dog but it does take time, because you don't want to risk injury. In this section, we teach the basics. If you and your dog turn out to be naturals at this type of trick, you can go farther on your own, perhaps one day winning at Frisbee or Freestyle Dance competitions.

To teach your dog to "Be a Parrot", first ask him to put his front paws on your back. You can do this by telling your dog, "Paws up" and tap on your back as you bend over. When your dog puts his paws on you, offer him praise and reward with a treat. Even if he only puts one paw up the first time you should reward him. If you cannot get the dog to put his paws up on you, you may need a friend's help. Your friend can pick the dog's paws up onto your back when you say "Paws up". Or he can stand on one side of you and keep the dog on the other. Then the friend can lure the dog to put his paws on your back with a treat while saying, "Paws up."

Just make sure that the dog understands he has to put his paws on your back in order to get the treat. The next step will be to get the dog to put all four legs up on your back when you say, "Up."

As your dog gets more and more comfortable getting on your back, start telling the dog, "Up," and praising when he climbs up on your back. To add some fun, start mixing things up. On one repetition, ask the dog to stand on your back; next time you can have him sit or even lie on your back. But take care that your dog has his nails short so you don't get scratched and **never allow your dog to jump off your back in a way that might hurt him.** Just take your time, get creative and have fun.

Catch the Frisbee
- the right way to play Frisbee to make dogs' behavior better without problems -

Frisbee is a great game for hyperactive dogs. Your dog burns off lots of energy, and the owner doesn't have to strain to keep up. All you need is a fenced area to practice and a sturdy dog-safe Frisbee. (Owners without fenced yards can (carefully) play Frisbee with their dog attached to a long (20-50ft) lead, or visit a park in your area where it's legal for your dog to run off-lead.)

We've included Frisbee here in the Balance and Coordination section, because running for and catching a Frisbee can present balance challenges to dogs that are new to the sport. Believe it or not, some dogs fall the first few times they try to catch the Frisbee. So, to avoid injury, start by throwing the Frisbee gently, from short distances. Then let your dog build up to more ambitious moves as he builds in coordination and overall physical fitness.

> *Teach your dog good habits (like bringing the Frisbee all the way back to you, and waiting calmly for you to throw it) from the first time you play!*

At first, take care not to throw the Frisbee too high for your dog to catch easily. Even a hyperactive dog that jumps on your family all day long may tumble like a bag of rocks in his overexuberance the first few times he lunges for the Frisbee. Just make sure that your dog has no physical limitations, play on a cushiony surface with no hazards (for example, choose grass over concrete). And, if your dog is on a long lead, never allow him to hit the end of the lead running full speed. To keep things safe at first, keep the Frisbee low and easy.

Not all dogs show equal interest in the sport of Frisbee. Some immediately go wild just at the sight of a Frisbee, jumping and trying to grab it out of their owner's hands. Others show some interest, but not enough to start jumping up and down. With a dog like this, you may want to wave Frisbee around in front of him to get him geared up and ready to go before starting the game. And some dogs show no interest at all in a Frisbee and choose to walk away. If this is the case, Frisbee may simply not be the game for your dog. Sometimes it helps to revisit the sport under different conditions, when the dog matures a little or when other dogs are also playing. But, just as some dogs are amazing stars at Frisbee, others just "don't get it" and shouldn't be forced or traumatized.

When first starting to play Frisbee with your dog, there's one good habit you should get into. Throw the disc only a few feet at first. When your dog grabs the disc, immediately call him back to you and ask him to drop the disc at your feet. You want this to become an immutable habit! When your dog drops the Frisbee, pick it up and then ask him to sit for you in non-demanding fashion before you throw it again for him to chase. Making your dog sit patiently teaches him not to jump and snap at the Frisbee while you are holding it. Not only is this real-life obedience practice, but teaching him to sit and to reliably surrender the Frisbee back to you short-circuits future dominant behavior in a symbolic language your dog easily understands.

If you don't make sure your dog retrieves the Frisbee for you, he may learn that *he* controls the game. Now you risk future defiance and you've created a monster that will happily chase the Frisbee and deliberately tease you with it, eventually dropping it far enough away from you that you'll get more exercise than he does! In contrast, if you set good habits from the very first time your dog experiences a Frisbee, the good experiences are likely to continue throughout his life.

Also get in the habit of always quitting games of Frisbee while your dog still wants to play. This will keep him motivated, interested and always wanting more for next time. If you've followed our advice, your dog's only chance to play Frisbee will be if he continues to properly retrieve it for you. If your dog ever acts obstinate and refuses to bring the disc back to you, stay consistent. Immediately end the game and put him away out of sight before retrieving the Frisbee yourself. Next time, throw the disc only as far as your dog's last successful retrieve. And, overall, have a great day with lots of fun, exercise and training for your dog!

Walk the Plank
- use the regulation agility equipment to increase balance & confidence
or construct your own -

We're not referring to what pirates used to make captives do; but rather about walking the plank in canine agility. This activity is good for many reasons. It builds a relationship of trust between owner and dog by having them work as a team and it also teaches your dog to be directed by voice commands only. Before starting this game, make sure your dog isn't afraid of heights. If he is, you'll have to work on getting him less afraid first or you'll set the dog and yourself up for failure.

The items you'll need for this activity are few, but not always readily available. Owners have two options to get what you need. You can find a local dealer that sells agility equipment and ask to buy a piece of agility equipment called a dogwalk. Be warned that this item won't be cheap; most cost between $199- $799. The dogwalk consists of one long plank raised off the ground with shorter angled planks leading up to and down from it.

If you're handy, another option is to build a dogwalk yourself with supplies you buy at a hardware store. First look over photos of dogwalks on dog agility websites or sites that sell agility equipment. Then start with three planks about 12-inches wide. The length of these planks depends on how high you want to build your dogwalk; just don't make them too short, because this will make the incline up to the top plank too steep. You'll also need wood to make a base for the dogwalk and non-skid paint so your dog won't slip going up the planks. Whichever way you decide to obtain your dogwalk, make sure it is made to a standard that's safe for the size dogs that will be using it.

Safety must come first, so if you don't have previous experience building things and your dog is large, we recommend that you buy your dogwalk or have an expert build it for a fee. Don't attempt to cut corners if a dog could get hurt.

The game "Walk the Plank," is actually very easy to teach if the dog isn't afraid of heights. Once your dogwalk is ready, bring your dog up near it and make sure to have a pocket full of treats he loves. At first, keep the dog on a long lead for control. Stand at his side and ask him to, "Walk the plank". Lure him by holding a treat in front of his nose while you walk along the dogwalk. Now cheer him on- up one side of the walk and then across the long flat plank to the other plank that brings him back down to the ground. If he completes this successfully, reward him with lots of treats and praise because you have a real natural!

"Walking the Plank" may sound easy, but there are some problems that may occur. For example, you may get your dog to the equipment and ask him to "Walk the Plank" and he may look at you as if to ask, "Who me? Are you crazy?" And then it may feel like you hooked an anchor to the end of your leash rather than your dog. Don't fret, since this reaction is very normal. Your dog may just need you to show him exactly what you want, or perhaps he's just trying to tell you he's afraid of this thing he's never seen before. Try offering him a particularly tasty treat or his favorite toy to lure him up the plank, along with lots of encouragement.

If this still gets no response, just set a few treats on the inclining plank and walk away. Let your dog wander around the equipment a little, sniff around it and maybe even take some treats off the plank. Once this happens, you can take him away and then try again the next day. Most likely your dog will now work with you more easily. Just never push your dog too hard or you could ruin him forever.

The next problem you might face is if your dog tries to jump off the plank. This is one reason why you'll want to keep your dog on a leash close to you, and take your time teaching the exercise. Always be aware and ready and leave enough leeway in the leash that, even if your dog ever jumps from the top of the plank, he can't hang himself.

During agility competitions some dogs like to jump off the plank prematurely on the way down. This is why, if you buy a dogwalk, it will have yellow painted areas on both ends. Make sure from the beginning to make your dog touch these yellow painted areas going up from the bottom and stepping off the other side. In formal agility competitions dogs must touch these areas or lose points. This rule was made to keep dogs from jumping and jarring their hips and shoulders trying to make better time. And you should teach your dog the habit of disembarking safely as well.

If your dog seems afraid at any point when practicing "Walk the Plank" just take it slow and go at his speed. This is a challenging activity, but one both you and your dog will feel very proud learning to master together.

Stack
**-   standing like a show dog helps posture & muscle tone,
while building respect for owners -**

Have you ever watched show dogs as they stand proudly for the judge on television and admired them simply as objects of beauty? Did you know that your dog can stand up regally in the same fashion, displaying his grandest potential even if he's not a show dog? "Stacking" in competition stance occasionally will improve your dog's posture and his muscle tone, self control, mental focus, attention span and calmness. And it also increases his sense of pride, purpose and self-esteem while improving his connection with his owner.

When you start practicing "stacking", or show posing, your dog should already know how to walk politely on a leash. Knowing the command to "stand" until you allow him to break will help as well. Make sure your dog's exercised and loosened up before posing, but not too tired. Walk him in a few precise graceful circles as you would in a ring. Then bring him into the spot where you want him to pose. For example, this could be in front of a friend or family member who will be acting as a mock "show judge". Or you might allow your other dogs to act as a well-trained audience, awaiting their respective turns to pose.

You can also pose each dog in front of a mirror if you lack an assistant. While most dogs won't really understand the concept of the mirror, posing in front of it may formalize the command for them. And certain dogs may even glance at themselves proudly, perhaps understanding that you have some special game afoot.

Command your dog either "Stack", "Pose" or just, "Stand" in an encouraging tone of voice as you adjust your dog's stance and every aspect of his or her pose. You could even murmur words like, "Look pretty" while making miniscule adjustments and then praise your dog by murmuring something like "What a pretty dog!" Start easy. For some dogs, especially puppies, just standing still for a few minutes is an accomplishment, so give lots of legitimate praise. At each practice, challenge your dog to remain posed longer, and to improve in style. Getting it perfect is part of the fun, and you can always refine your dog's presentation over a number of years

Stacking is healthy for most dogs as it provides a good stretch and improves body alignment. But make sure your dog is in perfect health , with no skeletal injuries or chronic ailments like hip dysplasia or arthritis before you attempt to physically adjust him into a pose. If your puppy or adult dog resists slightly as you attempt to pose him, this is the point of the exercise, and you'll gently work to increase his comfort zone at subsequent practices. As your dog learns, expect better poses each practice over the course of years. There is no need to hurry because posing your dog is strictly for fun!

The best way to get your dog started is to first lure him into a pose like what you want with treats or a squeaky toy. (Observe how professional handlers do it.) Then very gently stroke and adjust him into the desired show stance. Also practice lifting his gums and gently palpating his abdomen. **If at any time your dog strongly resists, squeals or shows any signs of distress when you attempt to adjust him into a pose, stop immediately**. It's possible that he's feeling real physical pain. The fault might also be yours if you're not posing him correctly and you must recognize this and refine your skills.

Professionals take years to learn how to show dogs and it's a challenging pastime. To do it right, not only should you practice with your dog, but you need to research the proper procedures for posing your breed. It's also useful to read books on dog training and dog physiology, attend dog shows, enroll in professional show-handling classes or learn from videos. As you practice you'll also want to watch yourself stacking dogs on videotape. Then, if your dog is a registered purebred with good conformation, you may excel at show posing enough to start entering dog shows. But you can also practice stacking just to increase dog/owner bonding.

If practicing at home, you may wish to allow your "mock judge" to handle your dog as a show judge would. **But first test out that your dog will not bite the "judge"** Accepting handling by a friendly stranger is a sign of a dog with a good, balanced temperament, but no one should assume anything about their dog's behavior if they're not sure. There have been cases of dogs biting judges in the show ring. And you certainly don't want an unfortunate incident like this to happen when a friend or neighbor has kindly volunteered to help you with your dog!

If your dog *does* do great allowing a pretend " show judge" to handle him, this is a sign that he may also be a candidate to pass the Canine Good Citizen Test. Canine Good Citizen is an AKC designation offered to dogs that are able to behave well in the face of dog and human distractions. These standardized trials are offered at many dog shows, and the Canine Good Citizen title can be earned by mixed breeds as well as purebreds (see the Book section in Resources).

Once your dog learns the skill of "Stacking", you can show him off at every family reunion (rather than letting him make an impression on the relatives by jumping on them!) After your dog masters a grand show pose, it might also be a great time to employ a professional dog photographer or artist who paints canine portraits. Pose your dog and have the magnificent work framed, and display over the mantle for future generations of the family to be impressed!

Teeter Totter
- this challenging agility obstacle is ideal for balance, confidence & muscle building -

Have you ever played on a teeter totter (or seesaw) when you were a child? And would you ever think that one day your dog would be using the same equipment in agility competitions? Or in your backyard? You can buy a Teeter Totter over the Internet along with other agility equipment. Or you can just make a small triangle out of wood for a base and put a 12-inch wide plank on top of it. The 12-inch plank on top should be six to eight feet long with bolts holding it to the base in a way that it can tip from one side to the other as the dog's weight reaches a certain point.

The difference between human and dog seesaws is that kids play with one child at each end to shift the weight, while they bounce up and down. In the dog version, however, only the one dog is on the teeter totter, using his balancing skills so he can walk down the other side and walk off. The dog learns to slowly move across the totter to the other side to get off without the totter slamming down. The dog should learn to shift his weight smoothly so that the jar of the end of the totter falling is not too intense.

This is just one of the many obstacles your dog must master if he wants to be an agility champion, and it is one of the most challenging. Benefits of mastering the teeter totter include increased confidence and focus and the ability for the dog to completely trust his handler and take direction effectively. It teaches your dog to learn how to use his weight in an effective way in life. He'll be less likely to get injured hurt when jumping or making sharp turns running because he'll more accurately use his body weight to his advantage.

Using the teeter totter is a challenging activity that could strain the joints, so first clear the activity with your veterinarian just like you should for any of the other more challenging agility activities. Never push a dog that appears terrified or in pain to try the activity, or you may create fears or injuries in a dog that just wasn't ready. Avoid using teeter totters with elderly, ill or physically compromised dogs, especially those with bone or joint problems.

Using the teeter totter is good practice for puppies whose balance and musculature has not fully developed. Just carefully assist so that the pup does not get hurt or become frightened. For puppies under six months, either use regulation equipment lowered to an extremely low height, or create your own (safe) low surface that tilts. Keep a firm hold on your puppy as he masters the challenge and always make the game fun.

Double Hoops
- more challenging variation on the easy, popular game keeps dogs interested & looking beautiful -

In Chapter 9, Problem Dog Games, you are introduced in detail to the hula-hoop as a way to exercise your dog in "Ring of Fire." To make the activity more graceful, more challenging and more fast-paced, simply introduce a second hula-hoop. Move the hoops in graceful sequences as your dog jumps or climbs through. Your dog will twist his body around, doubling back to the second hoop after he has climbed through the first.

If you own several dogs that work well together, you can even teach the dogs to intertwine with each other, exchanging the hoops that each goes through. Watching the dogs "perform" is quite entertaining, and it's invigorating to be the person manipulating the hoops. Try this with graceful long-haired dogs like Papillons or Afghans and ask a friend to videotape. Watching your dogs just might take your breath away!

Spin Circles
- doesn't just make you laugh; it burns energy, teaches control & is useful in other activities -

Some owners of high-energy dogs will want to teach their dog how to spin in circles on cue rather than just letting the dog chase after his tail on his own! As long as the activity is not taken to excess, it can burn up a little energy and make everyone smile, even on the most forbidding day and without ever having to leave your apartment. (This is one workout for which you only need a tiny bit of space!) Spinning on cue like this is also a good skill for your dog to acquire better balance and control- and also to learn when it's appropriate to get worked up and when it's appropriate to stop.

As long as your dog has no medical or balance problems that you know of, you can easily teach your dog to spin on cue by using treats. Move a treat around the dog's body so that your dog follows it as you command, "Spin". If the dog follows the treat and spins on command, reward him with the treat and tell him, "Good Spin," along with praise and petting.

As your dog gets better at spinning on cue, you and your family members can make things more challenging by asking him to spin left or right, and coordinating the movements into dance routines. (See "Dancing Dogs/Freestyle in Chapter 5, Indoor Games.) Dancing like this, indoors and outdoors is an ideal exercise for healthy high-energy dogs of every size. It works for small spaces and small blocks of time and spinning is a basic move used as a building block in many professional routines.

Also, just like this method helps with some other unwanted repetitive physical behaviors and habits, teaching a dog to spin on cue when you command him can actually keep him from doing it on his own at inappropriate times.

Ch. 7- Multi-Dog Games & Activities:

"Lead your pack with positive activities so the inmates don't 'run the asylum'".

Introduction

Duck, Duck, Goose

Simon Says

What's My Name?

The Long, Long Stay

Obedience Competition at Home

Agility Competition at Home

Home Agility One By One

Dancing Dogs

Sit on a Bench

Limbo

Under/Over

Also Try These Ideas From Other Chapters for Multiple Dogs:

Puppy Activities (Ch. 3): Follow the Leader, Which Box Has the Fun In It?, Tunnel Crawl, How Do I Get What's In There?, Walk This Way, Obedience Practice

Mental Games & Activities (Ch. 4): Movie Star, Watch Me, Wait, Hold That Position, Listen, Move Slow

Indoor Games & Activities (Ch. 5): Hide & Seek, Agility Inside, Dancing Dog (Freestyle), A Room of His Own, Doggie Gymnasium, Basketball

Balance and Coordination Activities (Ch. 6): Will the Real Dog Stand?, Play the Seal, Walk the Line, Walk Like a Man, Catch the Frisbee, Double Hoops

Problem Dog Games (Ch. 8): Catch, Ring of Fire, Go to Your Place, Take a Bow, Up and Down, Stop Barking on Command, In the Army Crawl, When I Move, You Move, Race

Therapeutic and Senior Dog Activities (Ch. 9): Party in the Storm, Show the Puppy Obedience, Change of Scene, Help His Comrades

Activities for High-Energy Dogs (Ch. 10): Agility, All-Terrain Run, Hiking, Backpacking, Snow Games, Race, Weave Poles, Water Run, Hurdles, Track and Field, Sand Run, Flyball, Rally, Tracking, Ocean Swim (two handlers), Run In Snow

Water Activities (Ch. 11): Kiddie Pool, Chase the Hose, Dog's Own Pool, Water Walk

Useful Activities (Ch. 12): Pack Animals, Check the Perimeter, Find the Missing Person, Follow the Scent, Work with Livestock, Personal Bodyguard.

Family Activities (Ch. 13): Rally at Home, Races, Playground Built with Dog Games, Junior Grooming Salon, Assess a Dog, Petstar at Home, Test Obedience

Activities for Owners with Limited Mobility (Ch. 14): Dog Walker, Balloons, Bubbles, Play in the Snow, Be Creative.

Multi-dog Games & Activities- Introduction
"Lead your pack with positive activities and the inmates won't 'run the asylum'".

If you own more than one dog, you may have felt at times that "the inmates were running the asylum" in your home. Life may have been great when you owned only one dog, but then you decided to bring a second or third dog home. Now, several large dogs may play constantly and uncontrollably inside your home. Suddenly, the whole house seems to rock, precious possessions tumble and you may frequently get knocked off your feet. All day long the dogs may leap on each other, biting on each other's fur and even engaging in "socially indelicate" play- such as mounting or sniffing each other's private parts.

You may even notice that your better behaved dog has gone downhill since you brought home the more rebellious canine. Suddenly, a dog that had good manners for years starts to imitate the bad manners of his new companion. Now you have two dogs engaging in sports like "counter surfing" and digging flowerbeds.

Ironically, many owners bring home a second dog motivated by love or compassion. They may enjoy their first dog so much that they want a second, or perhaps they want to do a good deed by adopting.

Other multi-dog owners are motivated more by impulse. An example is the young working couple who've never owned a dog before deciding to buy a puppy for their preschool kids. If they buy from a pet store in their local mall rather than a reputable breeder, they may start out with problems. Since many pet shop puppies are bred in "puppy mills" the owners will likely have to deal with multiple health and behavior problems as the dog grows up. And often the naïve owners may make their challenges worse by buying two puppies at the same time!

Families frequently call us for help after bringing home two puppies of approximately the same age, a situation that lends itself to disaster because of the way young dogs think and develop. Unfortunately, most owners don't learn these facts until it's too late.

It's understandable if an owner worries that their dog will become depressed if they leave him alone during eight, ten or twelve-hour workdays with nothing to keep him occupied. So rather than changing their schedules, they reason that another dog will solve the problem by providing needed companionship. The truth is that adding another dog can only help if you own the right combination of dogs, since not every two dogs get along well. (For example, although it seems counterintuitive, littermates of the same sex are especially difficult to raise together. And certain breeds are known to create problems when combined.)

Owners can face two different types of problems when dogs live together in their homes. Sometimes the dogs learn to like each other *too* much. If the owners fail to interact with the dogs enough, the dogs may bond more closely to each other than to people. This is a complex behavioral issue, but owners should be aware that if they wish to raise pups together into adulthood, they must socialize the pups properly and frequently with people.

Dogs that spend too much time alone with other dogs are likely to engage in lots of wild "doggy" behaviors that drive owners crazy. They may forget their house manners, and even soil your house by marking over each other's urine indoors. And dogs that are socialized too much with other dogs and not enough with humans may grow up to act insensitive to humans, or to act skittish about human touch and affection.

Sadly, this is often the case with puppies raised in "puppy mills". Through no fault of their own, these pups are deprived of human contact during crucial developmental stages and they receive all their learning and feedback from dogs. Dogs like this that do all their youthful socializing with dogs may not understand humans. One example is that these puppies often bite humans too hard in play, not understanding that human's skin is thinner than dogs'.

It's easy to understand how crowded puppy mill conditions can create this dog-directed behavior. But owners are often unaware that if they bring home two puppies of the same age, they may create similar problems at home. In either situation, the problem can respond to remediation, but it requires intense effort on the part of the owners; so it's better to start out fresh with the right socialization.

Another common problem occurs when owners bring home a new dog, assuming their existing dog(s) will like him and instead they're shocked when dogs hate each other. An example is owners who notice their senior dog acting listless and depressed and decide to bring him home

> *Owners may wonder why other handlers have such great control of large packs, while they can't even stop two dogs from running in a circle! The answer is proactive thinking- and your "pack" can function seamlessly.*

a furry little companion that they hope will infect him with its uncontained energy. In some cases, instead of perking him up, the new young dog may make the last years of your older dog's life completely miserable for him or hasten his demise!

Some older dogs just don't have the patience for a particular younger dog, and sometimes the younger dog is too big and boisterous for an appropriate playmate. A large puppy of almost a year old can seriously injure a delicate geriatric dog just during normal canine play. Remember that, in the wild, wolves are not always gentle with each other, and much of their play is actually mock fighting, complete with tooth, claw and flinging the weaker dog around.

Sometimes the situation at home deteriorates into worse than play if the younger dog challenges the older for dominance and the older refuses to back down. Suddenly the older dog may lash out at the younger in violent anger, perhaps even drawing blood. And then, if the torch of canine control isn't passed smoothly, the younger dog may retaliate and the dogs may fight again, day after day, doing serious damage to each other.

Each time owners bring additional dogs into their home things can get exponentially worse. Even if male dogs are neutered and generally friendly, they may start fighting each other over a new bitch. And some homes move along smoothly for years with four dogs in the family pack, but the moment they adopt a fifth dog, this may be the catalyst for violence. The new dog may suddenly attack their existing dogs, or the instigator may be one of the existing dogs in the household- one that previously acted sweet.

None of these canine social difficulties would be a mystery to us if we were dogs ourselves, because canines operate in a complex social system that keeps their packs running smoothly. Just like humans understand human body and facial cues like crossed arms, yawns or smiles, dogs understand their own indicators- a raised lip, bristling hackles, a straight up tail or even the smell of another dog's rear end or urine markings around the territory.

In order for a canine pack to function as an effective hunting unit, it's important that the animal controlling the pack and making all their decisions remains the strongest and wisest. This is why, in the wild, dogs fight each other for the privilege of leading the pack. Even those who are not pack leader fight for their own positions in the hierarchy and weak animals are not tolerated.

As much as we humans would like dogs to be "humanitarians" as we understand it, this is not how canine life functions. Dogs do not help old ladies across the street, or hold doors for the weaker animal, nor do the weaker animals of the pack eat first. In fact, it's exactly the opposite. In the canine world, the strongest animal pushes his way through small spaces first, causing the pack to follow along behind him. He also eats first on kills, growling at any lesser animal that tries to intrude and then biting, if the growling doesn't stop the interloper. Canines in the wild are even known to abandon elderly or ill animals that can't keep up. Harsh as these methods seem, dogs do not possess government as we do, and these methods are the only way for their pack as a whole to survive and flourish.

This doesn't mean that in the wild dogs or wolves constantly kill each other. That also would be non-productive. Dogs locked in a home with each other with humans interfering are much more likely to fight constantly and do serious damage to each other than a legitimate pack of dogs or wolves in the wild. Again, you must think like a canine to understand. It wouldn't help the wolf pack much if the wolves constantly fought with each other to the point of inflicting injury. If that happened too much, then nobody could hunt. Instead, the animals engage in many signals- sounds like growling, or physical gestures like raising hackles or rolling over in submission to avoid conflict and establish the social hierarchy in everyday situations.

Once an owner learns more about the behavior of wild canines, they can easily recognize the same social posturings in their own pack of dogs right in their living room. But, although the insight can be valuable, the owner may still feel sad. We've all watched other owners managing groups of dogs in their homes without problems. We may have relatives or neighbors with assorted groups of dogs that behave wonderfully in their homes. We've all seen handlers on television controlling multiple working dogs; and some of us have met these people in real life. Examples range from show handlers, to hunters, to shepherds- and of course individuals who handle a dozen sled dogs at a time. In each of these cases, the pack of dogs works together seamlessly, while stills showing tremendous love and allegiance to their owner.

The answer is proactive thinking. Dogs naturally wish to follow a pack leader and to act together as a team to produce positive results. In order to bring out the best in multiple dogs, an owner should constantly provide clear leadership and provide all the dogs with a clear idea of what they *should* be doing at all times. Of course, many other factors come into play, and the choice of dogs you bring together will always influence results. Some dogs cannot live together in peace without the intervention of a professional, and some dogs are so dog-aggressive that bringing them together could be dangerous.

Assuming you make the proper selection to start with, how well the dogs behave depends on how well you teach them to look to you for leadership. And the more they look at you the less they will attempt to squabble with each other.

You can make up wonderful games for your pack of dogs to engage in- or else you can let them make up their own games. Unfortunately, the games they initiate if they're bored may include running wild through your home- or worse. It's preferable to interact with your dogs and show them the games you want them to play.

In this chapter we describe several exercises (like Sit On a Bench, The Long, Long Stay, and What's My Name?) that help teach your multiple dogs self control. These exercises, while fun to practice, also teach the dogs to take their cue to act from you, rather than from each other and this habit will then tend to carry over into everyday life.

Other selections (like "Simon Says", "Limbo" and "Under/Over") teach control as well, but they're also great party games. These are ways to participate in the fun with your dogs and to get your children involved as well. Or read the sections on Obedience and Agility at Home to add even more exercise to your dogs' daily agenda, while still having fun and keeping things controlled. Also use the Ideas from Other Chapters for Multiple Dogs. This will give you hundreds of choices for planned activities with your group of dogs. Once you begin practicing together as a team you may be happily surprised. Instead of creating a feeling of chaos, your group of dogs will now make life more exciting. After all, it is in the nature of dogs to work wonderfully as a team. It's just up to the owner to channel that ability!

Multi-Dog Games & Activities:

Duck, Duck, Goose
- teaches your dogs to stay with distractions -

This is a game that will keep your dogs thinking and working hard the entire time they play it. To win at the game, the dogs in the family will have to learn to control their bodies, keep hyperactivity in check and only move when you indicate it's their turn to follow you.

First teach your dogs to stay. Then put all your dogs in a "long down" or "sit/stay" and walk around the room or the yard where you are playing. Walk past each of the dogs, then touch (or tag) one dog of your choice. This dog should immediately break the stay and follow you, heeling at your side as the other dogs remain in position. Move around the room or yard with the dog you touched. Reward the dog with a treat, then put him back in a stay and start the game over, choosing a different dog for the next round.

This is a good advanced game to practice your dogs' "stay" command and to build their self control. If your dogs can play this challenging game effectively, it would take a lot to make them break a "stay" in a normal situation. And think of the pride you'll feel when you know the sound of your voice alone can make your dog wait and just the touch of your finger is enough to make him follow you.

Simon Says
- teaches your dogs to do anything you say by using their drive to get your attention

If you have a multiple dog family you probably know how jealous dogs can be about who is getting your attention at the moment. You also probably know that controlling many dogs when you are home alone can be a Herculean feat, especially if one is a troublemaker. When one dog constantly pushes for attention, it makes controlling the pack that much harder. And many multi-dog families seem to have one or more dogs that tend to be a little hardheaded, refusing to work when you want them to and preferring to control interactions themselves.

Rather than getting mad, why not start playing a new game that gives you control of such dogs? In "Simon says" you use your dogs' drive to seek your attention to your advantage. You may have noticed how each dog always wants to be the one that gets the treat or love from the owner. When you play "Simon says" you first give all your dogs a command. Then you give immediate praise, petting and a food reward to the dog that performs the command the quickest. Give the other dogs more or less attention depending on how quickly they do the command, but withhold treats. Now give another command and again give a food reward only to the dog that performs that command the quickest. Alternate many different commands to make the game more challenging.

If one dog is much slower at the command than the others and appears reluctant, just give a slight nod of your head or a smile when he finally does it, but offer no real praise. If he doesn't attempt to do the command at all, withhold attention entirely, and he will likely try harder on the next round. But make sure all the dogs know all their commands well before starting "Simon says". It wouldn't be fair if one dog was competing and always losing just because he needed review sessions. The challenge of this game should be performing the command the fastest, not learning the commands!

After playing this problem-solving multi-dog game a few times you'll start to see all your dogs obeying their commands more quickly and concentrating on you more. And this can lead to greater control and confidence on your part. Soon you can expect dogs that refused to do commands trying to be the quickest because they want the treat and petting. After playing "Simon says" a few times, it's not unusual for an irritating attention-craving dog to quickly transform from class goof-off to class-pet, just to get your attention first!

What's My Name?
- a good way to work on a dog that won't come when he's around other dogs -

You can do this alone or with multiple people and any number of dogs. First, be sure that each dog is trained to know its name, as well as the "come" and "stay" commands. Then put each dog in a long stay, or have a person hold each dog. Next, call out one of the dogs' names, along with the command "come". Only that dog should come to you. Interrupt any other dogs that try to get up with your palm up in the air and a sound like "Uh-uh". Reward the dog that you called lavishly when he gets to you at the same time as you gently take hold of his collar.

Now, put that dog in a "stay". Walk around the room and select another name to call- or have your helper call another dog. Only the dog that was called should come running to you, and all the rest should remain staying. This game is good because it teaches your dogs restraint and how to pay attention and it increases their mental concentration. Practiced slowly and carefully, it's a good obedience exercise. If you want to make it more complex, add in different commands, such as "sit" or "down" or "heel" rather than just "come". Direct each command to only one dog at a time by first saying the dog's name, and only reward a dog that gets its name and command right.

Now, if you wish, you can speed up the process. The humans may start to laugh and both humans and dogs will get a good mental and physical workout if you play this game very precisely and very fast with a large group of dogs. At highly advanced levels, you can bring this game to any level of complexity or rapidness; you can alternate hand signals with verbal commands and you can call out commands from other rooms or off-leash in a fenced outdoor area with increasing distances. You can also use any number of people or dogs.

Playing this game sharpens communication between pack members, and your dogs learn to work with you just as they would orchestrate their actions with a canine pack leader during hunting. Practicing this "game" will also help later on if all your dogs try to push forward at once and you need restrain them to perform a task one at a time. (for, example, waiting patiently at feeding time.)

For an ultra easy and fun variation, line the dogs up in a line at as far distance as your yard allows and then you and helper will call them back and forth between you by name. This variation is great for exercise, indoors or out. The amount of physical workout depends on speed, distance and length of time played.

The Long, Long Stay
- Can your dog stay the longest? This competition is based on self-control -

When your dogs lie down next to each other for long periods, this can also help reduce dominance flare-ups.

This is an advanced game of mental concentration and your dogs should know their long stay command well before starting.

The game is simple- a competition of who can keep their stay the longest. Put all the dogs in a long stay and watch for who breaks first. That dog is then eliminated, and so forth with each dog that breaks. Once eliminated, if your other dogs can stay relatively calm, they can watch the game and/or serve as distractions for the dogs remaining in a stay.

The dog that keeps the stay the longest, breaking it only when released by you, will get a lavish reward, including lots of love, a large, tasty treat or maybe even a small rawhide or toy that will be his. (Only offer such big treats, however, if the longest stay will last very long (over ten minutes) and you're playing "one round". And supervise carefully making sure your dogs won't fight over this rawhide or toy. Otherwise, stick to treats that are more easily consumed.) Another option for rewarding the winner after a competition is a special walk or outing just for him.

Play one very long round (ten minutes and up) for dogs that are highly advanced and know their "stay" command well. (Some dogs can keep "stays" for an hour!) For less advanced dogs, you can play this game not so much as a competition, but as a way to practice the "stay" command. In this case, play many short rounds in succession, rewarding the dog that stays longest each time with a small treat. Try to play long enough that each of your dogs can win a round. You should also practice "The Long, Long Stay" with puppies under six months but, since they have naturally shorter attention spans they cannot be expected to stay for long periods of time.

For dogs that are advanced, introduce distractions- jump around and act silly, walk your other dogs around or enlist human helpers to make staying tougher.

Also note that the Long, Long Stay is more than just a game. Along with a full program of remediation tailored to the individual case, the Long Stay exercise, practiced frequently can help mellow some dogs that act defiant to owners or unfriendly or domineering to other dogs in the household.

Obedience Competition at Home
- **get ready for the dog show at home; or avoid the stress & cost and have the show at home –**

Any pet owner serious about obedience understands that you should frequently practice your obedience commands with each of your dogs at home and, as each dog becomes more proficient alone, you should practice with the dogs together. Obedience sessions are great to burn off mental and physical energy indoors and the more dogs involved at a time, the greater the challenge for each dog to concentrate.

But if you want to really take obedience to the next level, consider a competition at home. Start with dogs that are already highly proficient and plan your competitions when you have a decent chunk of free time (at least a half hour to as much as a whole afternoon.) You can use the activity to practice for "real" obedience competitions at dog shows or as practice for your young "junior handlers". But, even if you never intend to compete at dog shows, you can duplicate the same demanding level of obedience competition at home.

First, study up on the rules and techniques of competition obedience, ranging from beginner to advanced. And next train your dogs so that you have several that are qualified to compete. If you don't have enough dogs in your home, you can also enlist family members', friends' or neighbors' dogs for the competition. To make it even more of a challenge, select a qualified impartial "judge" who won't be competing this time around. Or you can ask different participants to judge different events. Then proceed as you would in a real obedience competition at a dog show.

Videotape the event if you like, and award a plaque or prize to the human winner and an appropriate prize to their winning dog. But every dog should be a winner just for competing, so provide treats for all at the end of the event.

Hosting obedience competitions at home can be fun & educational for a dog-loving family. You can host frequent mini-events for your immediate family and the dogs in your "pack" and bigger competitions at events like family reunions or neighborhood parties.

Agility Competition at Home
- make home agility more challenging & fun and see how your dogs focus with a crowd around -

If you've followed our advice and used a backyard agility course for your dogs, you're probably already overjoyed with this great form of exercise. And you're probably already using your agility course for your multiple dogs. So why not go to the next level and have your dogs compete?

Different family members can coach each dog, and you may also wish to invite friends over with their friendly and well-behaved dogs. You can plan a formal agility competition as a neighborhood party and you can host the competitions as often as you like. Family members, including youthful "junior handlers" can become very committed and really enjoy the excitement during the competition.

Proceed as above for "Obedience Competition at Home". But please note that in a home competition dogs are not evenly matched in body type, nor are they equally suited for agility! Adjust the obstacles as much as possible to suit the different dogs' body types. But also make sure that, regardless of whether each dog wins a timed event, there should be enough praise and reward to keep everybody motivated. (Also see sections on agility and agility equipment in Chapter 10, Activities for High Energy Dogs, Chapter 5, Indoor Games & Activities and Resources.)

Home Agility One By One
- increase fun & challenge by working with more than one dog -

Even if you don't want to conduct a formal competition, you can practice on your home agility course with several dogs at a time by having them complete the course one following the other. One owner can operate as many as four different dogs, each running through different stations in the agility course, all at the same time. This is challenging and exhilarating for all. But it requires exact timing! Two dogs trying to squeeze through one obstacle at once might get hurt, so build up to several dogs working the course with many small, careful sessions. And make sure you have perfect control before attempting this at full speed without a helper.

Dancing Dogs
- it's like *Dancing with the Stars* except it's with dogs. Sublime!

This idea of dancing with your dogs (also known as Freestyle) is not only great exercise for dogs, but it looks amazing! And choreographed dancing with your dogs feels exhilarating for the soul. (See the "Dancing Dog/Freestyle" in Chapter 5, Indoor Games, for a more detailed description.) You can teach all the dogs in your household to dance if they seem interested. And you can dance with them for exercise, for fun, for bonding and for teaching respect and obedience. You can even go on to competition with your multiple dogs (see Resources.)

Just make sure that you only practice this activity with dogs that enjoy it; and never force dancing on a dog. Also, you may notice that different dogs in your household have different learning- and dancing- abilities. One dog (maybe even the one you least expect) may take to Freestyle like Fred Astaire. Another dog may be eager to dance, but he may not have that same grace or control over his body and may get frustrated if he frequently makes mistakes.

Since you are the choreographer, you can easily adjust the routines to draw on each dog's strengths. For example, you could teach several of your less coordinated dogs to simply move around, highlighting the steps of your star performer. The good thing is that dogs are not ego-driven like humans, so none of the dogs will be resentful that one of the pack gets star billing. They will each be excited and proud to be doing their jobs, and Freestyle dancing is tremendous fun for everyone. If you have multiple dogs that excel at dancing, it is a great opportunity to get the family involved as well. Your kids can teach their dogs basic obedience and then start teaching "dance" moves. Then the whole family can cooperate to choreograph an amazing routine.

Freestyle dancing with a group of dogs takes lots of practice and it's great for exercise and building focus as well as a healthy way for dogs and humans to have fun together. If the routine that your family works on is really professional, you can show off for extended family, or perform at a neighborhood gathering or fundraiser. Some families may even want to videotape their accomplishments and/or enter contests.

Sit on a Bench
- even relaxing can teach your dogs impulse control -

This is just another quick way to achieve some calm and control for multiple dogs. Having your dogs stay in a "sit/stay" or a "long-down" next to each other is great for lessening aggression and promoting harmony in your pack. And sitting up on bench together and holding the pose for any length of time can enhance that effect.

Use a small garden bench outdoors, or use any appropriate bench or table inside. The easy way to train is to first teach each dog individually to jump on the bench and then sit pretty, remaining in a stay. Reward the dog for its satisfactory performance and then teach the next dog the same. When you are confident each dog can hold a stay on the bench, try two dogs at a time, then three and then more if you wish. You will be astonished as all your pack sits pretty in a row, just perfect for taking a picture. Practice this "trick" often and remember it isn't magic; it's just basic obedience!

Limbo
-how low can your dogs go? Up-tempo party game can include the dogs-

Humans love playing the popular party game known as "Limbo", where a line of party guests dance to Caribbean party music while passing underneath a limbo stick that's lowered at each round. The winner of the game is the person who can pass under the stick at the lowest setting without touching the stick or the floor. The lighthearted game of Limbo seems to make everyone laugh and easily lowers inhibitions while engaging the competitive spirit.

So now your "party animal" canines can also enjoy the game. You can use a broomstick for a Limbo stick, and you'll need one helper as well as two or more dogs. You can also play with only one dog. And humans can play also. Dogs aren't as music-driven as we humans are. But some pleasant, perky music can serve to set the mood for everybody.

A game of Limbo can be a reward for a day of good behavior and obedience and it's good mental and aerobic exercise on days when the weather's not great. Dogs can be easily trained to pass under or over the limbo stick using treats to lure them. Practice the first few sessions using treats, and then reduce the use of treats to only intermittently. Eventually your dogs will want to jump or crawl just for the sheer fun of the game.

Limbo's also a fun way to get your high-energy dogs and your kids playing together in a contained and organized fashion. Let your kids set up and teach the game. But first make sure that no dog they work with is aggressive or fearful. The dogs should know basic obedience and be respectful of your children's commands before the children attempt to teach a potentially confusing or frustrating series of activities like those involved in "Limbo". **You should also check with your veterinarian if you suspect that any of your dogs might have physical problems that would prevent them from jumping or crawling.**

Crawling under the Limbo stick as it's lowered closer and closer to the floor calls for extraordinary self-control and this is why successful practice helps skittish dogs build confidence and overcome fears. But only play Limbo if your dogs seem to enjoy the game. Forcing a dog to participate in any game when he's in full-blown panic will obviously defeat the therapeutic benefits of the game.

If your dogs are approximately the same size, shape and fitness level, they may appreciate direct competition with each other when they play Limbo. In this case, you'll only reward the dog that makes it under when the stick is lowest. But you don't have to make Limbo a competition. If your dogs are widely different sizes, ages or fitness levels you can just reward each dog for his own best efforts, and simply let the dogs take turns with each other. Unlike people, dogs will enjoy doing the activity together and likely won't get too stressed about competition.

Under/Over
- an exhilarating "mini agility practice" indoors, without the equipment or space -

Imagine this easy jumping game in various different incarnations. It's a great indoor game, to be played with one or more dogs. It's relatively simple, yet requires the dog(s) to use mental discernment, bodily coordination and split-second obedience to their owner's commands. Play it with one dog and it's like a mini agility practice without the need for obstacles or a great deal of space. Add more dogs, and speed up the pace enough and it becomes a zany and fun party game, while still acting as a serious obedience challenge. And, even with more than one dog, if you play carefully, you can still enjoy the game in the center of your living room.

The only equipment needed for "Under/over" is a long stick (for example, a broomstick, curtain rod or bamboo pole) plus two willing people to hold it up for your dogs to jump over or crawl under. (Or, if you're alone, just find a safe place to wedge one end of the pole.) The only other prerequisite to playing under/over with a group of dogs is that you first train each dog to respond to his name, and his name only. Don't worry if the dogs aren't yet perfect on this, though. Playing will give them practice and it's one of the reasons playing this particular game is so helpful in increasing owners' control of a pack.

Make sure you have some basic control of all the dogs before playing this game in a group. If your group of dogs bounces off walls uncontrollably, you will probably want to practice "Under/over" (this chapter) with each animal individually first, and then bring them together as a group only after each individual can accomplish the task calmly.

Once you are at this point, assemble your calm dogs together in the room where they will play. Before starting, give a cue like, "Hey, guys, let's play under/over!" Call the first dog to you as you hold the pole close to the ground and lure him over with a treat as you command "over". Once he steps over, praise lavishly and let him eat the treat.

The first few times you practice you'll probably want an assistant to hold the other dogs back until you call each individually. Send the first dog back to the assistant, then call the next. Command "over" while luring, then praise and offer the treat after the dog steps over. Repeat with each of the dogs.

Next, you will start the process again, only you will raise the pole a little higher, so that each dog will need to jump a bit this time. **Use caution. There's no need to raise the pole too high. Dogs with medical conditions and some breeds with short backs, long legs or**

large breed puppies should not be jumping at all. For them it is possible to still participate in the game along with their buddies in the pack, but only raise the pole a few inches off the ground for them, so they do no more than step over.

If practicing with healthy longer-legged dogs, use common sense when setting the height of the pole. This game is more about discernment and control than it is about athleticism, so there's no need to raise the pole higher than each dog's shoulders. You should also use care when asking dogs to go "under" the bar. Make sure the dog's height allows it to crawl, otherwise simply let the dog walk underneath the bar when commanded. If you're ever not sure what's healthy for your dog, consult with your veterinarian.

It may take several sessions for all your dogs to master the "over" command with the raised bar. Once they have, no longer use treats to lure them. Just give the command, "over" and then offer praise and reward after the dog jumps. Next, start rewarding with treats only intermittently, offering treats only to mark the quickest and best performances. Eventually the fun of playing the game, along with your fervent praise, will become its own reward and you should only offer treats at the completion of a successful game.

Once all the dogs have mastered the "over" command, you can now play the game in an advanced, but simplified, version by having your assistant set the dogs free. The object is for each dog to quickly come to you and jump over the pole when you call his name. Meanwhile, the other dogs should wait patiently. The game will progress smoother and quicker the more the dogs focus and cooperate. It will feel exciting and fun and the dogs will enjoy your smile and lavish praise as you all become more accomplished. You can hand out occasional treats for exceptional jumps. And, at the end of the game, you will cuddle, praise and reward all the dogs.

Once your dogs have mastered playing in a group with the "over" command, go back to the beginning and teach the "under" command to the dogs individually, luring with the treat again if necessary. For the next few sessions play the game only as an "under" game, until the dogs get great at it. Using your imagination, you can probably see that teaching a group of dogs to play this game perfectly can take a long time. And this challenge is part of the beauty of the game. (For example, just imagine your preteens teaching this game to your high-energy dogs during summer break…)

Once the dogs are perfect alternating with each other at your command to do both "overs" and "unders", it's time to go back again and teach each dog individually how to alternate "unders" and "overs" at your command. Some dogs' brains might "lock up" a little on this, or they might seem to acquire "four left feet". So be patient. Remember that this is only a game, and it's one meant to build coordination and mentally acuity, so expect it to be somewhat of a challenge for your dogs at first.

Once each dog has accomplished both commands on his own, alternating with no predictable pattern other than what you ask him, it's now time to bring all the dogs in and try to trick them about which dog you're going to call when, and what you will ask them to do. **You will be calling the dog's names indiscriminately, followed by either "under" or**

"over". For example, "Sammy, over!", Saki, under!", "Anna, under", "Saki, over!", "Good dogs!" Expect a lot of stumbles, a lot of false starts, a lot of panting, a lot of wagging and a lot of giggles from the humans.

If your dogs stand at different heights, you and your assistant(s) will be constantly adjusting the height of the pole, so keep yourselves sharp as the pace of the game increases. At first, things may get a little hectic and the dogs may swing wide as they circle for their next jump or crawl. So, at this stage of the game, you can practice on the lawn, if necessary.

But we believe a true connoisseur and their well-trained pack of dogs, plus a willing assistant, will want to hone their skill to the point of such fine control that they can play "Under/Over" at top speed in the living room with four, five or even six dogs. Imagine playing the game during a winter blizzard or under air-conditioning when the temperature is over a hundred. And then imagine the alternative- the same pack of dogs running around freely in the home without structured activity, and yourself with

Bonnie & Clyde-"No longer outlaws"

no way to control the dogs- and no way to get out! Yes, "Under/Over" played with a large pack of dogs may be highly challenging but certainly more fun than the alternative!

Ch. 8-Problem Dog Games

"Specific positive activities can help emotional and behavioral problems."

Introduction

Catch

Ring of Fire

Go to Your Place

Take a Bow

Up and Down

Stop Barking on Command

Kisses

In the Army Crawl

When I Move, You Move

Drop It

Jump Over

Interactive Toys

Wacky Walking

Also Try These Ideas From Other Chapters for Problem Dogs:

Puppy Games & Activities: Follow the Leader, Tunnel Crawl, How Do I Get What's In There?, Let's Play Doctor, Shopping Spree, New Learning Every Day, Walk This Way, Obedience-minded, Soft Mouth

Mental Games & Activities: Watch Me, Wait, Hold That Position, Listen, Move Slow

Indoor Games & Activities: Agility Inside, Get That Pose, A Room of His Own, Doggie Gymnasium

Balance & Coordination Activities: Walk the Line, Stack, Double Hoops, Different Surfaces

Multi-Dog Games & Activities: Duck, Duck, Goose, Simon Says, Sit On a Bench, What's My Name?, Long, Long Stay, Obedience Compaction at Home, Home Agility One by One, Under/Over

Therapeutic and Senior Dog Activities: Massage, Meditation, Swim, Party in the Storm, Talking Toys, Kong Time, A Change Of Scene

Activities for High-Energy Dogs: Doggie Treadmill, Backpacking, Snow Games, Retrieve in Water, Weave Poles, Water Run, Track & Field, Sand Run, Flyball, Tracking, Ocean Swim, Run in Snow, Hunting Trials

Water Activities: Continuous pool, Dog's Own Pool, Water Fetch, Water Walk

Useful Activities: Dog Pull, Pack Animal, Sled Dog, Check the Perimeter,

Family Activities: Circle of Love, Diversity Training, Playground Built with Dog Games, Different Handlers, Assess a Dog,

Activities for Owners with Limited Mobility: Long Lead, Ball Launcher, Dog Walker, Playdate (only with professional guidance), Try on a Dog, Be Creative

Problem Dog Games- Introduction
"Specific positive activities can help emotional and behavioral problems."

Do you own a "problem dog"? In our line of work we often hear people complain that their problem dog is driving them crazy with his bad behavior. They tearfully tell us, "This dog has to change or he's going to the pound tomorrow!" Often the dog's problem behavior creates a vicious cycle. The owner has so much trouble simply struggling to control the behavior that they cannot think of interacting with their dog in other positive ways. In other words, they simply do not know what to do with their dog and opportunities for positive interaction slip away. These dogs do not get exercise, play or learning opportunities with their owner and this feeds into the vicious cycle, making the dog act even more wild and hard to control.

The problem with the dog in question may simply be that he lacks focus or is bored out of his mind and is making up games of his own just to keep occupied and avoid a case of Useless Dog Syndrome. Sometimes the fix to a problem that has plagued owners for years is as simple as trying something new. After introducing some of the activities in this chapter, owners may find that the crazy dog they needed help with ends up being the best dog they ever owned.

Does your problem dog lack the ability to focus- even for a second? Is he a problem barker? Does he have much too much energy? Does he always jump on people? Or is your dog the dreaded dog that takes you for walks rather then the other way around? Activities in this chapter can help all the suffering owners out there with dogs with these problems and many more, and help you and your dog become a happier team in life.

Some activities in this chapter specifically benefit those dogs that can't focus. Try games like "Catch" or "In the Army Crawl" so that the dog has to start looking towards you to see what you want from him. If your dog has too much energy for you to deal with, try "Interactive Toys", "Up and Down" and other activities that help him use his mind, both from this chapter and from the list of games from other chapters. For dogs that jump too much, try teaching "Take a Bow", "Ring of Fire" or "Go to Your Place". And for the dog everyone in town calls puller, try "When I Move, You Move" and "Wacky Walking" so he learns a new way to interact with you, with you taking the lead.

Many common behavioral problems can be solved right from this book. But if adding some games to your dog's day doesn't immediately help and you suspect your dog's behavior problems may be more serious, you should have your veterinarian examine your dog. Some of the more serious behavior problems can actually be symptoms of serious physical illness. So it's possible your dog is acting out because he feels bad physically and is asking for help.

Other serious emotional disorders (including severe clinical separation anxiety) may not be physically caused, but they may also require the help of an expert behaviorist with scientific background. With the exception of serious cases like this, most behavior problems start out small, so families can usually make a difference if they present their "problem" dog with positive alternatives to the undesired behaviors as soon as possible.

> *Let's start making every problem dog in this country an Awesome Dog*

Trying some of the activities in this chapter (and activities from other chapters that are cross-referenced as great problem-solving games) may make an immediate difference in quality of life. As you watch your dog's behavior improving daily, you may want to look around at other dogs on your street and think about what activities might help their owners. And maybe even give your neighbors a copy of this book with these games which can help teach leadership, so that our dogs can learn by fun rather than by fear or punishment!

Problem Dog Games:

<u>*Catch*</u>
- keeps your dog on his toes doing something he loves, so he'll ignore distractions

This is an easy game that teaches a dog that is easily distracted by everything to look at you whenever you want him to. It can help make a dog calm down and pay attention to you. And, if your dog is more motivated by toys or balls, you can use these items rather then treats when you play the game of "Catch".

To teach this game, you'll first teach your dog to watch you. You can do this by putting a treat in front of your dog's nose and slowly bringing it to your face. The second your dog looks into your face, say "Good watch" or "Good look", and give him the treat. When your dog gets good at this, start saying, "Watch," or "Look", from a distance.

Now, when your dog looks at you, quickly toss him a large easily visible treat (or a small favorite toy) while saying, "Catch!" and allow him to catch the treat in his mouth and eat it (or catch the toy and play for a moment). After he's successfully caught toys and treats like this a few times, all you'll have to do is say the word "Catch" and your dog will look right at you because he'll be waiting for the fun to start.

Not only is this easy-to-teach game good for mental focus, it also improves reaction time and sharpens senses like dogs' close-range vision, which tends to be a natural weak point. And it teaches dogs some patience and self control and not to "jump-the-gun" by lunging for the treat before it's thrown by you. Regularly focusing your dog on playing the simple game of "Catch" can help calm hyperactive dogs. It's also great for interesting and stimulating bored, lackluster or depressed dogs, and it sharpens puppies' reflexes, judgment and intelligence as they grow, so dogs of every age and stage will thank you for it.

Ring of Fire
- just start with a hula hoop- easy, cheap & fun for almost every dog and owner -

This game helps stop dogs from jumping up on people by teaching them an alternative behavior. First find an old hula hoop. (You can also buy them new at discount department stores, and we've found small hoops, perfect for smaller dogs, at some Dollar Tree locations.) Keep one end of the hoop on the ground and lure the dog to go through the hoop using a treat or calling him, while saying "Jump". As the dog learns to go through the hoop without fear, bring the hoop higher and higher until you're holding it at the height that you want the dog to jump. (If you suspect that your dog has any physical problems with jumping, you can either keep the hoop extremely low or ask your veterinarian what height he or she recommends.)

"Ring of Fire" is, of course, a good trick to show off at parties, and your kids will enjoy it. But the best part is that now your dog will know when you want him to jump, so he won't be as likely to jump at every random moment. This game is great for high-energy small dogs like Jack Russell Terriers, and all the other dogs that love to jump up at you. And, if you're wondering, this is also how they teach the tigers to jump through the "rings of fire" at the circus!

Go to Your Place
-essential & easy command that teaches dogs to go where you want them; not underfoot-

In this game you teach your dog to go to any set place in your home, so he won't interfere with the activities of family and guests. You can choose any place where you think your dog will be comfortable, but not be underfoot. For example, your dog might like a certain corner of the room near the fireplace or the back door. Or you can teach him that his designated "place" is a particular red rug, and this way you can move the rug to any place you need to. Your dog will have a comfortable place to lie down and stay for a while, and you can avoid some household chaos.

Start teaching your dog to, "Go to your place" by pointing at the "place" you desire and giving him a treat as soon as he walks to and stands on the spot. You might have to start with the dog on a leash so you can show him exactly where you want him to go, or you can throw treats onto the spot (for example a rug or dog bed) to lure him. Once he gets the idea that you want him to go to the particular place, you now teach your dog to go to the place you indicate from farther and farther distances. Next you'll start phasing out treats, only offering food treats for the best performances- when he goes to the place the quickest or remains there calmly the longest.

At first you should teach only one spot, so you don't confuse your dog. But you will be surprised that your dog will soon be able to learn spots with different names. (For example, "Go to your bed," "Go to your red rug".) A lot of people make good use of this command for when their dogs try to jump up on guests or bark at the windows. But don't ever use it as a punishment. Keep the command fun for your dog and let him think of his "place" simply as a place he can relax and get his thoughts together, near but not right on top of the chaos of overstimulating family activities. You may find that your dog actually learns to *like* to go to his place, and he may often do it on his own at all the right moments!

Take a Bow
- a polite alternative to jumping on guests -

> *While jumping on guests is one of the behaviors that bothers owners most, dogs usually respond well when you teach them alternatives.*

This is a game that's fun to use when you want to show off at a party with friends. It also helps with a dog whose problem is jumping on people that first come into your home. Instead of jumping up on people when he first meets them, you can teach your dog to "Take a Bow." And this will make your guests smile and laugh, rather than run for the hills. When you dog "takes a bow", it looks like the dog is getting ready to lie down, but he only puts the front part of his body on the floor. This makes it look just like when a prince or princess bows out of respect to someone. So rather than your dog looking like a ruffian, he will more resemble royalty!

The trick to teaching your dog to do this trick is to first get your dog doing "downs". And the best way to teach him to lie down on the floor is either by luring him into position with a treat or waiting to "capture" the behavior, and then offering a treat.

Next, you may or may not need a helper depending upon how well your dog works with your touch. As you tell your dog to lie down or use a treat to get your dog to go down, either you or your helper will gently hold up your dog's belly so he can't go down all the way. (Obviously, you should only do this with healthy dogs and you should not press too hard!) The moment the dog's front legs bend as if doing a down, eagerly say, "Take a Bow!" and reward him with a treat. (You can also use a towel to keep your dog's back end up if you are by yourself, but follow the same safety precautions.)

Each time you practice, try to get your dog to wait in the "Bow" position longer and start releasing the dog with a word like "Okay." The next step is to get a visitor the dog usually acts calm with to walk in your front door and then ask your dog to "Take a bow." The friend should be instructed to only greet your dog when he is in the "Bow" position. Once your dog is consistently "Bowing" for this visitor, you can work on the cue with other people that he usually finds it harder to control himself with. After a surprisingly short amount of time, your dog should act like royalty whenever you ask him to "Take a Bow".

Up and Down
- this basic exercise is a favorite to help highly distractible dogs pay attention -

This game helps people with dogs that just don't want to pay attention to them. First you'll want to teach your dog to reliably do a "sit" and a "down" at your voice commands. Next, to teach him "Up and Down" (also commonly referred as "Doggie Pushups") start moving your hand up when you ask him to sit, and moving your hand down when you ask him to lie down. After each cue that the dog follows correctly, immediately reward him with a treat and praise. Practice bringing your dog from "down" back up to "sit" and from "sit" to "down" until he's completely reliably. Next, teach him to change positions based on the movement of your hand. Start offering food rewards only after your dog moves from a "down" to a "sit", and then back to a "down" again just following the move of your hand.

Your dog will like this exercise because he's getting treats and seeing you smile. And what owners like most about practicing "Up and Down" is that this simple exercise is sometimes the first thing to easily break through with a highly distractible dog and get him to willingly and happily do something that you want. Perhaps for the first time, you'll see your dog really look at you and focus on you. And then you can take it from there, expanding to other desired activities.

Stop Barking on Command
- more than a party game. This prevents problem barking-

Barking is one behavior many owners find particularly tricky to deal with, but **teaching a problem barker to quite down can be much easier than most people believe it is. All you have to do is teach the dog what you want in a manner he understands. But first you may have to get rid of some common misconceptions.**

People often yell at their barking dogs, but this is one of the worst things to do. If you read "I Bark, You Bark, We All Bark" in Chapter 2, "Games 'Useless' Dogs Play on Their

Owners", you'll see why yelling at your barking dog can backfire. Your dog may think you're joining in and supporting him and it will only increase his barking!

Sometimes owners become so frustrated with their dog's barking that they hit him or throw things at him. This is like attacking a family just because they alerted you that they saw an intruder outside! Unfair physical punishment like this creates an unstable dog- one that's more likely to become agitated, aggressive and even *more* likely to bark!

The first thing to understand is that your dog is not necessarily bad because he barks. In wild conditions, it's normal for canines to vocalize as one way to communicate what's going on in their environment. It's an interesting scientific fact that, amongst canines, different pitches and sequences of barks mean completely different things. For example, when a dog happily welcomes a comrade home it sounds recognizably different from a dog warning the pack of serious danger. Barks associated with states like anger, fear, physical distress and even boredom are standard enough in dogs to be easily interpreted just by sound. When we explain to our customers how different barks work with canine body language for communication, they usually start viewing barking from a more realistic perspective, because they learn what each bark means.

We doubt anyone would really want their dog to give up barking one- hundred percent. The dog would no longer function well as a watchdog and he'd be giving up an important aspect of communicating- his unique way of talking. The key is for your family to agree on when you want your dog to bark and when you don't- and then teach the dog these limits.

Unfortunately, some misinformed owners can get even more forceful in their desperate attempts to stop problem barking- to the point of cruelty. This includes using electric collars, also known as "e" collars or shock collars. It's hard for us personally to imagine painfully shocking your dog that loves you unconditionally. It's possible the collar might stop the barking. But a bad experience with a shock collar might also cause lasting physical, emotional and personality damage to your puppy or dog, even to the point of making him fearful or aggressive. And we don't feel this is worth it when positive training methods work just as well!

We're also horrified when we hear of people paying veterinarians to surgically stop dogs from barking, and even individuals who've tried to stop barking by shoving pipes down their dogs' throats. People capable of senseless cruelty like this should never be allowed to own dogs!

Usually when a dog barks all day, it's because he's in distress. For example, he may be tethered outside without food, shade or water. If you hear a neighbor's dog barking like this, perhaps it's time for a call to the police or your local humane society because the dog is very unhappy. Even though *some* barking is natural for dogs, barking shrilly for ten hours in a row is not. If a family that leaves their dog untended like this for extended periods then silences his cries for help with a shock collar, it only compounds their wrongdoing!

Like us, our readers probably feel horrified at the cruel ways some owners try to stop barking. But what should you do if your dog is a problem barker?

Owners may be surprised that, **before you can teach your dog to stop barking, you'll first want to teach him to bark on cue.** One easy way to teach your dog is to wait until you can catch him doing it. As soon as he gives a bark, immediately say "Speak" or "Good speak!" and offer a treat. Repeat the process until your dog makes the connection that when you say "Speak" you want him to bark.

If your dog rarely barks except when he's barking excessively at some outside stimulus, you may have to get creative and act very silly to get him excited enough to bark for your cue. (Sometimes holding the dog back on a leash while a helper teases him by holding a favorite toy just out of reach will do the trick.) Once you get the first bark, say "Speak" or "Good Speak". Repeat the process until your dog makes the connection that you want him to bark on command each time you say the word.

Now that you've taught your dog to bark on command, you can teach him to stop barking on command. First command him to, "Speak," as described earlier. Next bring a finger to your lips, make the "Shhhh!" sound and wait for your dog to stop barking, no matter how long it takes. When he stops barking, wait 2 seconds, so your dog recognizes that not barking gets positive attention from you. Then reward him with praise and treats. After practicing a few times you'll notice that your dog stops barking quicker each time you ask.

Rather than using the "Shhh" command and gesture to silence their dogs, some people prefer to use the alternative commands, "Enough" or "Quiet" while crossing their arms in front of their chest like an umpire indicating a baseball player is safe. You can always try both the "Shhh" and the "Enough" or "Quiet" versions of the command and see which one your dog responds to best. Now your dog, literally, has learned to stop barking on command! Using these commands and gestures is usually enough to teach your dog to stop barking.

For some dogs with a more defensive temperament, you might consider respecting their heritage and desire to protect you. And there's always a chance your dog may be alerting you to a real problem. Next time your dog suddenly runs to the window barking as though someone's outside, we recommend that you get up and check to show that you're responding to his alarm bark. This is not about giving in to a dog's problem barking. If nothing is amiss, give your dog respect by thanking him out loud for alerting you. But then follow with either the "Shhh!" or the "Enough" or "Quiet" command and gesture. With this combination of respect and control most dogs easily stop barking when you want them to.

There are a few other alternatives to stop dogs from barking. For example, most dogs are unwilling to bark annoyingly from a lying down position, so give your dog the "down" command whenever you think there might be a problem.

Another good method to stop your dog's barking is to mimic the same gentle admonishment a mother dog uses if she needs her pup silent for the family's safety. When your dog starts barking, simply lay one hand on the top of his snout and say, "Quiet," in a quiet voice filled with conviction. Then praise him the second he stops barking. The object of teaching a dog to be quiet in this particular manner is to mimic the intervention a mother dog uses with puppies. ***Never* grab your dog's snout and squeeze. This practice is cruel and** squeezing the dog's muzzle painfully will *not* make your dog stop barking; it will just make him not want you to touch his face. And hand-shy dogs can bite!

A better idea if you have a dog that goes right back to barking at the window is to **distract him and teach him to focus back on you rather than barking. Do this in a positive fashion by simply calling him away from the distracting item seen in the window and offering him a treat or toy that you know he likes.** Praise him lavishly and reward him for each success he performs. Eventually you will have largely weaned your dog off the food treats, and your dog will still comply with your commands for him to stop barking.

Also start to get your dog out into the world for more new experiences because many barking problems come from a lack of confidence or boredom. So the next time your dog barks, maybe he's just saying that you both need to get out for a nice long walk in the beautiful world outside your door!

Kisses
- teaches dogs and pups to kiss hands, rather than nibble on them -

"Kisses" is a game that helps dog owners who are having difficulties with a "nipper" or a "mouther". Your dog will learn to be gentle with human flesh and kisses feel a lot better than nips. To teach the command, call your dog to you and have some honey or peanut butter spread on the back of your hand (as long as your dog has no allergies). As your dog starts licking your hand say, "Give kisses," and praise. Practice a few times. Next, call your dog to you and just say "Give kisses." As your dog starts licking your hand on cue, immediately offer a treat and lots of praise. Now practice frequently, gradually phasing out treats, so the dog receives a treat only occasionally. After this point, if your dog ever looks like he's about to nip, instead command him, "Give kisses". (**Please note for safety that "Kisses" is only meant to help dogs and puppies with minor nipping problems relating to play or overexcitement . This game is not intended for dogs that cause injury, break skin or show any signs of aggression or unfriendliness towards people, especially children. Dogs that show these signs could be dangerous, and may require assessment and treatment by a professional.**)

In the Army Crawl
-an adorable & easy command that also helps your dog calm down -

This game is helpful for a dog that tends to be very rough with his body and has no idea there is any such thing as grace. We all know the dog that wants you to pay attention to him, so he runs into you like a load of bricks. Everyone runs when they see this dog coming, knowing they'll get bruised if they're lucky, or end up at the hospital if they're not. But a dog can't hurt you or do much damage when he's at a crawl, so this exercise is perfect for slowing down a dog like this!

There are many ways to teach your dog to crawl. One way is to first put your dog into a "down". Then hold a treat just out of his reach and ask him to "Crawl". If he moves even a few inches, let him have the treat and praise. Each time you try this with your dog, ask him to crawl farther for you.

Another way you can teach a dog to crawl is to have the dog on one side of you as you sit on the floor and encourage the dog to crawl under your legs to get the treat. Praise him as he does and say, "Good crawl". For a more advanced dog you can challenge your dog to crawl under a long coffee table.

You can even get to the point where both you and the dog can crawl under a net stretched a few inches off the ground like they do in the army and pretend that you both are commandos! This skill can also be used for your dog to win in games of "Limbo" (see Chapter 7) or just to make people laugh. If someone puts a stick up for your dog to jump, surprise them by giving a hand cue and your dog will crawl under instead. Be forewarned that a clever dog may try to play on your emotions with this trick, knowing just how cute he looks. When your dog gets down and crawls towards you, your heart will likely melt and you may want to give him anything!

When I Move, You Move
- teaches your dog to fine-tune his excitement, even when you play with him -

This is a good game for owners who have trouble controlling their dog when he gets excited. It also helps owners and dogs who work together at serious tasks or frequently practice obedience because they can break loose on occasion and experience some spontaneous joy together.

In this game, the owner goes from acting relaxed to suddenly busting loose and jumping, dancing or spinning while encouraging their dog to jump around with them. Then, when your dog is really worked up, you command, "Stop," and both of you come to a complete stop. Make the dog "sit" or do a "down" until everything is completely calm and controlled again. Now, give the cue that it's okay and both of you can start jumping around and having fun again. Stop and start this game frequently so that your dog learns how to quickly turn his excitement on and off. This gives him better control over his body and his state of mind and it also assures you that you can bring him back into control even when he is highly worked up.

Drop It
- essential command that can save your dog's life (and your sanity). Learn it now

The cue "Drop It" is a command we feel all owners must know. One day the command may save your dog's life by getting him to drop something poisonous, while sparing your fingers! Have you ever given your dog a bone and then he refused to give it back to you? This possessive behavior is dangerous, and an owner must be able to take anything out of their dog's mouth at any time. One day the item your dog refuses to drop may be something that could kill him- a chicken bone, a fishhook or a poisonous snake!

Don't listen to trainers who tell you to take items by force; this is not the best way to get something out of a dog's mouth. Some dogs may learn to fear you if you use force or intimidation to take things away from them. A dog like this dog may learn to run from you every time he has something he thinks you may want to take. He may not want to come to you at all and this will undermine the bond between you.

Some dogs may have existing problems with food or possession aggression. A dog like this needs careful rehabilitation so that he can learn to drop possessions at your command. But suddenly using force against a dog with this problem could be dangerous. And some owners are not aware of the danger of "redirected aggression". This means that, if you use excessive force or intimidation, your dog may no longer give you any problems when it comes to letting you take items out of his mouth, but he may suddenly turn on other dogs or other people- even children.

An owner may instinctively grab for an item to try to pull it away from their dog unless they know a better way. But the alternative is so much easier. Practice teaching your dog the command "Drop it" by giving him an item (perhaps a toy) that does not have an extremely high value to him. After he begins chewing on it, show him a particularly yummy treat or item that you know he likes more. As the dog drops the first item to get the more valuable item, tell him "Drop it". Offer the treat and lots of praise, and then give the first item back again. (This way the dog learns that by giving you what he already has, he can get something better and may even get the first item back.)

> *Teach the Drop It command before your dog needs it!*

When the dog gets more and more predictable with the command, "Drop it," you can move on to practice with items the dog holds in higher value. Practice frequently, and carry some treats with you on walks so that you can start practicing in real-life situations. But do not offer a treat every time. You want the payoff to be unpredictable. You will only offer a treat every so often and eventually your dog will no longer need treats to obey the "drop it" command.

Jump Over
- one of the easiest ways to get a flighty dog working well with his owner -

You can help a dog that has problems controlling his body in the house by teaching him how to jump over a stick on cue. Try the game with a light stick, a baton, a bamboo rod or any similar household object. Bend, kneel if you're physically capable, or sit on a low stool and hold the stick out straight with one hand quite close to the floor.

Lure your dog over it with a treat and simultaneously command, "Over", or "Jump". When your dog climbs over, reward and praise. Next raise the stick a bit higher and encourage your dog to jump in a more lively fashion. Soon he'll be jumping several times in a row and you will only offer a food reward at the end of each session.

You can raise the stick a bit higher now (as long as your dog has no physical limitations) and make the performance flow like ballet set to music as you hold the stick near your body and cue your dog to jump. You can also introduce a hand signal, rather than the verbal command if you wish the performance to appear more seamless.

"Jump over" can certainly be used as part of a "Freestyle" or "Dancing Dog" routine (see Chapter 5, Indoor Games & Activities). But it's also a way to enjoy time with your wild or hyperactive dog, exercising him while focusing and controlling his uncoordinated or inconsiderate body movements. A naturally high-energy dog that tends to get overexcited will also tend to enjoy games like "Jump Over" that properly channel his energy. But make sure that when you practice the game with your dog, he appears to be having fun, panting gently and wagging. Look out for symptoms like fast panting or trembling. These are symptoms that the dog is either exhausted or stressed, and this or any demanding game should be stopped immediately.

The "Jump Over" game can accommodate dogs with short legs, overweight dogs or dogs in less than perfect physical condition. You just have to hold the stick low and simply concentrate your dog on stepping over like a slow ballet move. (But make sure to always check with your veterinarian on what's safe for your particular dog.) Don't allow your dog to jump if any physical condition prohibits it, or if he appears to be in pain or seriously hesitant to jump. And don't practice this, or any jumping game, with large breed dogs until their bones and joints are fully mature. Even at that point, you do not want giant breeds doing high jumping.

Ideal heights for holding the stick for all breeds are relatively low, for example at the owner's knee height for medium and large breeds, and lower for smaller breeds, with the owner sitting, bending or kneeling. And always practice any jumps on a cushioned surface.

The average owner should probably avoid teaching their dog to jump higher since it might lead to improper stress on bones and joints, and possible physical injury or long-term damage. If your dog is a healthy athlete, however, and you intend to compete in events like Freestyle, you might train him to jump significantly higher jumps, but get your veterinarian's medical clearance first.

Note that "Jump Over" is an especially great indoor game. Your dog circles around you again and again, jumping over the same stick or even over your arm, and you and he use up no more than a tiny circle of floor space. Meanwhile the game exhausts your dog in a healthy fashion both mentally and physically and you may not even have to change out of your pajamas!

Interactive Toys
**- modern-day essentials in the war against boredom;
may also help separation anxiety -**

Separation anxiety, a disorder where a dog experiences severe stress whenever the owner leaves the home, can sometimes be serious enough to require the intervention of an animal behaviorist and/or veterinarian. Symptoms of separation anxiety include whining, barking, excessive panting, self-mutilating and damaging owners' possessions. Even adult dogs that do not suffer from clinical separation anxiety often destroy possessions out of boredom. Sometimes a change in lifestyle, a new job or more hours away on the part of the owner will set off the problem, and the unsuspecting owner may return home to find possessions destroyed- anything from a designer shoe to a whole leather couch.

Your dog does not have to have full-blown clinical separation anxiety to show some of the symptoms. A frustrated or bored dog may chew on household objects just like a person would seek for something to occupy himself if he was left in a house all alone. People have the option of surfing the Internet, calling a friend, working on a craft project or popping in an exercise video, so it's difficult for us to imagine the kind of boredom an unoccupied dog can feel. But think of how quickly children get into mischief if they're left without proper toys and projects to occupy them.

If you own an adult dog that chews your possessions out of boredom/frustration or even mild separation anxiety, training will help. And so will toys known as interactive toys. An interactive toy is designed to dispense a reward if your dog manipulates it correctly. The reward could be a sound, another toy inside or, most commonly, a food treat. Interactive toys come in all levels of difficultly, all sizes, shapes and prices and they are available at most local and chain pet stores, as well as through pet catalogs. Some are shaped like rubber balls that your dog can roll or throw around, and the reward falls out through a hole. Others feature flashing lights, glow in the dark, funny sounds or even a recorded voice.

Perhaps the best known interactive toy is the highly popular rubber Kong. The classic red Kong comes in sizes ranging from tiny to extra large. It's cone-shaped, with an empty cavity in the middle, which the owner can stuff with treats of their own choosing, a specially made paste or fillings like peanut butter or cream cheese. (Make sure, of course, that your dog has no food allergies before selecting treats or filling.) Depending on how tightly the owner stuffs the Kong with treats, the dog may work at it diligently for minutes or even hours, and most dogs seem to like them. Other varieties are available for puppy teething, and even for senior dogs, and they come in stick shape as well. There are many other brands of interactive toys available that work on similar principle- keeping your dog busy working for his treats while you are away or occupied. For the purpose of this section, we will refer to them all as Kongs.

"Kongs" are quite popular, and some of our client's dogs have had good success with them. What we like is that they are made of an especially tough material, so they're safe for most dogs to be left alone with for long periods. (We have heard of one rare instance of a dog chewing up a Kong. So, owners should use care and know their own dog. You can err on the safe side by using a Kong toy made for the toughest chewers.)

If you don't want to buy an interactive toy, you can create your own version to use for when you are home with your dog supervising. But, since dog's teeth are so strong, store-bought alternatives specially made to stand up to hours of chewing are probably the best bet.

Not all dogs will maintain interest in a single Kong, or similar toy, after all the treats are gone. One alternative is "Kong Time", a unit which dispenses multiple Kongs (see Chapter 9) over a period of time. Another alternative is to introduce more challenging interactive toys including some created to look like children's puzzles, which require much more work and thought to dispense each treat. The two interactive toys that we most commonly personally recommend for our customers are the Busy Buddy and the Buster Cube (see Resources).

The more intelligent your dog, the more complex interactive toys he will enjoy. And these toys are not just good for leaving your dog alone, but also for dog-owner playtime. You can cheer your dog on to figure out the puzzle when you are spending time together or offer the toy, loaded with goodies, as a reward- for example, after a successful obedience session. You can also set the toy down when you want some quiet time. It helps your dog's focus and means you do not have to constantly give attention to a rambunctious dog or puppy.

A really easy trick to quickly slow down a hyperactive dog or puppy is to offer him a Kong or similar toy filled with peanut butter. Watch the dog immediately stop flinging around the house, lie down calmly and begin licking the toy. Similar to the use of mood altering medication in humans with emotional disorders, this first moment of calmness may be enough to help the owner break the hyperactive cycle and then set the stage for further therapy and training. What an easy way to train a dog and to give an owner a short break!

Interactive toys are also a smart choice for puppy teething, because they occupy puppies much longer than non-interactive toys. Some are also made specifically for chewing. But be careful. Select a toy made specifically for puppy chewing and for a dog of your pup's size. It's always better to err on the safe side. If your puppy is almost grown and appears to be a very tough chewer, use the adult version of the toy and/or one of a larger size or tougher material. And, while interactive toys are good, they are not a substitute for properly supervising your dog. Make sure to thoroughly "dog proof" any room your puppy will be left alone in, and never leave your puppy alone unsupervised for long periods of time.

Wacky Walking
- stretchy leash makes walks easier for some owners -

Boing, boing, boing! What is that strange sound? Most owners have never seen this intriguing leash made of stretch rubber called a "Wacky Walk'r", available in pet shops and through mail order. (See Resources). Just like flexible exercise bands (the principle behind its design), the Wacky Walk'r leash is designed to stretch if your dog pulls. You can use it as an immediate measure to make walking more comfortable and it's good for owners who have hip, shoulder or back problems. But using this leash is not a cure-all or substitute for training for dogs that pull extremely. You should wean yourself off the Wacky Walk'r as you teach your dog to heel properly.

And be advised that **what's good about this leash can also make it dangerous**. If you attempt to use the wacky walker for leash corrections, you are out of luck! Just like it stretches when your dog pulls, it also stretches when you pull. So, **if your dog rushes at another dog, you cannot stop him with this leash!**

We recommend you use the Wacky Walk'r only in relatively safe and mellow situations. You might use it long term with a dog that's already a good (if not show-perfect) leash walker. Imagine this in situations like walking a quiet path every day around the golf course in your gated community. As long as there are no unexpected surprises, an hour-long walk with the Wacky Walk'r can make your dog's presence on the other end of the lead light as air.

Our Bella-" Learned to carry herself with grace and pride"

Ch. 9- Therapeutic & Senior Dog Activities:

"Physical or emotional challenges no longer have to limit quality of life for dogs."

Introduction-

Massage

Meditation

Stretching

Swim

Hydrotherapy

Talking Toys

Kong Time

Look in the Leaves

Bring Me the Puppy (Caution)

Doggie TV

Party in the Storm

Show the Puppy Obedience

More Learning Every Day

Visit With Seniors

Doggie Stairs

A Change of Scene

Help His Comrades

Doggie Wheelchair

Also Try These Ideas from Other Chapters for Therapeutic & Senior Dog Activities:

Puppy Games & Activities: Follow the Leader, Find the Treat, Which Hand?, Find Mommy, Which Box Has the Fun In It?, How Do I Get What's In There?, Let's Play Doctor, Shopping Spree, Walk This Way, Obedience-minded

Mental Games & Activities: Watch Me, Listen, Doggie Einstein, The Shell Game

Indoor Games & Activities: Hide & Seek, A Room of His Own, Basketball (with caution)

Balance & Coordination Activities: Walk the Line, Stack

Multi Dog Games & Activities: Simon Says, What's My Name

Problem Dog Games: Go to Your Place, When I Move, You Move, Drop It, Interactive Toys

High Energy Activities: Doggie Treadmill (with caution), Weave Poles

Water Activities: Kiddie Pool, Pool Float, Dog's Own Pool, Water Walk

Useful Activities: Follow the Scent, Volunteer Your Dog, Lap Dog

Family Activities: Circle of Love, Assess a Dog, Demonstrate Tricks

Activities for Owners with Limited Mobility: Treadmill, Playdate (with caution), Cat Toy, Bubbles, Games on the Floor, Dog Stairs, Rehab Together, Be Creative

Therapeutic & Senior Dog Activities - Introduction
"Physical or emotional challenges no longer have to limit quality of life for dogs."

These days we have learned that mind and body are made up not only of substance, but of energy, able to constantly change. And this is true for dogs as well as humans. It accounts for the fact that individuals can recover completely and quickly from serious illness or injury and the fact that they can change their fitness level and/or physical appearance at any age if they are motivated. The connection between mind, body and energy also accounts for some of the seeming "miracles" of recovery, when people strong in faith and/or willpower completely recover from conditions where doctors gave them a death sentence.

Dogs can possess this same kind of willpower for healing in their own way. But, in order to move forward or to heal, it is vitally important for a dog to feel engaged in life- to live with mental and physical stimulation and a daily sense of purpose. Dogs, or their canine ancestors in the wild, had to face extremely challenging hunts every day. They had to migrate distances up to fifty miles a day and sustain their "families" by each playing their part in an evolved social structure. Specific dog breeds as we know them today were also created for demanding tasks, most involving steady physical exertion along with mental discernment and judgment. And dogs thrived on this demanding life, working side by side with their humans.

Although dogs of today may have it easier than their forefathers in terms of physical comfort and amenities, some of today's dogs seem to suffer the most in terms of spirit. Yes, a dog can be patient and relaxed waiting for his owner at home. But no dog is meant to sit alone hour after hour, day after day, often in confined spaces, with nothing at all to do and then be set out in a tiny, blank yard with no new stimuli and nothing to sniff other than his own waste! Being left with no diversion or purpose affects dogs of all breeds, ages and physical conditions, depending upon how busy the owners perceive themselves to be and how well they selected a breed to fit with their lifestyle.

Certainly many dogs are bored. But we wonder if they experience it in a more existential way- as feeling profoundly useless. Although feeling useless might not manifest in a dog like a human, it may affect vitality, drive and even the strength of the animal's will to live.

Most boredom and frustration problems can be remedied simply by owner awareness. Owners must educate themselves and plan a daily schedule of activities to share with their dogs, including, but not limited to leashed walks, obedience practice, structured play and introduction of new stimuli. And we'll assume that, since you're reading this book, you're an educated and concerned owner, willing to make an effort to provide activities that are good for your dog.

But you may be faced with a challenge. Let's say you're used to sharing physical exercise with your dog daily but now he's getting old and suffering from arthritis, and physical games that used to give him pleasure now cause stiffness and pain. Or your dog may have been injured, or may be recovering from an illness. Some chronic illnesses may require a change in activities for the remainder of a dog's lifespan as medical treatments advance and owners keep their dogs alive longer and longer.

The key is finding the right activities for your dog, just like a human, to live as an "active senior". Not only is continued play and movement for your dog's body vital, but so is constant stimulation for his mind, especially if he seems less alert. You can take active steps to improve the quality of your dog's senior years. Mental stimulation, as included in many of the games in this chapter (as well in Chapter 4, Mental Games and Chapter 3, Puppy Games) has amazing effects, perking up your dog's mind and strengthening his body at any age.

If your dog is recovering from illness or injury, a feeling of being needed by his owner will provide him with strong willpower to push his recovery. He may not see it in the philosophical sense we humans might, but he will react in the same way. Other ideas included in this chapter (and also some from other chapters, like Chapter 14, Activities for Owners With Limited Mobility) will help you to keep your dog active, even if his disability challenges him in old activities.

Recent years have created a boom in products like "Doggie Stairs" (see the section in this chapter and Resources) and special harnesses that assist with hip or arthritis problems. These products allow your dog to stay involved in activities he cherishes to continue mental and physical stimulation.

In addition to physical rehabilitation, some dogs require rehabilitation with serious emotional problems that interfere with effective living and cause acute distress. Veterinarians and animal behaviorists are still in the research/debate stage as to whether dogs can suffer from "real" psychiatric disorders in the sense that humans do. At the same time, they treat many dogs with human psychotropic drugs. And just like human psychiatric patients who sometimes injure themselves, some highly anxious dogs compulsively chew on dangerous objects or mutilate their own bodies to the point of injury or hospitalization. As trainers, we treat many dogs that owners complain are "bouncing off walls", too frightened to be touched or just generally unreachable.

Some of these dogs lost their ability to relate properly with people because the owners left them for months with no structured activities, stimulation for body or mind or vigorous exercise. (Excessive crating is a common cause of the syndrome.) Another component of the problem is early life. Dogs that come to their new owners as rescues from shelters, pet shops and puppy mills have often been given the very worst type of husbandry during their critical early weeks and this can have a formative effect on all their future behavior.

Breeding plays a part as well, and these same irresponsible breeders don't breed for sound temperament. We see serious temperament problems too many times in pet shop puppies for the problem to be a coincidence. Some of these puppies cannot thrive with simply a normal level of care that the average family would commonly provide. Their agitation level is so high that they require specific intervention to calm themselves. Often these puppies present with glazed-looking empty eyes, along with all their other physical signs of imbalance and unrest.

If your dog started life in a pet shop, or if you suspect he came from a puppy mill or "backyard breeder", you will want to pursue intense veterinary treatment and thorough screening throughout the dog's life to head off physical problems that may develop as a result of irresponsible breeding or early lack of husbandry. Puppy shop dogs almost always present with some sort of illness or physical genetic problems, and these can all have a huge negative role on behavior. There is no sense trying to play with or train a puppy that is in physical discomfort, so always take care of physical needs and remediation first.

Whether psychotropic drugs are needed for dogs with serious emotional disorders is up for debate. We feel an owner must make an educated decision based on input from their veterinarian, animal behaviorist and their own extensive reading and research as well as their experience with their dog. The good news is that, once any medical issues are addressed, changes in activities are sometimes all that is needed to make a dog with serious problems like fear, depression or dislike of people thrive and seem to "come back to life".

This chapter includes special activities to help integrate and energize fearful dogs, and gentle activities to renew mind and spirit in nervous and distrustful dogs. Additional ideas are also found throughout the book. For example, some dogs can benefit greatly from hands-on massage, others from a simple change of scene.

Owners will experience great delight and relief when they see life begin to head in a positive direction for their seemingly "hopeless" dog. No matter the dog's limitations, once they find activities they can successfully and healthfully engage in together, this opens up a whole range of possibilities and the owner has a clear direction to apply their energy. Watching a dog and owner that had both lost their verve turn this "corner" together and start moving in a positive direction gives us great delight as well. They can finally stop wrangling with difficulties and now spend their time together enjoying a whole new realm of possibilities!

> *Some chronic illnesses may require a complete change in activities as medical treatments advance and owners keep their dogs alive longer. The key is to find the right activities to keep your dog feeling active and useful.*

Therapeutic & Senior Dog Activities:

Massage
- outstanding health and emotional benefits when practiced with care -

Have you ever owned an older dog that had problems walking because of severe joint pain? It's heartbreaking to see a dog you've loved for all his years cry out as he tries to stand up first thing in the morning. When this happened to our Akita we cried uncontrollably ourselves as we carried our 115-pound dog to the car to rush him to the vet. After our visit to the vet we also learned a lot about preventing and easing arthritis and hip pain.

We found that one of the things we could do to keep our dog out of pain was to learn how to give the right kind of massage to keep his old joints limber. And massage isn't just for older dogs; you can start massaging your dog the day you bring him home, no matter what his age. And, if you combine regular massage with other healthy lifestyle changes, you may even be able to prevent joint and muscle problems from ever happening. If you wish to use massage for therapeutic purposes, we recommend that you first check with your veterinarian to see if he has specific recommendations about what type of massage is best for your dog or if there are any movements you should avoid.

Next, you'll want to learn about the different types of massages you can give your dog. First is the type of massage people are most familiar with, where you simply run your hands over the dog's skin. This type of massage will make your dog start to relax and loosen his muscles, and this is the easiest method to learn. All you need to do is to get settled with your dog in a comfortable position, run your hands all over the dog's body and just watch your dog start to fall asleep in your arms. This massage helps improve bonding between dog and owner in a calm and positive atmosphere and it also helps keep your dog limber and keeps his joints loose to avoid injury.

Additional massage techniques work differently, targeting specific problems. For example, certain types of massage are meant to speed the healing process if your dog is recovering from an injury or surgery. Others types of massage not only help your dog to relax, but they help with serious behavior problems like fear or aggression. One technique of massage that helps both physical and emotional healing, called Tellington Touch, or TTouch, has gained tremendous popularity recently. Tellington Touch is a gentle intervention that not only works with dogs, but with cats, horses and zoo animals, as well. For example, the method was used in zoos by the founder to calm large cats that were hurting themselves from the stress of feeling trapped.

Tellington Touch massage is much more involved than the basic massage we first described. While performing TTouch, the masseuse uses many different hand positions and moves their hands on the dog's skin in specific patterns. In TTouch, each hand position is named after a different wild animal and is meant to make the animal you are treating feel better in a particular way. For example, the "raccoon" touch, which uses just the tips of your fingers, helps to make your dog feel more secure. In combination with our behavioral and psychological treatment, we have also used TTouch massage successfully to help calm dogs and help with certain phobias and certain types of aggression.

If you wish to try TTouch massage specifically, you can hire a certified professional or you can study the techniques on your own. Another option is to allow a highly qualified human masseuse to massage your dog, if no dog masseuse is available in your area. You can also ask your veterinarian for a referral. The same is true if you are seeking a professional to perform acupressure on your dog. Since the area of canine massage is unregulated, you want to make sure that whatever technique you or a paid professional choose won't harm your dog. This is why it's important to first mention to your veterinarian, or holistic vet, that you are considering massage for your dog and ask if there are any physical limitations before using any complex or deep massage technique.

If you are using basic massage that's only skin-deep, and your dog is healthy, you don't necessarily need to clear it with your vet, but you should always use caution and common sense. Start your first session simple, and work within your dog's comfort zone as you cover every part of his body. Some areas respond particularly well to gentle massage- including the ears, a little spot in the center of the dog's forehead and the feet. But these same areas are highly sensitive and your dog may not like them touched at first if he is not used to it. **Go slow, never push things and always respond to your dog's feedback.** If your dog pulls away from, or winces, when you touch him in a particular spot, this is your cue to ease up the pressure and/or move away from that area.

Serious signs of discomfort when you touch a certain area might indicate illness or injury, so you should stop massage immediately and report the symptom to your vet. You can use massage to cure minor discomfort like stiffness, but you should always watch your dog's expression. The more you touch, the more he should relax, even looking a little sleepy.

If your dog ever squeals when you touch him, stop immediately. Pressing certain areas on your dog's body could hurt or even kill him. Your veterinarian can advise you in detail, or you can research more on your own. **Also never push massage on a dog that appears to be unfriendly, angry, growly or snappy or any dog with an unknown history (such as a shelter dog) until you are sure of his behavior.** The safest rule of thumb for any pet owner who wants to massage their dog at home is to never push hard and never force anything if your dog appears to be in discomfort!

Always leave any deep massaging to qualified adults in the home and supervise your children carefully if you want them to practice basic massage on your dog. **Only individuals that are calm, with a gentle touch, should massage your dog.** And their calm gentle touch will lead to the dog becoming calmer and gentler as well. If you want to learn more about canine massage, see Books in Resources, check the Internet and talk to dog professionals about what's new in this fascinating realm. Your dog will love you for it, and it's a great way to spend time with him.

Meditation
- dogs help us feel more meditative; now we can help them. No reason not to try this!

For humans, meditation has been shown to adjust the body's brain waves, improve immunity, lower amounts of feel-bad chemicals (for example, cortisol) and to increase the amount of feel-good chemicals (endorphins). For people living in today's hectic society, meditation is virtually a requirement if you want to bust the daily cycle of stress naturally, without resorting to drugs. A meditative state also facilitates visualization, which can lead to greater effectiveness in physical or sports performance and in business. Meditative states are achieved during times of prayer, and can be built even stronger by several individuals reaching the state at once (for example the transcendent feeling after a particularly moving church service). Meditation can also speed the frequency of healing, and more and more traditional medical practitioners are including a prescription for meditation when their chronically ill patients leave the hospital and begin the hard road of recovery.

Those of us who seek a more Zen-like state have traditionally envied our pets for their natural ability to live "in the now". After all, that is what meditation consists of- a passive focusing on the now, without interpreting, worrying or striving- simply being.

Sadly, veterinarians and dog trainers today are seeing more and more cases of extremely stressed pets, some of them suffering from rather severe anxiety disorders that resemble similar states in humans.

Extreme stress in a dog can be manifested by signs of separation anxiety such as incessant barking, destructiveness, bathroom accidents or even self-mutilation. Some dogs are so fearful and anxious that even the casual observer will notice it. When faced with a new stimulus, such as a visitor, a dog like this may cower behind his owners' legs, visibly trembling and heaving for breath. Other dogs manifest anxiety through hyperactivity or pre-emptive aggression. Still others display severe fears and phobias (such as thunderstorm fear or fear of loud noises) and some develop compulsive behaviors (such as always lunging at a certain item like the vacuum cleaner.)

There are many causes and many treatments for these stress-related behaviors. There is also some disagreement whether behavioral methods alone are enough to help or if herbal or pharmacological intervention is necessary.

But one great practice to soothe and center your overly anxious or hyperactive dog is to practice daily doggie meditation sessions with your pet. Meditation may be the first thing to break the cycle of the hyperactive dog and the well-meaning owner who has problems relating to him. In fact, it may be the first time you see your pet willingly sitting still. This then gives you somewhere to build from to make all activities calmer and more effective with your dog.

The best time to start regular meditation sessions would be with a young dog, *before* the dog develops any problems. But no time is too late to start and there is absolutely no downside to the practice (as opposed to chemical interventions.)

The first step is to learn the theory of meditation, and practice meditation a few times on your own. The first few times you might feel silly and might experience problems getting fully relaxed and emptying your mind. But with just a few practice sessions it will become easier and you will begin savoring your time for meditation. You will also better learn your own preferences in terms of environment (for example, indoors vs. outdoors or music vs. no music). Start having your meditation sessions at a regular time of day, and encourage your dog to wander in and observe. The more relaxed you can remain, the more likely your dog will notice your positive energy. Dogs, who cannot communicate as we do verbally, are masters of reading energy signals, so this is no surprise!

Now, it's time to start including your dog in meditation. To make it easier, make sure that all his physical needs are met first. Take him on a long walk (or other activity) for exercise. Make sure his stomach is neither empty nor overly full and that his bladder and bowels are empty.

Now, clear the area! If you've already been meditating yourself for a while, you will know better how to do this. No television. No loud music (except some soft, New-Agey instrumentals, nature-sounds or a murmuring fountain). No loud washing machines or dishwashers. And no cell phones. Kids can participate, but only if they have a long attention span and have already been practicing meditation with you. Otherwise, this would be a great time for your partner to take the kids out shopping and for you to have the house to yourself. Early morning or early evening are also good times to feel undisturbed. You can be sure if you are worrying about anything in the home, your dog will also feel it and the meditation attempt will backfire.

Once you have created a tranquil environment, welcome your dog into the space with you. A nice embrace, a tiny kiss or slow gentle strokes on your dog's body would be appreciated, but don't get your dog too hyped-up by petting him too wildly or vigorously (see "Ruffle My Ruff" and "Pro Wrestling" in Ch. 15 of Dangerous Games.) You may hold your dog loosely on a leash beside you. This is only to guide and ease him, however. If he seems truly uncomfortable, you must let him go for the time being.

If your veterinarian has okayed stretching or massage for your dog, you can do some of this as well. Tell your dog that he's good as he relaxes and allows you to stroke him rhythmically. But do not speak too much. Pay attention to breathing, both yours and his. Both should be relaxed and regular. Dogs can fall easily into a naturally meditative state. Do not expect anything in particular of your pet. Allow him to look off into the distance, to stretch or to groom himself. Allow him to sigh if he wants to. If he looks to you, share an undemanding gentle glance, but do not stare at him. This is not a time for obedience practice or learning tricks. It is a time for the two of you to simply *be* together.

Enter your own meditative state as well, and allow yourself to go with the flow. One day, you may wish to stroke a sore muscle for your dog (see Massage above), or even groom him during a session. Another day you may not touch him at all. Another day you may find that your pet goes to sleep midway during the meditation. This is okay as well (but, next time, try to schedule at an hour when he's a bit more alert.) If your pet walks around the area, gently sniffing around, this is okay as well. A dog does not have to be lying down to experience a tranquil thoughtful state.

If, however, your dog becomes extremely "hyper" and his agitation seems to be building rather than lessening, you cannot force him to do meditation at this time. Simply excuse him from the area and complete meditation yourself. Do not get agitated or upset. You can welcome him back or try again whenever he is calmer. Even if he seems the type never to be calm this is all the reason to teach him meditation. But it may be a painstakingly slow process. You must build from a moment that he is calm and then encourage that calm to last a few minutes longer each time. (The principals of positive reinforcement training apply here.) Or you can start using the principals of meditation for other regular activities you share, like grooming.

Most dogs will come to love a brief daily meditation session. Don't make it too long. Go with your dog's attention span. When the session is complete, you can reward with a nice hug or a treat. Because dogs are so responsive to routine, it is good to schedule meditation at about the same time each day. Say to your dog, "Meditation-time", as you prepare the area in a ritualized fashion. Put on the soothing music, close some doors and lay out a cushiony pillow for your dog right next to yours. Your dog will come to recognize the sensory cues and he will likely lie down on the pillow next to yours, let out a sigh and pleasurably anticipate this time of tranquility and closeness with his owner.

If you like, videotape a successful meditation session to show your family that your dog really can relax. Some dogs, like our Akita Casey, are naturally meditative, and you may learn a lot from you dog. Some individuals may want to try aromatherapy during sessions. You may also want to try advanced meditation techniques like walking meditations on the beach together, or "howling" at the moon.

Just never break one golden rule. You should certainly encourage your dog to calm down more and participate in meditation. But you cannot *force* him. That would defeat the entire purpose.

Stretching
- done carefully this can reduce physical strain & emotional stress -

This activity will be of great interest to owners that like to run or hike with their dogs. These highly active dogs often have expensive veterinary bills. For example, surgery to repair a pulled muscle or a torn ligament can cost between three and five thousand dollars. But simple stretching before workouts can help prevent such injuries. If you own a sporting breed that hunts or retrieves, you should learn how to stretch your dog before activity. Stretching is also helpful for owners who enter their dogs in agility, Flyball or other high-energy competitions, because the rapid bursts of running, jumping and twisting required in these activities put dogs' joints and muscles under a great deal of strain.

Dogs are like human athletes; if they don't warm up they are more likely to get hurt. And most of the injuries could have been easily avoided by just stretching your dog. One great thing about stretching is that this healthy activity costs only time, not money. And it also helps you bond with your dog, in turn making him want to work better and more efficiently for you.

When you first start stretching your dog you'll want to take it slow. Get to know your dog's muscle tone and how your dog's body moves. Your dog will let you know what feels good and what bothers him as long as you pay attention to his feedback. And you'll want to learn exactly where he's tender, so you can focus on building up these weak areas so they're not as vulnerable to injury.

Start with a relaxed dog and have him lie down on a comfortable area on the floor. First just run your hands over the dog's body and see if there are any spots that the dog tries to have you avoid. These are the weak spots that need work, areas where there's the greatest likelihood for your dog to get hurt while working or playing. But do not push to work on these tender spots too quickly, or it may hurt your dog. And if this happens, your dog may learn not to trust you. **Instead, proceed slowly and carefully, guiding and encouraging each stretch, but not forcing it.**

We recommend starting your dog's daily stretching with the back legs. First, rub the dog's legs to get some blood flowing. Then bring one of the dog's rear legs up towards his body slowly and then stretch the leg back out away from the body so the leg is straight; also move the relaxed leg in a small circle to stretch the hip.

(Remember to only go as far as your dog is relaxed. If he starts to pull his leg away, you likely stretched him uncomfortably. You'll need to slow down and not move the leg around so much yet. Just like a human becomes more flexible with practice, so will your dog, so don't push too much at first. Stretching should be a daily activity and there's no need to do too much the first day when your dog will be the stiffest.)

After the first stretch, bring the leg back into the dog's body and start over. Do this a few times and you'll probably notice that the leg feels looser and more comfortable. Then move to your dog's foot and ankle. Gently rotate the joint in small slow circles and gently spread your dog's toes. After the dog feels relaxed, move to the next leg.

When all four legs are done see if you can get the dog to stretch his own back by sliding his front legs forward and lowering his the front part of his body. After a few days or weeks of your dog stretching you'll see a whole new dog, with better muscle tone. And all those creaks and groans will go away. Your dog will become stronger; he'll be able to jump higher and run and play more comfortably. And he'll have a new life in his eyes showing you how much he appreciates the time you took helping him stretch each day before exercising.

Swim
- great exercise for physically challenged dogs if practiced with cautions mentioned -

You often hear it said that swimming is the "perfect exercise" And this is just as true for dogs as it is for humans. You can read more about the benefits of swimming for play in Chapter 11, Water Activities, and its benefits as serious conditioning in Chapter 10, High Energy Activities. In the proper depth of water and with proper support, swimming is therapeutic for dogs recovering from injury (see "Hydrotherapy", this chapter). And it benefits any dog with delicate joints, arthritis or pain that makes weight-bearing exercise uncomfortable.

Older and overweight dogs benefit especially, but swimming is also great exercise for highly athletic dogs. Since swimming provides intensive exercise in a short amount of time, owners can adjust the length of their dog's swim to fit his physical condition- anywhere from a short, gentle swim of a few moments duration with the owner supporting the dog's weight, all the way to an x-treme canine athlete swimming laps, racing to beat his own best time.

Swimming also enhances dogs' emotional health because it builds confidence. It's a source of stimulation for all the senses for a lethargic animal, and it feels great on the body, bringing more "zing" into a listless or otherwise unresponsive dog's life.

It's also good aerobic exercise for dogs that tend to be susceptible to summer heat. Just like humans, dogs can exercise in the cool water in relatively hot temperatures or hot sun without overheating as quickly. This makes swimming a good vigorous exercise to select in summertime. Use care, however, and, even if the pool water is cool, restrict the midday sun on your dog's exposed snout and/or use a waterproof sun product safe for dogs. Also give your dog's head an occasional wet-down to cool him further and avoid heat indexes over 100 degrees if you want to keep your dog outside for any length of time. (One notable exception is if you don't have air conditioning in your home and water is the only way for your dog to get cool. In this case, you'll want to encourage the dog to swim, but restrict his exertion to a gentle dip on dangerously hot and humid days.)

You may have noticed that dogs tolerate cool water a lot better than humans do. If your dog likes cool water, then it's okay to let him take a quick swim in mild spring or fall temperatures, but let him enter the water of his own accord. Allow him to swim only briefly and then dry him thoroughly. The same applies to your swimming pool. If you've retired your pool for the season because it's too chilly for humans, yet your dog dips his toes and then decides he *wants* to go in, you can let him. Make his swim brief, watch for signs of shivering and dry him well. Breeds with thick coats, larger dogs with a smaller surface area to their weight, and dogs with a layer of fat may tolerate colder water better.

Your dog's own instinct is probably the best guide of what he can handle, but for older and more delicate dogs, we don't recommend water cooler than the mid-sixties, even to splash in. If you have any doubts about water being too cold (or any hazards in the water) don't toss your dog's favorite toy far out into deep water for him to dive in and fetch. His desire to play with you may override his reason!

Never force a dog into the water if he doesn't want to go! There are only a few downsides to swimming for exercise and one of them is that not every dog likes it. Some dogs have never encountered water, yet they can be gradually taught to love it. (For example, it is natural for wolves/wild dogs to swim in the wild on a limited basis and to feel comfortable with water.) Unfortunately, some dogs seem to be born terrified of water. Sometimes this is a matter of breed; other times it's just the individual. I**f your dog is otherwise emotionally healthy, but he seems to freeze up with terror when you try to get him to swim, you may simply choose to never confront the fear head-on and never include swimming in your dog's activities**. If your dog is otherwise healthy and happy, there's no need to push this one activity.

Some dogs immediately take to water on their own (Labrador Retrievers are famous for this) and the owner will have to do absolutely nothing to teach them to swim. In fact you may sometimes have to hold the dog back. The majority of dogs fall somewhere in the middle when it comes to water. Many dogs aren't terrified of swimming, but they are hesitant and cautious at first with the unfamiliar concept. Owners may find it worthwhile to take the time to slowly and carefully introduce a dog like this to swimming, especially if he has physical limitations like arthritis or hip dysplasia that indicate swimming for therapeutic purposes.

It's usually easier to first introduce your dog to water in a calm body of water like a pond where he can wade and play in the shallows and then work up to coaxing him into the backyard pool one step at a time. But algae and protozoa can pose a risk of disease in some freshwater ponds, so research the safety of the body of water and weigh risks and benefits carefully. Another idea is to first introduce your dog or puppy to wading and swimming in a kiddie pool (see Chapter 11, Water Games).

If you want to start immediately with your in-ground backyard pool, just make sure you introduce the dog slowly, allowing him to first hang out on the steps and then coaxing him into deeper water, much as you would a child. Most dogs will soon be able to cross the pool on their own, swimming comfortably in the deep water while supervised by their owners. A lifevest made for dogs (available in chain pet stores and catalogs) is a necessity if your dog swims in lakes, ponds or the ocean, and you should also use it in the pool if your dog is not a strong swimmer.

While some dogs take quickly to the deeper water, others may act reluctant. They may want to remain in shallow water, or on the pool steps, and owners shouldn't try to push them beyond their comfort zone too quickly. Some dogs won't ever be willing to go out into deeper water. (Although they may swim in a pool designed especially for dogs, as described in "A Pool of His Own" in Chapter 11, Water Games.) But most dogs can eventually be coaxed beyond their reluctance with the right training.

If you want to coax a reluctant dog to swim in deeper water in the backyard pool, you'll need two physically strong adults who are capable swimmers. First encourage the dog (wearing a lifevest) to play on the steps in the water, while he watches his owners taking turns swimming around and having fun. Reward his participation with lots of praise. Depending on how comfortable he seems, you can practice on the steps for several more sessions or, when he seems ready, have both adults ease him into slightly deeper water.

Let the lifevest support the dog or, if not using one, the adults should brace him- at arm's length- not up close! Avoid flailing claws! Stay near enough to function as a lifeguard, but let the dog swim on his own. Instinct should guide him. Spend only a few minutes with him swimming. Then gently steer him back to the steps, showing him how to climb out on his own. When he does, give him tons of praise! Proceed in this fashion until he's comfortable swimming for longer and longer periods on his own. Dogs vary from the timid to those who practically live in the family pool with the kids in summertime, so it's just a matter of finding your dog's own personal best.

Swimming can be a small or a large percentage of an exercise program depending on the needs of the dog and the owner. An older or physically compromised dog should be discouraged from stunts like jumping into the water off the side of the pool, or running on a slippery deck surface. And, just like kids, no dog should ever swim in a pool unsupervised! You should gate off your pool from your dogs when you're not there to supervise and this may be even truer for dogs that love the water. Your dog may dive in the pool when you're not around and then find himself unable to get back out! (Whether you gate your pool or not, you should provide adequate steps and/or purchase a special pool ramp made for dogs to prevent this.)

Swimming for therapeutic purposes can also help if your dogs are in great health but *you* have the physical limitations, because swimming is such a concentrated workout. Just ten minutes of swimming can be more intense exercise than an hour of walking. Let your dog get most of his exercise swimming, then take him for a brief leashed walk just for bonding and you can possibly forgo hours of exertion on your part and still maintain a physically and mentally fit dog!

The last thing to mention about swimming as exercise for your dog is its second very real downside. We've seen other books on dog exercise that tout swimming without mentioning that many, many owners won't ever be able to let their dog swim. A backyard pool is expensive, and not everyone can afford one. Renters, condo owners or homeowners who share a clubhouse won't be able to bring their dog to their community pool.

And not many of us have ponds or lakes on our private property. Meanwhile we often observe owners throwing sticks for their loose dogs to swim out and fetch in bodies of water in public parks. The problem is that this is usually illegal, no matter how tempting it seems! Even if dogs are allowed in your local park, they're probably required to be leashed, unless it's a designated dog park or dog beach. The majority of ocean beaches don't allow dogs and the few that do require leashes. And you must be fair to your neighbors and only allow your dog loose to swim in areas where it is legally permitted.

If you don't currently own a pool, this may be the time to give some thought to the future. Swimming can be immensely important to your dog's health, fun and fitness. So, if you know that you and your dog love water, you may want to install an in-ground pool. If this isn't an option, consider an inexpensive above-ground pool that your dog can get out of safely. (See "Dog's Own Pool", Chapter 11). And, next time you purchase or rent a home, you may want to start your search with homes with pools!

Hydrotherapy
-   physical therapy for dogs using water; can be done by a professional or, in some cases, at home -

Once again, a good holistic medical idea for humans is also a good idea for dogs. Hydrotherapy is simply the idea of using water, and/or water exercise for therapeutic purposes. Just like it can for humans, **water can take much of the weight off a dog's tender or injured joints.** Movement in water is great exercise for many reasons, but it's especially recommended for physically compromised dogs, including elderly animals and those recovering from surgery. Hydrotherapy allows dogs to freely move their limbs for exercise, without the pain or risk of additional injury that exercising on land would bring. **Hydrotherapy is great for dogs with joint problems including arthritis and hip dysplasia.**

Lately we see many dogs that already have serious hip problems when they are young (perhaps due to irresponsible breeding practices). Medication can reduce these dogs' pain, and medication, diet and supplements can sometimes slow the progression of their disease. But their owners are often left in a quandary- they know their dog needs strenuous physical exercise to keep his mind occupied and his body fit- yet they also know he is not supposed to stress his hips. Water exercise provides an ideal solution in these cases because it's a highly concentrated aerobic exercise that, at the same time, takes the majority of the stress off the joints.

Water exercise is also a good alternative for owners with overweight dogs who face a similar Catch-22. If a dog is heavy, too much sudden weight-bearing exercise could injure his joints or strain his heart before he reaches his ideal weight. Water exercise is a great way to start a fitness program for overweight dogs since it equalizes the excess weight they need to carry and allows them to move freely until they get closer to their ideal weight.

Water can also bring dogs a measure of joy. Although most breeds are not highly aquatic creatures, and some even fear water, the average dog, especially if he's been ill and inactive, will find gentle movement in water pleasurable.

There are professionals whose expertise includes administering hydrotherapy for dogs. If your dog is recovering from surgery, or has chronic illness or disabilities, your veterinarian is a good place to start for recommendations on how hydrotherapy can be a part of his treatment plan. He or she should be able to put you in touch with the nearest facility that offers a pool and hydrotherapy professionals. You can also look online (and see the Resources section for more information).

A dog doesn't necessarily need sophisticated equipment for hydrotherapy to work, although items like underwater treadmills are available through catalogs and online. Unlike dogs in perfect health, dogs that require hydrotherapy for physical rehabilitation may require assistance to support more of their body weight, to encourage them walk to in the water or for other specific purposes. They also do better in shallow water, sometimes in more controlled settings than the family pool, and they sometimes require professionals to work sessions with them.

Healthy dogs or dogs with less serious problems can receive hydrotherapy right at home, in the family pool, a wading pool or even in a bathtub. You can support the dog while using your hands and/or a lifevest and the dog can either walk in shallow water or swim, depending upon his therapeutic needs. Not all dogs will immediately take to the water (see "Swim" in this chapter). But most dogs can slowly acclimate to swimming or walking in water, and they will eventually come to like it.

In contrast, some dogs have serious phobias relating to water. So if your dog continues to be terrified and panicked even after attempts at gentle introduction, we recommend that you simply give up on the idea of water for exercise or rehab. The only exception is if your dog absolutely requires hydrotherapy to recover from an injury and there is no alternative. In this case you cannot introduce the panicked dog to water on your own, or you or he might get hurt. You would have to hire a professional to work hydrotherapy with an extremely fearful dog like this, and we only recommend this if your veterinarian offers no alternative for your dog's recovery.

Unless ordered by your veterinarian, never force a water-phobic dog into water, even if you feel it can help his condition. A dog in a state of panic like this is more likely to hurt himself and his fears could become worse than the original physical problem.

Moderate temperature water is best for dogs that are physically compromised, unless your vet recommends a warmer temperature. **Be extremely careful if you want to use your spa or hot tub and never use hot water with your dog.** Your vet might also recommend water massage, or jetted water. But do not attempt these methods without your veterinarian's recommendation, as they could worsen certain serious medical conditions. If your healthy dog seems to enjoy a gentle massage under the water jets, then allow him to enjoy this at his own pace as long as he can come and go as he pleases.

Talking Toys
- cool idea, just watch the noisemaking mechanisms around strong chewers -

Here's a good ideas with no downside that can help dogs with emotional problems when they're left home alone. Most owners already know that if your dog chews up your possessions it's a good idea to leave him with toys while you're away. But the bad news is that sometimes the dog ignores the designated toys, and tears up the house anyway.

Sometimes chewing progresses well beyond teething age, and the habit can become dangerous for the dog depending on what he ingests. In cases of clinical separation anxiety, destructiveness like this occurs as part of a cluster of other symptoms, and the dog may single out certain unlikely objects to fixate on and chew compulsively. A dog may even mutilate itself in its frustration, for example, chewing on its paws until they are bloody. True "separation anxiety" is a complex disorder and, depending on severity, it may require professional help. But the right toys can often help as part of a successful treatment program in many cases, preventing a minor problem from becoming severe.

The idea is to keep the dog's mind truly occupied. Just as humans become bored, anxious or depressed if left alone for long periods with nothing to do, so can dogs. Highly intelligent breeds easily become bored with the same rubber chew toy or ball day after day. Or the dog may make quick work of a rawhide.

"Talking toys" are included in the category of "Interactive toys" (see Chapter 8, Problem Dog Games) and these toys are special because they engage the dog's mind. These are not the simple squeaky toys of years past. Many of these toys "giggle", "groan" rattle or make other sounds as your dog rolls them around, trying to figure out how to get treats from inside. Other toys even allow the owner to record their voice. Even dogs that quickly become bored with regular toys happily spend hours investigating the mysteries of interactive toys like these.

Bring your dog to the pet store to select the interactive toys he likes best. When you're home, give him the talking toy only at special times like when he's completed a great obedience session or when you absolutely must not be distracted. Sometimes the toy alone is enough to focus the mind of a highly flighty, anxious or wild dog. Owners love watching the antics of their dog trying to "figure out" a talking toy. And, when used carefully, these toys can help enliven a depressed dog or calm an overexcited one. Talking toys can also be used to immediately refocus a dog's attention during training or play. Simply make a noise with the toy, and you're dog is likely to immediately focus on you.

You may only want to leave the special toy for your dog when you go out. In the mild cases of separation anxiety, fun toys that keep a dog occupied can sometimes refocus his mind to keep him calm. And your dog may not hate it so much when you go away because he enjoys getting the favorite toy; if fact he may be so busy when you put the toy down that he doesn't even notice you leaving.

Caution: If you intend to leave your dog alone with an interactive toy, you must be cautious about the toy's construction and carefully read warning labels. The manufacturer should let you know if the toy is safe for a dog of a certain size to be left alone with. But use their warnings only as a guideline and err on the side of caution.

If your dog is a gentle chewer, and he has been for years, you're probably safe to leave him alone with the toy if the manufacturer says it's safe. **But do not leave a small puppy, or any strong chewer alone with any noisemaking toy unless you are 100% sure of the safety of the toy's construction. Noisemaking toys contain small parts and/or electronic parts that can be especially dangerous if consumed.**

Kong Time
**-   this more expensive delivery system for the popular toys
sometimes helps big problems -**

One highly popular interactive toy is the "Kong" a patented rubber toy with a hole inside that can be stuffed with flavored Kong paste, peanut butter or treats. Most dogs will focus intently on getting the treats out, unlikely to get bored like they would with other toys, and Kongs are known to help occupy seriously bored, frustrated or destructive dogs. The makers of the popular Kong also decided to offer an even more x-treme invention to occupy dogs with more serious boredom and frustration problems when they are left for longer periods of time.

Leaving a single Kong toy for your dog is one line of defense against separation anxiety and destructiveness. But the problem with the Kong is that eventually the dog licks out all the paste, peanut butter or treats and then he can get bored with the empty toy and turn back to the possessions in your house for amusement. The innovative "Kong Time" machine takes care of this problem. It sits on a countertop and dispenses multiple treat-filled Kong toys over a period of time to keep your dog occupied, gently shooting them out from the machine onto the floor at intervals widely spaced enough to keep your dog guessing.

Kong Time may seem like a rather strange invention, and the cost (over one-hundred dollars) is somewhat pricey. But for some owners the machine is a real lifesaver. Dogs seem to love it, and so do many owners who swear it made the first difference in their dog's separation anxiety problem. And Kong Time isn't only for problem dogs. It can be a good idea to reward and occupy any dog that stays home while you are away at work, especially senior dogs that may benefit from the additional stimulation. Just don't use the toy as an excuse to stay away longer! All dogs need their owners' companionship as much as possible. Owners who stay away for a normal workday are already pushing their dog's emotional and physical resources almost to the breaking point. Interactive toys including Kong Time, and other activities described in this book can help. But, if an owner must ever be away for longer hours at a stretch than the normal workday, they should have a qualified person stop in to care for their dog.

Look In the Leaves
- cool game to stimulate shy, timid and listless dogs to act vibrant-

Have you ever noticed dogs' fascination with the mysteries hidden underneath piles of autumn leaves? Owners can't help but smile watching our dogs dig in the leaves, sending colorful leaves flying in the air while they always seem to be in great spirits. Digging through leaves is more than just fun for dogs; it also works for rehabilitation and therapy because it stimulates dogs' senses. You can see how the activity helps a young puppy, keeping him occupied while emboldening him and encouraging him to explore the world with several of his senses. For the same reason, this fun game also helps elderly dogs- it stimulates the senses and provides mild exercise.

To make the game more challenging, you can hide an object and make the dog dig for it. "Look in the Leaves" is also good for fearful or timid dogs because it tempts them to come out of their emotional shell and take action, thus building confidence. It helps depressed animals and those with medical conditions for the same reason. And it helps dogs with phobias learn not to be afraid of the sound of the crackling leaves.

Playing in leaves can also focus an overly wild or bored dog and take him away from destructive alternatives, such as mutilating your trees or digging up your flowers. It's also a truly fun way for dogs and owners, or dogs and kids, to play together. The only caution is to first check that there's nothing unsafe, like a snake, or barbed wire, hiding under the pile of leaves to hurt your dog (or your children) before you let them start to play. You should also be able to instruct the dog when the game is over and he should be willing to listen. We don't recommend letting the dog play in deep leaves unsupervised because of safety issues. And we doubt you'd walk away anyway- because you still must remember to do yardwork!

Bring Me the Puppy
- challenging task makes mature dogs feel useful, while setting your pup on the right path -

Not every dog will have the skills for this game, so don't demand it if your dog does not catch on right away. Other dogs may naturally excel at the task, since it builds on natural herding, protective and pack instincts.

Let's say you own an adult dog and also a rambunctious puppy that seems to vanish into hiding spots just when you're occupied and unable to run around looking for him. Wouldn't it be great to have some help in the form of a doggie "nanny"? Some responsible older dogs go looking for the puppy on their own, then come back whining to lead you to where the little trickster is hiding. It's the nature of puppies to follow adult dogs, so your older pet may be able to get the puppy out of the dark corner where he's hiding and lead him back to you. And you don't even have to leave your cooking in the kitchen!

The nice thing about teaching your adult dog to go get the puppy is that it gives the dog a truly useful task to do, and makes him feel assured of his vital place in the family- just what this book is about. If your dog gets good at finding the puppy on your command, or if he ever takes it on himself to help you before you even knew the puppy went missing, never forget to give loads of praise. You can teach, or encourage, the behavior by practicing when the puppy is not really lost. Give the command, "Where's the puppy?" or "Find the Puppy", substituting your puppy's name. Reward your older dog when he's successful in locating the puppy and/or leading the puppy back to you.

Teaching your dog this behavior is fun, but don't feel frustrated if he doesn't take to it. Only a small percentage of dogs will be able to accomplish this task, and an even smaller percentage will be able to accomplish it every time, including real situations where the puppy might be in trouble. For this reason, consider this as just a game or a little help around the house. Leave it for dogs that seem to naturally excel, and don't expect too much. And, if you ever send your older dog to look for the puppy and he doesn't return right away, or he returns appearing distressed, something may be truly wrong. The situation can no longer be left for the dog to take care of, and it becomes time for the owner to intervene, because it might just save your puppy's life.

Doggie TV
- should dogs watch television?-

When an owner hears the term "Doggie TV", they may think of the concept in several different ways. The first way owners may use television when they leave home for the day is simply to leave their television on, full volume, to "keep the dog company". We believe the merits of this idea can be questionable. That may be due to our bias that we like quiet during the day, and we're not fans of mindless daytime television shows playing one after another. We can't be sure whether dogs are also bothered by the sound of the television. We do know that dogs' ears are many times more sensitive than humans' and certain frequencies cause them pain. Studies have also demonstrated that the flickering light of television can even set off seizures in susceptible dogs.

For this reason, we don't suggest that average owners leave the television playing all day as "company" for their dogs. There are cases, however, where dogs may come to like the sound of television because they associate it with warm feelings when their owners are home. If you notice your dog behaving better if you leave him home alone with the television playing, there's probably no harm in it. Just make sure you adjust the volume low and leave the dog an "escape route" so he can leave the room if he ever feels uncomfortable.

An even better idea may be to try "doggie videos". You may have noticed that dogs don't watch television in the same manner as we humans do. Many dogs, if they notice television at all, will only do it at certain particular times- for example, when they hear a dog bark. This is all due to differences in dog's sensory perceptions. They hear television differently, and they see it differently as well. They usually do not do well when they get up close to the television (their near-vision is not as sharp as ours) and they tend to perceive only certain movements on television- therefore they cannot follow our favorite television shows in the same way as we would. To the rescue is a modern innovation- DVDs made specifically to occupy your lonely pets during the day. These are available in various styles, often containing animal noises, calming music and video specifically designed to catch your animal's attention.

We've never tried these DVDs ourselves, so we truly cannot recommend for or against individual programs. In general, a video made for dogs could be a good idea for a dog that stays alone for hours while his owners work. Anything that stimulates your dog's mind during the day in a productive fashion could be good for him. And stimuli that focus the mind tend to make dogs healthier. This is especially true for senior dogs that have lost some of their joie de vivre, or nervous dogs that may slip into the behaviors of separation anxiety if left unoccupied for too long.

So, why not try video programming made for dogs while you are home and watch your dog's reaction? If he focuses on the video and seems to enjoy it, you can play it for him when he's alone. Keep the volume relatively low and leave the dog somewhere else to go if he wants to exit the show. Spy on him with a hidden camera if you own one. Or simply observe if his demeanor seems more balanced on days when he's watched the show. Since you can buy "doggie videos" for ten to twenty dollars apiece, there doesn't seem to be much risk in trying them.

Party in the Storm
- this party is actually an intervention for thunderstorm fear -

As home trainers, we frequently treat cases of thunderstorm anxiety in dogs. This phobia often becomes worse over time, with some of the worst suffering happening in dogs' senior years. The intensity of thunderstorm anxiety can be mild, but some cases are so severe that the dog may seriously injure itself trying to escape to a place it perceives as safety. Owners may feel deeply distressed watching their dogs' misery but, unfortunately, this is one disorder where well-meaning owners can actually contribute to the problem.

For cases of storm anxiety that are not too serious, this intervention alone can sometimes help.

Storm anxiety is a serious emotional disorder, and we could easily devote a whole book to it. For the time being, one good book to consult to learn more about cures for storm anxiety and other fears, and products that may assist you is *Help for Your Fearful Dog* by Nicole Wilde (see Books in Resources). Storm anxiety can sometimes become so serious that veterinarians prescribe medication. And a complete behavioral assessment may be necessary to properly diagnose the causes and solutions to your dog's unique problem, so owners may wish to consult a highly qualified behaviorist who specializes in kind treatment of fear disorders.

Even though we can't come to all our readers' homes, nor make a diagnosis in a book, we can safely tell you that **the more anxious you act when you see your dog upset during a storm, the worse it can make your dog's problem.** Let's say your dog suffers from only a mild case of storm anxiety, or he doesn't show specific storm anxiety (yet) but he's quite high-strung and acts nervous around many noises or sudden stimuli, including storms. Counterintuitive as it may seem, the best thing you can do is to present as a strong pack leader, rather than acting worried and filled with pity. Show that you are completely relaxed and in control during the storm and lead your dog in positive activities as alternatives to the old fear-centered behavior.

The intervention in this section is only meant to work if your dog 's problem is mild. **If you catch the fear early enough, you can actually change the feelings your dog associates with storms by always using the start of a storm as a cue to have a party.** Start at the very first signs of the storm, before it's in full-force, get the family together and put on some upbeat music. It also helps to have another well-adjusted dog present to model relaxed behavior. Now you'll use various positive activities to get your dog's mind focused away from the storm.

For example, you can practice your dog's obedience commands or favorite tricks (you'll find many in this book). As the dog effectively performs the obedience routine or tricks, concentrating on your commands rather than the thunderstorm, reward and praise him lavishly. Include some physical activities like jumping over a baton (see this chapter), through a hoop (see "Ring of Fire", Chapter 9), or "Agility Inside" (see Chapter 5). **Activities that involve both the dog's mind and his body will best distract from the bad weather outside, and your dog won't have as much pent up energy to expend on his anxiety.**

Calmly praise your dog as he performs obedience and tricks. Don't show him any anxiety and don't focus on the storm outside. This is no time to be dignified. Play with your dog and act a little silly to get his attention. Break out your dog's absolute favorite toys only at storm time because, if you leave toys out constantly, they'll lose some of their novelty and appeal. Also try interactive toys, including toys that make noise, toys that wiggle or shiver or toys filled with treats (see "Interactive Toys", Chapter 9).

While you want to reward your dog's healthy behavior during the storm, one thing you do *not* want to do is inadvertently reward his anxiety by petting him when he's shivering or panting or he's showing other noticeable signs of distress. And *you* should never sound distressed by crying over him and repeating things like, "Poor baby." **Any distress you show will only heighten your dog's anxiety.** If you're not good at appearing confident or upbeat when your dog's upset or if *you* ever get nervous during bad storms, this would be a time for you not to interact with your dog and instead ask a more relaxed family member to occupy him during the storm.

If "Party in the Storm" seems to be helping, repeat it each time there's a thunderstorm, and make sure all family members are onboard. If you have to leave your dog alone during a storm, you can leave the same pleasant music playing and make sure to give him a comfortable place to retreat to. For example, a special bed inside a laundry room, bathroom or pantry may make some dogs feel more secure. Include his interactive toys (especially something like Kong Time (see this chapter) that is "time released"). And make sure to exercise your dog well before leaving him alone.

Practicing "Party in the Storm" is good for every dog. But, if your dog's thunderstorm fear is severe, threatens his safety or doesn't respond to this simple intervention, you should consult a qualified animal behaviorist and/or your veterinarian.

Show the Puppy Obedience
- help your older dog teach your new pup good behavior early, or you may regret it later -

Some owners are extremely lucky. They buy a new puppy hoping to put the spark back in their lackluster older dog's life and it actually works! In these lucky households, the dogs get along wonderfully and the senior dog does indeed perk up. But other owners try the same tactic and it backfires horribly. Sometimes a puppy's constant playfulness can bother a senior dog. This is especially true if the older dog suffers from serious physical problems like arthritis or if the dogs are badly matched in size and breed. Although dogs are social animals, and your elderly dog probably enjoys company, a younger dog suddenly joining the household could stress him. So owners considering adding a puppy should consider carefully, since the pup's effect on the senior is not guaranteed.

The effect your older dog will have on the new puppy is more predictable- the puppy will learn from him. This is how wolves learn in the wild, and it's hardwired into your older dog to teach and guide the puppy. The problem is, if your older dog is spoiled mischievous, defiant or dirty your pup will likely copy his habits. If your older dog is well-mannered and obedient, this will also rub off on the pup.

Since dogs are pack animals, they are constantly affected by other dogs in the home. Sometimes a stable older dog in the household is enough to help a newly adopted dog with serious emotional problems, or one that is recovering from past abuses. In some cases a puppy can be so rambunctious that his pestering stresses a frail elderly dog. But in other cases, guiding the new pup in his habits makes your older dog feel proud he has a job to do and just may give him that new lease on life you were looking for. It's also a lot easier for you to teach your new pup obedience when your older dog shows him every command first.

A few chapters back, we told you that you should practice a little bit of obedience every day of your dog's life. And this is a case where it will definitely pay off. Practice obedience with your older dog, and your tiny puppy will sometimes mimic the commands on his own- an incredibly cute sight to observe. Teaching the pup obedience will be so much easier when he's already watched your older dog happily obeying you.

Your multi-dog household will proceed in much smoother harmony if your older dog is obedient and well-mannered. And you may even notice him gently stopping the pup from bad behavior on his own! Life with a senior dog and a younger puppy *can* be a joy. If you notice your senior dog modeling good behavior, and the pup imitating, not only will you have reason to feel happy and proud- so will your senior dog.

More Learning Every Day (for Senior Dogs)
**-   however you do it, this makes an enormous difference
in your older dog's quality of life -**

Studies have shown that a good way for people to avoid senile dementia and retain memory and even IQ in their senior years is to exercise their minds and their memory. Experts suggest older people take adult education classes and work on challenging games and puzzles (like the *New York Times* crossword) every day. Seniors can also benefit from challenging hobbies and continuing their career skills by volunteering or consulting. And all these activities that keep seniors engaged benefit overall health and immunity in addition to mental faculties.

Just like humans, dogs can also experience diminishing mental faculties in their extreme old age, as well as problems in the senses and physical performance. Unfortunately, owners sometimes make these problems worse by "forgetting" their senior dog, and no longer including him in activities that were the norm in his youth. This is often due to a well-meaning owner who thinks that the physical activities the dog grew up with might be too demanding.

Owners sometimes get a new puppy when they fear their older dog will soon pass away and inadvertently they focus all their attention on the new pup. This is especially true if the puppy causes problems and the senior dog is well behaved. It's easy to think your older dog doesn't need attention if he's trained by years of doing exactly what you want in perfect sync with your lifestyle and if he seems to prefer spending his time lying around serenely. But, even though your geriatric dog may no longer be able to tolerate the strong stimuli he enjoyed when he was younger; and even though he may sometimes feel a little creaky and cranky and need an afternoon nap to rest up, he still needs stimuli and he still needs your attention! In fact, the amount you engage your older dog and stimulate his mind may make all the difference in his quality of life in his golden years!

From this moment on, think of your dog as an "active senior" with lots to still contribute to the world and lots to still teach you. With respect for any real physical limitations, start planning his days accordingly. Give your senior dog real tasks to perform for you, just as you would a younger dog. Choose tasks that don't demand as much brawn as they do wisdom, and activities that suit the unique talents he's displayed over the years. Keep him as physically active as possible in accordance with your veterinarian's recommendations. Include gentle daily grooming. And if your vet okays it, try daily massage (see the section in this chapter and see Resources) to stimulate his nerves and to keep his joints limber.

And go all out stimulating his mind. We recommend a new learning experience a day for every dog. If you haven't done this with your dog as a puppy, you can start now that he's already a senior. (See "New Learning Every Day" in Chapter 3, for suggested activities.)Your dog's mood may perk up immediately with the first learning experience you give him, starting right now. A task or learning experience could be anything new as long as it's health promoting and preferably has some real-world use (for example, many of the activities in this book.)

Your dog's new experience for the day could be learning a new word, or properly meeting and greeting a new person. It could be taking a successful walk in a new environment, learning a trick or an obedience command or playing with a new, mentally stimulating toy. By disciplining yourself to teach something entirely new each and every day of your dog's life, you will make his mind sharp and avoid "useless dog syndrome", a root cause of many behavior problems, anxiety disorders and psychosomatic ailments.

Watching your older dog prance around, proud of himself again, is an incredibly joyous experience. And, since you are formally scheduling yourself to spend a little quality time with him each day, you never have to worry about the myriad chores and tasks in today's busy lifestyle intruding. Family members can even take a little time together planning what they will teach the family dog the next day and then everyone can take turns teaching new tasks on different days of the week. Not only will these new activities make life more enjoyable for your dog, they will likely also remind the family members how much fun spending time with the dog can be.

Visit With Seniors (Therapy Dog)
- volunteer work helps keep some gregarious senior dogs active & involved -

You can find a more complete description of therapy dog work in the "Volunteer Your Dog" section in Chapter 12, Useful Games. And also see Resources for links to additional information.

You may have already heard about the emotional and health benefits to seniors when therapy dogs visit them in a nursing home setting. If you know a bit about therapy dogs, you may also know that some keep on working well into their own senior years- sometimes until the end of their lives. For the right dog, visiting elderly or sick humans to brighten their days also brightens the dog's days, giving him a sense of purpose. So imagine your older dog in an interesting scenario- cheering up older people.

If your dog is already working happily as a therapy dog, there's probably no reason not to let him keep working. Some older dogs do develop physical ailments, like arthritis or hearing or vision problems that might make petting feel annoying or uncomfortable. And intense handling might damage some frail dogs, so these dogs are forced to retire. Other dogs can continue their therapy work with slight changes. For example, as he gets older, you might switch your dog from working with children to working with the elderly or you might have him make his hospital or nursing home visits less frequently. Even if your senior dog no longer visits facilities on an official basis, you can still bring him on visits to elderly neighbors or relatives to cheer them up while making him still feel useful.

Most therapy dogs start their careers relatively early, but a dog could start at any age provided he is in good health, displays the right temperament and passes a test showing he is friendly and handles well around humans. You might be surprised that, in some cases, starting a therapy career gets a dog past a mid-life crisis and starts the most vibrant phase of his life. If you are also retired, yet in good health, this is another indicator that therapy dog work might be good for you to try. And the very best fit of all may be a senior dog, senior handler and seniors receiving the visits.

Therapy dog work is not highly physically demanding, but it engages a dog mentally and emotionally to a high degree. Seniors in a nursing home that receive the visits will likely feel inspired by your spirited old guy or girl still coming to see them with a wagging tail and possibly even demonstrating tricks or obedience to varied commands. In return, the seniors will give your dog lots of love and appreciation in a relatively relaxed setting. If you wish to volunteer, or work with, your dog as a therapy dog, a good place to start reading is the book *Therapy Dogs, Teaching Your Dog to Reach Others* by Kathy Diamond Davis (see Books in Resources). You can also find many resources on the Internet, including Therapy Dogs International (www. tdi-dog.org) and the Delta Society. (www.deltasociety.org).

Even if you don't formally use your dog in any kind of therapy work, think about the same concept informally, and some wonderful doors may open. Perhaps you have an older dog that you leave alone all day while you work, and he seems to be showing less vitality and interest in life. Perhaps you also have a nearby senior relative or senior neighbor who always compliments and pets your dog when you meet on the street. Maybe the two could get together for a visit every now and then and this could bring joy to both.

It's even possible that the senior you know would like to babysit for your dog sometimes when you are away. Maybe they don't want the full-time responsibility of caring for a dog, but watching your dog occasionally might fit their needs and abilities perfectly. You might pay your senior acquaintance for watching your dog; you might exchange favors or barter with them. Or you might just let your older dog visit with your senior neighbor for a few hours every now and then just for fun. The older person might cherish the companionship, your dog will find it fun and you won't have to feel guilty while you rush your kids to ballgames, go shopping in a distant town or engage in any prolonged Saturday schedule where your older dog couldn't accompany you.

> *Stairs are a low cost way to improve your dog's quality of life. Every home with a senior dog should own these. They also help with large dogs, small dogs & dogs with physical problems.*

Doggie Stairs (therapeutic for dogs)
- essential for homes with older or special needs dogs; buy them now to be safe!

What a wonderful invention! These little sets of carpeted stairs are available for sale in pet stores, over the Internet or on

TV, with prices starting at approximately $20 or even less (see Resources). Don't use doggie stairs to help your dog onto your bed if you do not want him to sleep there! Otherwise, these stairs are a miraculous help with senior dogs, small toy dogs, overweight dogs, puppies and dogs with joint disorders or other disabilities. They can help dogs with limited mobility get up on furniture, climb into your SUV or help them navigate any area in the house or yard where they would usually have to jump. Most importantly, these stairs provide your dog independence, because he can jump up and down without injuring himself. Doggie stairs may be just the thing to help your senior dog continue his former level of functioning despite arthritis or joint problems. You could also fashion a single step for your dog anyplace it's needed in the house. Just make sure that it is sturdy and does not slip.

A Change of Scene
- with proper caution, this could make the senior years the best time of some dogs' lives-

Have you ever considered applying the old adage, "A change of scene does wonders" to your older dog and his quality of life? It's true that your older dog may not show as much interest in the vigorous activities he used to enjoy. And he may even seem a bit grumpy or nervous or just plain tired and disinterested if you impulsively take him to a place he used to enjoy in his youth, like the park or beach. One reason for a negative reaction like this may be that you've let him lie around the house for so long and this has become his routine.

Another reason is that senior dogs, just like elderly people, may not feel their greatest every day or at every time of day. (Your dog may need more sleep than he used to or he may need to rest much more frequently after exertion.) Diminished senses might leave him feeling vulnerable around stressful stimuli like traffic or other dogs. Or he may have simply gotten accustomed to the constant routine of hanging around the home and, just like a puppy, he may need time to acclimate to the new place. If your senior dog shows negative symptoms around new things, it's all the more reason to get him out of the house every now and then.

Take him somewhere wonderful! As long as his health allows, you can even take him on a luxury vacation! It's easy to find lists of luxury human hotels that also specialize in pampering dogs on the Internet. Or read some of the newer magazines (like Fido Friendly) devoted to the subject.

Of course you want to follow reasonable cautions when taking your senior pet to new places, whether just around the corner or halfway across the globe. First **check with your veterinarian about your pet's ability to travel, and use common sense. Any trip will be somewhat taxing to your dog, so you have to weigh the benefit of the positive stimuli versus the exhaustion or stress factor. Never expose any dog to extremely hot weather during travel.** You may have to plan your entire vacation around your dog, but many owners are happy to do this. Dogs with chronic illness may not be able to travel by airplane at all, and susceptible dogs may be stressed by long car trips.

For older dogs with real health problems or dogs that have never done well with travel, we suggest you **keep trips short. You could simply take your dog on a short walk to the corner café, a five-minute ride to visit friends or a laid-back visit with nearby relatives.**

If your dog tolerates travel a little better, **you can try day trips**, rather than overnight journeys. But always plan ahead. Travel only during moderate weather, and map out pleasant stopping places (*not* hectic rest areas) for your dog to take breaks.

Pack cushiony bedding for arthritic joints, a comfortable containment method like a (soft sided) pop-up crate (for travel only), medications, treats and lots of water. A collapsible wire-style playpen is handy so your dog can rest, while still taking in scents and scenery in areas like beach pullovers and mountain overlooks. It also keeps unwanted strangers from forcing their petting on your dog! Too many encounters with new people could stress him when traveling. Exposure to brand new places also intensifies the effects of any exercise, so don't overdo.

If you are traveling a distance out of town, carry numbers for 24-hour emergency veterinarians in the area(s) you'll be visiting. And **plan every aspect of the trip carefully so every stop is a true pleasure to your dog. Maybe he's never seen a beautiful beach and this may be his last opportunity. Signs he's enjoying the adventure may include an inquisitively twitching nose, a waving tail, sparkling eyes and a grinning "doggie-smile".**

You know your dog well enough after all the years to judge if he's truly stressed. And, **if your dog is seriously stressed or deeply exhausted at any time during your journey, you may have to leave the particular venue. If he doesn't recover in a reasonable amount of time, you might have to terminate the entire trip.** But if your dog seems just mildly apprehensive, this can actually be a good sign. **Help him to explore at his own speed and build his confidence. Just the experience of mastering the new place may perk up his life at home for months.**

Meeting a few new dog-loving people, or even a few friendly dogs, can be an enjoyable part of your vacation. But these encounters can be highly stressful as well as exciting, so they are best in miniscule doses! Don't throw in too many human and dog meetings on a road trip. Meetings like this are best reserved for the half-hour jaunts closer to home. So you don't throw too many things at your dog at once, plan your road trip to include only the most relaxed and uncrowded parks, lakes, forests, fields and scenic downtowns. Or stop along the way at homes of friends and relatives who you know will make your pet feel pampered.

Don't go anywhere your dog could encounter lots of animal excrement. **And never take a senior dog to a public off-leash dog park**, especially in an unfamiliar community! Don't expose your senior dog to hot sun or marshy water that might host bacteria, dangerous algae, protozoa or mosquitoes. And be careful also of ticks in long grass. Any danger a younger dog is susceptible to can affect a senior dog more strongly.

Travel overseas could be dangerously stressful to a frail senior dog, and so can airline travel in general. In limited instances where the dog is healthy and already a seasoned world traveler, you may be able to take the risk. But make sure there's no chance your dog will encounter dangerous stressors like any quarantine situation during the trip. **Never transport older dogs as cargo**, except in a true dire emergency! If your dog is too large to travel as carry-on in your lap, you cannot justify making him ride in the cargo section just for vacation! Even though there are strict rules governing transport of animals on airlines, your dog will still encounter uncomfortable temperatures, odors, noise and vibration. He'll likely feel lonely and terrified and a trip like this will definitely stress him more than the vacation will bring him pleasure. The same is true if your dog gets so agitated during travel that you have to medicate him.

Once you've decided to travel with your dog, the great news is that the world has become much more "dog-friendly". Publications and guides feature venues of every price range that welcome pets. And some luxury hotels cater to pets in creative ways. No matter your vacation budget, we suggest you go as upscale as possible to provide pleasure and stimuli for your senior pet.

Even if you can't take your senior dog on a vacation, you can take him on a special outing just to the other side of town. Just choose somewhere delightful that your pet has never seen before. Your dog may like the autumn leaves near a country farm stand or wading on the edge of the ocean at sunset. Maybe he'll enjoy his first-in-a-lifetime dog massage at an upscale dog spa or maybe the chef at the new dog-friendly café will come out and treat him to a cookie. Years ago, some of these places didn't even exist, so why not treat your older dog to something new!

But never take your senior dog somewhere that could terrify him. All dogs like routine, so new stimuli should come in just the right dose and intensity. For example, **there's no excuse to take any dog to a fireworks event** or any event that includes loud amplified music. Dogs have a much lower threshold of loud than we do and these noises are seriously painful and traumatic to dogs, even if they don't show it.

Moderation is always the best idea. Some dogs enjoy short drives just for the sake of driving, but don't make trips all driving without frequent stops, or you may have a carsick and confused older pet. Don't set your dog down in an unfamiliar place where traffic whizzes past. And be cautious about massive street fairs and art and craft shows, even though they *seem* like good places to take dogs. A few extremely small art shows or charity events in ideal springtime or autumn weather might be pleasant for your dog. And *a minority* of dog-focused charity events might be small and calm enough to afford your fragile older dog a pleasant day. **But the majority of craft fairs, community celebrations and large dog-themed charity events are practically designed to give your older dog a heart attack!**

Hordes of people jostling in the hot sun plus the bombardment of noise and strange odors overburden a frail dog's senses. The next time you see a well-intentioned owner prancing a tired, stressed or nervous looking animal around at such an event, you might tactfully educate them about alternative *calm* venues in the same city that already have your dog's stamp of approval.

Help His Comrades
- observe your dog with weaker pack members; some dogs surprise you with their helpfulness -

There are some activities you can teach a dog, but others depend upon that dog's natural talents and disposition and we believe owners should encourage their dogs to achieve their highest potential. So never underestimate your dog's capabilities! One example of dogs acting like heroes is the way certain special dogs will help their weaker canine pack members. Perhaps one of your dogs is elderly and suffering from failing faculties like eyesight or sense of smell. You may notice that your other dog helps him- walking shoulder to shoulder to lead him to his food bowl, for example, or to a nice spot to lie down in the sun. Just like a dog can act as a "seeing-eye dog" for a human, he can help another canine, as well. If the older dog is weak or recovering from surgery, the "caretaker" dog may choose to bring him a toy, or whine to encourage him to get him up and moving.

The tendency for a dog to help a weaker dog when he needs it reflects canines helping each other in the wild in particular circumstances. For example, if several wolves are hunting a moose and the moose hits one with an antler, leaving him dizzy and vulnerable, the wolf's brother may distract the moose, deliberately leading him away until the injured brother can recover his strength or get to safety. And, of course, in the wild all dogs in a pack have some responsibility for taking care of the vulnerable pups.

When your thriving adult dog shows signs of taking care of your failing older dog, he may be like a wolf helping his physically frail, but still mentally strong, pack leader. Or he may be taking the adult role and helping the older dog as he would a helpless pup.

But canines in the wild are not always kind to ailing members of their families! In fact, in the wild, wolves and wild dogs often leave extremely weak pack members to die. And it's common for them to challenge the ailing individual in a fight for dominance. If an older pack leader fights, but loses, he may then be killed by the members of his family. Unlike humans, wild dogs and wolves cannot support chronically ill animals, since their lack of productivity and inability to escape danger may lead to the whole pack's demise. Humans looking on wolves or wild dogs may judge these actions to be unmerciful or unsentimental. But this is just the way of nature.

Your stronger dog at home may fall anywhere on the continuum when it comes to helping weaker dogs, and you may be surprised at how he acts. So **be cautious. If your older dog shows signs of failing, he and your younger dog, especially if they are intact animals of the same sex, may start brutally fighting.** You may be surprised at how cruelly your younger dog attacks the older, ill dog. Sometimes such fights may stop once a new hierarchy is established. Other times, your ailing dog, the former "pack leader", may really be in danger. The human may have to step in to establish a stronger dominance themselves, or seek the help of a professional experienced with dog on dog aggression.

The most likely scenario you can expect is something in between- no brutality, but no nurturing either. Your older dog may still try to play and keep up with your younger dogs no matter how weak he is, while your other dogs will likely ignore him and make no accommodations for the slipping of his health.

But it's possible that you own that special third kind of dog- the type that will step in and make your senior dog's last years pleasant and worth living by helping him. Even more so than the human owner, your younger dog may know instinctively just what is needed to help the older dog. He can lead the older dog if the dog is blind, choose the safest paths for delicate bones and defend the older dog from everyday dangers in the environment- like snakes, bees, hawks or even the claw of a feral cat concealed in the bushes. Your stronger dog can lick the weaker dog to groom an untended coat, massage away aches and pains or stimulate failing senses. He can also alert the owner when the compromised dog needs immediate medical help. Would you trust your ill or infirm dog with such a caretaker? You certainly should!

If you are a lucky owner whose dog decides he wants to take care of your older dog, go ahead and do everything to encourage the caretaker's behavior. Praise him, and by all means listen to him if he whines or barks oddly- perhaps trying to alert you that the older dog needs emergency help. Give your caretaker dog an honored position in the household. This is no time to deny him access to any room, or to lock him out of the house when the older dog needs him. **Of course, no dog should spend his days crated, and certainly not this "caretaker" who will provide real help to the other animal while you are away**.

But make sure that your caretaker dog doesn't devote all his time to the older dog so obsessively that he forgets his own needs. Give him food, water and time to play. Show him that you "get" what he's doing, and make clear that you are participating as a team in the older dog's care, so that he will not become too worried nor too defensive of the other dog.

Some herding dogs, bred to watch over livestock, may particularly show this type of concern for other animals, and some large dogs with sweet temperaments, especially those bred for rescue, may act as caretakers for a small dog that needs help. But the fact is, there is no absolute predictor for which dogs will show concern for their "wounded" comrades and which will turn away carelessly or even attack the weaker dog. If you are lucky enough to have a dog that volunteers for the role of caretaker, by all means recognize it, encourage it- and feel blessed!

Doggie Wheelchair
- don't give up. Innovative products help mobility-impaired dogs regain quality of life -

One of the greatest benefits of being a dog owner in the millennium is the variety of sophisticated equipment that's readily available for purchase. And one piece of equipment that's a godsend for dogs and those with disabilities is the "doggie wheelchair". Various models are available from different manufacturers, and they function just as a wheelchair or a scooter would for a human with difficulty walking. A wheelchair can be used for dogs with an amputation of one or both hind legs, dogs recovering from surgery or dogs that suffer from severe arthritis or hip dysplasia.

A wheelchair is indicated for dogs that are completely unable to walk, and also for dogs that will damage themselves further if they walk unsupported. Disorders that interfere with walking that might have been a death sentence years ago are now viewed differently by enlightened dog owners. Many owners will pay for involved surgery and will then be willing to follow through with whatever type of rehabilitation their dog requires. A wheelchair can aid in this rehabilitation because, after surgery saves the dog's life, the wheelchair can give the dog much of the pleasure of its life back. Since the dog is able to move around and exercise with the wheelchair, it also helps the blood circulate and promotes health and healing.

If your veterinarian treats your dog or does surgery, he may recommend a certain brand of wheelchair. One company we found advertised in the pages of *Dog Fancy* magazine was Doggon' Wheels, www.doggon.com. You can also search the Internet for other companies and see our Resources section. The company that sells you the wheelchair should give you general instructions for usage, and you will also want to cooperate with your veterinarian and your dog's care providers to use the wheelchair for his exact medical circumstance.

Acclimate your dog slowly, in a positive fashion. If your dog has difficultly acclimating, consult again with your veterinarian to make sure it is not a physical problem or a problem with the equipment. If it is not, you may want to consult with a professional, such as a trainer with experience working with dogs with physical barriers, to first start your dog exercising with his wheelchair.

Ch. 10- Activities for High-Energy Dogs

"Finding the right activity for high-energy dogs makes life a joy for owners with diverse needs."

Introduction

Agility

Doggie Treadmill (for conditioning)

Fetch

Frisbee

Monkey-in-the-Middle

All-Terrain Run

Hiking

Backpacking (for conditioning)

Run in Snow

Snow Games

Retrieving in the Water

Race

Weave Poles

Water Run

Hurdles

Sand Run

Ocean Swim

Picture Windows (Caution)

Flyball

Rally Competition

Biking With Your Dog (With Caution)

Skateboarding with Your Dog (With Caution)

Rollerblading with Your Dog (With Caution)

Driving With Your Dog without Him in the Car (With Caution)

AKC-Sanctioned Events (Field Trials, Tracking, Hunting Trials, Herding Trials, Lure Coursing)

Also Try These Ideas from Other Chapters for High-Energy Dogs:

Puppy Games & Activities: Find the Treat, Soccer, How Do I Get What's In There?, Walk This Way, Obedience-minded (Note: Some breeds of puppies, including giant breeds, shouldn't engage in intense physical activity, especially jumping. Check with your veterinarian to determine what type of intense exercise is safe for your pup.)

Mental Games & Activities: Watch Me, Wait, Hold That Position, Move Slow, Ring Toss

Indoor Games & Activities: Hide & Go Seek, Agility Inside, Dancing Dog (Freestyle), A Room of His Own, Doggie Gymnasium, Basketball

Balance & Coordination Activities: Will the Real Dog Stand?, Walk the Line, Walk Like a Man, Be a Parrot, Catch the Frisbee, Walk the Plank, Teeter Totter, Double Hoops

Multi-Dog Games & Activities: Duck/Duck/Goose, Simon Says, The Long, Long Stay, Obedience Competition at Home, Agility Competition at Home, Rally, Under/Over, Limbo

Problem Dog Games: Catch, Ring of Fire, Take a Bow, In the Army Crawl, When I Move You Move, Interactive Toys, Wacky Walking

Therapeutic & Senior Dog Activities: Massage, Meditation, Stretching, Swim, Talking Toys, Kong Time, Help His Comrades (with caution)

Water Activities: Continuous Pool, Chase the Hose, Submarine, Dog's Own Pool, Net Pull, Water Fetch

Useful Activities: Find My Keys, Wagon Pull, Sled Dog, Pack Animal, Sled Dog, Check the Perimeter, Find the Missing Person, Bark for Help, Be a Lifeguard, Work With Livestock, Personal Bodyguard, Real Dog Careers (some), Lifesaver

Family Activities: Jump Rope, Circle of Love, Rally at Home, Races, Doggie Playground, Demonstrate Tricks, Petstar at Home, Jump Over

Activities for Owners with Limited Mobility: Long Lead, Ball Launcher, Dog Walker, Bubbles, Balloons, Play in the Snow, Doggie Daycare (with caution), Service Dog (possible), Borrow a Child (with caution), Obedience/Agility Clubs, Try on a Dog, Be Creative

Activities for High Energy Dogs - Introduction
"Finding the right activities for high energy dogs makes life a joy for owners with diverse needs"

There are two types of owners who should particularly concentrate on this chapter. The first are the proud owners of high-energy dogs. And the second are "accidental" owners. Those of you who personally related to Marley the Labrador's wild escapades in the immensely popular book and movie versions of *Marley and Me* can certainly understand this feeling. So can the owners who describe their dog as "like a hurricane", "like a tornado", "bouncing off walls", etc.

Those of you who chose a dog because he "seemed to be mellow in the shelter", only to find yourself knocked off balance by his boundless need to run the second he found himself in a secure home may feel harried and overwhelmed. And you may find it hard to understand why someone would *want* an extremely high-energy dog. But consider the fact that your high energy breed may have been created for a high-exertion task like herding cattle or sheep, retrieving game for hunters, pulling sleds, rescue work or police work. These dogs' fitness and power is magnificent when you watch them in action performing the task they were bred for. They are meant to be athletes.

Uninitiated owners of working or sporting breeds should take time to go to all-breed dog shows, speak to breeders and observe agility competitions and herding or hunting trials if at all possible. A knowledgeable breeder might even introduce you to a farmer or rancher who will allow you to watch your breed of dog working. Many champion show dogs also work full-time, often on ranches with livestock, and they are splendid to behold in action.

Owners who purposely selected high-energy breeds will understand that keeping your dog in good condition is likely a priority. You probably know a lot about the breed and are prepared to devote a good amount of time and energy to exercising your dog. Provided there are no medical limitations, high-energy dogs should be kept fit and their athleticism should be encouraged. So we encourage any activities that are safe, consistent and enjoyable for you and your dog. (Just avoid being a "Weekend Warrior", as described in Chapter 15, Dangerous Games.)

Many ideas in this chapter are novel enough to break up boredom, exercise new muscle groups and encourage the dog/owner bond. And you might want to take your dog's fitness to the next level and use him for work. As long as you practice good husbandry, a true working lifestyle can be the most fulfilling for very many breeds of dogs. And we applaud you for being able to provide this lifestyle to your dog in this high-tech day and age.

Other owners may exercise their high-energy dogs frequently, but they may live in metropolitan areas and feel saddened that their dog may never herd or retrieve anything more than a tennis ball. This is the time to explore novel options like Earthdog, hunting or tracking trials, Agility or Flyball competitions (see Resources). Some owners even pay ranchers to teach their dogs to herd.

This chapter also includes enough varied terrain and X-treme sports to challenge physically fit, adrenalin-driven owners. If you select the right breed, your dog will always be beside you, up for another outdoor sporting adventure. As long as you take proper care of your dog's health and prevent injury, you can shape him into the true athlete he was meant to be!

In contrast, other owners aren't so physically fit. Maybe you chose an athletic breed to "force" you to get up and exercise or to occupy your active kids. But you may not have understood exactly what you were getting into. The dog may act so wild that you feel unable to exercise with him or he and your kids may be in constant conflict. Other owners may have been told the breed they decided to adopt was "active" but may not have fully understood how much exercise the dog required.

Wolves travel over thirty miles a day while hunting. And your high-energy breed is likely to require at least one hour of running or the equivalent every day, if not much more. You should check with your veterinarian, read up extensively on your breed and contact several reputable breeders for additional recommendations about exercise.

Some owners might have hesitated before buying or adopting a particular breed if they had researched this extensively beforehand. Average suburban families usually do better with *medium* energy dogs, since they have trouble providing the extreme everyday exercise that *true* high-energy breeds require. Space is also a challenge. If you have a small yard or no yard at all, you will have to get creative and make an extra effort, since many active dogs were bred to work on large properties.

The first step towards improving things is to know your dog's true exercise needs. If you're committed to making your family more physically fit as well, now is the time to work some of the high-energy activities in this chapter into your family's schedule. If time is a problem, we suggest activities like swimming and the treadmill as shortcuts for more concentrated workouts than walking or running.

Mental challenges can also make your dog's workouts more intense. For example, because of the intense mental focus required, agility practice may be all the exercise your dog needs on a given day. As your family makes activity with your dog a bigger priority, you should start experiencing more of the family fun you craved when you bought him.

But what if you're the third category of owner? What if you are completely inactive and you had no idea that the particular dog you chose would need extreme exercise every day? Maybe you adopted the dog from a shelter or from an online ad that referred to him as "highly playful". Or you may have bought a tiny puppy from a pet shop, knowing nothing about his breed. Maybe you couldn't resist because you thought the dog was adorable, or maybe you hoped to save him from a terrible destiny. But now the dog's energy needs have your family's life in turmoil and you feel helpless, with literally no idea of what to do.

The list of the extremely high-energy breeds is long, and it starts with Labrador Retrievers, the most popular dogs in America, and Lab mixes. Also extremely high energy are: Pit Bulls and Pit mixes; other retrievers; most herding dogs, including German Shepherds and Border Collies; many hounds and sporting dogs; many working dogs, notably Boxers and Dobermans; most sled dogs and most terriers, in particular highly popular Jack Russells. These breeds and mixes may sound familiar- because these may have been the most common breeds you saw in the shelter on the day you adopted your dog. And this is not a coincidence, since many owners drop these breeds in shelters when they interpret the animal's simple physical frustration as uncontrollable behavioral illness.

Many of the high energy breeds are also somewhat large, and owners frequently give up when they feel they can't handle them. But when you choose to rescue a dog, you also take on his energy needs. Even if you already own the dog, you should go back and research his breed or breeds' exercise needs now. Then if you have the physical ability, try some of the high-energy activities suggested in this chapter with your dog. You may be surprised at how good it feels to get out in nature and give this breed of dog the kind of activity he thrives on.

If you don't have a lot of energy or if you have some physical challenges, you can try less demanding games from other chapters like Chapter 14, Activities for Owners with Limited Mobility; Chapter 9, Therapeutic & Senior Dog Activities and Chapter 5, Indoor Games & Activities. Novel ideas can be the perfect compromise for you and your dog, and many of the activities in this book are designed to provide a good workout for the dog with almost zero exertion for the owner. And don't be afraid to ask for help. A trainer and/or veterinarian may be able to educate you better about your dog's exact exercise requirements. You can also hire a dog walker specifically to provide a complete workout every day. Or you may have friends or family members who'd be happy to run around and play games with your dog.

> *Some owners might not have chosen a particular breed if they fully researched the breed's daily exercise needs. Average suburban families, even if they are active, usually do best with medium energy dogs, since they have trouble providing the extreme everyday exercise that true high-energy breeds require. If space is also a challenge, you may have to get creative to make the most of your dog's energy and start relating to him more positively.*

Focus on the positive, marvel at your dog's athletic feats and, don't forget, dogs know nothing about Primetime, and slumping in front of the television is no dog's idea of fulfillment!

Activities for High-Energy Dogs

Agility
- fast-paced obstacle competition burns energy & builds teamwork with owners -

Formal agility competition is *the* hot event for owners of high energy dogs. It was first seen at the Crufts dog show in 1978 with only two teams competing. John Varley, a member of the show committee, devised the competition as a way to keep the public's attention during a break in the show, and the first AKC agility event was held in 1994. Agility has now become immensely popular, with more and more dogs competing in ever increasing venues. Agility competitions take place at most dog shows and there are also many agility-only competitions, with clubs all around the country and the world.

Competing in agility events or joining a club is not only for high energy dogs, but also for energetic owners who'd like to have some fun and work with their dog as an efficient team. Great cooperation with your dog is essential if you want to excel at agility competition. You can have the best dog in the world for the event, but if the handler doesn't communicate well with that dog, they will not win at the higher levels.

Some people are so serious about winning in agility competitions that they have been tweaking dog's breeding specifically for dogs to be great at this event; but according to rules, any AKC breed can compete. Some breeds of dogs are physically more likely to excel because of their physiology, but any purebred can participate and even win in the AKC events. And even if your dog is a mixed-breed, many clubs other than AKC will allow him to compete.

Some of the most popular breeds commonly entered in agility are high-energy with a very strong need to please their owners. Some of the best known breeds for the event include Border Collies and Australian Shepherds. Ironically, as home dog trainers we often see these same breeds presenting with behavior problems because of lack of exercise even though they are bred to want to please their owners.

The reason these breeds can have such wonderful traits, yet still present such a challenge, is because they were bred in particular to have a job to do in life and because they are so well suited to working. The highly involved task of herding sheep all day long according to handlers' instructions has been taken away from these breeds in our modern world. But the physically and mentally challenging sport of agility can reduce frustration and once again give the dogs a purpose.

In agility competition, your dog performs many instinctive activities he probably already loves to do, including jumping, running and climbing. The event is judged on speed and accuracy and some of the obstacles can be tricky. But each obstacle gives dogs and handlers the chance to show off particular abilities.

Your dog's experience as he moves through an agility course begins with your dog waiting in a sit/stay at the starting line. Most courses have you first call your dog over a jump or two. Then the order can change for each course. You may send your dog through a tunnel, a line of weave poles and a chute (a tunnel the dog can't see through). He may climb up and down an A-frame, maintain balance on a Teeter Totter and pause on a Stay Box (or table). He'll perform a tire jump and a long jump and sometimes dogs jump over a small wall. With each course a judge sets how the course must be run, times the dogs and decides how well the handler worked with the dogs.

Not only does agility take a lot of energy, it also takes a lot of work at home to train your dog to compete. People sometimes work with their dog for years to make him a stronger competitor. And this is good because every moment working together strengthens the dog/owner bond. Agility practice is also good because a tired dog equals a happy owner!

Even if you don't want to compete in events officially, teaching your dog to run an agility course at home or to use some of the equipment is great for exercise and training. You can also form your own club, or get a group of neighbors or friends together with their dogs to enjoy the sport in a social atmosphere. For more details on agility at home, see "Agility Competition at Home" in Chapter 7, Multi-dog Games; "Agility Inside" in Chapter 5, Indoor Games; and sections in other chapters that detail uses for particular pieces of Agility Equipment. These include "Teeter Totter" and "Tunnel Crawl" in Chapter 6, Balance and Coordination Activities and "Hurdles" in this chapter.

To find out much more about agility, you can go online and Google "agility" or start out with the American Kennel Club (AKC) website (see Resources) and/or sites that sell agility equipment. You can also find books on the topic through your local library or sites like Amazon.com. However you decide to use agility as part of your dog's physical routine, it's lots of fun and a great way to bond with your high-energy dog.

Doggie Treadmill (High-Energy)
- the very best idea to burn excess energy in many cases, but not safe for every dog -

The secret's out. For years, only owners of show dogs regularly exercised their dogs on treadmills to improve the dogs' physical conditioning. And a hundred years ago dogs were actually made to walk on treadmills to provide a power source in sawmills! Thankfully, nobody does that anymore. But today many owners are catching on that walking/running their dogs on treadmills can be the best way to keep their dogs healthy, in great condition and calm and centered rather than wild and frustrated.

Some dogs simply need more physical exercise than the average owner can provide, and you don't have to be embarrassed if your dog is one of them. One notable example of a breed with tremendous exercise needs is the Labrador Retriever- the most popular breed in America. Every single Labrador owner we've served has complained of difficulty providing their dog with sufficient exercise! Another popular breed with unusually high energy requirements is Pit Bulls, or Pit mixes. And the list of energy-intensive dogs goes on and on, including many of the popular hound and herding breeds.

Part of the problem is that many owners are happy to take their high-energy dogs on hour-long walks on a Sunday when they are off from work, but their weekday schedule simply does not provide enough time to do this Monday through Friday. Weather is another very real problem, not just an excuse. Some breeds want so badly to run that they would do it in any weather. But, especially in the Southern and some of the Western states, temperatures along with humidity can get so high that prolonged vigorous exercise could physically damage your dog.

Unfortunately, lack of daily vigorous exercise can make your dog unhappy and emotionally unbalanced and it can even shorten his life span. The treadmill can help with weather or scheduling challenges since ten minutes running on a treadmill can provide similar intensity to forty-five minutes running outside. Using the treadmill also focuses your dog's mind and can help make him calmer and more balanced. It's even better if his beloved pack leader is walking on a treadmill right next to him!

We recommend that owners always acclimate their dogs gradually to the treadmill and then continue to supervise sessions, even once the dog is comfortable on the machine. As long as you keep one eye on the dog when he is exercising, it is okay to do some undemanding multi-tasking, but stay nearby in case of an emergency.

Daily sessions on a treadmill are great for any dog with high exercise needs. And of course the treadmill is appropriate for show dogs or those training for athletic events. As your dog's condition improves, you can gradually increase speed, incline and or length of sessions as tolerated.

If exercising on a treadmill will be an important part of your dog's fitness routine, we recommend you use a treadmill specifically built for dogs (see Resources). These are usually more expensive than human treadmills, but they are designed to contain and protect your dog, so you don't have to supervise quite as carefully. You can also use manual treadmills for dogs. While manual treadmills have some significant drawbacks, you never have to worry about the speed getting away from a dog. For this reason a manual treadmill can be the best choice for highly nervous dogs that are fearful of treadmills when the electricity is running.

For additional information and cautions about exercising your dog on a treadmill, please also see the treadmill section in Chapter 14- Activities Owners with Limited Mobility. Always first check with your veterinarian to clear your dog's health for running on a treadmill.

Fetch
- learn how to play right to keep your dog behaving and obeying, even when you're done -

We all know this game. In fact, for many of us, it's the first game we learn to play with our family dogs when we're kids. Fetch is a great game to play in a limited space to get your dogs nice and tired without exhausting yourself. The way it's supposed to happen is all you have to do is to grab a stick or ball, throw it and then let the dog do all the work.

But sometimes we encounter problems. One example is the dog that watches the ball sail to the far side of the yard or park, and then looks back at us with nothing but suspicion. "What do you want me to do now?" this dog seems to ask. "If you want to throw the ball, then *you* go get it!" This type of dog watches his owner chase after the ball, getting all the exercise. And then he appears to laugh at us if we're silly enough to throw the ball for him a second time, and retrieve it again ourselves when he ignores it. This is obviously a case of a dog teaching an owner how to play fetch!

Even though playing fetch can be a great pleasure, you should follow a few simple safety precautions and just because people commonly play the game certain ways doesn't necessarily make it right. For example, some owners love to throw sticks for their dogs to retrieve, yet this practice can be quite dangerous. We've heard of cases where a stick lodges in the ground, impaling a dog that runs into it! Dogs can also chew the ends of sticks so that splinters lodge in the dog's stomach or esophagus, causing internal bleeding.

And when throwing balls for your dog to fetch, never use tennis balls. Dogs tend to chew on tennis balls, trying to compress them. If a dog makes the ball small enough, the ball could slip into the dog's mouth and then expand again, closing off his throat so he can no longer breathe. So make sure to only play fetch with items large enough that the dog cannot put the whole fetch item in its mouth! Dogs also eat fibers on the outside of tennis balls, causing intestinal blockage. Since traditional tennis balls are so unsafe, you may wonder why you see them in every pet shop. Unfortunately, this is because the balls are popular and most owners are not aware of the danger.

Of course, tennis balls are not the only toy or treat in pet shops that can be unsafe for your dog. It's always the owner's responsibility to be extra cautious, because not every toy can be regulated and not every pet shop owner or employee is aware of the potential dangers of every product.

When you walk through the pet store, you can easily find many safer options than sticks and tennis balls for your dog to fetch. For, example, the same company that makes hard rubber Kong chew toys also makes specific variations intended especially for Fetch, including a rubber Frisbee. Or try a dumbbell (like the kind made for obedience), any large sturdy ball or any toy specifically designed to be safe for dogs that are strong chewers.

If you want "Fetch" to be more enjoyable, teach the game correctly from the start. The best time to teach your dog how to retrieve items is when he's a puppy, but the right technique also works well for older dogs and even for those dogs that usually look at you like you are silly when you throw a ball.

First put your dog on a long leash (20-30 ft), find an item that your dog really likes and toss it a foot or two in front of you. When your dog runs out and seizes the toy, eagerly call him back to you, drawing him to you with the leash if needed. Now, ask the dog to drop the toy (see "Drop It" in Chapter 8, Problem Dog Games.) When your dog drops the item, give him a treat along with praise and gentle petting.

(Don't get too wild with praise and petting. Whatever you use as a reward must be something your dog likes and feels comfortable with. So if you pat your dog extremely vigorously on his head and he flinches away like he's grimacing, do it more softly next time. If an owner's petting is too intense, the dog may not view it as a reward, so it becomes harder to teach the desired behavior. Especially with commands where your dog must come to you, it's important that you keep things positive and upbeat, but never act so excited that it scares your dog.)

Now, once your dog gets better bringing the item you've thrown back to you when he's leashed, add some more challenging variations like a longer toss or asking the dog to sit when he brings the item back to you. Once he excels at these variations, try asking him to retrieve an item off lead. To make this easier at first, only throw the item a short distance and let your dog know that you are holding a treat to reward him with when he brings it back to you. Soon you will throw the item much greater distances, and you will phase out the treats as just playing the game becomes its own reward.

To keep the game of Fetch fun for you, never throw an item farther then you know your dog will bring it back to you. And always call an end to the game before your dog is ready to stop. This way your dog will know you're in control of the game and he'll always be eager to play again next time. Although it might seem cute to give in when the dog pushes his favorite ball at you to throw it, in the canine world this is actually a sign of weakness! Only the pack leader decides when to start and end games, so you should always be the one to start and end the game of Fetch.

Also, **when playing Fetch, make sure your dog always brings the item all the way back to you.** If you start to let him drop the item two or three feet away from you, then the dog may get in the habit of never wanting to bring it all the way back. If your dog does drop an item too far away from you, ask him to pick it up and bring it all the way. If he refuses, then just say, "Game Over!" Walk the dog back to the house or car, and don't let him see you go pick up the fetch item. He will clearly understand that if he refuses to play by your rules, then he doesn't get to play at all.

Another sign of a dog that is acting too dominant with his owner is if your dog tries to steal an item away from you. If your dog ever tries to grab the Fetch item out of your hand, then you must make him sit and wait patiently until you say it is okay for him to

chase the item. Even if your dog barks demandingly, you must not throw the toy until he sits and waits calmly. This last rule is important because you never want your dog jumping up and biting at your hands or arms. Making the dog wait patiently for you to throw item helps prevent dominant behavior on your dog's part and it's also a good way to work on your dog's obedience.

Try asking your dog to do a command like "sit" or "down" each time before you throw the fetch item. When he complies with the obedience command, he gets to chase the fetch item as his reward. Dogs enjoy learning to master self-control in this fashion, and it's a great way for you and your dog to learn to work together better, while having lots of fun.

Frisbee
- you may even want to compete- once you get your dog to stop chewing the Frisbee!

In Chapter 6, Balance and Coordination Activities, we spoke about the benefits of Frisbee for your dog's coordination. In this chapter, we will emphasize its advantages as a game for dogs with naturally high energy. Frisbee is a great game to burn off some of that extra energy so that your live-wire dog won't want to tear up your home. (For example, we once read about a dog that did $10,000 worth of damage to his owner's house in ten minutes. This poor owner might have saved himself saved himself $10,000 just by playing ten minutes of Frisbee with that high energy dog! There's a good chance the dog would have been tired enough to sleep through that terrible ten minutes rather than causing the damage he did!)

One problem owners sometimes have is that their high-energy dog can go through Frisbees quicker than they can buy them. Two ways to fix the problem are to either change the dog's behavior or to change the Frisbee. It's a good idea to teach your dog to use a "Soft Mouth" (see Chapter 3, Puppy Games) when he grasps the Frisbee. Show your dog the Frisbee and tell him to be gentle. If he holds the Frisbee properly in his mouth without biting down too hard, smile benevolently, ask him to drop the Frisbee and offer a treat as a reward. If the dog tries to bite down hard on the Frisbee, give him a slight vocal correction and remove the Frisbee. Then try again saying, "Gentle." Praise when the dog holds the Frisbee rather than biting it.

Another way to protect your Frisbees is to go to your local pet shop and buy a Frisbee made for hard biters by Kong or one of the other brands. This is no substitute for the first option, but it may make it so you don't keep going through Frisbees before the dog learns to use a soft mouth.

Frisbee isn't just for the backyard anymore. If you own a high-energy dog that loves playing Frisbee and doing tricks, you may just want to work with him and join a club that sponsors Frisbee competitions (see Resources for Skyhoundz competitions). If you and your dog practice diligently, one day your friends may see you on television wining awards!

Monkey-in-the-Middle
- a tried & true favorite for zippy dogs, small yards and very tired owners -

This is a good way to wear your dog out quickly while you, your dog and a buddy to have lots of fun! All you need is a dog in good condition that *really* loves playing catch or fetch. You can use any size ball (one slightly larger than a tennis ball specifically made to be safe for dogs is ideal. Choose something your dog can hold comfortably in his mouth without swallowing.)

Find an open space in an enclosed area, and start with a relatively short distance. The idea is for you and your human buddy to throw the ball back and forth to each other, while your high-energy dog races back and forth between you, salivating at the thought of catching the ball if one of you lets it fall. This game wears a dog out quickly! Just make sure your dog gets ample opportunities to catch the ball to keep him interested. Every time the ball flies out of bounds, your dog will likely retrieve it, meaning even less running for you! Of course, you can play this game with any number of people and your dog. Calibrate your throws to how fast your dog can run in order to keep things exciting. If you want your dog to run more, you and your buddy can back away to farther and farther distances. It's best if your dog actually gets the chance to catch and carry the ball at times. And, to spice things up occasionally, you could also use a football thrown far distances or a soccer, or (dog-proof) beach ball, kicked on the ground.

Just make sure not to overdo it. Playing this game for any period of time at high intensity like this is intended only for healthy and physically fit dogs.

All-Terrain Run
- one of the best for healthy dogs- builds strength, alertness and dog/owner bond -

Running over varied terrain provides more physical challenge, more mental stimulation, and more chances to bond for you and your dog.

This is an activity we highly recommend for all healthy athletic dogs and their athletic owners. **You may already take your dog jogging or running with you. But introducing varied terrain is a way to increase the challenge of the workout, build muscles in a different fashion than usual and also stimulate your dog's senses.** And surfaces like grass can actually be easier on his joints than pavement!

You can take your dog for an all-terrain run on your own property or a friends' or you can travel to public hiking trails or state park forests where dogs are permitted. A winding dirt trail is a lot pleasanter to run on than flat, sun-seared concrete and each wild scent on the breeze will invigorate your healthy athletic dog's senses, bringing him pure joy. And you'll feel pleasure sharing his pleasure, making exercise exciting rather than boring.

Your dog should run beside you, not ahead and he can be leashed or free. If your dog's leashed (or on a long lead), jog slowly and carefully enough that he does not tangle up around trees. If it's legal to have your dog unleashed in a public area or if the property you're running on is private and enclosed, your dog can run free beside you. But only try this if he's well trained to stay by you off-leash, and you're confident he will not run off to chase wild game.

Start your initial runs with easier terrain, working up to more challenging terrain gradually. Mastering the uneven surface underfoot will be a challenge, so you'll achieve the same intensity of exercise in less time than if you ran your dog on a flat surface. You can incorporate moderate inclines or declines; you can run on grass or through sand, splash around through shallow water or run through areas of snow. You can even work your dog on parts of the "fitness trails" in certain parks.

Part of the joy of running on new terrain is how invigorating it feels, since you never know what's around the corner. Obviously, you do not wish to run full-speed in this situation; sometimes your run may slow to a walk as you proceed carefully through trickier obstacles or a rougher surface underfoot.

And we must advise you to **use caution when running with your dog over novel terrain.** Don't start out immediately trying to be a hero. Only take on woods or terrain that you know you and your dog are fit enough to handle. And come prepared with supplies including a compass, water for you and your dog and a cell phone if you can get reception. If you're a dedicated woodsman and your dog has been running with you off the beaten path for years, then hilly terrain with a little brush may be okay and you can also run in a greater range of weather.

Dogs and owners that aren't highly fit or highly experienced should run only in temperate weather on relatively easy terrain. Avoid extremely steep or stony mountain terrain, where hazards may include falls, exhaustion and sudden blizzards. Also avoid remote desert terrain, where hazards include thorns, snakes, scorpions and sudden flash floods, plus the danger of deadly heat and scorching sun. You must learn each area slowly over time before getting too adventurous. We recommend that you initially travel any new area you will be running in with an able-bodied human companion to first familiarize yourself with it. And always let a friend know if you're traveling to a remote area to run with your dog and when you're expected back.

No matter how accomplished you become, whenever you travel through truly wild terrain alone with your dog, you should take basic safety precautions like checking for snakes before stepping over fallen logs, checking for hornets' nests, poison toads and poison ivy and making sure your dog doesn't step into deep piles of leaves where you cannot see the bottom.

Check the Internet, the public library and local parks' service publications for more information on specific hazards in your area. For example, during hunting season, you and your dog should wear orange and/or neon to protect from possible shooting!

Never trespass on posted land. You should also avoid countryside where cougars or wild hogs are likely to frequent. **People who aren't serious woodsmen can elect to avoid the more challenging and remote areas and run with their dogs along the many gorgeous trails, woods and fields intended for human visits within minutes of your home. Instead of a dull jog around your residential area, try going off the beaten path occasionally for a more exhilarating and memorable experience for you and your dog!**

Hiking
- share the best for body & spirit with your dog if you follow cautions described -

Hiking increases aerobic conditioning, builds muscle and heightens sensory alertness and problem-solving capabilities for dogs. And you can feel proud that you selected a high-energy athletic breed if your dog loves hiking with you!

Hiking gives you a chance to view remarkable wild vistas that other people can only imagine, while experiencing yourself in an elemental state, in tune with nature and the world. Many of the most magical places are inaccessible by car, protected from the indignities of traffic and gaudy tourist traps. If you appreciate hiking you can understand that your active dog will also find fulfillment in excursions into the wild. His demeanor when you first bring him out into nature will tell you this clearly, even though he may not be able to put his feelings into words.

Before going hiking with your dog, please read all the safety precautions in the "All-Terrain Run" section, in this chapter. Follow all local laws, carry necessary safety equipment and only attempt trails where dogs are permitted. And don't attempt too much on the first day out. When you exercise your dog on flat terrain, he may easily be able to walk for hours. But flat terrain doesn't compare to the steep or uneven terrain you'll confront while hiking.

If your dog is not athletic and a full-grown adult in perfect health, then he probably should not be hiking. This also applies to certain short-legged or toy breeds, young puppies or elderly dogs. These dogs may be able to accomplish a tiny hike just to see a vista beyond some trees in a public park, and they might appreciate the sights and smells of woods and the different terrain underfoot. But you should not take a vulnerable or out-of-shape dog on miles-long hikes where the only way out is to forge ahead.

If your dog is already healthy, muscular and in great aerobic condition, he should be able to hike along beside you even on challenging excursions. After all, dogs are descended from wolves, and wolves travel all day long! But problems show up when an owner works at a sedentary desk job all week and then pushes too hard on the weekend. Hiking without adequate preparation like this sets both the owner and their dog up for exhaustion or injury. Instead, you should exercise at home every day preparatory to the big hike and then only attempt what you and your dog can comfortably accomplish.

When hiking, it's okay for your dog to pant, just like it's expected for you to breathe heavier as you both get an aerobic workout. But while you're walking remember that you should still be able to carry on a conversation. Your dog's eyes should remain sparkly, his attention bright, his tail wagging and his gait still springy. Take frequent breaks, keep well hydrated and hydrate your dog, but don't overdo with too much water at once in order to avoid bloat. The difference between exercising on your neighborhood street versus hiking in a state park that's miles away from civilization is that once your dog shows visible signs of exhaustion or overheating it will be too late to get help. For this reason, you should think proactively, and make progress in small slow increments.

First build up your dog's condition just as you would your own on shorter, less challenging hikes. Then once successful, you can attempt longer treks. A healthy athletic dog will prove the perfect companion. Provided you are physically up to it, and are already an expert hiker, and if you pace your dog and keep him well nourished and hydrated, it would not be impossible to spend weeks at a stretch together in the woods, conquering obstacles that most modern pet owners haven't even dreamt about!

Backpacking (for conditioning)
- not just for hiking; it's an easy way to strengthen & center your dog during walks -

You've already taught your healthy, high-energy dog to travel over challenging terrain, and you've taken him hiking with you in some of the country's most remote and beautiful spots. And your dog has thrived on the experiences. His muscle tone and aerobic conditioning have built up and sometimes you think he even outstrips you a bit on your wilderness adventures. So you wonder how you can make his hiking experiences even more challenging, and even better for his conditioning. So why not add a backpack intended for dogs? (See "Pack Animal" in Chapter 12, Useful Activities for more details.)

Having your dog carry his own pack while hiking will serve two functions. First there's the obviously useful function, since it allows you to pack in more supplies (like water for the dog) and thus stay out longer. The second function is that carrying additional weight increases your dog's conditioning and makes any exercise more efficient.

Doggie backpacks are not only great for hiking trips, but for everyday exercise as well. Just be careful and only increase the weight carried in line with your dog's strength and conditioning (check with your veterinarian for specifics if you're not sure). You can shorten your dog's walk or jog if he carries a backpack and he'll still get the same health benefits, just as you would carrying wrist or ankle weights.

The weight your dog carries should be just enough to build conditioning, but never enough to hurt his back or to exhaust him, and you should choose a backpack specifically designed for dogs (See Resources). Your dog should remain jaunty while carrying the pack, always appearing to enjoy it. And consider shortening the length of his workout at first, because the weight makes every movement tougher.

If you have the kind of high-energy dog that sometimes acts "hyper", a backpack can provide an additional advantage. The feeling of a little weight, and the fact that the backpack gives the dog a real task to perform, will often "center" a dog so that he'll walk along beside you perfectly, rather than jumping around in every direction. Just this one little change sometimes transforms a dog that pulls on walks to one who'll walk beside you calmly.

Run in Snow
- power workout & great for healthy dogs with proper caution-

If you live in a cold climate and you own a fenced property, you've probably already noticed how much dogs love to run in deep snow. And running in snow intensifies exercise benefits- more work for the muscles and the cardiovascular system in a much shorter amount of time than running on grass or concrete.

Dogs also love running in snow for the same reason that kids do- because it's a novel situation that's very stimulating to the senses. And exercising in snow is bred into the genetic makeup of many northern breeds. If you ever want a highly efficient workout that's a little different, you can allow your leashed dog to make his way through the snow beside you while you walk on a path or you can play fetch or other games with your dog when he's off leash in a fenced area.

Some dogs love chasing snowballs. And as long as you're healthy, it's a great fun to put on your snowsuit and snow boots and jump right into the snow to play with your dog!

But only exercise your dog in snow with caution and common sense. **Since running or any exertion in snow is incredibly taxing, reserve it for dogs that are in top physical condition and checked by a veterinarian**.

Even healthy dogs can suffer if left out too long in cold and snow. And walking in any accumulation of snow is inappropriate for puppies, elderly dogs or dogs with physical problems. In some instances a dog suddenly thrown into unaccustomed vigorous exercise in snow will experience dangerous hypothermia or exhaustion. Certain breeds have extremely low tolerance for cold, and others are simply not big enough to make their way out of extremely deep snow on their own. If your dog is bad in snow, he may need a cleared path and a coat, sweater or booties for wintertime walks.

Other breeds thrive on vigorous exercise in snow. But, even in these cases, we caution against leaving the dog outside unsheltered in snow and cold for extended periods. And running in deep snow is many times more taxing than running on flat terrain, so make exercise sessions in snow shorter.

Observe your dog's demeanor. If he appears energized and happy, then include running in snow in his exercise routine. But if you have to drag him by the leash to step into deep snow, and he flounders around in a panic, find different ways of adding additional resistance to his exercise routine!

Snow Games
- dogs enjoy this so much it's fun to watch; an easy way to add variety & intensity -

Please read "Run in Snow" above for specific cautions for exercising high-energy dogs vigorously in deep snow, and the section "Play in the Snow" in Chapter 14 for cautions about types of dogs that should *never* be exercised in snow.

Once you fully understand the cautions, consider the fact that exercising with your dog in the snow opens up a whole season of activity when many owners and dogs might be hiding out inside, letting their muscles go slack and their aerobic capacity fade away. And it's natural for many dog breeds, especially long-haired and northern breeds to exercise in snow and crisp weather. Exercising on relatively mild winter days is healthier for most dogs than playing furiously on hot summer days. And snow and cool air feels quite exhilarating to a curious individual with a natural fur coat!

Play in the snow also introduces many new games to keep exercise interesting and keep your high-energy dog occupied. It's fun for owners as well, and many adults forget how freeing it can be to put on a snowsuit and jump around in the snow!

If you have children, they'll likely introduce you to plenty of fun games the family can share with dogs in the snow. These include running, jumping or rolling around together, playing "Fetch" or "Frisbee", hiding objects for your dog to find in the snow or having him chase loose-packed snowballs.

A larger dog may happily pull a sled to help you with groceries or firewood. And, as long as you use proper caution, you may even be able to teach him to pull your small children. (Please read the full cautions in "Sled Dog" in Chapter 12- Useful Activities).

After a new fall of snow you and your dog could walk together on the edge of the woods to marvel at the winter wonderland. A working or guarding breed dog is a great partner to look out for you if you have to slog along through deep snow to take care of chores.

If you got lost in a heavy snowfall on your own property, many working, sporting or hound breed dogs could actually safely lead you home. Training a dog specifically for this type of work is complex and would be the subject for a different book, and you should never force your average pet dog into a situation where he must save your life unless you are already *sure* that he can do it. But if you want to encourage your dog's snow rescue abilities just for fun, you can practice hiding behind a snowdrift. Have another family member command the dog to find you, and then praise him lavishly when he does.

Or walk a little distance away from your house while a thick curtain of fat snowflakes is falling, then command the leashed dog to "Go home" so he can lead the way. To be safe, don't go too far, don't actually get lost and make the task easy. Then praise your dog lavishly when he succeeds and you arrive home together safely.

Just don't confuse these basic, fun exercises with serious training. *You should seek in-depth professional training for tracking/lifesaving if you seriously wish to rely on your dog to save lives in snow.*

Modern owners tend to baby dogs, and some overcautious owners hesitate to take healthy athletic dogs out in snow at all, forgetting that dogs are animals whose ancestors thrived in varied weather. We like to remind cautious owners that snow games *can* be safe- for people and dogs- and most dogs benefit from playing in the snow *in moderation*.

But make sure not to take the idea to the other extreme, however. Unless your dog is an active working dog, bred and trained for the conditions and cleared with a veterinarian, you should **avoid putting your dog outside off leash on below-zero days or in blizzard conditions**. Allow him out, leashed, only long enough to empty bowels and bladder on such days. This applies even if he is regularly active and usually likes snow.

On days when the temperature is a little warmer, but still below freezing, most dogs can run free in a contained area, but only briefly. Stay around to call your dog inside, and **never forget your dog in the yard when the temperature's below freezing**! Leaving a dog out for hours in a yard with no escape from deep snow or freezing rain can also be dangerous. Even for healthy active dogs, short periods are best for snow play. And every dog needs a chance to warm up and dry off, preferably indoors.

Supervising, and/or going outside with your dog to play is the best way to make sure that his energy stays up and he benefits from the full winter workout without overdoing. Any exercise in snow is a *lot* more exerting than the same motions on dry ground. So when your dog begins to pant and looks yearningly toward home, and if you feel exhausted as well, it's probably the right time for both of you to head inside and curl up beside the fire…

Retrieving in Water
**- super-high intensity workout for dogs; fun but not so much work for owner-
just use caution -**

This is a perfect activity for owners with high-energy dogs bred for retrieving fowl. You may have noticed that, as long as these dogs are healthy and fit, they have endless energy and sometimes not even the longest session of playing fetch is enough to get them tired! To teach your dog to retrieve in water, all you need is a safe item that will float rather than sink.

Search pet stores for a variety of safe toys or farm supply stores or catalogs for retrieving decoys specifically made for this purpose.

Before asking your dog to retrieve in water, first practice "Fetch" (see this chapter) on land until you're absolutely sure that your dog can and will bring the item back to you every time. This is one time you don't want to have to go out and get the fetch item yourself unless you are a good swimmer with a lot of patience!

Retrieving in water makes your dog work twice as hard for each throw, exercising different groups of muscles and making the task more stimulating because it includes swimming in water along with running on land. It's great exercise for most high-energy breeds and it feels particularly natural and exhilarating for the breeds genetically shaped and bred for retrieving.

If a dog is in otherwise good health, yet he has slightly compromised hips or other joints, retrieving in water can provide him with hours of high-quality aerobic exercise while taking the strain off. Just make sure to avoid belly flops or violent launching into water. And if you suspect your dog may have any illness or disability, check with your veterinarian for his particular limitations. If your dog has no current health problems, using vigorous water exercise as part of his conditioning program when he's young may protect his joints later in life because the workout is so low-impact.

Many dogs naturally love retrieving in water. Others don't show interest at first but can be taught to like it with a careful introduction. **But don't try to force a dog to retrieve if he is afraid of water or a weak swimmer.** When first starting any dog on retrieving, use a lifevest and keep him attached to a long lead close to shore until he proves his swimming abilities. You can then release the dog from the leash and let him swim out farther on his own, but continue to supervise carefully with another qualified adult around if you should ever have to make a rescue!

If your dog is retrieving in your backyard pool, you won't ever encounter certain problems. But all freshwater bodies of water (lakes, ponds, rivers) may present certain natural dangers along with their natural appeal. Whenever you go to a new spot, you should check out water quality and underwater hazards to keep your dog safe. Risks include predators like alligators, poisonous snakes, deep spots, frigid currents and hazards left behind by humans (fish hooks and barbed wire). Jagged or slippery rocks or even quicksand or overly soft muck can also hurt your dog. And the very worst hazards are the biological ones-bacteria, protozoa and some forms of algae that can sicken or kill you or your dog.

With all these hazards, you may wonder why you would even consider freshwater swimming. But many freshwater bodies are perfectly safe. Your local or state parks departments are good sources of up-to-date water quality information. Not only will they be able to tell you where the water is safe, they can also help you find a great spot where your dog will be welcome. Some private lodges and campgrounds offer safe private swimming holes for dogs and your dog may even be able to swim with friendly, well-screened canine companions while you socialize with the other human guests.

Another option which avoids the danger of infection altogether is to have your dog retrieve in the sea where he has to work against the waves and current. If you wish to do this, check with local lifeguards to make sure that it's safe and legal. Many municipalities also offer a free hotline that you can check throughout each day for current beach conditions.

Race
- teach your dog to race with you rather than running around when you don't want him to -

There are two types of exercise for dogs- generalized running around versus focused exercise and sports, which provide a more intense and concentrated workout in every way. For example, dogs love to race and you see them running alongside each other all the time. But when you structure a formal race for dogs, it makes it more explosively powerful. Racing is great for building speed- especially the explosive quality of athletes' muscles. It focuses the mind, plus it's very enjoyable and satisfying, both for humans and dogs.

You can teach several relatively well-matched dogs to race against each other, enlisting the help of a human helper or two if you need them. First, command the dogs to stay, but if they're overeager, ask a helper to help hold them until you're ready to give the signal to run. This signal could be the sound of a clicker, a gesture or the word, "Go!" Once you give the signal, the dogs will race to a designated spot. You can have another human helper wait at the finish line to praise all the dogs and perhaps offer the winner a food reward.

Human family members can run in the race also, or you can even race your dog one-on-one. Set a prize up at the other end of the field where you will be running- maybe a toy you both like. Then train the dog to hold back until the signal to run. Or you could set an oven timer to go off to make things totally fair.

The only safety cautions involve common sense- run your dog only as fast and as far as his health and physical conditioning allow. For example, racing short distances can be a good activity for puppies. It fascinates them and keeps their minds out of mischief. It also teaches puppies discipline, as they learn to contain themselves waiting at the finish line to channel boisterous energy properly, running in a straight line toward a goal. (Note that some giant-breed puppies shouldn't run too hard while their hips are still developing, so check first with your veterinarian for his or her recommendations.)

Racing is a sport for truly athletic dogs, and it shows them at their finest. Greyhounds are, of course, bred for the sport, and they will thank you for racing with them for fun. You can easily imagine whippets and other sighthounds racing, too. Racing is also great for high-energy terriers like Jack Russells and Pit Bulls, herding breeds like Border Collies and Australian Shepherds, sporting breeds like Vizslas and working breeds like Dobermans. But any healthy, high-energy dog will benefit from this kind of exercise. When you see how fast your dogs can run, it will probably amaze you!

Weave Poles
- easiest, cheapest and most versatile agility move to fine-tune control of your dog at home -

Weave poles. What is this crazy thing we hear that dogs love? Weave poles are one of the regulation obstacles that dogs work through during formal agility competition. As quickly as possible, the dog must thread or weave his body in and out of a set number of sticks coming out of the ground. This takes intense discipline and self-control, and perhaps dogs thrive threading through weave poles because it brings back natural instincts to run through the woods dodging trees.

In agility competition, the handler has to teach the dog to enter between the first two poles on the right and weave his body around each pole until he gets to come out at the last pole, moving as fast as possible. The dog must not miss even one pole or he must start at the beginning again.

> *Steal this trick from agility competition and modify it - it's one of the best.*

This can be challenging and fun for both you and your dog and your dog will burn up lots of energy running through the poles. Since he must move his body carefully, navigating the weave poles also makes him have to think. This gives his brain a refreshing workout along with the physical workout for his body. Threading through weave poles will mentally tire your dog out, but it's quite simple and doesn't take long to teach.

Your healthy dog naturally knows how to run in the woods and not run into trees. But at first he may not know what these strange poles sticking out of the ground are, and he might run right through them, knocking some poles down.

There are many ways to teach your dog that you want him to move through weave poles. We recommend training with treats because this helps the dog love the game and love to work for you. First keep your dog next to you in a sit. Then use a treat to lead the dog to the poles and use the treat to lure the dog to weave through the poles one at a time. This could be a five-minute job, but some people need to work for days or even weeks to get their dog to approach the poles. Just don't rush your dog if he's frightened.

As you teach your dog to run through the weave poles, both you and he will start having great fun and a hyperactive dog that was driving you up the walls may just become the magnificent working animal you always imagined he could be!

Weave pole practice is not just for formal agility competition. You can also practice with your dog in your backyard as a highly easy and versatile exercise option. There is virtually no downside and weave poles are good to use with almost any dog. Or use poles or traffic cones spaced more widely to practice keeping your dog closer to your side as he heels. You can buy weave poles online, or through catalogs that sell agility sets. But there's no need to spend a lot. As long as you're not practicing for formal agility competition, you can make your own weave poles that are easy to move around the yard, simply by using discarded traffic cones, or PVC lengths attached to a base. Your weave poles will fit perfectly in the smallest square of yard and when you're finished, you can easily stow them away.

Water Run
- add this for cross training & saving time on running -

This game can be played two different ways, depending upon your dog's level of fitness, and the intensity of workout you're looking for.

Dogs that can't tolerate strenuous exercise on land because of physical conditions will benefit from running gently in water. The novel stimulus of moving in the water can stimulate the dog's senses and increase both calmness and alertness at the same time. Water also increases the intensity of any exercise without increasing strain. If you wish to rehabilitate elderly, obese or physically compromised dogs, please read the "Hydrotherapy" sections in Chapter 9, Therapeutic and Senior Dog Games, and Chapter 11, Water Games. Also see Resources. The additional resistance of the water magnifies healthy strain on the dog's muscles and cardiovascular system without hurting his joints.

If your dog is healthy and athletic and needs ever intensifying workouts to build muscle mass, strength and cardiovascular fitness, running in water can jump-start his exercise routine. You can include this activity with your dog's regular cross-training. And it can be especially useful in summer months when the water may cool your dog enough to allow him a safe cardio workout during daytime hours.

If you want a cardio workout, you can lead your dog on-leash as you jog through the water. Keeping your dog on leash helps you protect him from hazards and allows you to better control distance and speed for structured training. If you do wish to take your dog off-lead, just make sure it's legal wherever you're running.

If the length of your beach or lakeside shoreline allows it, you can run straight for a long distance. But you can still get in a good run even on the shore of a small backyard pond by just running for a bit and then doubling back again and again.

Keeping the distance short is also a good idea for your initial water runs when you don't know your dog's exact tolerance. Also have your beach umbrella, towel and water bottle nearby if rest is needed. Some days are just too hot for the beach and, with enough sun exposure, a dog *can* get heatstroke on the beach, even if he's wet. To avoid this risk, don't choose noontime on the hottest day of summer for your dog's first vigorous water run. And don't make him run in very cold water either; save this activity for temperate weather!

Start with a brief run, and watch how your dog adapts. Moderate panting, bright eyes and perkiness are good signs and your dog should be able to keep up with you without lagging behind. Keep each session brief enough that your dog still seems perky as you sit down to rest. Ten minutes of water running can be long enough to stop for the first rest and even stopping after five minutes wouldn't be unreasonable for the first session. After you rest, you can run for a while more and then rest again. As your dog's condition builds, you can increase the length and difficulty of workouts and/or the depth of the water.

Keep in mind that when you run with your dog, you may be wearing rubber-soled "sand shoes" or you may be barefoot, which is not as advisable. But your dog always runs barefoot, so it's your responsibility to check the surface under the water before letting him run! Jagged rocks can hurt your dog and so can broken beer bottles or fish hooks left behind by irresponsible beachgoers. Clear water and smooth sand is safest. Your dog may be able to tolerate a slightly gravelly surface under the water, so consider each case individually. You might even be able to find a rubber soled bootie that fits your dog well enough that it will stay on in the water. Just use common sense.

And consider this: you may not need much room at all to run your dog in the water, and you may not have to leave your home. Smaller breeds and puppies can even go for their "water run" in large plastic kiddie pools, or even in a pool installed specially for dogs! (See "A Pool of His Own" in Ch. 11, "Water Games")

Hurdles
- another popular idea borrowed from agility, burns extra energy & aids coordination –

Do you have a dog that loves to jump like most high energy dogs do? Well why not put all that jumping to good use and teach the dog to jump hurdles? A hurdle is another popular canine agility activity, similar to those used in track and field events for humans. In formal agility competitions, hurdles are made with two posts that have pins at different heights to adjust the height of the jump each dog has to make. But, if you're just practicing at home, you can construct hurdles for your dog out of just about anything that's safe. Avoid anything sharp and make sure the hurdle will fall over if your dog hits into it so he won't hurt his legs.

Even if you own a larger dog, like a Labrador Retriever, you should start with very low jumps. Even if the jump doesn't look quite high enough for your Lab, it won't scare or hurt him the first time he jumps hurdles. You also should not have dogs of larger breeds jump hurdles before they are one year old, because it can hurt their growing bones which can't withstand the impacts of the jumps. And make sure to first check with your veterinarian if there is any chance your dog has physical limitations that might make jumping dangerous.

If you have a high energy dog that loves to jump it should be no problem teaching him to jump over a hurdle. Put the item you are using as a hurdle on the ground and stand on the opposite side of the hurdle with a treat or toy while a friend holds your dog about two feet behind the hurdle. Now have your friend release the dog, as you call him and encourage him to jump across the post to get to you. It's okay if your dog simply steps over the hurdle gingerly the first time, but do not allow him to walk around it to get to you. As soon as he steps over, give the dog treats and lots of praise!

Practice again and again with loads of excitement and encouragement until your dog actually jumps over the hurdle with some energy. Congratulations! Your dog just made his first jump! Keep repeating the process, making the jump an inch higher each time, but never going too high. If your dog knows the "Stay" command, you can also teach him to jump hurdles without the help of a friend, but remember to keep the hurdle low at first. If your dog gets hurt the first time he jumps, he may not ever want to try hurdles again without professional intervention.

Jumping hurdles is an easy activity to set up in a small space outdoors (or even indoors) with almost no expense. And it offers many benefits for dogs. Since your dog learns to jump on command, he's less likely to jump when not asked. And he'll get to let out extra energy by running and jumping over hurdles, so you can do your guests a favor and use hurdles for your dogs' jumping rather then their laps! Both your guests and your dog will thank you for it.

Sand Run
- another intense cross-training move for your canine workout buddy -

Are you in great condition? And do you love running on the beach for exercise? Reasons to love running in sand include the fact that sand offers much more resistance than flat terrain, for a shorter, more efficient workout. It also stabilizes the body while working muscles from every angle and providing cushioning to the joints. Running on the beach in the invigorating sea breeze also stimulates the senses and provides a wonderful feeling of freedom and oneness with nature. And your dog can enjoy all these benefits also!

Running in sand provides a highly challenging workout that is appropriate for high-energy dogs that are in perfect health and great physical condition. Dogs with lesser conditioning, young puppies, older dogs or those with minor health problems may benefit from a brief walk or gentle jog of a few minutes duration in sand. But you should first check with your veterinarian about any workout in sand if your dog has any physical limitations.

If your dog is healthy and high energy, you can easily adjust beach runs to his conditioning needs. As he becomes stronger and more aerobically fit, increase the speed, length of the run or the depth of the sand (the less depth, the easier the workout). Since most public beaches don't allow dogs to run off leash, you'll likely be running right beside him.

Use common sense about sun and temperature. Hot sun and sand can burn your dog and some breeds are particularly prone to heat exhaustion or deadly heat stroke. Vigorous exertion increases the likelihood of these problems tenfold, so select times for beach runs carefully. (Your local beach patrol may provide a free beach conditions hotline.) We live in South Florida and we spend time on the beach almost daily. The secret is coming out only when there's a nice breeze and before or after peak sun hours. And some days are cooler than others. We recommend running during overcast or hazy conditions or when the sun drops a bit.

A beach or lakeside is the only place we'd personally run a dog in sand. But if you want to run your dog on desert sand, just use the same cautions for sun and temperature. Since desert conditions can be harsh, only attempt to run with your dog when the temperature is cool, but not too cold, and always check weather reports before embarking.

Use your own feelings of exhaustion while running in sand as a guide and observe your dog's demeanor to know when to cut short a session. You want your dog to seem focused and effortful, but still happy, normal and alert. Never let your dog tremble, heave for breath or pant extremely (see symptoms of heat stroke in the "Hot Dog" section in Ch. 15). And respect your dog's reluctance if he just seems to want to lie down. Allow him rest and a chance to cool off, but also monitor his vital signs in case he needs medical attention. Initially, work your dog in sand only a few minutes at a time and build the length of his run gradually as his condition increases.

Ocean Swim
- why you'd want to do it, and how to keep your dog safe -

This is one highly X-treme dog exercise. Since there are many milder forms of water exercise, we'll assume that if you want to swim your dog in the ocean, you already know your dog is an excellent swimmer, physically fit and perfectly healthy. You should also be fit enough so you can swim with your dog with a lead attached to a harness or lifevest so you can help him if a current threatens to pull him out. If you're not both in prime shape before attempting your ocean swim, you can practice in the family pool until you build your physical fitness.

Before starting, become familiar with the ocean conditions in general for your area. Always swim in front of a lifeguard and check with him about weather conditions for the day- rip current and sea pests, for example. And, of course, make sure that dogs are allowed by law on your stretch of beach. Here in South Florida, the water is completely calm on many summer days, so on these days even a dog that's a novice could try his first ocean swim. But, even here, conditions can change quickly and the waves can be treacherous, so don't expect too much of your dog. And never go out when the surf is really rough (red flag) even if you and your dog are experienced swimmers.

Fighting even small waves in the ocean provides an immediate and intense workout for your dog's muscles and his cardiovascular system. So, you won't need more than a few minutes of this for his cross-training. Stay near your dog, but distant enough so that you allow him free movement and you do not get scratched. Make sure that he's not swallowing excessive water and that he's swimming eagerly and not going into a panic.

If your dog ever panics, gently encourage him to follow you to shore, pulling on the lead attached to his harness or lifejacket, if necessary. Don't get into a battle with a struggling dog, or you will both go under! Some breeds of dogs are literally bred for swimming, and you'll know if your dog is a candidate if he acts completely fearless and joyous in the ocean. If your dog shows more than natural caution with the unfamiliar and his anxiety does not subside, there's no need to try again. Ocean swimming is not appropriate for every dog.

If your dog loves the ocean, but he's not the strongest athlete, there's no need to go into deep water for him to benefit from the exercise; he only needs to be in deep enough to swim. And be conservative in every way. Frigid winter weather and high waves are dangerous, so choose days that are pleasantly warm- typically late spring, summer, or early fall.

If you're swimming in Florida or one of the Sunbelt states, remember that just because your dog's working out in water doesn't mean he can't suffer heat illness (See "Hot Dog" in Ch. 15.) Your dog will be extremely tired after even a short ocean swim and will need to rest. So choose reasonable days when temperature and humidity are warm, but not stifling hot, and provide the shade of a beach umbrella if you plan to keep your dog out on the beach for any length of time.

Picture Windows (Caution)
- **Controversial. This can brighten a dog's day or agitate him;
read & decide for yourself -**

This can either be a great activity, or a dangerous one, depending on your dog's reaction to novel stimuli he views outside the home when he's home alone. And some dogs should never be left to look out open windows. Trainers often recommend you close off the view from all of your windows if your dog is a problem barker, overly aggressive toward strangers or if he shows symptoms of separation anxiety. In those cases, a cozier den-like environment can make your dog feel safer.

If your dog has problems controlling himself while looking out windows you may have already found torn-up Venetian blinds and scratched windowsills. Or your neighbors or your mail carrier may complain that your dog flings himself at the windows, barking aggressively whenever they pass.

But this chapter is not geared towards problem dogs like this, but rather healthy, athletic dogs whose worse problem is boredom and bottled up energy. If your dog is left with time to kill during the day and you're sure he has no fear or aggression problems when he watches passersby, one of the nicest things you can do for him is to leave him a view when you are away from home. Leaving views out windows in different parts of the house will also keep your dog moving while you are gone, rather than simply sleeping away the day. This is even better if some rooms are upstairs or if some rooms are in the rear of the house and others in front, because the dog will have to walk back and forth.

The best way to know what your dog may do when you leave him alone is to observe what he does when you are home. Does he run to the French doors and cock his head, giving a little "yip" at the antics of squirrels playing in your yard? Does he jog upstairs and stand with feet on the window frame diligently watching the pool man service your neighbor's swimming pool? If his actions seem manageable when you are around, then you can take a chance on leaving him a view while you're away.

If your dog has never made an escape attempt, and your windows have good locks you could even leave one or more windows cracked a tiny bit so he can sniff the world. A simple breeze wafting in is an amazing stimulant for your dog, since he gets so much of his information about the world from his nose. (For example, if you were on foot, he could probably smell you a mile away when you returned home from work!)

Modern society with its hermetically sealed windows and drawn drapes has effectively subjected dogs to sensory deprivation while owners go away to work for eight or more hours each day. So it's not surprising if your dog feels a little stir-crazy when you're gone, especially if he's a high-energy or a guarding breed. Provided he's trustworthy, and you do not get any negative reports, why not allow him a little freedom each day? You may be surprised how much simply moving around the house all day with some feeling of purpose takes the edge off his store of bottled up energy and frustration.

Make sure to use "Picture Windows" with care and reasonable discretion and "dog-proof" your house if your large dog has free run. Even if your dog is exquisitely behaved, you never know when an unwelcome solicitor or even a would-be burglar playing with your lock may send your normally placid pet into a frenzy. If your dog weighs one hundred and twenty pounds and he comes flying downstairs at full gallop, it's really not his fault if a precariously placed crystal vase on the coffee table topples over and shatters.

Most well-bred and well-trained adult dogs that have been raised with respect and love will likely show surprising respect for your possessions and won't *deliberately* destroy anything. But dogs combine the traits of being fast-moving and yet somewhat clumsy by human standards. So, if you wish to leave your dog free in the home with an unobstructed view, you should give him a fair chance by removing fragile valuables from pathways and areas near the windows.

You can also make things easier on both of you by blocking off some stressful views, while leaving mellower views open for his enjoyment. For example, watching distant waterfowl or golf carts along the course behind your home might be somewhat entertaining, but not enough to trigger your dog. But watching your neighbors' dogs playing in the yard only ten feet away from yours might be too much for him, especially if he can hear them barking through an open window. If you know that watching your neighbor's rowdy dogs gets yours barking, you can close off that window, or even that room, when you're away. And just leave him the golf course view that he's more comfortable with!

Flyball
**- super high-intensity sport that many owners haven't heard of;
your athletic dog might love it -**

Do you have a high-energy dog that really loves to run and chase tennis balls? If so, a high-speed organized sport called Flyball just may be the sport of choice for you. In Flyball, your dog burns off energy running as fast as he can over a set number of hurdles to get to a launch pad which he hits to release a tennis ball. He then runs back to the handler. It sounds easy, but this sport takes a lot of practice. Your dog will be one of four dogs on a team that must cooperate to get the fastest time. And his team will compete against several other teams.

Quite a bit of strategy goes into the sport of Flyball. First there is the fact of timing- to get the fastest time you must learn the precise moment to let the next dog go. Then there is strategy. There is a line on the floor that the first dog must past before the next dog passes the line. But if you wait too long and let the first dog get all the way back to you, it may cost you those seconds that could have won the round for you.

You might think that to win at the sport you'd want to use the biggest, fastest dogs you could find, but you often see one small dog on each Flyball team. The reason for this actually has to do with the official height that hurdles are handicapped at and it's all part of the strategy. Because of the small dog, larger dogs on each team (like Border Collies or Shepherds) are able to run at top speed since they only have to jump over very small hurdles. But if the team had all large dogs, the hurdles would have to be set higher.

Flyball is a very high-intensity, high speed and highly charged sport for all involved, so it isn't for the faint at heart. If you're up to the challenge and want more information on Flyball, go online and Google the sport or see our Resources section for the AKC (American Kennel Club) website.

Rally Competition
- like Curves for dog obedience, these competitions keep it moving -

"Rally" refers to an AKC-sanctioned version of obedience that is faster paced than regular companion dog competition. In Rally trials, each team, consisting of dog and handler, moves through a course consisting of twenty different obedience stations where points are either added or deducted based on successful completion. The teams move through the course in a continuous fashion, one after the other, after first walking the course in a preview. Obstacles include jumps and retrieving dumbbells and dogs stay beside the handler, but not in a strict "heel" position.

Dogs can obtain different levels of Rally titles, and the sport is intended to reward dogs who would handle well in real life. And since the Rally trial consists of going through the stations in a dynamic fast-paced fashion, this sport definitely suits high-energy dogs. While allowing dogs to burn energy and exercise physical skills, the mental components and discipline involved in Rally competitions also focus dogs' minds. For more information on Rally trials, see Resources and consult the AKC, or American Kennel Club, website.

> **Safety Note: Please consider using the four exercise options that follow only with caution. And never let children attempt these methods.** *If not completed properly, each activity carries risk of serious injury to yourself or your dog; however, many owners of healthy high-energy dogs have had great success with each of the activities. Before continuing, you should clear the activity with your veterinarian and consider your dog's temperament and the environment (for example, how many people and other distractions are present.)*

Biking with Your Dog (with caution)
- if you can do it safely, you can't beat this for dogs with super-high energy -

It's tough to find a suitable public trail where exercising your dog off-leash is legal. If you can find such a location, and you're sure your dog will run beside you without straying or disturbing people or animals, then try bicycling with your dog off-leash, the way this exercise works best.

Otherwise, your dog must be leashed, so it's safest to use an inexpensivel device made for hooking your dog up to your bicycle (see Resources). If you choose to use a regular leash instead, hold it loosely as you pedal with your dog running parallel with you. **Do not wrap the leash around your wrist or affix it to the bicycle.** If you do, and your dog takes off after some distraction, he will topple you over! Other potential disasters include the dog becoming entangled in your wheels as you fall. So, even if your dog is always careful, always wear a helmet and knee pads!

The great thing about bicycling with your dog is that it's the only way that certain breeds can reasonably get the hours of running they need outside. A reasonably fit owner will enjoy their outdoor workouts on the bicycle, while the naturally stronger dog, will get the equivalent workout for his needs.

Unfortunately, as trainers specializing in dog's emotional and behavior problems, we haven't yet found a single dog and owner who can safely bicycle together in public places! But we do often observe dogs and owners bicycling happily, notably one senior gentleman who sedately pedals around his neighborhood, allowing his little Miniature Pinscher to jog for a block or two. Halfway through their daily journey, he lifts the dog up into the bicycle basket, offering appropriate exercise and rest.

Other owners of small dogs won't do well with this method of exercise because they can't resist going all-out on the bike. But no matter how energetic a small dog is and how much they like to run, it's hard for them to keep pace for very long because of their size. Therefore we don't recommend bicycling with small dogs unless you make your trips slow and short, or ride your dog in the basket part of the way if the trip is longer.

Bicycling together is best with healthy adult medium and large breed dogs that are comfortable running long distances at high speeds. (Examples include Pit Bulls, German Shepherds, Weimaraners, Ridgebacks, Labradors, Dobermans, Boxers, Border Collies, Australian Shepherds, Great Danes, retrievers, hounds and sighthounds.) **Push-nosed breeds, short-legged breeds and some giant and/or extremely hairy breeds physically can't keep up or easily overheat. And you should avoid bicycling with young puppies or skittish dogs of any age.**

Never bicycle with a dog that acts overly prey-driven or dog-aggressive. Other dogs and owners *will* pass and, i**f your dog lunges, you *will* suffer a fall!** You should first **test your dog extensively with every type of distraction (including loose dogs and squirrels)** *before* attempting a bike ride in a public area.

Your dog should be absolutely obedient running beside you on a loose leash before you head to the park with your bicycle. Practice repeated trial runs in your driveway or cul-de-sac before bicycling with your dog in the real world. When you've tested him with many planned distractions and he proves reliable, then take him to the park! Carry lots of water and give your dog frequent breaks. Start out with shorter distances and gradually increase. Remember, your dog's getting approximately twice the exercise he would if he jogged with you, and about ten times as much as on a walk lasting the same amount of time!

Skateboarding with Your Dog (with caution)
- **whether you can pull this off safely is debatable. When it works it's fun & burns lots of extra energy -**

If you're a fan of popular television dog trainer Cesar Millan, aka *The Dog Whisperer*, you've likely witnessed *this* activity. But, **if you try it, make sure you're an expert skateboarder and that your dog is healthy and robust, not skittish around the skateboard and appropriate in public places.** It's hard to find any private trails for skateboarding, since you *must* be on pavement, so plan for serious distractions including traffic and pedestrians.

Skateboarding can give your dog's workout extra oomph and equalizes dog's and owner's ability to exert themselves. Just make sure to follow all the safety precautions in the "Bicycling with Dog" section above. Also be considerate and make sure wherever you exercise is legal for both dogs *and* skateboards. Avoid streets overly crowded with pedestrians and avoid darting through traffic and creating a hazard. If introduced correctly, all the distractions your dog encounters while skateboarding can actually build his confidence around new things.

Rollerblading with Your Dog (with caution)
- not always safe nor easy, but definitely burns energy for the highest energy dogs -

As with the activities above, rollerblading with your dog can equalize a moderately fit owner with a dog with off-the-charts exercise needs. Just follow all the cautions in the "Bicycling with Your Dog" and "Skateboarding with Your Dog" sections. When you are up on rollerblades, holding your dog on a leash, even though you probably feel quite exhilarated, you *are* off balance. Your dog must be perfectly obedient and he should not be swayed by distractions, since rollerblading frequently takes place in crowded public areas.

Practice first in secluded private locales to make sure your dog is reliable. **Never try to make your dog pull you along, even though you may have seen it on television!** Teaching your dog to pull you when you're 'blading is a bad idea. It can make your dog have trouble distinguishing when you *want* him to pull you from all the times you don't. And it could injure your dog, especially if he's wearing a choke collar or other neck collar. Unless your dog is massive, and wearing an appropriate harness, the best way to rollerblade is with both you and your dog moving side by side, each on your own steam.

Driving With Your Dog Without Him in the Car (with caution)
-       **You decide. Is this abuse or simply a practical way to give the most athletic dogs the workout they need?**

Please note that this activity can be extremely dangerous so, although we describe it, we do not actively recommend it. Dog owners who elect to try this activity should proceed at their own risk, using extreme caution.

Of all the extreme exercises for high-energy dogs, this is one of the most extreme. And if you heard it described at a cocktail party, you may have thought it was a myth or an urban legend. Perhaps you've heard of owners driving slowly, holding their high-energy dog's leash out the window so the dog can jog.

While we personally can't recommend the method, we *have* actually watched it performed safely. For example, we once observed an owner jogging his robust adult Pit Bull along the winding drive of a park with the dog's leash extended out the window of his moving car. The dog ran, appearing quite happy, and the owner controlled him appropriately, driving slowly enough to make the process safe. He also allowed the dog frequent breaks in the warm weather and, in this case, the dog seemed to benefit. But this doesn't make the activity safe for everyone.

Dangers of exercising your dog this way start with the **possibility of running your dog over! Also if you drive too fast or too long, you could exhaust your dog to the point of serious injury or death. And some dogs will panic if forced to run beside a car.**

Other potential drawbacks include the horrified stares you'll likely get from neighbors and the possible complaints to your local Department of Animal Cruelty called in by concerned witnesses with cell phones. We honestly don't know if exercising your dog out a car window is even legal!

If you feel you have compelling enough reason to still try this form of exercising your dog, first make sure that you have complete control of the dog. Practice first on out-of-the-way streets, parks or private property where you can safely drive very slowly without risking faster traffic rear-ending you or hitting your dog. **While you concentrate on your dog, you may not pay full attention to driving, even at five miles an hour, so don't cruise along where you might hit a pedestrian! You also have no control over your dog while you're in the car.** If a squirrel runs past and your dog tries to chase it, this could cause disaster before you could stop the car. **You can make the process a little safer by asking a helper to drive while you hold your dog from the passenger seat.**

With this exercise method you must also be cautious not to overwork your dog. You'll be getting about a hundred times less exercise in the car than your dog will on the pavement, so go easy on him! **Let your dog set the pace and don't travel at more than a few miles an hour.** Build up the length of sessions very gradually as your dog's conditioning improves. **But never even begin this technique unless your dog is vibrantly healthy in every way and is already a fast and natural runner!** The best way to gauge how much exercise your individual dog needs is to ask your vet. If your veterinarian is willing to condone this extreme method of exercise, then you may be on the right track to try it. **If your vet recommends against this type of exercise, please follow his or her recommendations and avoid it!**

AKC-Sanctioned Activities: Field Trials, Tracking, Hunting Trials, Herding Trials, Lure Coursing
- these less familiar sports are great for certain breeds & can be adapted for at-home -

The main intention of this book is to provide activities for the do-it-yourself dog owner to enjoy with their dog at home. But for owners of high-energy dogs, we'd like to also mention several formalized field events, judged by the AKC, and other organizations, that test dogs in sporting tasks they were bred for. If you own a sporting breed, you may want to find out where trials are being held near you and then go at first to observe.

You may be surprised to find that your purebred dog can compete in one of these activities formally. Even if your dog's not purebred, you can make contacts with a club or trainer who can help you learn to use sporting activities as exercise. To get started, check the American Kennel Club (AKC) website (see Resources) or Google each activity individually.

Novice owners of purebred sporting breeds should know that some of the above activities do use actual game for the dogs to retrieve. Some owners would feel uncomfortable with this, so there's no need for them to participate in particular activities or seek particular titles. Tracking, where the dogs search for a lost individual by following a scent trail, and lure coursing, where dogs follow a mechanical lure, are some alternatives that do not involve the use of any killed game, although they do invoke a dog's inherited prey drive and provide intense and mentally challenging workouts.

Lure coursing as a formal sport is only available through AKC to purebred sighthounds (including Greyhounds, Whippets, Ridgebacks, Borzois and others.) But you could adapt the idea for any dog with high prey drive and set up your own lure for your dog to chase. If you wish to use a vehicle like an ATV to trail the lure, use extreme caution. Consult first with a professional about the best way to use the lure with your dog, and ask a helper to watch the dog as

Clyde- "Loving his first beach run."

he chases the vehicle and to give you a signal if you need to stop or slow.

Even if your dog will never compete in any trials, just learning more about these sports can open your mind to his tremendous athletic potential and give you many new ideas for exercise.

Ch. 11- Water Activities

"Water activities are diverse enough to help, and to entertain, almost any dog and owner."

Also Try These Ideas from Other Chapters for Water Activities:

Therapeutic & Senior Dog Activities: Swim, Hydrotherapy

Activities for High-Energy Dogs: Ocean Swim, Water Run, Water Walk, Retrieve in Water

Useful Activities: Be a Lifeguard

Activities for Owners with Limited Mobility: Continuous Pool

Water Activities- Introduction
**"Water activities can be diverse enough to help, train and entertain
almost any dog and owner."**

Do you own a dog that loves water, or a dog you just can't tire out no matter what you try? Does your dog have hip problems or difficulty supporting his weight because of injury or old age? Water activities in this chapter can help all these dogs. And vigorous water exercise is an alternative for "dog days" of summer when too much land exercise could quickly send your dog into heat illness.

Adding a regimen of intense water exercises like "Water Walk", "Net Pull" and "Continuous Pool" can take the edge off for high energy dogs that keep getting into trouble no matter how far you walk them. Other dogs that particularly crave water exercise because they were bred to retrieve in water will enjoy games like "Submarine" and "Retrieving in Water" (see Chapter 10). And they'll love splashing around whenever they like in a "pool of their own".

Water exercise can also be a lifesaver for dogs that are injured, recovering from surgery or suffering from hip problems. Your veterinarian will likely advise you to rest your dog for a short time after surgery or injury; but if your dog's problem is chronic you'll need a way to provide him with healthy exercise without straining his bones and joints. Rehabilitative water activities (see "Hydrotherapy" sections in this chapter and Chapter 9) can speed your dog's healing. Hydrotherapy can strengthen muscles surrounding the weak area, stimulate the dog's mind, improve his mood and energy level and even bolster his immune function. Water rehabilitation can sometimes work miracles- to the point that dogs people thought would never walk again are soon up and walking on their own.

Read on in this chapter for some cool ways to have fun with your dog on hot days. Once your dog learns to love water, use your imagination for many more ways to incorporate water into his play and exercise routines.

Water Activities:

Kiddie Pool
- works in almost every household; very cheap, very easy & very much fun –

This is one of the easiest, cheapest and most stress-free ways to entertain your dog in the summertime, and dogs love it! A kiddie pool- the kind you can buy in discount stores and some pet stores for less than $10- is great for dogs of any size and any age. You can use it to acclimate puppies or shy dogs to water or use it for a relaxing, yet stimulating, activity for senior dogs or dogs with physical limitations. You can even use it for hydrotherapy for smaller dogs.

Another nice benefit of owning a kiddie pool is that it provides your dog the chance to cool off in hot weather, allowing him to play outside a little longer, in slightly hotter temperatures.

It's great fun to watch dogs playing in the kiddie pool, especially if you have more than one. You may also want to get creative. Buy some interesting water toys and teach retrieving from your lounge chair. The water entertains your dogs, and keeps their minds and bodies stimulated, even when you don't feel like expending a great deal of energy.

If you get inspired, you and/or your kids can splash around in the kiddie pool with your dog. Just use clean water of a moderate temperature, and make sure the dog is clean, healthy and pest and parasite free. **Your children must never get the water in their mouths when the dog's been in the kiddie pool, and you should always provide adult supervision for kids and dogs whenever they play in water. For safety purposes, you should also make sure to empty the pool when not in use.**

The kiddie pool idea also helps owners with limited mobility. Not only can an owner with physical limitations use a kiddie pool in their backyard. But, as an "off-label" use, an owner who is unable to exercise the dog on the street during hot weather could use a kiddie pool on a condo balcony or screened porch with small dogs. The kiddie pool could bring a taste of summertime to a safe shaded area and allow owner and dogs to bond for hours. Just make sure that the dogs are supervised and that splashes of water have an appropriate place to drain so that nobody slips and you do not damage your home or other units.

Continuous Pool (With Caution)
-   not for everyone, but good for a tougher workout or
if you don't have room for a full-sized pool -

A "continuous pool" for humans provides the option of a constantly moving current to swim against for exercise. This saves space and these compact pools are usually installed indoors, so you can swim laps all year round. Some owners may also consider exercising their dog in a continuous pool if he's high energy and a confident swimmer or if he can't do other exercise due to climate or physical limitations. Used correctly, the mild current in a continuous pool can also help with a dog's physical therapy and rehabilitation.

Use caution if you wish to try a continuous pool with your dog. Never make a continuous pool with the current turned on your dog's first experience swimming. We only recommended this type of pool for dogs who are already experienced and expert swimmers with no fear of water. Always supervise swims in a continuous pool very carefully, train your dog to the activity starting with the weakest current and don't push your dog if he seems afraid. Because of the resistance, this type of swimming is very exhausting, so keep sessions much shorter than regular swims, perhaps a quarter of the time. And supervise your dog continuously, since he could have difficulty escaping the current on his own. Stay right next to him while he swims to assist- just stand back far enough that you don't get scratched! And make sure your dog always wears a lifevest.

While a continuous pool is an investment, it can be much cheaper than a full-sized conventional pool. And the fact you can install it indoors multiplies its value because it allows for year-round swimming.

Comparison shop on the Internet to learn more. Also check the Resources section of this book. Next check with your veterinarian that your dog will physically benefit from this kind of swimming. Installing a continuous pool is a serious investment. If your dog is the primary reason you want to install the pool, first "rehearse" with him in a sample continuous pool to make sure he can use it comfortably before you install one at home.

Chase the Water
- silly water fun; start with a garden hose -

Have you ever tried to water your grass with your dog around? Every time you try to spray the grass your dog interferes, chasing the stream of water and swallowing so much that more goes in his mouth than on the grass! The good news is that this dog will love to play the game called "Chase the Water". It's a great little silly game to play with your dog on a hot summer day. And it can also help you bond with your dog and make him love to pay attention to you.

There are some rules to keep your dog safe when playing the game. First, you *must* teach your dog to never put the hose itself in his mouth. It isn't a game anymore if he starts biting the hose. If your dog does acquire a taste for chewing on the garden hose, the least you may lose is your hose. But you may also someday have to rush a dog with this bad habit to your veterinarian's operating table. So, discourage hose chewing from the start by letting the dog know all fun ends the moment he touches the hose with his mouth.

Also teach your dog to wait for your signal to start and end the game- otherwise your dog may think that you're playing whenever you try to water the grass! If your dog already interferes with you whenever you use the hose, teaching him to wait for your signal like this can actually cure the problem, as he will only try to play when you give the go-ahead.

"Chase the hose" is very easy to play. All you need is a garden hose and a water-loving dog for lots of fun combined with lots of exercise. Just ask your dog if he wants to play "Chase the Water". Then squirt a stream of water into the air and your dog will try to catch it. (Some Boston Terriers love this game so much that they'll jump six feet in the air to catch the water!) Angle the water into different parts of the yard (while watering the grass) and your dog will run all over chasing it, quickly tiring himself out for the day.

At first keep the water at a steady stream as your dog learns to follow it. Then, you can teach him to keep his attention glued to you by only spraying the water for him to chase when he looks into your eyes. This teaches your dog that looking at you makes him have more fun. And, at the end on the game, remember to tell your dog the game is over with a word like, "Game over," or "Enough".

As an advanced variation, if your dog really loves this game, you can also pack up your own water supply in a large squirt gun and head out to the park. Playing the game he loves is a good way to keep your dog's attention focused on you in this more distracting environment.

Hydrotherapy
- for more details, see chapter 9 -

Hydrotherapy refers to using water for physical rehabilitation for illness or injury. Just as the use of hydrotherapy is increasing in popularity for humans recovering from surgery or suffering from chronic ailments such as arthritis or joint disease, the use of physical movement in water is also becoming increasingly popular to treat dogs with similar medical conditions. Water has many benefits, including relaxing joints and keeping most of the weight off injured limbs while still allowing range of movement. Since water exercise isn't overly strenuous and can be used to target problem areas, it's also helpful for elderly and overweight dogs.

You can buy special hydrotherapy equipment for dogs (for example, slings to support weight and underwater treadmills) and/or visit centers around the country staffed with physical therapists specializing in canine hydrotherapy. Another alternative (in less complex medical cases) would be to use your own swimming pool, bathtub or kiddie pool for your dog's hydrotherapy, or to simply include swimming as a form of summertime exercise as part of your dog's "get healthy program".

Please read the fully detailed description of "Hydrotherapy" in Chapter 9, Therapeutic and Senior Dog Activities, and see Resources for more information. If your dog is elderly or overweight or suffers from injuries, illness or chronic medical conditions you should first check with your veterinarian before you start water exercise or hydrotherapy at home.

Submarine
- for strong healthy dogs that are able to dive; intense activity that some dogs love -

Once you find out that your dog loves water, you can choose the activity that best suits his abilities - from splashing in a kiddie pool, to a task like diving that is highly challenging.

We all know dogs love to swim, but did you know you can teach your dog to retrieve items off the bottom of the pool for you? Ray was shocked the first time he saw this happen. He was watching his friend's 100 pound Labrador Retriever swimming in the backyard pool and then, the next minute, the dog was gone. Ray jumped into the pool thinking the dog needed to be rescued, only to find his friend laughing and the dog, now surfaced, looking at him like a fool who stopped him from doing what he loved most. Ray asked his friend how he didn't have a heart attack whenever his dog went under like that and the friend just laughed and said it came in handy when he dropped his sunglasses in the pool.

For the rest of the afternoon Ray watched in awe as the Lab repeatedly dove under the water, grabbing items off the floor of the pool and bringing each of them back to his owner. The dog truly loved this extreme game. And it's no coincidence that the dogs that love diving the most seem to be the sporting breeds. Many dogs can learn to enjoy water, but there's no sense in even trying to teach this challenging activity to dogs that do not already have natural leanings to retrieve.

Start with a strong healthy dog that loves water and only practice in the shallow end of the pool. You first need to teach the dog to fetch whatever you throw and have the dog build a strong retrieve drive, so start outside the pool. (See "Fetch", Chapter 10.) Then have your dog retrieve a ball that you throw into the pool and make sure that your dog can easily climb out of the pool to bring it back to you.

For the next step, you should be in the pool with your dog out on the pool edge. Then toss a sinking item in the shallow side, and ask the dog to retrieve. Your dog will jump in and you should stay close by so you can help in case he panics and needs help surfacing. If the dog comes up with the item on the first attempt, praise him lavishly. If he tries, but can't retrieve the item, it's possible the water may be too deep for him at the moment. Try tossing the toy onto a step, so the dog can get it easily and then praise when he does.

As your dog gets better at the game you can make it harder by tossing a few toys into the pool and then asking him to retrieve them in the order you ask. You'll be amazed how good your dog can get, but remember to always use caution with a dog who's learned to retrieve items from the pool. No dog is safe unsupervised, especially dogs who are likely to attempt acts of daring. Make sure to gate your pool and never leave your dog by the pool alone without a human there to watch.

Pool Float
- FYI- the pros and cons of pool floats for dogs -

What could be cooler than relaxing on a big neon pink pool float in the center of your crystalline swimming pool, enjoying the rhythmic drifting of the currents and the feel of the sun on your back, as you slip into a state of relaxed tranquility? Some might say the only thing cooler would be your dog enjoying the pool float, or sharing it with you!

Some dogs will happily climb up on a pool float on their own to take a break from swimming. But, for the average dog, the feat may prove challenging. You can help your dog by choosing a float with a thicker than average rubber-type skin, and you will really do him a favor if you can find one with a built-in uninflated piece that can act as a step. If your dog is a natural born swimmer and he does climb onto the pool float on his own, praise him lavishly and get out the cameras! Then let him relax and let him make the decision when he wants to jump back in the water. If your dog climbed up confidently but then seems nervous getting down, you can provide some assistance, or pull the float over to the steps.

It's also okay to help your dog onto the float as part of his water play with you. But only attempt this if your dog seems to *want* to get onto the float, and remains calm and happy. Lying on a pool float will only feel relaxing for those dogs that are already completely at home swimming in the pool. Some dogs will never feel comfortable on a float, and that's okay.

Use caution and never let your dog jump into the family pool when he's alone and unsupervised. And don't leave floats out in the water when he's unattended. A pool float will not save a drowning dog's life and it may provide a temptation for him to jump recklessly into the pool. And all pet owners should fence their swimming pools and install suitable steps so that their pets can climb out if they ever fall in accidentally.

Water Walk
- add this to speed up vigorous workouts, greater interest & intensity and less strain -

You may have already read about "Water Run" as an Activity for High Energy Dogs (Chapter 10). Walking in water can be used for intense exercise as well but, depending on how you do it, walking in water can provide your dog a very gentle workout. If you ever walk in water yourself, you'll notice it gives more resistance than walking on land. You have to "push" really hard and the water gives all your muscles quite a workout, even little-used muscles. Your heart and lungs also get an intense cardiovascular workout- even chasing after a drifting beach ball!

But walking in water can provide an incredibly gentle form of exercise if you do it differently. If you walk at just the right depth, you'll notice that the water supports your weight, making walking feel easier, especially if you have joint problems or if you're overweight.

Another pleasure of walking in water is that it keeps you cool. You can get a good workout walking along the shore *in* the ocean in summer and you likely will not even feel hot. Try the same walk on the sand *out* of the ocean on the same afternoon and, even if you don't suffer any heat illness, you may end up feeling broiled, woozy and exhausted. You could have worked harder and more intensely in the calm water and come onshore feeling energized! Walking in water is also fun and different, so it can add some spice to a flagging outdoor workout routine that tends to hit the doldrums come summer.

For dogs, walking in water can provide all the same benefits as it can for humans. Walking your dog in water may seem like a slightly eccentric concept but if you've read this far we don't believe you're raising your dog right unless at least a few of the neighbors raise their eyebrows! Walking in water is fun because it *is* different, both for you and your dog.

This "Water Games" chapter is intended for owners whose dogs love water. And the same is true for walking in water. If your dog is deathly terrified of any type of water, he certainly won't be thrilled that you drove hours out of your way to take him to the nearest beach. What starts as a novel idea can become a struggle. So if you have to drag your dog to get him into the water, this is not an exercise for him.

Most dogs, however, will appreciate walking in water to some degree, so this is a good "starter" activity if you want to get your dog used to water. The shallower the water you start with, the more comfortable your dog should feel. And while a few rare (one in a million) dogs enjoy battling waves with their surf-champion owners, most dogs prefer natural bodies of water that are calmer.

For this reason, lakes, ponds, rivers or creeks (as long as they're bacteria and algae free) might be more enjoyable for your dog than the ocean in many areas. Your veterinarian can advise you if he believes your local freshwater sources are safe for your dog to walk in. And the ocean *can* be a great place for your dog's water walk in summertime. Just make sure it's not too wavy or keep the dog beside you in very shallow water.

You should walk with your dog on leash beside you for the "water walk" exercise. It's the only way to keep him walking right beside you and it allows you to check for underwater hazards or sudden drop-offs.

The depth you choose for your dog's water walk will determine how much exercise he gets. Water that's only inches deep will not be that different than walking on land for most dogs, but it will add excitement and stimuli to the workout and cool you and your dog a bit. Water that hits at chest level will likely give your dog the toughest workout. Go slowly so as not to overexhaust him, and work for only a brief period. This is a very tough cardiovascular workout, and fifteen minutes can substitute for hours walking on land. Walking at this depth is suitable for dogs that are healthy (cleared by a veterinarian), and in prime physical condition.

> *Walking in water is easier on your joints while tiring you quicker, and it's the same for your dog. Water Walk can benefit both high-energy dogs and dogs with bad joints.*

If you take your dog into slightly deeper water, the water will start to support his body weight, so this can actually reduce resistance. Walking more slowly is also easier. So these variations can make this exercise possible for dogs that are not in prime physical condition. Walking slowly in water is also a great substitute for walking on land because it cools your dog and protects him from heat illness. It also protects vulnerable joints. Just check with your veterinarian if your dog has existing health problems or limitations.

You don't always need a natural body of water. If your dog is very tall, you can walk him up and down the shallow side of your in-ground pool. Or if you own a shallower pool or a pool made for dogs, your dog can stay in the water while you walk around guiding him on the leash outside the pool. You can do the same for tiny dogs by walking the circumference outside a plastic kiddie pool while your toy breed walks circles in the water. You may get some funny looks from the neighbors, but your dog will appreciate the novel exercise!

Do only what feels comfortable for you and your dog. Remember that some days are simply too hot and humid to exercise outdoors, even when you and your dog are immersed in water. A good rule of thumb is that when something doesn't feel good it isn't good (this applies to every activity in this book and to life in general, in our opinion!) Water should provide enough natural cooling to make exercise feel good. If you get in the water and still feel queasy from the heat or sun, then this isn't a good time for your dog to exercise, any more than it is for you. Wait for the sun to drop, the breeze to pick up, or wait for another day. Head inside the air conditioning with your dog, and curl up with a good book. Or, better yet, read chapter 5, and substitute some great "Indoor Games & Activities".

Net Pull
-   if you fish, you and your dog will be fascinated by this working activity you may never have heard of -

Do you live by the coast, and own a Portuguese Water Dog, Newfoundland or other large breed dog that loves the water? In the past fishermen used to use their dogs to help them pull in heavy fishing nets that were dropped overboard. These fishermen needed these dogs because the nets and the fish they caught in them were their livelihood- if they lost a net they lost their only way to live.

You probably don't depend on your dog for your livelihood like these men of the past. However, if your dog has lots of energy you may be interested in giving him a job to do and a healthy way to burn energy that's in line with his heritage. To teach your dog to pull nets, first you must have a dog that loves to swim. Next you have to teach your dog to hold the net in his mouth. Do this by first showing your dog the net that you will want him to hold. Then put an end of the net in your dog's mouth and say, "Hold." After the dog holds the net for a second or two, ask him to "Drop it" and then give praise and treats. Once the dog will hold the net for a minute or two, ask him to pull the net towards you a foot or so and then say, "Drop," and praise.

Having the dog pull the net on the ground will start to build your dog's strength. You might be surprised how quickly your high-energy dog gets tired the first few times he pulls the net. This is why you should first build him up on land; you don't want your dog getting tired the first time he pulls the net in the water or he could drown.

Once your dog is stronger, you can start working with him in the water. Start first in very shallow water your dog can walk in and then move to deeper water where he needs to swim. Practice for very short intervals at first and then increase the length of the practice session as your dog's endurance builds. Soon you may even be able to hold one end of the net in a boat and have your dog on the other end and see if you can make a catch!

> *Pulling a net isn't just for dogs that were bred for this job. Just like a backpack can make a nervous dog feel like it has a job. Pulling a net for the owner can do the same, making the nervous dog more a confident dog.*

Dog's Own Pool
- **alternatives at various price points; can be worth it for your dog's quality of life over the years -**

We always find it fulfilling to advise clients how to modify their properties for the most positive interaction with their dogs, and it surprises us that many other dog trainers never address environmental issues! Perhaps it's because of money. Installing a pool or fencing a property can cost thousands of dollars. But costs in terms of lifestyle are harder to measure. What would fifteen years of happiness, versus fifteen years of stress with your pet be worth to you? And what if a simple environmental change could also save you thousands on trainers, doggie day care or vet bills just by providing your dogs a way to exercise?

Though not many people do it, why not take the plunge and professionally install a small pool for your dog, right next to your own swimming pool? A well-designed dog pool is similar in size and design to a kiddie pool. And some homes already have existing children's pools or spas that can be re-purposed. To cut expenses, owners should do extensive research and consider many designs and options, focusing primarily on function, before they commit to a project.

A shallow dog pool addresses the danger of your dog drowning in deep water in the family pool, or drowning because he cannot get out. With a pool designed for dogs you don't have to watch your dogs as diligently as you would in the family pool, and they can get in and out easily at any times, increasing safety. A shallow "dog" pool is much better for small dogs and it can be used with some older puppies as well. (Just make sure to observe puppies carefully.)

One design decision depends on whether you plan to use swimming as a primary source of aerobic exercise for your dog. If so, you'll want to make sure one side of his pool is deep enough so he can paddle, and roomy enough for laps and wading. If you don't plan on your dogs swimming as important source of their exercise, you could get by with a much smaller pool just for fun and splashing.

If installing new, you can design your dog pool to any size and specifications you want; for example, you could include shallow steps all around, spray or waterfall features or nighttime lighting. You could build in massage jets and/or a comfortable seat for humans if you'll be helping your dog with hydrotherapy. And don't forget fencing and/or a pool cover to keep kids and animals out when you can't be around to supervise.

With a designated doggie pool, you may feel more comfortable hosting "play dates" with friends' dogs. They can splash around in their pool while you float indolently in your pool with a Pina Colada and paperback, and they won't bother your guests who may not be comfortable with dogs swimming near them. Using a dog pool prevents your dog scratching, bumping or acting rowdy with your children in the family pool and it really helps in multiple dog households.

Some people also have hygiene issues and feel squeamish about swimming in the same water with dogs. An extra doggie pool satisfies these concerns, plus you can install a heavy-duty filter and practice more frequent cleanings of the dog pool filter if you have several long-haired dogs. And, if you close your own pool down for the season in late summer, the small dog pool can remain "open" a while longer without as much expense in maintenance. Your dogs, less sensitive to water temperature and less likely to stay immersed for long periods at a time, can enjoy splashing around well into the fall.

Due to the expense, not all readers may be able to install a dog pool, but the concept is worth mentioning because it opens up whole new ways of thinking about lifestyle with your dog. Think along the lines that, if you can dream it, there's somebody out there who will help you design it and install it! It's your life, and even though your neighbors may not do it, why not try something that makes your lifestyle most fun for *you*?

For example, you don't even have to have a family pool to install a compact permanent dog pool in your yard. If your dogs are water-loving breeds and a plastic kiddie pool is too small or inconvenient to keep setting up, you can install a dog pool designed completely to fit your own needs. You can build it just like a regular in-ground pool, but you may be able to use a shallow pool intended for humans' above-ground use to keep the costs down, rather than making it fiberglass or concrete. (Of course, first consult with your local zoning department and a qualified contractor before installation.) And always make sure steps are ample and securely fitted, since dogs can't use ladders.

Another idea is to use a spa as a canine pool, sunken in-ground or in fitted into a deck. Spas with massage features can be great for dogs that require hydrotherapy. Just make sure the spa has stairs your dog can use comfortably and that aren't too slippery. You might have to add rubber grips, padding or a ramp. And, if using a spa, make sure your dog can't turn on any hot water on his own!

Other homeowners have used fountain kits or small pond kits to design little "swimming holes" for their dogs. In this case you'll want to filter the water and/or make sure it's treated with harmless substances to forestall bacteria and fungus, but not an algaecide that's poisonous to dogs. As long as you first consult your veterinarian and your pool expert on how to keep it safe for dogs, a man made "swimming hole" can turn out wonderfully. And some dog owners with large properties will want to go all out and install a man-made pond big enough to accommodate dogs, plus fish and a rowboat! Imagine the blissful life your retrieving breeds will enjoy playing here at every hour of the day. You and your dogs will never want to leave your property!

Ch. 12- Useful Activities:

"It's easy and vitally important to make your dog feel useful, because helping you was what he was bred for!"

Introduction

Find My Keys

Sled Dog

Get the Mail

Wagon Pull

Pack Animal

Watch Your Children (Caution)

Check on the Baby

Check on Grandma

Check the Perimeter

Find a Missing Person

Help Your Special Needs Family Member

Bark for Help

Be a Lifeguard

Volunteer Your Dog (Therapy Dog)

Work with Your Livestock

Personal Bodyguard

Also Try Ideas from Other Chapters for Useful Activities:

Puppy Games & Activities: Find Mommy, Shopping Spree, Let's Play Doctor

Mental Games & Activities: Discern Objects by Name, Go To a Person by Name

Therapeutic & Senior Dog Activities: Bring Me the Puppy, Visit with Seniors (Therapy Dog)

High Energy Activities: Backpacking

Water Activities: Net Pull, Submarine

Family Activities: Junior Grooming Salon, Doggie Bakery, Assess a Dog

Activities for Owners with Limited Mobility: Service Dog, Rehab Together

Carry My Purse

Open a Door

Lap Dog

Real Dog Careers

Movie Star (for pay)

Lifesaver

> *Most dogs are happiest when they are doing something useful to assist their owners.*

Useful Activities-Introduction

"It's easy and vitally important to make your dog feel useful, because helping you was what he was bred for!"

We hope this chapter gives owners a new perspective when they look at their dogs. Owners mean well, yet if their dog was bred for demanding outdoor work like hunting or herding, they often feel confused about what to do with him every day in the suburbs or city. So we like to introduce other useful tasks that their dog can do to help them out in any environment. The fact is that most dogs are happiest when they are doing something real to assist their owner. Both dog and owner benefit- the owner gets much-needed help, while the dog stays healthy, happy and content. The key is to discover the right activity that works with your dogs' talents, but also realistically fits your schedule and meets the needs of modern life.

Someday, you might like to read up on the origin of your favorite dog breeds. Every breed we know today was originally bred to do a highly specific task for a specific type of owner, whether the breed was created thirty years ago or thousands of years ago. Today's dog owners may cherish the appearance or temperaments of a particular breed, yet may find the task they were made for antiquated or distasteful. (For example, most of us don't want our dogs hunting rats, even though this is exactly what many terriers were bred for!)

This is the time to think creatively to channel your dog's drives into more relevant tasks that you *do* need help with. For example, families are pleased to find out that their high-energy terrier that was originally bred to chase rats can just as easily search out the car keys lost under the bed or clean up all of his own toys after playing.

Often owners wonder what tasks are appropriate for their large working breed dogs in today's world. Sometimes these dogs can still perform the task they were bred for in a modified fashion to meet their family's needs. For example, you may not need your Bernese Mountain Dog to pull jugs of milk as his breed originally did in Switzerland, but you might like him to pull a little wagon to help you with the groceries. And, provided you do it with care, you can even let your child take a ride in the wagon! If you own a Husky or Malamute, you're likely aware of the dog's sled dog background and you could train him for real sledding competitions available in many cities. But, if you don't want to go this far, your dog will also be happy hauling firewood at home.

Other working dogs are bred to be guardians, and these guarding instincts could someday save your property or even your family's lives. But protecting your family and checking on family members is not limited to guard dogs. This chapter includes suggestions for how to properly encourage dogs of any breed to look out for your family and to aid your peace of mind. And encouraging your dog with activities like "Check on Grandma" and "Check the Perimeter" can also make the difference between a bored, frustrated dog and an engaged, confident dog that carries himself with a sense of pride.

When reading this chapter, you should also consider all the things that dogs can do for their communities and the world at large. A dog can make people happier, healthier and less stressed and can actually boost your immunity in the privacy of your home, simply by being an accommodating "Lap Dog". An assistance dog can help you with tasks of independent living if you face a wide range of challenges (see "Help Your Special Needs Family Member"). And you may be able to train the dog you already own as an assistance dog depending upon his particular abilities.

If your dog is friendly and loves people, you might also want to volunteer his services as a therapy dog. You and your dog will visit hospitals, nursing homes and other facilities and your dog will brighten the lives of everyone he meets, including the elderly and children with terminal illness (see "Volunteer Your Dog", this chapter and "Visit with Seniors" Chapter 9.)

Dogs' usefulness doesn't stop at just physical and emotional contributions- because some dogs actually bring money into their households! Read the sections on "Movie Star" and "Real Dog Careers" to learn about dogs that get paid for their work, or account for their human families' livelihoods by the work they do. And always keep an open mind- one day *your* dog might start bringing in the big money and then *he* may start asking *you* to bring him his slippers!

Useful Activities:

Find My Keys
- complex activity builds skills of retrieving and scent work -

Are you one of those people that frequently lose your keys in your house or front yard? If so, it can become frustrating to have to hide one set of keys under your car bumper and another set under a rock in the backyard just to make sure you can get back into your house. But did you know if you own a dog you may no longer have to worry? A dog's nose is designed for finding things, and your dog can learn to love finding keys, just like search and rescue dogs find fulfillment in locating lost children. Your dog will enjoy the search a lot more than his frustrated owner who's tired of walking in circles, wishing someone would come up with GPS for keys.

A dog's skills can rival GPS at finding whatever you need! And there are the added benefits- he won't get low on batteries and he'll give you lots of love when your keys are found. All you have to do is first train him the skill.

Dogs that do best at finding keys include hunting and working breeds. Some breeds that immediately come to mind are Bloodhounds, German Shepherds and Beagles, but any breed can learn to do the task. Just allot adequate time to teaching the activity. Don't start training your dog by immediately throwing your keys in the woods behind your house and telling your dog, "Find the keys," with no preliminaries. Unfortunately, if you try this you will definitely need that extra set of keys you just made for your house and car!

The correct way to begin training your dog for this task is to start the training inside your house. You only need three things to start: your dog or pup, your keys and a bag of treats. If you want your dog to carry the keys back to you, rather than to simply sniff out their location, you will first want to train him to retrieve objects in general. (See instructions in "Get the Mail" in this section, and other sections in the book which deal with retrieving.) Train your dog to retrieve items first, so that when you teach him to find missing keys you can also ask him to pick up the keys, bring them to you and drop them into your hand.

Once you've taught your dog to retrieve, you can now teach him to sniff out and locate the keys by name. First, get your dog's attention and shake the keys until he notices them. Then toss them a foot or two from you and tell him, "Find the keys!"

As soon as your dog grabs the keys, call him back to you and praise by saying, "Good find the keys!" and rewarding with a treat. Next time, toss the keys a little farther from the dog and repeat the cue. Continue to practice and, if your dog ever has problems, go back to the difficulty level where he last succeeded and work up more gradually from there or point out the keys and repeat the cue to give him a little assistance.

Once your dog is succeeding ninety percent of the time with you tossing the keys in the same room, next time hide the keys in a different room in the house. Now give the cue, "Find the keys," to the dog and see what he does. If the dog runs straight to the other room and brings you back your keys, praise him lavishly and offer a handful of treats. (If your dog succeeds this quickly, he may be a natural for finding not only missing keys, but missing people as well!)

If your dog won't look for the keys, or if he can't find them when you first place them in another room, help him out a bit. Walk around the house with him, saying, "Where are those keys?" Your dog will likely show great interest and he'll probably find the keys with a little help or hint from you. As soon as he finds the keys, praise him. If your dog continues to have trouble, try hiding the keys in much "easier" locations until he starts to show consistent success. Then increase the level of difficulty until he's locating the keys close to one-hundred percent of the time. Doing this successfully is a great accomplishment and, if the house is the only place you tend to misplace keys, this is as far as you have to go.

But if you frequently lose your keys outside you may also want to teach your dog to find the keys amidst the distractions of the great outdoors. To start the training, first leave your keys on the ground in full view near a tree or stone where you can easily find them again. Next bring your dog outside, give him the cue to find the keys and see if he can find them on his own. If he finds them immediately the first time, praise and reward lavishly.

If he has some trouble locating them, you can offer a little help in the same ways that you did inside. As his skill gets better, make the locations progressively more difficult. You can keep your dog off-leash during the activity if he's off leashed trained and/or your property is fenced or you can keep him on a long lead while he searches. Practice on different days until your dog is finding the keys every time.

Now it's time for an even greater level of difficultly in which you'll throw your keys someplace outdoors and neither you nor your dog will know exactly where they land. (If you're alone during the first practice sessions, you can tie a long string to the keys for insurance, just in case your dog can't find them. Or you can have a helper hide the keys.) Once the keys are placed, bring your dog out, give him the command and let his nose lead you to the keys.

Later you can make things harder by kicking a little dirt or leaves over the keys or, if you live in the North, you can even have your dog look for the keys in the snow. If your dog will find your keys in all these environments you'll never have to worry about losing your keys anymore- as long as you can find your dog!

Sled Dog
- teach your strong & healthy dog to pull the *right* way & he will love it -

Some dogs love to pull sleds! This includes dogs specifically bred for pulling sleds like Huskies and Malamutes, some working breeds like Newfoundland and many muscular high-energy breeds, including Pit Bulls. If you want to try this great exercise with your dog, follow reasonable precautions. **First clear the activity with your veterinarian, ask him for weight limits and never make your dog pull anything extremely heavy.** This is only an activity for healthy dogs that can tolerate cold well, and it's intended to be fun, not a serious way to haul cargo.

To start, buy your dog a well-fitting harness that bears weight across the front of his chest- his strongest point. **Never attach a sled to a buckle collar, choke or pinch chain**! Once your dog is wearing his harness, gradually introduce him to the sled so he doesn't panic. For example, you can walk with the dog, pulling the sled along beside both of you at first. Next attach a very light sled with no weight on it for your dog to pull a short distance and reward and praise him once he accomplishes this. Build up distances and weight over time. Make sure your dog enjoys this task and that he's comfortable outside in cold weather, or else choose another sport. Some dogs may hate the sled, so forcing it on them defeats the purpose of this exercise. You also don't want to keep your dog out too long or work him in extremely low temperatures.

On a nice winter days, however, an athletic large dog can easily help you pull a bag of groceries home from a short trip to the store, retrieve a small load of firewood or even pull your small children around (with you closely supervising and able to stop him at all times). Dogs love these activities because they recognize they are genuinely helping. (And you can even use a plastic tray-style sled on grass with a reasonably light load.)

There are many safe and healthy ways your dog can help you by pulling items on a sled. But pulling a full-grown adult around is not one of them! Tempting as it may seem, unless you possess a professional dog sled, the expertise to use it and a team of dogs bred and trained for the sport, never climb onto the sled yourself!

Get the Mail
- cute multi-step task, easily applied to other functions -

Have you ever watched a dog on television run out to the mailbox and bring the mail back for his owner who sits back resting in his recliner? You can easily teach your dog to do this for you. The training method that most people use to teach the skill is called chaining, in which the dog is taught the last part of the activity first. This same method of training can also be used by people with disabilities to teach their dogs to bring them a variety of items, and it's also a popular technique used to train dogs for movie roles.

If you want to teach your dog to retrieve mail for you, the first step is to start with a dog that you know loves holding items in his mouth. First, encourage the dog to gently hold a piece of mail in his mouth and to then drop it into your hand at your command. The second the dog drops the mail into your hand, praise him and offer a treat. Next teach the dog to walk a few steps toward you with the mail in his mouth and then drop it.

If your mail is regularly dropped through a mail slot, the next step in training would be to instruct your dog, "Go get the mail". Walk him over to the mail slot and encourage him to lift the mail gently in his mouth. Then have him walk back to your recliner before dropping it in your hand. Give him loads of praise and treats, and practice until he can walk all the way to the door on his own and pick up the mail at your command.

If you want your dog to go farther and get the mail out of an outside mailbox, you will either have to open the door for him, or you may want to install a doggie door. Either way, when you first practice, you can do all the steps above, but have a friend hold the mail just outside the doggie door.

A dog that learns to get the mail like this from your friend can also take the mail from the mailman, if you want him to stand inside the fence and meet the mailman every day. More likely, you will want to teach him to take the mail out of your mailbox. So your dog can do this, make sure the mailbox is mounted low enough that he can get to it and that the handle is easy for him to maneuver without breaking any teeth. Continue the "chaining" process by starting with your helper giving him the mail standing right next to the mailbox the first few times. Next leave the mail just on the lip of the open mailbox. Your dog must now also learn to grab the mail and then set it down for a moment so he can nudge the mailbox shut with his nose to close it. Finally, teach him to open the box on his own. Eventually your dog will learn to run out and complete the entire process whenever you say, "Lucky, go get the mail!"

As you can see, training a simple task like getting the mail is actually an involved process that will likely take weeks of practice. Once you train the skill with the mail, you can also apply it to similar tasks like getting the newspaper. Training your dog to retrieve items like the mail keeps your dog busy, and when he masters the skill, you'll both feel a real sense of pride.

It's interesting that teaching this skill sometimes has a remedial function. Some frustrated dogs love to shred papers, particularly mail that the mailman drops in the slot every afternoon. If you train your dog that he receives treats for picking up the mail and placing it, undamaged, into your in-box, then treating the mail gently will become a habit. Practice repeated times with old junk mail until you're sure you can trust the dog, and then let him try with the real thing. Now every day when you come home and find your mail waiting for you in perfect condition, thank your dog and give him the praise and treats that he deserves.

Wagon Pull (With Caution)
- don't let it scare you; healthy dogs can thrive on pulling a cart when done right!

Dogs love to pull. In fact, if you own a dog that pulls inappropriately on the leash, you may notice how easily he pulls a hundred-fifty pound adult off your feet to drag you down the sidewalk! But there's a much more productive way to channel your dog's power! Carefully using weight pulling for therapeutic purposes can center a hyperactive dog's mind and can help with behavior problems. And as your dog becomes steadier and more emotionally balanced you can start introducing pulling for useful tasks.

If your dog is a problem puller, before trying weight pulling therapeutically, you should check with your veterinarian to make sure your dog's hyperactivity isn't caused by illness. Also check that the dog has no physical limitations (such as bad hips). And never allow a dog with behavioral problems to attempt pulling with children involved. Note also that we don't recommend formal weight pulling competitions for dogs, even though competitions have become a popular sport. Certain highly athletic dogs thrive on pulling increasingly heavier weights in competition, but we feel the sport could prove too risky for the general public to try it with their pet dogs.

Instead, we recommend that you have your dog pull moderate (but not heavy) weights as a useful everyday function. If you have a strong healthy dog, he may really love helping you out with some simple everyday chores. **First check with your veterinarian that pulling is okay for your dog and ask him for a suggested pound limit.** Next buy a harness that provides good support across the front of your dog's chest. **Never use any neck collar for your dog to pull weight; only use a harness designated for this purpose.**

First accustom your dog to pulling very small weights and see how he takes to it. **The dog should show signs of enjoying himself. If he ever seems uncomfortable- stop!** Try again later with lesser weight or a different task.

You can gradually build up the weight your dog pulls, in accordance with his size. You can hook his harness to a small cart with well-oiled wheels, a plastic sled or a small lightweight tarp, depending on what you want him to move. But unless your dog is very big and very strong, haul only lightweight objects. Your dog's help will still prove very useful. For example, imagine him helping you haul tools and homegrown produce back to your house after you've worn yourself out working in your garden.

Having your dog help you pull items is easier than juggling your dog on a leash while trying to juggle all the items in your arms. And it's certainly better than having a high-energy dog jumping around feeling useless and left out of chores and hobbies. Instead, let your bundle of energy feel useful and truly integrated in your lifestyle. Dogs love to help their owners when given a chance; it's part of their essential nature. Even a dog that's used to running around and constantly annoying the family can be trained and channeled into more productive pursuits.

A larger dog could help you by pulling bags of groceries in his cart, (one at a time) from driveway to kitchen, and this could really help a senior or busy mom. Or imagine your loyal companion carting back your fishing supplies and a proud day's catch! Your dog will happily bond with you during these activities, which harken back to a canine pack going hunting together.

When selecting the right cart for your dog to pull, you can experiment with the many different wheeled garden carts, file carts, kids' carts and utility carts on the market today. Some of you may have watched video of large breeds like Bernese Mountain Dogs or Swiss Mountain Dogs happily pulling small children in carts. Such breeds were actually created as draft dogs. And, if you own a big perfectly trained dog of reliably placid nature *and* your kids are lightweight and highly cooperative, you *can* successfully enjoy this activity at home.

Please note, before allowing your large breed dog to pull children in a cart, your dog must be thoroughly obedient and resistant to any distraction. Two strong adults with fast reflexes should supervise the dog and kids carefully. Never let kids try this on their own and lock the cart away when not in use so children cannot use it unsupervised.

Pack Animal, Useful Version (With Caution)
- **highly recommended for "centering" pulling dogs on walks; more owners should own these packs-**

This is a variant of the activity above. It's another way your dog can help you carry items, only this time he will use a doggie backpack designed specially for this purpose. You can find these for sale on the Internet and in chain pet stores (and check our Resources section). And you may have seen doggie backpacks featured on *The Dog Whisperer* for the purpose of exercising out-of-control dogs. Using weights in the backpack increases resistance, making exercise more efficient, while centering a dog's mind.

We highly recommend the backpack. But, rather than stuffing it with weights, we suggest you fill it with *your* stuff instead! Picture your dog accompanying you on a hike in the woods, toting some of his own supplies. For example, if a swim in the lake is also on the agenda, he could carry his water jug and lightweight bowl, some treats, a towel, a comb and his doggie life preserver.

On the walk to the water's edge from your beachside vacation home, your dog could pack doggie sunscreen, a long lead, a small popup sun tent or lean-to for himself and bottled water. He could even help tote some kids' toys and a paperback for you.

Follow special cautions for the beach. Never combine exertion like backpacking with hot days or hot sun. Only allow your dog to carry items in the backpack on cool hazy days or before or after peak sun hours. And never walk your dog on sand that feels hot to your bare feet! He could get seriously burned. Rubberized dog shoes can help, but the best alternative is to simply choose a cooler day. Backpacking anywhere increases exhaustion for your dog, so use common sense on warm or sunny days and never backpack at all on very hot days.

Adding weight in a backpack also means you should drastically decrease the length of the walk for every bit of weight added, and also decrease speed. Walking with a weighted backpack in steep or uneven conditions makes the exercise even more strenuous for your dog, so adjust the speed and length of walk accordingly. Just like a human, a dog will gradually build endurance. **Start out with extremely small weights to get your dog used to the backpack.** Then build up the weights slowly over time. **Check with your veterinarian that your dog is fit to backpack** and ask for a recommended weight limit for what he can carry.

Never rig a human pack onto your dog's back. Dog backpacks are specifically made to distribute weight properly for a dog's skeleton.

Packing weight is great exercise and it increases focus and a feeling of usefulness for high-energy breeds including many of the terriers. Just use common sense since these breeds were not bred for packing, and they are small! If you want to try backpacking with a smaller dog, use an appropriate sized doggie backpack and you will find little ways he can help. A smaller dog can carry smaller items, like a clutch purse, baby bottle, cell phone or camera or he could carry his own supplies.

Backpacking makes your pet feel useful and appreciated for helping you. So, with his help, why not try out simple living for a change? Instead of navigating freeway traffic to drive through at Dunkin Donuts on a lovely Sunday morning, imagine ambling downtown with your dog and stopping at a quaint family-owned bagel place that is walking distance from your home.

Now imagine purchasing the Sunday *New York Times*, aromatic fresh-baked bagels and homemade cream cheese and then selecting strawberries, freshly picked herbs and a dewy head of Boston lettuce at the local farmers' market. Next you'll chat with a few neighbors and slip some of your bounty into your dog's backpack so he can help you carry it home. Human and dog working in unison like this is a beautiful picture and, when you bring your dog up like this, helping you becomes a lifetime habit.

For more details on the backpacking as exercise, please read the "Pack Animal" section in Ch.10, Activities for High-Energy Dogs

Watch Your Children (Use Caution)
- can dogs safely "babysit" kids? Read this for important suggestions & cautions -

Experts each have their own opinion of whether young children and dogs should spend time unsupervised and there's not necessarily one right answer. A lot depends upon the dog, the children and the situation. If you're lucky enough to have a dog with a "caretaker" personality you may have noticed that your dog not only is good around your kids, but that he actually takes on the job of babysitter. The dog may nudge the children to keep them out of trouble, growl if a stranger approaches your kids when they're in the front yard or bark for your attention if your baby falls down on his backside crying.

Acting protective and nurturing is nothing unusual for a dog; the dog is simply taking care of your children like it would its own puppies. In fact, as a small child Ray was "raised" by his German Shepherd Alfie. This K-9 trained dog acted wiser and gentler than a human mom and never once made a mistake, and she's part of the reason Ray grew up with a lifelong intuitive connection with dogs.

Some breeds (notably herding breeds) and female dogs that have already had puppies are more likely to be nurturers. But any dog can show the behavior. **In contrast, other dogs will NOT show nurturing behavior toward your kids. In fact, some dogs act rowdy or uncontrolled around children and they need professional training in order to learn to contain themselves.** (We see plenty of these dogs in our practice!). **Other dogs may even act aggressive and bite children under certain circumstances, and many dogs simply act indifferent to children. So never assume that all dogs are good with kids. Even if your dog usually acts sweet, an adult should supervise whenever the dog is with young children.**

If you're lucky enough to have a dog that shows concern for your kids, you can capitalize on this natural tendency. Allow your dog to watch over the kids when you are all together and encourage the behavior. A dog should always have a purpose in life and focusing on the kids and their well-being is a highly fulfilling job. It will give the dog's life meaning and prevent frustration and depression.

Praise your dog sincerely when he checks on the children. You can teach the dog each of your children's names and teach your dog to go to a child on command. If, for a moment, you lose sight of a child, ask your dog to find her. Teach your dog the skill during downtime and then, if a crisis ever does occur, your dog can help you find your child in an instant whenever you ask.

If your dog ever runs to you and starts barking stridently, trying to lead you towards one of the kids' rooms, follow immediately! Your dog is definitely trying to tell you something and performing one of the most vital tasks he has been bred for. Dogs that are big, small, young or ancient can all help look out for your children. Even if the dog calls you on a "false alarm", praise him for his concern.

There's a wide variety of useful tasks for dogs, and not every dog is suited to every purpose. While every family dog should respect children and act appropriately, the skill of acting as a caretaker for kids is a special one. It can be encouraged in dogs that already have the natural inclination, but it can't really be trained. Learn to discern if your dog is really showing caretaker behaviors around the kids. If he is- it's just one more thing to be proud of and one more way to let him help you.

Check on the Baby (Use Caution)
- how to tell if your dog wants to take responsibility for your baby & whether it's safe -

This skill goes along with "watch your children" above and parents should proceed with caution. We *do* recommend that dog owners encourage their dogs' natural tendency to care about an infant but we don't recommend that parents use their dog to take care of their baby rather than doing it themselves. **And never allow dogs around babies unsupervised.** Some dog trainers take an extreme view and tell parents never to allow their dogs near their babies at all. For, example, they'd say a dog should never enter the nursery.

> *In the past the Japanese used their Akitas as babysitters for their children. These parents never had to worry about anyone hurting their babies while their Akitas were on duty.*
> *If trained properly, dogs can be safe around babies but always use caution!*

We advise moderation. We believe that dogs *are* part of the family, and we also believe well-behaved dogs can be trusted around children under most circumstances. **But we advise parents to always supervise diligently whenever even the best behaved dog is with the baby. And only sweet, well-trained and well-behaved dogs with no behavior problems should be allowed around babies and young children at all, with no exceptions**. Despite our own backgrounds growing up intimately with dogs, this **is one area where we advise zero tolerance.** If you're expecting a baby and you know your dog displays behavior problems like jumping or nipping, you **must** treat those behavior problems before the baby is born. **Dogs with active behavior problems cannot safely be around young children at all.** And, unfortunately, keeping dog and child separated is not an adequate or long term solution.

Crating in particular can make small behavior problems much more serious, especially in cases of aggression, so don't think crating an unsafe dog in the same home as a baby makes it safe long term. Ideally, couples who plan to have children will first socialize their dog to act gently around children in various situations so that they feel completely confident in his temperament. However, once their baby is born, if the parents seriously believe that their dog shows aggression or even unfriendliness towards the infant, to be totally safe, we advise that they re-home the dog to a qualified new home or rescue society (making sure to advise the new owners of the potential problem). Another possible solution would be to immediately remove the dog from the property until he completes treatment with a caring applied animal behaviorist with an advanced degree. In contrast to a regular "dog trainer", an applied animal behaviorist is educated at the doctoral level to make the best assessment of the dog's temperament around children and his potential for recovery. They can also prescribe medication. Unfortunately, if you cannot find or cannot afford an applied animal behaviorist, sending a dog that has problems around young children to many old-school trainers who board and train dogs could be disastrous. Harsh conditions and harsh training at many of these facilities can backfire and make aggression worse.

The good news is that it's not that hard to find dogs or puppies that will act sweet around children and some are highly nurturing. Loving behavior around kids is in the nature of many dogs. And owners should look for this quality or potential for this quality when initially choosing a dog, taking into account breed, specific genetic background and history of early upbringing (as well as history of behavior in past homes if the dog is an adult). After that, bringing the dog up kindly and training and socializing him conscientiously is usually all that's necessary to make sure he'll welcome the new baby. The parents can then shape their dog's behavior even more once the baby is born.

Assuming that your dog is generally well-behaved, parents should consider the subtleties of the dog's temperament and ability to control his body movements when they determine how closely they let him interact with their infant. For example, you may choose to allow your dog to walk into the nursery as long as he cannot reach the crib, you may block the nursery door with a baby gate or you may choose to keep the door closed when the baby is sleeping, depending on your dog's behavior and your ability to supervise.

Some dogs take it on themselves to look out for babies. (This is the kind we grew up with.) If one day your dog runs from the direction of the nursery, barking in alarm and tossing his head trying to get you to follow him, your baby may be in trouble. The dog may be alerting you, so it's best to follow him back to your baby- at a run. The same is true if your dog wakes you in the middle of the night, leading you to the nursery. Never discount these behaviors. Instinct wakes dogs immediately when there's trouble so, even if the dog led you to the nursery on a "false alarm", don't scold him. Instead, praise and pet him. Perhaps the baby was whimpering and the dog was concerned. If the dog tries to lead you to the yard or pool area and your baby is not within sight, follow him immediately. The baby may be in trouble and the extra few seconds the dog gives you in finding him could save your baby's life. Sometimes a dog may come through in a crisis even if you've never seen him show much concern for the baby before.

As in any nurturing behavior, looking out for a baby can't really be taught. And many dogs are on the opposite end of the spectrum. Some act too roughly around infants, others just don't understand the concept of an infant and some dogs will even bite an infant. It's up to the parents to know their dog's individual temperament completely, and to always safeguard appropriately even if your dog appears to be good with infants.

If you're lucky your dog may be one of the special ones who will go the extra distance to help you look out for your baby. You can help a nurturing dog like this out by teaching him the baby's name. Always encourage him (as you would any dog) to be patient and appropriate when you care for the baby; allow him to stay around, but make him learn not to act pushy. Give him extra praise and encouragement any time he tries to alert you to danger, because someday a dog like this dog really may save your baby!

Check on Grandma
**-   there are many ways your dog can help the seniors in the family;
start with this command –**

Time and time again throughout the book we've stressed that the best way to enjoy living with a dog is if your dog is a real family member. Dogs were originally domesticated and bred not just as companions for man, but also to help man. Many of us who live alone with a dog understand how easy it becomes to communicate with each other with the same daily give and take that you would with a human family member.

Just as people speaking different languages can develop a commonly understood slang that incorporates words from both, you can also develop a language to communicate with your dog. This language may combine words, movements, sounds, emotions or even smells so that the two of you spend your day in constant communication and your dog is always at your side to assist you. Your dog can be a helper and an encouragement to other family members as well, and some dogs have a natural inclination to help the weaker members of the pack, including senior citizens.

If a senior is a part of your household, the right dog can be a joy to them. From the time the dog is a puppy, he should spend time with the senior family member. They can play together and your senior family member should also practice obedience commands with the dog. Even if the senior is physically limited, you can use suggestions from Chapter 14, Activities for Owners with Limited Mobility for creative alternatives.

Never separate the dog from the family. The (well-mannered) dog should be integrated (safely) with every member of your family and should learn to give respect to each family member. Starting when the dog is a puppy is the best time to get your dog in the habit of frequently visiting the senior member of your family, especially if grandma or grandpa has physical limitations that keep them confined to a chair or bed for much of the day.

How great for them to receive spontaneous visits from the puppy or dog! Dogs can lift depression, keeping seniors focused and interested. And they even have beneficial effects on blood pressure and immune function! Of course, your dog does not know that he's doing grandma or grandpa a favor. Your senior family member may be your dog's favorite person and your dog will enjoy stopping in to be petted, to play games, practice obedience or nap at their feet. Or your well-behaved toy dog may curl up in grandma or grandpa's lap or at the foot of their bed.

Not only can a special dog act as a companion to the elderly family member, they may also act as a helper. (See the "Help Your Special Needs Family Member" section in this chapter). The dog may also alert you if your elderly family member needs help or if something is wrong. In a true emergency such as a health crisis, many dogs will become upset when they notice the elderly family member in trouble, and they will bark or come running to get you.

This is instinctual behavior in many dogs and it doesn't need to be taught. But always respect it if your dog "calls" you in this panicked fashion, and immediately follow him to check on grandma and grandpa. Even if the situation turns out not to be a true emergency, but just something a little different that had the dog worried, you should praise your dog for his actions. This way, he'll feel encouraged to repeat the potentially lifesaving behavior if a true emergency ever comes up.

Sometimes your senior family member may need to talk to you, but they may not feel they can walk to another part of the house or yard to look for you. Your dog should know both the senior person's name and your name. If your grandmother needs you, she can command the dog, "Go find Kathy!" and the dog will go running to find you and get your attention. To train this behavior you would practice repeatedly. Each time the dog finds you and brings you back to Grandma, your grandmother would praise and reward her with a treat. Gradually you would phase out the treats and just use praise, except for rare occasions.

You can use a similar technique to teach your dog to go to the grandparent's room by using the command, "Go check on Grandma!" Both these behaviors can easily be taught through repetition, just like you can teach your dog to retrieve specific items for the senior member of the family. But remember, the desire and judgment to assist a senior in trouble with no specific prompting depend more on a dog's inborn character than they do on specific training. If your dog is a natural nurturer, you've probably noticed that he already tries to look out for the senior in your family.

But whether your dog is a natural born caretaker or not, certain actions on your part can help build character and confidence. Follow all the suggestions throughout the entry, making sure to integrate the puppy with all family members at a young age. Teach the dog basic obedience, and always reward the dog when it shows responsible and helpful behavior.

Also frequently practice the exercises above, teaching your dog the senior person's name, how to go to their room and how to send them to find you. Anytime your dog "calls" you to the senior's room, you and the senior family member should praise her lavishly. And showing respect and trust whenever you train her or interact with her will make her more likely to come through for you in a crisis.

Considering how much companionship and life-saving help a dog can provide a senior, we advise against confining the dog to a crate. A dog must be free to follow its senses and intuition to check on the senior and perform its lifesaving function. If there's any doubt that the dog would be too rough or rowdy around a frail senior, you must either train the dog yourself and or get professional training from an expert behaviorist. Crating is never a long-term solution. Training is a better solution, but it must be done perfectly. **Only allow the dog to interact with frail seniors when you're certain he will behave gently. If you allow a large dog or dogs to leap on or nip at a physically frail senior, even in play,**

it could result in life-threatening physical injury that the senior might never recover from.

This warning might seem obvious, but we've been called in to help families where a physically delicate senior is frequently jumped on by a large dog and their physical safety is in jeopardy. Often the senior hesitates to complain and the adults in the household allow the behavior to continue. We strongly suggest that when you select a new dog, you ask the senior in your household what breeds they'd work best with. Next, consult books and reputable breeders about what breeds are usually best with seniors. And, before making a final decision, introduce your senior family member to the specific dog you're contemplating bringing home to make sure they're comfortable together.

Despite appearances, not every small breed is good with seniors and not every large breed is bad. In fact, some of the relatively larger breeds (for example some Collies, Golden Retrievers and Standard Poodles) are known to be excellent with seniors, but they are also versatile enough to keep the whole family happy. Within each breed, certain individuals will shine when dealing with seniors and, if you provide proper training and shaping, your dog should make life much happier and more comfortable for the seniors in your household.

Check the Perimeter
- easy foundation activity for working or guardian breeds. Pleasant to do every day –

Check the perimeter? This is an activity especially for the owners of guardian breeds. Many of these breeds give their owners problems because they are high energy and have been created to do demanding jobs, but in today's world those jobs are no longer needed. These dogs still desperately need a job to do, and for many of them checking the perimeter of your property may be just the job they were made for. In this activity, you teach your dog to walk the perimeter of the property making sure everything is as it should be and giving a warning bark if something is out of place.

People may feel cautious and worry that a job like this could make their dog vicious. It is true that some guard dogs become too aggressive. But this is usually due to owners who don't fulfill their responsibility of adequately socializing the dog when he is young and continuing to do it throughout his life. Proper socialization at a young age is necessary for all dogs, but it's absolutely urgent in the case of large guarding breeds that may become emotionally unbalanced to the point of becoming dangerous. These dogs should have opportunities to meet friendly strangers in a positive fashion out in the world. If a dog is locked up his property for his whole life and never exposed to the world, he may become overly territorial. The same is true for guarding breed dogs that are given no structure or obedience training, and are basically ignored by their owners.

Before you train your dog to check the perimeter, he must first be properly socialized and obedience trained. At this point, channeling his natural guarding instincts in a controlled activity like checking the perimeter will actually make the dog a better canine citizen. It will focus his mind, make him obey the desires of his owner (rather than choosing how to handle situations on his own) and most importantly, having a real job to do will prevent frustration.

And not only does frustration cause many bad canine behaviors ranging from jumping on people to digging holes, it's often a contributing factor in aggression. Never ignore or forget about your dog. When you leave a working dog abandoned in the yard with no attention, no structure and no tasks to perform, you are not doing him a favor, even if he has adequate room to run. An intelligent and naturally courageous dog must also have something to engage his mind, and the best tasks for working breeds are those in which they feel they are helping their human family.

Teaching your working breed to check the property lines feels natural to your dog and it's a pleasure to accompany him on "the rounds" to show him exactly what you want from him. All you need for this activity is a dog and a leash and some time. You and your dog can walk your property lines as a team once a week, several times a week, once a day or as frequently as several times a day. You'll get a nice walk, and you can also check all the corners of your property, pick up debris and attend to any overgrown brush or damaged sections of fence. All you need to do is to put your dog on leash and start walking confidently around the perimeter of your property. You must encircle the entire property every time, and never step over your property line. This teaches the dog in a manner he easily understands where your family's property begins and ends. He will be more likely to stay within the confines of these boundaries, and he will tend to defend within these boundaries.

If you plan to walk the perimeter with your dog unleashed, then we recommend that you fence your yard regardless of the exact wording of local laws. If your yard or your property is unfenced, then you should walk your dog on leash, and you should also keep him under physical control at all times. As your dog walks around the edge of the yard, encourage him any time he notices something that seems out of place and calls your attention to it with a bark (for example, if he spots trespassers on a neighboring property).

Don't scold your dog if he barks at wildlife, but if he gets overexcited you will want to recapture his attention. Tell the dog, "It's okay," and then walk him away from the distraction. As soon as he calms down, you can praise him and offer him a treat. You will be shaping him to understand when he should and shouldn't give the alert.

You or your other family members should regularly walk the perimeter of the property with your dog to reinforce the boundaries and sense of ownership. And soon you will notice that your guarding breed dog will start regularly patrolling the perimeter on his own. Suddenly a previously bored and frustrated dog will now have an important job to focus on- watching for anything strange that approaches his property.

Not only will this job give a lackluster dog spunk and confidence and make him feel more secure, but it will also teach the dog sound judgment. You will teach him that his job is only to *bark* if he sees a stranger approaching the property line, and not to do anything else until his owner arrives to give him guidance. A dog that regularly practices this will be under his owner's control and he'll be less likely to bite. Practicing walking the perimeter with your dog and discouraging inappropriate outbursts will also help him contain himself when he sees animals- he'll understand that you don't want him to overreact each time he sees a squirrel.

Another benefit of walking the perimeter is that a dog that has done this since puppyhood is less likely to try to run away- it's a dog's nature not to run from an area he knows he's responsible for watching. You can also start this activity with mature dogs and it will help them to become more responsible and balanced and less likely to run away. And it helps immensely to calm jangled canine nerves. But, **for safety, owners of all large breed guarding dogs must keep their property and their dog secured at all times. Never allow anyone to come onto your property uninvited/unannounced or your dog might bite, mistaking them for dangerous intruders and you may be liable.**

A well-trained dog will almost always behave responsibly according to what you trained him, but if the dog is loose and a stranger walks onto the property unannounced, you cannot expect the dog not to treat this person as an intruder. Either fencing the property or securing the dog at all times is necessary if you wish to stay safe and remain a responsible neighbor.

Find a Missing Person
- take time to teach your dog this complex task; for his benefit and to possibly save a life

Find a missing person is one of the most important tasks you can teach your dog. Imagine your dog being able to help find a little girl from your neighborhood who's wandered off and can't find her way home. A skill like this will win a lot of good will for dogs, because it demonstrates the heroic tasks our dogs are actually capable of. And, even if there's no real crisis, a dog that's trained to track the children by name can save a worried parent a lot of stress.

If you want your dog to learn to find someone who has wandered off, you don't need special training equipment. All that you need is a long lead, some time and the patience to teach your dog a skill based in an activity he likely already loves- putting his nose to the ground. If you own a hound or a hunting/scenting breed like a Bloodhound, it's important to include work on finding things in your dog's activities. If you don't give your hound something productive to do with his nose, he will likely use it to get into mischief. So why not teach him a challenging task that could one day save a life?

If you have a hound dog that you might want to use for tracking, start scent training the moment the pup comes into your home. Start by playing puppy games like "Which Hand?" or "The Shell Game" (see Chapter 4, Mental Games.) which require the pup to use his nose to

> *It takes time and devotion to properly teach your dog this skill. But if you give him the time to learn, you'll likely be amazed. Your couch potato dog may display great scenting talent, which could someday help save a life.*

find a treat. Next start hiding treats around the house and telling your dog to find them. Praise the puppy when he starts putting his nose to the floor looking for the treats. At the same time work on getting control of the puppy so he won't follow his nose on his own, but instead will wait for your command.

As your puppy grows older and you are able control where he puts his nose, start working on more challenging games. Some good games to work on are, "Find Mommy" (see Chapter 3, Puppy Games) or "Find My Keys" (this chapter). The next step would be to teach your dog to distinguish different scents. To do this you can use rubber gloves to put some dumbbells on the ground so your scent isn't on them, or have a friend put out the dumbbells without your scent. And then put down one dumbbell that does have your scent.

Next have your dog sit at your side and have him smell an item with your scent. Next instruct him to, "Go find!" If he finds the correct dumbbell that matches up with your scent, praise and give him treats. If your dog grabs the wrong dumbbell, just shake your head, tell him, "wrong" and then command "Go find," again. Once he is consistently picking your scent out, repeat the same process with the scents of some friends. It may take a few times for your dog to get it right at first, so don't rush. You want your dog to be able to consistently find the right scent before you move on.

The next step is to get your dog to be able to stay on a path with a person's scent on it. This is why you need the dog to be able to distinguish different scents and to follow only the scent you instruct him to. You can't have a dog looking for one person and then start following another scent of an animal or other people. To teach your dog not to get distracted by new scents, you will first practice using a 30' long lead. (This will prevent a loose untrained dog from getting so engrossed in a new scent that he runs away!) Start by having a friend walk away in a straight line and then hide behind a tree twenty or thirty feet away. Next show the dog a glove with your friend's scent on it and instruct the dog to "Go find".

At this point in training you will know exactly where your partner walked. So, if your dog stays on the scent praise him. But if he goes off the scent or looks confused, just use the long line to bring him back to the scent line and then praise him when he picks the scent trail back up. When your dog finds the training partner, have the partner praise and thank the dog for such a great job and reward the dog. After a few practice runs when you are sure your dog can find the partner easily, start having the partner make turns in his path before he hides. When you first send your dog out, never let him go far off the scent without helping. But don't overcompensate either, because later on you won't know where the path is yourself and you will need to depend on you dog's nose.

So far you have only left one scent at a time for your dog to follow, but now it is time to make it harder for both you and your dog. You will stay in your vehicle with your dog and you will enlist two training partners to lay a path for your dog to follow. This time, the friend whose scent the dog will be following will walk a twisty path, while meanwhile the second person will deliberately cross the trail to see if your dog will be distracted and take off on the wrong trail.

At this time you will have to depend on your dog, because you won't know where your helpers walked or where they are hiding. Only the helpers will know where you and your dog should be going and the pattern of the scent. At this time it will become clear if you trained your dog with care or if you overcompensated for your dog. Watch for the telltale signs that your dog has lost the trail, including walking in circles or looking to you for help. This may happen the first time he encounters the second scent crossing the first. If your dog looks like he isn't sure which trail to follow and needs help, have him smell the sample scent item again and ask him to, "Go find."

Your helpers can tell you after your dog gets to the end of the trail where you went wrong or how well you did. If you are working with experienced tracking partners they can help tell you where and why the dog lost the trail and give you tips for improvement. Don't get discouraged because this is a very hard task for a green dog to do. Just think how hard it would be for us to find someone hiding if all we tried to use was our noses!

Once your dog can keep a trail no matter how complicated it is you can move on to using older scents over different terrains, including hills, snow and rainy conditions. Some police dogs can even follow a scent if a person got into a car and then backed out or if they crossed a river on foot. So, if you have a well enough trained dog on someone's trail there's no way they will get away. Many pet dogs become good enough at tracking that they can help you in everyday situations, and even in the occasional crisis. But if you train your dog to become a true expert at tracking you might consider volunteering his skills for search and rescue work, because you may have a truly special dog in your possession!

Help Your Special Needs Family Member (Assistance Dog)
**-   dogs can help owners with various disabilities both in an "official"
or an informal capacity -**

Everyone knows about guide dogs for the blind, but do you know that assistance dogs also help owners with many other physical and psychological challenges? For example, assistance dogs can help diabetics avoid life-threatening changes in blood sugar and epileptics avoid or prepare for seizures. Assistance dogs can act as ears for deaf owners; they help owners confined to wheelchairs open doors and reach objects so that they can live more independently and they even help owners who suffer from panic attacks or emotional disorders like agoraphobia go out shopping comfortably.

Do you also know that these assistance dogs can be of widely varying breeds? Some assistance dogs may be as small, frail and unexpected as a Chinese Crested. All that's necessary in the dog is a certain temperament and a certain talent. You can purchase an assistance dog that's already trained for the specific type of help you need and then do additional training together. Or if the dog you already own is suited in talent and temperament, he can be trained and then tested in order to be certified as an assistance dog. If you wish to find out more about certification, the first step is to research assistance dog certifying organizations.

Please see the Resources section, and look for more on the Internet or at your local library. These organizations will happily give you more information about the specific tests your dog will have to pass to be certified. Or contact the local agencies in your community that advocate for the disabled. As a rule of thumb, your dog must be able to focus on tasks without being distracted by people or dogs in public places, and he must be trained to do specific tasks to assist with the owner's disability. Having a good disposition with no aggression, fear or bad manners (like jumping on people or pulling on leash) is also essential.

Once your dog is trained as an assistance dog, he'll legally be able to go with you into all public places, including staying with you at hotels. By law, even if your handicap is not visible, people have no right to demand to know the nature of your disability (this would violate your civil rights), nor do they have the right to deny access to your dog just because the nature of your disability is not visible. The law is on your side, so if your dog is already an assistance dog, or you are thinking of training your dog as an assistance dog, learn your rights! If an uniformed business owner ever gives you a hard time, you can first try educating the person through friendly conversation. If the problem continues, the next step is to contact your local advocate for the disabled and the next step is to call a good lawyer!

We believe that, in future, more and more dogs will become assistance dogs and they will perform more sophisticated tasks. Once the general public can keep more open minds, assistance dogs could provide their owners ever greater opportunities to become more independent and productive. And, unlike technical or mechanical aids for disabilities, an assistance dog can also provide non-judgmental and cheerful companionship. This makes overcoming difficulties more pleasant and more dignified.

Depending on the nature of the work your dog will be doing, you may be able to train him yourself or you might need to hire a professional. Some assistance dog work is fairly basic, so any highly qualified professional trainer that uses gentle methods may be able to help you. (Examples include teaching your dog to lift objects for you or open door handles for you if you are in a wheelchair.)

Other assistance dogs need to perform highly specialized tasks, so you would want help from someone who is not only familiar with the particular physical challenge, but is also familiar with training assistance dogs to work with that challenge. An example of this might be if you are deaf. You might want to start with an advocacy organization for the deaf to see if they can suggest a qualified trainer. You can also go in the direction of first contacting a national dog trainer's association (such as the Association of Pet Dog Trainers, APDT) for referrals for specialized trainers in your area. Another suggestion would be to consult the local organization that certifies assistance dogs in your area, and they can refer you on if needed (see Resources.)

Even if the task the dog will need to you with specialized, you often *can* train it yourself, perhaps with the help of a dedicated friend or family member. Also consult the best materials on the particular subject, including books and DVD's.

Some parts of an assistance dog's work really can't be trained and an innate talent for the work must be inborn in certain cases. You may first realize you are blessed with a dog with an uncanny talent to help with specific challenges the first time he saves your life! For example, a dog may sense when an owner is about to have a seizure, and he will bark or act up in some other noticeable way. Once he does this a few times, the owner will likely make the connection that this particular dog has a unique "sixth sense" and is able to sense the seizures coming on. If the owner decides that they wish to use the dog as an assistance dog, they can then work with the talent and use training to channel it properly.

Even if your dog has no amazing talent persay, if he's friendly, well-balanced, kind, loving and loyal, great with obedience and always seems eager to help his owner(s), he may be able to help a family member with physical or emotional challenges. Your dog does not have to be specifically certified or work full time as an assistance dog in order to be of help. Think for a moment about your "wish list". List the kinds of help you could most use to accomplish your daily activities. And now imagine that your dog already is an assistance dog. How many of these activities could your dog theoretically help out with?

It will help to read about assistance dogs and some of the varied tasks they perform (see Resources). Then stretch your imagination as much as you want at first to come up with as varied a list of activities as possible. Assuming that you've read plenty of books on dog training, you can now brainstorm as to how you can use specific training methods to train the activities you want most.

Some of the "useful games" described in this chapter, such as "Find My Keys", "Get the Mail" or "Bark for Help" might prove useful to a person with physical limitations. Using the same training techniques as you would to teach your dog to retrieve the mail, you can teach him to pick up other objects as well. Your dog could even learn to retrieve your cell phone or bring you a snack from the kitchen if you teach him to combine retrieving techniques with "Soft Mouth" from Chapter 3, Puppy Games & Activities.

If you will be depending solely on your dog to help you with complex tasks, or if you want to train the dog to help a disabled family member, this book is just a starting point and you will then want to read much more in-depth material on the theory and practice of training dogs. And read about training other animals as well, because some of the same techniques used to train sophisticated tasks in dogs are also used to train other species. Just make sure to always use gentle, positive training methods. If you need more help, you can also consult local dog trainers and select a knowledgeable trainer who will come to your home and coach your dog in the exact tasks you want trained.

Bark for Help
- how to encourage this behavior that can save your family in an emergency -

This is another lifesaving skill your dog may possess. You may not even know that he can save your family's lives by barking for help until the day comes that he is called upon to do it. Of course, acting as a watchdog and sounding the alarm when danger threatens is natural for dogs, especially certain breeds. Many dogs (not all) will bark whenever a potential intruder approaches the home, or in various other situations where the dog perceives danger to human family members. The behavior, in excess, may seem a little annoying, but most families are grateful because of the dog's superior senses and ability to perceive danger.

Sometimes a dog may bark for other lifesaving reasons. For example, in an instant when you were occupied, your toddler may have wandered out of the house, slipped through an open pool fence and fallen into the pool! You'll likely notice if your dog ever barks for a reason like this because his bark will probably sound different- agitated and insistent. He may also "dance" and toss his head as though leading you. In a situation like this, some dogs even attempt to drag their owner by the sleeve or pantleg. No owner should ignore a summons like this, especially if it comes from a usually placid dog!

A dog with an elderly owner may also tend to watch over the owner. If the owner falls asleep with a pot boiling, the dog may bark to wake her or he may grab her by the sleeve, as above. If for some reason the owner doesn't wake, the dog may start barking frantically. If the owner still doesn't wake, the dog may run to alert another family member. And if there is a way outside like a doggie door, he may even run out to try to get a neighbor's help, barking frantically and imploringly.

As in the entry about dogs helping special needs family members, above, your dog won't, in most cases, be professionally trained to bark for help unless you obtained him trained for this purpose already. If he does bark to get help when his owner needs it, he will likely do it out of natural instinct, and his instinct will tell him when the time is right.

You *can* train commands like "Check on Grandma" in this chapter and "Bark on Command" in Chapter 8, Problem Dog Games. *If* you have a responsible dog with good judgment, you can combine the two commands by teaching the dog to bark to wake Grandma or to get her attention. (Teaching the average rowdy young dog to bark at your grandmother or to tug at her sleeve to wake her may not be appreciated! So try this only with a mature dog that you know will only do it either at your command, or on his own judgment if a problem arises.)

As with the other commands involving helping, assistance or rescue there's no way you can proof the activity one hundred percent. In the end, your dog will bark to help a family member in a life threatening crisis only if he knows he should. Some breeds are more apt to be protective or nurturing with their owners, but this rule has many exceptions- in the end, how your dog reacts in a real crisis depends on the right training *and* the right dog. You can't *force* a dog to act heroically on the day a real crisis occurs. But you can *encourage* him to act like a hero, and even a tiny toy dog can do his part when it comes to barking for help.

To encourage heroic behavior in your dog you must raise him with love and respect. You should also actively build his confidence while teaching responsibility. Basic obedience trained with gentle methods is essential, and the family members must be involved in the training. **If you want your dog to someday use his own judgment to save your family, you should never train him with harsh corrections or by intimidation or he might feel too afraid to act in a crisis. It's essential that your dog learn to think when there's a novel situation and Mental Games & Activities (Chapter 4) will help this.**

You should also ask a lot of your dog every day if you want him to step up when there's a crisis. Training the dog to do any type of helpful task around the home will teach him that he has a real part in the family's well being. If your dog does alarm bark if he sees a strange car pull up, do not punish him. First take a moment to check if anything is wrong. If there's no real danger at the moment, respectfully signal your dog that everything's okay and it's time to stop barking now. Or distract him to a different task.

Obviously **you should never use any frightening or hurtful method (for example, shock collars or "e-collars") to stop the dog's barking, or he will never bark when you need him to.** If your dog ever does bark to alert you of a problem, reinforce the behavior. For example, if your teenaged daughter screamed because she saw a spider and the dog came to you barking this would be the perfect time to praise and reward him for an appropriate reaction to her distress. You could say the dog's name and something like, "Good Bark for Help".

If you want your dog to protect and watch over the family by barking, he should have as much free access to all areas of the house as possible. (Just prevent unsupervised direct access to infants or small children without an adult present.)

Some houses are very large. As long as you train your dog properly, your adult canine family member should never hurt himself or hurt or annoy family members. Nor should he destroy possessions. There is no substitute for the peace of mind you will feel when you know that your dog is roaming every corner of the house all night long, checking every family member, every door and every window, checking for any bad sound or smell, and never even waking you until that one night when you may need it most. No, there is absolutely no guarantee that your particular dog will react by barking and will save your life in a crisis. But there *is* a guarantee that **a dog in a crate absolutely CANNOT bark to save your life if he is not free to roam the house and evaluate the situation.**

Be a Lifeguard
- you can train some dogs to act as a backup to the human lifeguards whenever your family swims -

Do you have a dog that loves water? If so this may be just the game for you. There are dog breeds bred specifically to save people in the water. An example is the Newfoundland. These dogs used to jump into frigid waters to save fishermen who fell overboard. You can teach your dog to do the same for your family if you have a swimming pool or live by any body of water. But be forewarned that you will need to teach your dog that not everyone in the water wants saved, some just want left alone to swim in peace!

First you have to make sure your dog really loves water. This activity is not for dogs who hurry out of the water whenever you persuade them to get in. You'll want the work on this command only with dogs that happily jump into the water all the time on their own. Your dog will not only have to love to swim, he will have to possess the judgment, the will and the strength to pull a person to the side of a pool or boat without hurting the person. Your dog must also learn to be very gentle with his mouth (see "Soft Mouth" in Chapter 3, Puppy Games).

Any breed of dog can learn to be a lifeguard as long as they are large enough to stay above water when they have hold of a person. But if you are going to have your dog work as a lifeguard in any large body of water, you will want the dog in tip-top shape. Don't be silly and take a poor Labrador that's used to being a couch potato and throw him into the lake to save your 10 year old child. A dog like this may not have the strength or endurance, and both your dog and your child may be in danger. Always start off small, practicing in a shallow pool first, and then work your way up to lakes or the sea.

While your dog is in training to become a powerful swimmer, you will also be training obedience and "Retrieve" commands until your dog is perfect. (See "Fetch", in Chapter 10). Start lifeguard training at the edge of the family pool. Have your dog sit at your side, then throw a mannequin that looks like a person into the pool. (You can purchase a mannequin specially made for lifeguard training (see Resources). Or you can use a CPR dummy, a large kid's doll or an old store mannequin wearing a lifevest). Give the command "Save 'em!" or similar words and encourage your dog to jump into the pool and retrieve the dummy. Encourage your dog at every stage. Once your dog grasps the mannequin by the arm, call him back to you with great encouragement. When he reaches the edge of the pool, pull the mannequin out and give your dog intense praise.

(If your dog has trouble at any point, you can get in the pool to help him. If he doesn't want to put his mouth on the dummy, you can show him how by "targeting". First teach him to touch the dummy and reward him, next reward him for grasping it with his mouth, next only reward him when he drags the mannequin through the water and finally only reward him when he reaches the edge of the pool.)

Next you want to make sure that dog is using a soft mouth on the dummy. This will let you know how he will hold a real person. If he bites too hard just show him the marks and tell him to be gentle. When the dog has no problems bringing the dummy back, start adding weight to the dummy to make it more like the weight of a real person. After your dog masters this you can move on to a real person.

The first person your dog practices saving should be light, because it's easier to pull a dummy to the edge of a pool than a real person who might be unconscious or panicked and might fight the dog. Have the person working with your dog help the dog at first. But if the dog puts too much pressure on the person's arm, the person should scream. This will teach the dog to keep a soft mouth while trying to save people. Even a dog that is great "saving" the dummy may panic at first when he sees a real person in the pool. As your dog gets more proficient at saving the person, the victim will want to fight the dog more and more. Human lifeguards train this way also, because drowning victims are never calm and often fight like you're the one trying to drown them!

Give your dog tons of encouragement. A benefit of teaching your dog this highly challenging task is that he'll enjoy the feeling of having an important job to do. We hope that your dog will never have to use this skill in real life. But, if you practice his water rescue skills, your dog will always be ready for the day you need him to be a lifeguard. This will keep the dog happy and the bond you have with your dog will flourish, knowing you have a dog you can be proud of.

Therapy Dog (Volunteer Your Dog)
- some dogs can help the ill, the elderly or kids in need
just by visiting and being adorable -

> *Therapy work has become so popular that one of the larger non-profit organizations has over 20,000 registered dog/handler teams*

Therapy Dogs are some of the best known "useful dogs", and they can provide a wonderful service to humans in need just by being their loving and lovable selves. But there are some skills your dog will need to possess before he or she can qualify as a therapy dog. Make sure to read "Visit with Seniors" in Chapter 9. We also recommend you read *Therapy Dogs*, by Kathy Diamond Davis, a good book to help you get started, and also a good reference for obedience and husbandry. Also see the Resources section for some websites for therapy dog organizations, or do your own Internet search.

If you wish to volunteer, a local therapy dog club can help you evaluate whether your dog has a suitable temperament, and they may be able to help you train the dog specifically for therapy dog work. They can also test and certify your dog as a therapy dog and then they can match you and your dog up with appropriate local volunteer opportunities.

You and your dog will visit people in need, often seniors in nursing homes, children with serious illness or hospital or hospice patients. Some individuals that a therapy dog visits may be severely disabled. Some may not even be able to speak and some may be severely depressed because of their illness. Interaction with the dog may be the first positive interaction the patient has had in a very long time, and people tend to relate to animals on an instinctual level that transcends their disabilities. Sometimes petting a dog can actually improve immune and cardiovascular function, aiding healing. And sometimes playing with a dog can be the first step in bringing an autistic child out of their shell.

Therapy dog work has been widely publicized in recent years and it's a popular cause that everyone can get excited about. If you wish to volunteer your dog, it's probably because you know you own a friendly dog that loves people and loves being petted. Some dogs even seem to show a special care and concern for people in need and it seems like they truly want to help.

Books about therapy dog work and your local therapy dog organization can help you decide if your dog has the right temperament to train for the work. Individual dogs of almost any breed have been known to make good therapy dogs. Exceptions are some of the rarer guarding breeds like Fila Brasileiros (Brazilian Mastiffs), Presa Canarios (Canary Dogs) and Black Russian Terriers that have been bred to protect aggressively. No matter how much owners want these dogs to be friendly, it is unfair to try to use one of these rare-breed dogs in a capacity that goes completely against their nature.

Other commonly known guardian breeds like Pit Bulls, Dobermans and Rottweilers can be used as therapy dogs, provided the individual dog has a reliably soft temperament. A potential volunteer must also consider the public's perception of certain breeds and whether there are some facilities where a large working dog might not be welcome. If the volunteer does use a working breed as a therapy dog, and the dog behaves perfectly, he'll act as a great ambassador for his breed. So make sure he behaves beautifully.

Some working breeds may not be appropriate as therapy dogs because they tend to have a quiet or aloof temperament. An ideal therapy dog should enjoy being petted by large groups of people and thrive on it, rather than simply tolerating it. And some dogs are simply too rambunctious to act as therapy dogs. Beyond being perfect in basic obedience, a dog must have sound judgment and act mellow and well balanced. Your eighty-pound Labrador may love people, but if he gets so excited that he sometimes jumps on people, he simply can't be around kids or seniors using walkers. And some dogs are too delicate themselves, including tiny toy breeds. Some larger toy dogs might qualify, as long as they are matched with volunteer opportunities where the patients are able to handle them delicately.

Although working as a therapy dog and handler is not usually paid work (there are some exceptions, and some therapy dogs and handlers are paid for their services) it is highly involved work. It can also be tremendously fulfilling. It will give both dog and handler a sense of purpose. But never make so many visits so that you and your dog "burn out".

Instead, therapy dog visits should make not only the patients feel uplifted, but should make you and your dog feel uplifted as well.

Work With Livestock
**-   the most common dog career not too long ago. Lots of dogs
would still love to do this task!**

Despite living around some ranches and farms, over the years we've never once gotten a call from a customer who wanted us to train their dog to work with their livestock. This is because training dogs to work with livestock is part of a way of life. If you're a working rancher or farmer, you may have learned the skills and traditions from several generations of family members who owned and ran the property before you. And many generations of working dogs may have grown up on the property as well- herding dogs like Border Collies or Australian Shepherds, for example or flock guardians like the Kuvaz or Anatolian Shepherd. And your dog doesn't have to be purebred to herd your sheep, goats or cattle. Many dogs were simply made for it. There is nowhere they'd rather be than outdoors with their owner, running circles around his flock of sheep or goats or cattle to bring them home safely from the far pastures before a storm.

Watching a dog work with livestock as many of them were meant to do will leave most city people awestruck the first time they see it, especially if it's their dog! They may have never imagined his capabilities until they enroll him in a program on a ranch where he is taught to herd. Being active and productive like this can, in itself, cure many dog behavior problems that are rooted in boredom and frustration. The exercise is healthy for the dog's body, and the many strategies and judgment calls stimulate the dog's mind.

This entry is not aimed at those of you who already work your dogs with livestock, but rather those folks who may not know anything about the ranching lifestyle, but are curious. The first thing to do is to research your dog's breed and learn about the types of work he may have been bred for. Then watch videos of dogs like yours working. Next, you can contact some local farmers or ranchers. They may have a working dog on their property and they may welcome you to watch him. (Some might even be willing to train your dog, for a price.)

If you're not comfortable approaching farmers or ranchers, you can also get information by contacting championship breeders of your dog's breed. If your dog is a herding or working breed, many of the top show dogs of his breed also work full time on their properties when they're not winning shows. You will likely be amazed what the dogs are capable of, and the best breeders will be happy to talk with you. Or you can check some of their websites to watch videos of the dogs at work.

These breeders should be able to direct you to the best local resources for someone who can train your dog to work with livestock. Not every dog will adapt to it. Remember, dogs are generations away from their working past. Sometimes prey drive will get out of hand and your dog may be less than gentle with an unfamiliar animal like a calf or a goat. If you are a hobbyist farmer, you should choose your dog specifically for a proven ability to work well with livestock. If you impulsively bring home a dog with unknown history, your livestock may be in serious danger!

If you own the dog first, most dogs can be trained to love farm animals that you purchase, but proceed carefully. Even if you have just one animal like a cow or a goat, your dog will likely enjoy herding it and protecting it. **But put safety first. Dogs and farm animals can be unpredictable.** This is a situation where you must introduce your dog to the farm animals and observe in a safe situation before bringing the animals home. Unless he naturally gets along with them perfectly, you should hire an experienced farmer or rancher to train him proper manners. Only then can you bring the farm animals home.

In a little while, your dog may truly amaze you. A few months earlier, you may have been stuck in a high-rise cubicle staring at a computer all day long. Now, you strike out to live your dream in the country, farming or ranching for a living. And perhaps the biggest surprise is when you find your dog who never did much more than sit beside you on the couch, now moving around like the wind, herding your animals and helping you in your work- just like he was always meant to do!

Personal Bodyguard
- your dog guards you out of instinct and love, so why not encourage it in a safe & healthy fashion?

In a chapter of useful activities, we must mention that the way in which some dogs are of the greatest assistance is by protecting their owner from attack by other people. A canine bodyguard will protect you every hour of every day, every day of his life and ask absolutely nothing in return; he'll protect you simply out of devotion and love. Your dog can hear things humans can't, he can smell things from a great distance and he can use unflinching intuition to decide if a stranger "just isn't right", or means his owner harm.

Of course, certain breeds have been designed specifically to work as guards; other dogs are bred to be more friendly and outgoing to strangers. But most dogs have some protective instincts and will tend to stand up for their owners in a true crisis. For this reason, owners should act responsibly when it comes to their dogs guarding them.

First, learn about the breed you plan to buy or adopt. Many dogs do not need any specific "attack" training in order to protect their owners under ordinary circumstances. One of the benefits of formal protection training is that it gives the owner the ability to "turn off" their dog if he is attacking, just as they can turn an attack on with certain commands. But training that teaches your dog to bite humans is something to be approached with utmost caution. Unfortunately some irresponsible owners enroll dogs of an already defensive breed in attack training with the motive of scaring or hurting people.

Other irresponsible owners don't follow through properly after the training; they may isolate the dog, tease the dog, use painful training devices, cruel corrections or house their dog in an unsafe fashion where he can hurt passersby, including children. Unfortunately some irresponsible owners like this have given dogs of some guarding breeds (for example Rottweilers or Dobermans) a bad reputation.

Some attack trainers, including police and military trainers, are highly qualified and highly responsible. They will not agree to train your dog to attack unless he is of sound and suitable temperament and you have decided on this type of training for the right reasons, and they will train your dog safely and carefully. Unfortunately, some of the very worst dog trainers have been known to gravitate to attack training for their own sense of personal power. These amateur attack trainers may not be truly qualified, and/or they may use cruel training methods that could cause dogs to become dangerous. This is why, **if the average family ever purchases or adopts a dog that has been previously attacked trained, they MUST learn all the specifics of the training and how to safely and appropriately handle the dog. It's a safer idea for average families not to purchase dogs with this background and to avoid attack training altogether.**

If you want adequate protection for your family and a dog that will alert you to intruders and stop intruders if necessary, simply choose a large guarding-breed dog and provide great husbandry and training. Treating your dog with respect and using positive training will allow you to control his actions, and it helps your dog develop confidence and a feeling of being a trusted and valued part of the family.

There are many guarding breed dogs beyond the better known ones and many guarding breeds are actually surprisingly gentle with your family members, including your children. To make sure your dog's guarding tendencies will come out at appropriate times and he'll react strongly enough to stop an intruder while still showing gentle behavior every day with your family, it's essential that you pick out the right puppy.

This is one case where **you must carefully investigate your dog's breeder before buying. You should learn how to assess the puppy's temperament in contrast to his littermates, meet the puppy's parents, check how the pups are housed and handled during critical early weeks of life and learn what the breeder has done to select for temperament.** If this is your first guarding breed dog, the breeder is also a good place to start for information about raising, handling and training the breed. A reputable breeder will share enormous amounts of information and will likely want to investigate you as thoroughly as you investigate their kennel, especially if they are selling you a dog that is capable of doing physical damage. **Any breeder who sells a guarding breed dog to a novice without full exchange of information is not reputable. Buying from such a breeder will almost always lead to bad consequences.**

If you want to bring home the right dog to protect your family, the best way to ensure temperament is to buy a young puppy from an informed breeder and then raise him properly. If you do choose to take home a full-grown dog and wish for him to protect you, you should likewise find out as much about his temperament as possible. If you cannot find out enough information to be sure about this particular guard breed dog's temperament and how he was treated in his previous home, then bringing him home and encouraging him to guard your family is a foolhardy idea for a novice. Many such dogs that end up in shelters are wonderful and function wonderfully as companions and they also guard properly and courageously in a pinch. But only an expert should take a stab at encouraging a strong guard breed dog with uncertain history to protect a home. The outcome is just too uncertain.

No matter where you obtain your dog, it's essential that all owners who choose a guarding breed first read up on their breed, as well as learning about defense in dogs in general. Large guard breed dogs are best for owners who are experienced and well-studied. As you study, you will learn amazing things about your breed of dog's physical power and protection capabilities over the centuries.

If you and your family are not up to bringing home one of the larger, more intimidating and tougher breeds of guard dogs, there are many other breeds to choose from that will also provide some level of defense. This is a time to do extensive research: read books as well as websites where information may be incomplete or slanted and consult many professionals, not just one who may be biased towards certain breeds or philosophies. All your efforts will pay off many times over in a dog who will be the perfect companion for your family and who may also save your family's life!

Carry My Purse
- cute task & the skill transfers to other objects -

Some dogs love to hold items in their mouths, and a well-trained dog can be taught to hold your purse when you need a little help. For example, when you're juggling your infant's stroller and a set of house keys, an extra set of helpful teeth to hold up your purse might be just what you need. And some dogs are happy to help. The same concept applies to any object you want your dog to carry in his mouth. Just start with an emotionally balanced dog with basic obedience training (one that likes to fetch objects is even better).

First, teach your dog to hold onto the desired object by encouraging him to touch it with his mouth, then quickly offer him a treat and praise. Next, gently insert the object, (like the purse handles) between his teeth, and simultaneously give the desired command, for example, "Carry it." Praise your dog if he willingly holds the object for any length of time, even a few seconds, saying, "Good carry it". Then release with the word "Okay", and remove the object from his mouth. (If your dog knows the command, "drop it" you can use that command here.) You could offer a treat now but, in order to avoid confusion, we suggest simply praising when your dog carries something for you and then giving treats only at the end of a successful session.

Through praise, repetition and treats at the end of each session, you can build up to your dog holding the desired object for longer periods of time and/or carrying the object to you from a distance. Adapt the idea to your own needs. Just make sure the object you choose to let your dog carry is not heavy enough to put any strain on his neck. As easily as you can envision one dog carrying a purse, you could just as easily see a different dog helping to carry a toolbelt or a picnic basket, so use your imagination, and allow your dog to feel proud that he's helping out   .

Open a Door
- teaches skills for your dog to help you overcome physical challenges in different situations -

This is a game that has real-life benefits for handicapped people who cannot use their hands for tasks like opening doors. These people might feel trapped inside their homes, except for their assistance dogs that go through years of training to help them with many tasks of independent living. But even if you're not handicapped in this manner, and even if your dog isn't an assistance dog, he can still help you out with many daily tasks when you need it- including opening doors.

> *You can also use the "targeting" skills in this section to teach your dog to control other functions- a light switch, doorbell or elevator button- or anything that is controlled by touch*

For safety reasons, only teach this skill to a mature dog you are sure you can trust, and only if you feel the benefits will outweigh any possible risks. **NEVER** teach this to any dog that might let himself, your other pets or your children out of the house without your knowledge or permission. Once your dog learns the skill, you cannot go back. So make sure to teach the dog to only open a door after you've given the command. You may also want to install a "failsafe" lock on your exterior door high enough that your dog cannot reach it in case there's ever a problem. (This also helps with those clever escape artists that learn to open locks on their own!)

Another way you can determine whether your dog will be able to open the door is by the type of handle you choose. Some highly dexterous dogs with strong jaws are able to open round door handles or deadbolts, but don't expect this. Most dogs can only physically work "paddle" style handles, so you may want to install this style handle on any doors where you will depend fully on your dog's help to get in and out.

You also need to be realistic and not expect your dog to do the impossible. A handicapped owner living with an assistance dog will usually retrofit their home so door handles are low enough that the dog can effectively work the locks. Make sure if you want your dog to open doors for you that you install handles low enough that the dog can grab them. (Our amazing Akita Casey could unlock a high deadbolt and then turn a round knob with his mouth! He taught himself the skill with no help from us but, consistent with the gentleman he was, he never used it except on our command, to courteously help us out of the house!)

When training your dog to open the door, you first have to teach him to hold the handle in his mouth. For some dogs this won't be too hard, because dogs love to mimic their owners. But if your dog doesn't already try to open doors on his own, you can teach him. **One way to teach the behavior is a method called "targeting". You would start by first teaching your dog to touch the door handle by using a piece of colored tape. First put the tape on your finger. Give the command, "touch" and the moment the dog touches the tape, reward him with praise and a treat.**

Once he's learned the command "touch" on your finger, you will now transfer the tape to the door handle. Praise and offer your dog a treat each time he touches the tape on the door handle. Next shape his behavior by withholding the treats unless, rather than just touching, he actually pushes the handle a little with his face. Get him consistently pushing the handle and then, once he does this, withhold treats unless he takes the handle lightly in his mouth.

Practice at this level for a while and then progress to the final step. This time the dog has to do more than just mouth the handle to get a treat. Only reward him with a treat now when he grasps the handle fully and opens the door! At this point you will always use the command, "Open the door!" whenever you want him to open a door and discourage him strongly and effectively if he ever attempts it on his own. (The only exception where the dog should open a door without your command is if he is performing a lifesaving service if you are unconscious and require help.) ONLY allow your dog to take this initiative in lifesaving circumstances like this. This is one "game" that should only be taught to mature dogs with dependable judgment. Do not allow children or any other family member to teach this game to a dog solely for "laughs".

If you have an assistance dog, in addition to teaching him to open doors with handles, you can also teach him to open automated handicap doors for you in malls and public buildings. You can use the "chaining" process here as well. Start by teaching your dog to touch a piece of tape on the tip of your finger. Give the command, "touch" and offer praise and a treat as soon as the dog touches the tape. Next put the tape on the floor, give the cue, "touch", and offer a treat and praise as the dog touches the tape.

Once your dog consistently achieves success, move the tape to one of the round triggers that open the door in the mall and give the command "open the door". The moment your dog gets this right, we don't have to tell you to give a ton of praise! This is one game that really shows the amazing ways a dog can help his owner, and it can serve as an inspiration to teach your dog many more helpful activities.

Lap Dog
- doing this right can be vital to owners' well-being, but not every dog does it right!

Throughout this Useful Dogs chapter, we acknowledge many dogs that perform tough highly physical work for their owners. But the forgotten heroes are often the toy breeds-particularly "lap dogs" like Pekingese, Papillons, Maltese, Japanese Chins and Tibetan Spaniels. The work these dogs were bred for actually involves sitting in their owners' laps! (This wasn't such an easy task for Pekingese at one time in history. Their purpose was to sit in the sleeves of Chinese monks and deflect unfriendly strangers. But during the Revolution the monks were violently ousted from power by the Communist Army. The monks' Pekingese maintained their haughty loyalty- and the breed was almost slaughtered out of existence!)

A good lapdog does its job with class and precision and in consideration of its owner's every move, so never take its services lightly. While cuddled on your lap, your professional lapdog shouldn't snap or nip or yap. It should tread on its owner lightly, even if the owner is delicate. It should graciously allow cuddling, stroking and grooming. Owners should understand the difference between spoiling the dog (allowing it something it tries to force or push on you) and utilizing it for its job (close companionship and healing cuddles).When the toy dog suspends some of its natural "doggy" tendencies and allows us to cuddle it like a Kewpie doll, we must understand that this is part of its work and give it credit for acting appropriately.

This does *not* mean we should spoil our toy dogs. For example letting your toy dog sit on the table and eat off your plate can lead to seriously unhealthy behavior. We must also respect that the dog should only "work" so many hours a day. Give it some time to be a dog! It should walk on the floor much more often than it's up in the air, it should have walks outside and it should not be crammed into clothes or carriers constantly, groomed roughly or with harsh chemical products and should not be handled roughly by the kids, even if it tolerates it, or stroked constantly by you. Give your hardworking toy dog a little room to breathe!

And, remember something else. You will note the list above included only a few breeds that we would call "lap dogs". A few other breeds like the Chinese Crested were not originally bred as lap dogs, yet they have many years behind them working happily in this capacity. **But not all dogs that are classed as "toys" were bred to be lap dogs! Some were bred to hunt and kill!** Some terriers are small enough that they look like lapdogs. They are not! They may be ratters or watchdogs. And **you will set yourself and your dog up for absolute misery if you attempt to force a dog into the lapdog capacity just because he is small.**

Unfortunately, some of the most widely purchased small dogs today have feisty temperaments and are not suitable for lap dogs. But unrealistic owners hold this expectation for them, leading to a lot of unhappiness. To find the perfect companion, you must carefully research your breeds *and* test the individual dog or puppy's temperament to determine how closely he'll match the work you want him to do. A good rule of thumb is to put as much time into researching your choice of dog as you would when purchasing a home, since statistically, you will be with your dog longer. And remember, only special dogs excel at the task of being good lap dogs!

Real Dog Careers
(Tracking, Herding, Hunting, Service, Therapy)
- don't forget that, even today, a small percentage of dogs perform jobs for their family or community -

Arguably the number one reason dogs of today seem to behave worse than dogs owned by previous generations is that most of our dogs are bored- in the deepest, most existential sense. They simply do not have a job to do. In the wild, wolves work every day as part of a functioning pack, with duties ranging from hunting, to navigating journeys in new territory, to protecting and educating young. Domestic dogs were bred with such variety to serve man in widely varying functions- everything from water rescue (Newfoundland), to killing rats (Jack Russell Terrier), to defending tax collectors (Dobermans), to hunting bears (Akita) and, in previous generations, dogs were expected to work hard every day to serve their owners.

In fact, the amazing variety in the appearances of different purebred dogs is actually deliberate breeding that was intended to make them more suited for their particular work task. (For example, look at the Komodor, a large flock guardian from Turkey. This breed has been around several thousand years and looks like a gigantic white mop, with its hair growing naturally in yard-long dreadlocks. The reason Komodorok were bred with this unusual appearance was so they could fool predators by blending with the sheep!)

As recently as a hundred years ago the majority of dogs in our country worked. For example "farm dogs" commonly guarded and herded livestock that family farmers depended upon for their existence.

A working dog is happiest working, and almost every single breed was bred to work in some capacity. (One notable exception being the Chow, whose disturbing original use we will not elaborate here since it is highly upsetting to dog lovers). Perhaps the nicest thing you can do for your dog is to allow him to work with you, as a true household contributor, every day. Cesar Milan, in his book *Cesar's Way* mentions that you never see a homeless man with a bad dog. This is because the homeless man's dog understands that he helps his owner in a real daily struggle for existence.

Even in our modern world many people still depend upon dogs for their livelihood and/or survival. Therapy dogs are one example. Police dogs are another. Hunting dogs another. Here in America, farmers (both large and small) still depend upon dogs to herd and guard livestock. And around the world, in less developed countries, man's continued dependence on dogs is much greater. In some areas, breeds of dogs like the Caucasian Ovtcharka (in the Caucasian Mountains of Russia) or Anatolian Shepherds (in Turkey) still guard livestock just as they did three to four thousand years ago. And every day dogs around the world are used in search and rescue work, saving lives. So this section is simply a shout out to all those dogs that are still working hard every day to better the lives of mankind!

And, even though your pet dog may not be a professional, why not look carefully at his breeding one day when you're in a philosophical mood? Blink your eyes and picture the creature in front of you as a hero in another day and age! Think of him this way every now and then to help you envision ways that you can integrate and depend on him more as a functioning part of your family every day and not just a freeloader. Find ways that your dog can help you out in day to day life and expect his cooperation and obedience. Believe it or not, your dog has just been waiting for you to ask!

Movie Star (for pay)
- if you've ever considered your dog having a career in movies -

Is your dog a wonder at doing tricks? Has he already breezed through many of the advanced tricks and games in this book? While all of the skills mentioned in this book are intended for hobbyists, we also mention ways you can use your dog's skills professionally. So you may find it interesting to discover that all of the amazing stunts you see dogs perform on television and movies are just an extension of regular training. Examples include teaching your dog to shake his head yes or no, or retrieve various items. Training involved in stunts for movies uses the same theory, but just requires a tremendous amount more patience and repetition.

Not all dogs have this kind of patience or ability, even if they are good family dogs. Some dogs more easily learn a variety of seemingly meaningless tricks, and some dogs are more relaxed than others in stressful environments like movie sets. Dogs that uncomfortable or unfriendly around new people, other animals and busy settings don't qualify. You are looking for a dog with high intelligence and a personality that can't be ruffled. A proud owner may have their dog appear on film once or twice, just for laughs. But there's also the possibility that the two of you might possibly make a career out of it, with your dog appearing in movies, television shows and/or commercials.

Just like with people, a few select dogs are naturally oriented toward being stars. It's not necessarily dependent on breed, although breed can influence temperament, as well as the demand for your dog in movies. The worst thing an owner can do is to try to be a "stage mom". Never ever force your dog to appear in movies if you're not sure he loves every moment of it! Only an extremely small number of dogs can actually succeed in this career or are actually meant for it. (And you might also invest more time and money trying to get your dog into movies than you'll ever profit monetarily, unless you already have professional connections and experience.)

Whether your dog does succeed depends not only on his trainability and "stage presence" but also on his looks, whether you live conveniently near a studio or can travel easily, whether there are openings available and how strong the demand for your dog's breed is at the moment. Just like if you wanted to pursue a movie career yourself, you may wish to start by obtaining a talent agent for your dog. You can learn more in the book *How to Get Your Pet Into Show Business* by Captain Haggerty or *Star Pet; How to Make Your Pet a Star* by Bash Dibra.

You will also have to decide whether you're determined to act as your dog's trainer for film appearances. Training pets for movies is an involved career with lots of competition for a relatively small number of jobs, but it's not impossible. You're much more likely to succeed if you know the right people and have years of relevant experience and great credentials. Rather than preparing for the career yourself, you may choose to let professional movie trainers work with your dog on the sets, while you simply travel with your dog as a chaperone to make sure he is well treated and never stressed.

Even if you don't want to have your dog work in real movies and commercials, you may feel frustrated because you're sure your dog has the potential. The great thing is that your dog doesn't know if a million viewers are watching him or not. Just for fun, observe some of the tricks and stunts dogs perform on TV, carefully breaking down the components of the task. And then consult books for step-by-step examples of how to teach the behaviors at home, or simply apply the principles of reward-based behavioral training to teach your dog any behavior you like. (In this chapter, for example, "Find My Keys", "Put Away Toys" and "Open a Door" describe such important training techniques as "targeting" and "chaining".)

Teaching your dog "movie" stunts will be a challenging and enjoyable family project that will flex your dog's physical and mental muscles. Have someone in your family film a seamless performance once your dog gets the stunts perfect and you will have home movies that all your family and friends will really want to watch! (See "Movie Star" in Chapter 4, Mental Games.)

Lifesaver
- every day dogs save lives; here's how to encourage it -

Perhaps the most amazing and admirable trait of a dog is the fact that your dog probably loves you enough to lay down his life for you! Since the time men started living with dogs, there have always been stories of dogs acting as lifesavers- protecting their owners from intruders in the home or saving them from fires or natural disasters. Dogs can also alert neighbors if their owner's been hurt or suffered a stroke, heart attack, seizure or diabetic coma. Dogs often alert parents when their baby is ill or having difficulty breathing and this intervention has saved quite a few babies' lives!

Sometimes even the tiniest dogs and puppies perform amazing feats of strength to rescue or assist their owners. Popular television shows and books have recently fascinated the public with dramatic stories of dogs saving their owners. Although some of the stories might seem like tall tales, we have to remember that what seems like superpowers in your dog is just your dog following his natural instincts without second guessing himself like a human might. This is the power of nature unadulterated by the softening and confusing effects of civilization.

Whether a dog can be trained specifically to save your life is difficult to one-hundred percent guarantee. A dog's desire to help his owner(s) is primarily instinctual, and what he does in a real-life situation could be different from what he does in practice. Of course, dogs can be trained to guard, and certain working breeds defend more strongly than others. But often even the "softest" breeds will stand up against formidable intruders to save their owner's life.

Some breeds, usually working dogs, have been bred and expertly trained to do specialized types of rescue work- in snow, in water or searching for missing persons. And dogs trained as service and assistance animals may save their owners' lives every day (for example, taking the initiative to prevent an owner with poor vision from stepping out into traffic). It's obvious that the more specialized training a dog is given, the more skill he'll have saving lives in specific situations. But there are stories every day of dogs with no training at all that rescue their owner's child from drowning in the backyard pool, or that wake their elderly owner in time to stop a neglected pot boiling over on the stove from setting the house on fire.

What makes these dogs act as heroes? Simply the fact that they are dogs and that they love you!

Will every dog save every owner's life in every situation? Unfortunately, it can't be guaranteed. You can increase your chances that your dog will take initiative to help you in several ways. First, you can carefully research breeds and breeders. Select a dog that is bred to help you in the lifesaving fashion you most desire, and then turn to the best breeder, who breeds for temperament and working ability. Next, get the dog specific training for lifesaving and follow through at home to reinforce the training.

If you don't think you need the specific training, but only want to encourage your dog in his natural tendencies to be a lifesaver, then the best thing that you and your family can do is to be good to him. Give your dog good diet, health care and exercise. Don't spoil him. But rather train him in obedience and give him lots of love and praise whenever he supports owners in their activities. The dog should also be involved with the family in many ways, like regular walks and going out in public with the family in varied situations to help build confidence.

Always be consistent with the dog. If you'd like him to bark in an emergency, then acknowledge him when he barks at other times by checking what is going on. Only when you assess that nothing's wrong should you instruct him to "Be quiet," in a firm, yet kind voice. Don't yell at the dog if he tries to help; for example, if he comes from the baby's room, barking at you in an agitated tone. Give him the benefit of the doubt and check out the situation. Always be kind, play with your dog in ways that stimulate his mind and give him affection when he's good to build his confidence. **There is no absolute way to know if your dog will act to save your life, but dogs that do are well-balanced and confident dogs that feel they matter as a functioning part of the family.**

Note: There is one thing many American families do these days that absolutely guarantees your dog will NOT save your family in an emergency- and this is crating your dog! A dog in a crate is completely helpless to assist you if you need him. He may not be able to hear or smell what's happening at the opposite side of the house, and you may not be able to hear him if he barks to alert you of trouble. A dog in a cage certainly cannot pin an intruder and, once the intruder sees the dog is helpless, his barking won't scare the intruder away. In fact, it will probably make a sadistic intruder laugh.

Trainers or so called dog "professionals" who tell you that crating is the best or only way to live with a dog are simply taking a shortcut to hide their own inability. A dog should live as a healthy- and helpful- member of his family every day. And, with proper husbandry and training, every healthy dog should be able to live in harmony in their owner's home.

(If a dog's behavior problems are so severe that an average family truly fears to let him out, they should get immediate professional assistance. Constant crating will only increase alienation if your dog doesn't cooperate with your family and it won't solve the problem of what to do when he's free. It also won't teach him how to "read" his human family to gauge if anyone is in distress.)

Don't let anybody, whether a friend or so-called professional, no matter how respected, convince you that a dog is happiest in a cage. Although some proponents of crating cite wolf studies, scientific fact, including the study of wolves, supports just the opposite. The only wolves that live in dens are tiny puppies; after two months they are out exploring the world. Adult wolves spend much of their life on the move, in the company of their pack. And the place your dog is most comfortable is with your family, able to help out if he's called upon. **Never put your dog in the most painful position of his life- seeing his owner in deadly jeopardy and finding himself locked behind bars with no way to help!**

Ch. 13- Family Activities:

"You don't have to give up the American Dream of fun with your family dog."

Introduction

Circle of Love

Jump Rope

Rally at Home

Races (Dog/Human)

Diversity Training

Playground with Dog Games

Jr. Grooming Salon

Doggie Bakery

Different Handlers

Junior Handlers

Assess a Dog

Demonstrate Tricks

"Petstar" at Home

Test Obedience

Also Try These Ideas From Other Chapters for Family Activities:

Puppy Games & Activities: Follow the Leader, Find the Treat, Find Mommy, Soccer, Let's Play Doctor, Shopping Spree, Obedience-minded

Mental Games & Activities: Movie Star, Go To a Person

Indoor Games & Activities: Hide & Go Seek, Limbo, Agility Inside, Dancing Dog), Doggie Gymnasium, Basketball

Balance & Coordination Activities: Catch the Frisbee

Multi Dog Games & Activities: Duck, Duck Goose, Simon Says, Dancing Dogs, Obedience Competition at Home, Agility Competition at Home, Rally

Problem Dog Games: Ring of Fire, When I Move, You Move, Jump Over

Therapeutic & Senior Dog Activities: Massage, Meditation, Stretching, Swim, A Change of Scene,

High Energy Dog Activities: Bike, Rollerblades, Skateboard, Hiking, Backpacking, All-Terrain Run, Race, Monkey In the Middle, Snow Games, Ocean Swim

Water Activities: Submarine, Kiddie Pool

Useful Activities: Wagon Pull, Pack Animal, Sled Dog, Check on the Baby, Find the Missing Person, Help Your Special Needs Family Member, Watch Your Children, Work With Your Livestock

Activities for Owners with Limited Mobility: Ball Launcher, Playtime with Other Dogs, Obedience/Agility Clubs

Family Activities- Introduction
"You don't have to give up the American Dream of fun with your family dog."

Family is a subject that elicits high emotion. And some of our strongest passion is not just for our spouses and kids, but also for the canine members of our families. Better than fame and fortune for many of us is the simple American Dream- a comfortable house in the suburbs, a balmy Saturday afternoon and our kids and dog playing happily in the backyard.

But what if that dream sours because of a dog that turned out very different from what we expected? If our dog fails us, it can feel heartbreaking and we may fear that no one else can understand. It's embarrassing and deeply disappointing to confess the profound alienation we may feel.

Owners may be fascinated by our dogs' marvelous, and sometimes mysterious, capabilities and the fact that they are wild creatures, just as we once were. But we also struggle to understand them. We wish to impart in our cherished children the feeling of an intuitive and joyous link with nature. But it's difficult in our modern world, where children are separated from wild things except in zoos, and parents' hectic lives prevent us from enjoying enough play and educational time with our kids in nature.

Ideally, we'd like to think that times with our family dog would be a joy and that the dog could provide the family a link with nature, as he indeed is capable of. But what happens when it goes awry? We purchase a little puppy that is so cute and dear, and his good intentions and sweetness seem to shine through his innocent eyes as he lies cradled in our arms. Our children react with excitement and joy when we bring the dog home, and this is one moment of true family bonding in the chaos of today's demanding world. We may take photos on that first day of homecoming, and those adorable photos may make both spouses' hearts swell with warm emotion, while tears of tenderness actually come to our eyes. We love this puppy, we truly do!

But, for some families, the dark side may come as soon as that night as behavior problems show up. The puppy may soil or destroy possessions, chew your hands constantly until he draws blood or run around so wildly that you literally cannot hold him. You suspect that these problems are beyond normal puppy behavior and life seems to swirl out of control, as you ask yourself, "What have I done wrong?"

The most deeply disturbing problem for most parents is when your children and your dog don't get along. Your dog may chase the kids, jump on the kids or constantly nip at their heels. Or the kids may play too roughly with the dog. And these problems may last well beyond your dog's puppyhood, continuing for years. Instead of feeling like the all-around happy American family you had perhaps naively perceived yourself to be, you now start doubting yourself. You may experience a literal tightness in your stomach when you come home and your kids ask you painful questions you cannot answer, like why the dog doesn't play with them the way they want it to.

The problem may manifest more subtly. There may be no obvious behavior problems, and yet your kids don't seem to be living with the dog as happily as you remember living with your dogs in childhood. Maybe your children seem more interested in staying inside, playing video games or texting their friends while the dog digs holes in the backyard, ignoring them. Something is wrong in a deep profound way but your family may feel too ashamed to seek help. In fact, couples are often more open to visiting a marriage counselor than finally airing their problems to a dog psychologist.

It's true that you might need to consult an expert behaviorist or veterinarian because not all canine problems are easy to solve. And certain serious behavior problems may be health related, or require extensive intervention. **But the majority of the canine deficiencies that concern us most are simply a malaise of our times! With simple lifestyle changes, you can easily change the tone of your family's existence with your dog and retrieve a piece of that lost "American Dream".** Part of the solution is finding activities that involve your dog in your family's daily life and that make him feel useful. The best "games" to enjoy with your dog are fun, yet not frivolous, and they feel natural to you and to your kids.

Even in this stressful era, we believe kids still possess a powerful inner compass that leads them towards what's healthy and good. Once you open the door to educating and having fun with your dog in novel ways, your kids may feel free to share many more creative suggestions of their own! **While kids shouldn't be expected to control a dog that's already out of control, they often have remarkable natural ability with animals- if you, as an adult, cultivate it properly.**

Always supervise your kids and dogs. We recommend that you also educate yourself in-depth on canine development, behavior and breed as well as child psychology and development in order to learn how kids and dogs can best play and learn together. But we strongly caution you *not* to passively accept word-of-mouth information and advice about dogs including information you may come across on Internet chat rooms, Craiglist, cocktail parties or even behavioral advice on individual cases casually dispensed online. Your researches should go further, and it's healthy to stay skeptical because the wrong training/ husbandry advice often hurts dogs and families. Always look for true scientific evidence to back up any fact, at the same time not losing sight of common sense.

"Regular" suburban families *can* become experts about dogs, and the more you know personally, the more comfortable you will feel, even if you end up knowing more than some of the paid dog professionals in your area. The science of canine behavior is highly complex, so take it as a red flag if an individual dictates that their knowledge is absolute with no further explanation or if they act defensive or dictatorial, yet have no scientific or written support for any of their ideas.

Dog owners should feel comfortable scanning information and deciding what's most realistic and useful for you. And the best way to do this is to skim through a variety of in-depth dog books. Start reading books at either your local library or through inter-library loan (which allows you to request books free from anywhere in the country). You can also flip through every dog book at your local bookstore and only purchase the select few that are most scientific, practical and compassionate. If you're on a budget look for the titles you like used, via Amazon.com, or at your county library system (most will let also let you search online). Let all your new information empower you to intentionally plan a program of healthy developmental activities for your kids and dog together, rather than always leaving their time together unstructured. You'll enjoy an enormous payoff in your family's quality of life.

To thoroughly research dogs, we suggest you read not only college-level books on canine behavior and psychology, but also breed books which include at least a hundred breeds and their photos. And don't forget illustrated veterinary manuals. You don't have to absorb all the information at once, but instead keep these books handy for all the family members to consult over time. Use *The Cure for Useless Dog Syndrome* as part of your library so you will always have hundreds of novel suggestions for healthy, smart and easy activities to share with your dog.

Structure family time with your dog and your dog will likely surprise you with improved good behavior. As soon as you bring your puppy home, your family can play the simple game "Circle of Love" which teaches dogs to want to come to you and not run away. When your dog's a little bigger, your kids may enjoy exercise games like "Jump Rope" or "Rally at Home" or creative games that bring also bring out a little competition ("*Petstar* at Home"). Most of the versatile activities described in this chapter are also appropriate indoors, to keep children and dogs active during the downtime of hot summers or snowy winters.

And also look for selections from other chapters that are ideal for the whole family. Some are good for any weather. Others, like "Diversity Training" or "More Learning Every Day" can increase your kids' world view and comfort with the world at large, while helping in a similar fashion with your pet.

Most kids will enjoy playing for a day at "Doggie Grooming Salon", or "Test Obedience Responses". But some children, when introduced to these activities young, may actually surprise you with a boundless talent with dogs and the start of a dream vocation. It's possible that your kids' native skill may literally make them famous as "Junior Handlers", exhibiting championship dogs. Your little puppy and the decision you made to buy him may someday make you proud, and bring tears to your eyes, as you watch your child and dog win awards together in the show ring. And that really is the American Dream!

Family Activities:

<u>Circle of Love</u>
- **highly recommended for every family, easily teaches dogs to run to you rather than run away -**

Many families call us because their dog runs away or refuses to come to them when they call him. This is why you should practice teaching your puppy to come to you from the first day you bring him home. Even if you have an older dog that you got from a shelter or rescue you need to start getting that dog to come to you when you call. This may one day save the dog's life.

Owners often complain that their dog won't come to them. One possibility is that the dog or puppy is too stressed at that moment. So you will need to address any underlying issues first. (For example, you should make it a habit to never call your dog to you for anything unpleasant.) If, at the moment, your puppy simply refuses to come, allow him to rest for a while and then try again later. Then call him to you from a short distance while he is on lead while showing him a treat. The fact that you have control of the lead will mean that you can guarantee the dog comes. If he comes on his own to get the treat, give him tons of praise. If he does not, gently reel him in to you on the lead.

Getting your dog to come to you may be the most important thing your dog will ever learn, but if you try to rush it or force it you could make it so the dog never wants to come to you or your family. **The dog should always associate coming to his owners with happiness and reward.**

Many owners have no idea of what happened to their dog in his former environment before he came to them. If you were careful enough to buy your pup from a great breeder, the pup may know how to come when called when you get him home. This makes your job easy as long as you continue to keep the experience positive throughout the dog's life. Unfortunately, less reputable breeders just breed dogs to make money; they can make things difficult for the new owners by not interacting with pups at all during the critical early weeks of life and not teaching the pups skills like coming when called.

Uncaring puppy-mill breeders or abusive former owners may have scared or hurt your puppy whenever they called him, making it very hard to teach the dog to come to you later in life. But if you are gentle, and above all patient, you can eventually teach even an undersocialized or skittish dog that the greatest things in life happen when he comes running to you.

One way we teach a dog this is to play the game called "Circle of Love." This game helps even dogs with a history of bad owners learn that coming to you and your family brings good things.

First get the whole family together and form a small circle around the dog, with the dog on a long standard-width leash, fifteen to thirty feet long. (Do not use thin, filament-style retractable leads, which can be dangerous when your dog is running.) Each family member should have a handful of small soft treats. One family member holds the dog to keep him waiting until the signal, while another person holds the looped end of the long leash. The person holding the end of the leash then calls the dog to them, acting extremely happy and enthusiastic and backpedaling if necessary to make the dog run towards them. When the dog reaches them, the person makes a big fuss over him while touching his collar and offering treats.

Next this person holds the dog and tosses the leash to a different member of the family so they can call the dog. Each person will repeat this process, taking turns. Since the dog is getting loads of treats, attention and exercise, you can see why he'd enjoy the game. If he ever does not want to come, just reel the leash in gently to get him started. Start with a small circle. As your dog or puppy gets better coming to you from short distances, you can make the circle bigger, so he has to come farther to get to you.

If you have a fenced-in area you can next take the dog off the leash and call him from all corners of the yard. But don't try without a fence, or you may defeat your purpose and the dog could run away before he's fully trained. Practice "Circle of Love" frequently, including around distractions. Kids love this game and it's great at family barbeques and reunions. Outside, playing the game with a long lead and a big circle of participants will provide exercise for your dog. And you can also play inside, with different family members calling the dog from different parts of the home. If you spend enough time practicing this game, you'll start to notice your dog coming to you faster and faster each time no matter where you are.

Jump Rope
- challenging to teach, but lots of "wow factor" if your dog has no limitations -

Agile dogs (including breeds like Australian Shepherds, Border Collies and Jack Russell Terriers) seem to love this game and so do kids. And jumping rope has the added benefit of improving your dog's focus, timing and coordination as well as his overall physical agility. Children or teens who are virtuosos can teach your dog to jump rope, but adults should supervise younger kids. And bring out the video camera, because this is one game with lots of "wow factor". This is one game that will certainly perk you up after a wearying day and you may be surprised to find your whole family happily hanging out together, laughing and wanting to take turns jumping.

Like with other new games, you should start out small and make sure your dog is suited to the game. **"Jump Rope" is not safe for dogs with joint problems, bone problems**, seriously overweight dogs, senior dogs, dogs with medical conditions, inactive breeds that have problems jumping (Bassett Hounds, Dachshunds, Pekingese), giant breed puppies that have not attained their full growth or extremely skittish dogs who may fear the approach of the rope.

You can judge your dog's interest in jumping rope by how excited he seems as you and your kids jump first. Let him watch a few rounds as two family members hold the ends of one long jumprope and another family member jumps. You can use the words "Jump Rope" as human family members jump just to get your dog more accustomed to the name of the game.

Now it's your dog's turn. You need three people; two on ends of the rope and one to handle and encourage the dog. Rest the rope on the ground between your two family members, and call your dog over, urging, "Come on, Sammy, jump rope!"

Your dog may seem a bit bewildered at first. Or he may step over the rope pretty much by accident. If he does this, immediately praise and/or reward with treats, saying something like, "Good Sammy. Good jump rope!" If your dog does not take an interest and wander over the rope on his own, you can lure him, either by holding out a treat or simply calling encouragingly. Make sure the rope stays down on the ground at this point. As soon as he moves over the rope, act excited and praise him or offer a small treat if you wish. Eventually, you won't use treats except at the conclusion of a successful session; your praise and the excitement of the game will prove incentive enough for your dog to joyously participate.

Like many activities, the key to training your dog to love jumping rope is patience. After he successfully steps over the rope as it lies on the ground the first time, you may be tempted to hurry things. But a little patience will pay off. Have your dog crossing the rope as it lies on the ground several times, in both directions. (You can increase difficulty by speeding up the pace or starting to provide treat motivators only on every third repetition.) Once your dog masters the rope on the ground, lift the rope up a bit, but keep it hanging still; don't attempt to move it yet.

You could use a leash to guide your dog, but keeping him off leash (in a secure area) is the best way to ensure he remains focused and fascinated with jumping rope. If the dog walks away, the human family members can resume the game for that session on their own. You may be surprised that after your dog has sniffed around a bit, he'll come back to play again. Simply pick up where you left off. Or try the next day. This game is only fun if your dog really loves it.

Once you've trained the dog to jump over the rope when it is off the ground, this will probably be enough to impress the neighbors but some dogs become even more talented at jumping rope. If you know your dog can handle it, two family members can slowly swing the rope as your dog jumps over it. Do not swing over his head at this point. Offer him tremendous praise and attention the first time he makes it over a moving rope!

With some dogs, your two family members will eventually be able to swing the rope completely around and over the dog's head, and then gently swing it under his feet so he can execute the jump. Not every dog will have the coordination to accomplish this! If your dog is adept at jumping even after you've passed the rope over his head, you can make the demanding sport a bit easier for him by swinging the rope close to the ground as he jumps, giving the command "jump" as the rope approaches and intentionally moving the rope gently and somewhat slowly. You can build to several repetitions in a row.

Toy dogs (like Miniature Pinschers) and small terriers (like Jack Russells) can be great jumpers and some really love jumping rope, even indoors. **But you must be extremely careful when playing this game with tiny dogs, because tiny dogs have tiny little legs that can easily become entangled.** A combination of a rope swinging too fast and a little dog becoming panicked can easily lead to a broken leg. For this reason, when working with smaller or frailer dogs, it's best to have adults or capable teens or 'tweens on the ends of the jumprope rather than younger children.

Remember that the goal is your dog getting fun and exercise while making everyone smile. A dog jumping rope should not be forced to jump with a fast moving rope or several ropes like a daring human jumprope champ! Even the most talented rope-jumping dog cannot keep the same focus or balance as a human. Keep his number of jumps in a row short. When your dog loses his rhythm, the human handlers on both ends of the rope should be paying close attention. If each and every swing of the rope is slow and gentle, even if the rope hits your dog's legs, the handlers can simply snake it safely away, avoiding any entanglements.

Always try to end the session on a successful jump and lavishly praise your dog. After the dog is done with his turn, the human champions can try some of the more challenging routines if they wish. Or, if you happen to have another dog that is up for the sport, he can now take his turn.

Rally at Home
- modify this fun fast-paced obedience competition to work your dogs at home-

Here's a "game" you can play with the whole family, or even with the whole neighborhood, and you don't even have to travel to an AKC dog show to do it. Simply visit the AKC website for information (see Resources), observe a few Rally obedience competitions at dog shows if this is possible and then set up your own unofficial rally course and competition in your back yard or throughout your house.

Rally is a particular style of obedience competition that takes place with dog/handler teams circulating through a course and completing standardized tasks like retrieving a dumbbell in a set order. (See "Rally" in Chapter 10, Activities for High-Energy Dogs). Because of the quick flow of the competition, Rally Obedience lends itself to excitement, thus it would be a good choice for teens or preteens who want a challenge.

Or maybe you'd like to set up a Rally competition just for fun as an activity in your gated community, or at your next church picnic. If you plan to compete in Rally Obedience competitions at AKC shows, then you would want to set up a regulation course and judge according to the standards you'd be facing at competition so you can benefit from practice. Meanwhile you can still bring all the (friendly) dogs in your extended family or on your block to practice together at your home.

Many of us have dogs who know some obedience, but not really enough to compete at Rally. For dogs like this you can get together and make up your own rally-style competition. Include only tasks and stations your dogs are good at and borrow the idea from Rally to move through the indoor or outdoor course in continuous fashion. This may not be exactly the way the sport was intended to be practiced, but we guarantee it will be fun!

Races (Dog/Human)
**-   your kids may already want to try this. It's fun and great for
burning energy if done right -**

Dogs love to race, since it's in their nature, and it's even better when you get the whole family involved. **Before racing, you should first follow careful health and safety precautions for both humans and dogs**. Dogs with health problems, very young or old dogs and dogs of certain breeds should not be running at full-throttle and dogs shouldn't run in extreme weather, especially heat and sun. Check with your veterinarian if you suspect your dog has any limitations, and don't forget to check with your doctor and/or your kids' pediatrician before starting your family on any vigorous exercise program.

As long as everybody is cleared physically, every single dog and family member can participate in races. Just don't force very unequal contestants to compete against each other unless you wish to offer a handicap. There won't be any official winner of these dog/human races anyway, but it's more fun if an active adult or teen takes on a sleek active dog or a feisty, fast-moving terrier. A less fit adult could race at a jog with a smaller, heavier or longer-bodied dog (make sure to heed doctor's and vet's orders). And your younger children could race a puppy who still has not reached his full coordination. You can race one human against one dog, one dog against several humans or one human against several dogs.

One of the most important things that racing with you teaches your dog is to control his boundless energy, to use it only at the appropriate minute at your command. Teach this when you start each race by you or a helper holding the dog back at a "Stay" or a "Wait" position with a verbal command and/or by gently physically blocking him. Then give the release command in an excited voice, for example, "Okay, race!" Release the dog and start to run and he'll soon get the idea. When he sees his owner running, the dog will want to run, too, because running in a pack is wired into a dog's genetics and dogs race against each other all the time to play.

There may be a few notable exceptions- for example, the Pekingese. No self-respecting Pekingese would ever race for anything! A good Pekingese knows how to use a blend of regalness and total adorability to make sure that the *owner* is the only one ever racing- to fulfill all of the dog's needs! We say this jokingly and fondly, but some breeds like the Pekingese are really not meant for racing. If your dog doesn't seem to enjoy the activity, then just don't do it. Dog/human races are meant to be fun and never stressful.

You should also use caution if your dog loves to race *too* much. A dog with this problem often runs away, won't let you catch him and won't return to you immediately when you call. In this case, the dog is forgetting your status as pack leader, and the fact that, other than during the occasional game, *he* should be following you. **Running away is a highly dangerous behavior, likely to cost your dog his life, so you must train him a proper recall prior to enjoying other off-leash activities.** You may need to seek professional assistance. For dogs that tend to run away, you should not attempt dog/human races except under a professional's advice for specific therapeutic purposes.

Owners should always conduct dog/human races in a safely fenced or enclosed area. Not only is this abiding the law, but it also makes it easier to control your dog in the rules of racing. If your dog could just keep going, he might not want to return to the finish line for the next race! (Read more about racing as exercise for your dog in "Race" in Chapter 10, Activities for High-Energy Dogs.)

Diversity Training

**- important suggestions for how your kids
can help properly socialize your puppy
(adults too) -**

Socialization (especially around the ages of 7-12 weeks) is important for your puppy to encounter the larger world and become comfortable in it. Proper socialization helps your dog mature without developing fears or aggression when he encounters new stimuli,

When you socialize your puppy, he becomes versed in different stimuli, different environments and different people. As long as you do it right, he'll become a much more balanced adult

and so it's vital that you take time to properly socialize your young pup. Unfortunately, as home trainers we're often called to work with grown dogs that weren't socialized properly as pups and were never taken outside their backyards. The owners then struggle with adult dogs that go completely out of control when they see other dogs or people on basic neighborhood walks.

Owners also create problems when the only thing their puppy ever sees is the same block in the same neighborhood with the exact same stimuli every single day. The first time the owners attempt to take a dog like this out into the larger world, the dog may panic, lunge and act "rabid" in response to the sight of anything different- people of different ages or races than they're used to, children on bikes or skateboards, a baby in a stroller, an adult in a wheelchair- or even a man wearing a cowboy hat!

In contrast, a puppy that has encountered all these different people under relaxing circumstances when he was growing up will understand that they are benign, just different facets of the world he lives in. The owner will enjoy outings more and the dog enjoys outings more as a better canine citizen.

Unfortunately, many people confuse the concept of canine "socialization" with the kind of socializing that humans do at a party. But seven to twelve weeks is very young and a puppy cannot, and should not, tolerate too much sensory stimuli. Too much at a time will overwhelm the puppy, and your efforts to make him like the larger world can actually create fears. So make sure to keep all encounters with new people and places short and pleasant!

Puppies at this age also have not completed all their vaccinations, and their immune systems are not as strong as older dogs'. Therefore your young puppy shouldn't physically come in contact with strange dogs, nor should he contact their waste or their bodily fluids. And you absolutely cannot risk him being bitten, so public dog parks are completely out of the question for dogs of this age.

Even though you must protect your puppy from contagious diseases, you *should* make sure he *sees* all sizes and shapes of dogs at a distance during this impressionable period. Carry your puppy, or walk him where he can *look* at other friendly dogs, and make sure he enjoys the experience. For example, you could pet him or offer him treats or a favorite toy, along with lots of verbal encouragement.

At this young age, it's also important that your puppy meet different people and it's okay for him to have physical contact with them under certain conditions. Since puppies are so cute, the people he meets will likely give him lots of friendly encouragement, but you'll have to make sure they don't get too exuberant. You can hold the puppy, or keep him on the floor. Make sure he is comfortable, and stop all encounters on a high note.

Many puppy owners may try to act polite and not realize that **not everyone you meet should be allowed to touch your dog.** Your pup can learn to like people, and learn to be comfortable with them just by seeing them. Walk or carry him past new people and give him encouragement as described above with dogs. Have your puppy pass by people of all different races, ages, shapes and sizes and engaged in varying occupations and leisure pursuits. Walk the pup past, or carry him past cars, bikes, motorcycles and skateboards. But don't put the puppy at risk and don't stress him. The idea is to make him feel comfortable around many different sights and sounds, and you should teach your children how they can help while still keeping the experiences positive.

If a person you encounter knows how to pet a dog properly *and* your puppy seems to like them, you can invite them to pet your puppy. Pleasant encounters like this will show your puppy that people are his friends, and he'll learn to feel comfortable when people touch him.

He should also meet children, **but only if they are supervised and know how to handle dogs gently.** This cuts both ways. You can let your five month old Labrador "look at the nice baby" but **never force your dog to physically sniff, lick or paw at some poor passerby's child just because you want your dog socialized. Both parties should mutually agree on any physical meeting involving a dog and you will be liable for anything your dog does!**

If you take your puppy out in public, he can see many people, but we recommend you limit physical petting sessions to one or two strangers a day. You can always bring the puppy out the next day for more. Make your pup's excursions out into the "real world" frequent, but not overwhelming. For example, we recommend you bring your dog to small quiet public events, like a local fair sponsored by your church, rather than huge regional art shows with hundreds of vendors, citywide street parties or county fairs. And one of the worst places you could ever take your dog is a gigantic fireworks display! This immerses most dogs in more stressful stimuli than they can tolerate and may cause lifelong damage. The truth is, it's usually better to take your dog out with you on everyday outings and then leave him home during highly crowded special events like this.

As long as you stay reasonable, the task of socializing your puppy can become great fun, especially for your kids. Explain the mission to your children but make sure they feel assertive enough to fend away strangers that reach out to pet the dog without permission. This will be difficult for kids younger than preteen age, and kids this young shouldn't be left alone in busy public places with the puppy.

In your presence however, you can let your kids hold the puppy and make "diversity training" a game. Encourage the kids to think of new places the family might encounter different people for your puppy to see for the first time. Maybe your kids will spot a pullover near the beach where the pup can observe skateboarders, or a quiet section of a local park where older gentlemen play checkers. Or they can bring the puppy with them when they visit friends of different races.

As long as you don't bother anyone, you and your family could approach a family with a child in a wheelchair and explain politely, "We just wanted to get the puppy used to seeing the chair as he explores the world. Is it okay if he says, "Hi'? Their child will probably be delighted to meet your puppy and everyone will learn a bit more about people with different abilities. With you supervising, your kids and your puppy could also politely introduce themselves to an older neighbor who always uses a walker when she gets her mail or they could even say, "Hi", to the postman as he drops the mail off.

An adult should always supervise every meeting, since it is not safe for a child of any age to approach strange adults when you are not with them. Regrettably, today's world can be dangerous, and children must be educated that polite neighborhood meetings are usually good, but that meeting adult strangers without you there could be dangerous or even deadly. Just because the child is with a dog doesn't make things safe, nor does it give strangers the right to push themselves on your child or the puppy if either is uncomfortable.

Practicing in nice situations, supervised by you, will show your child how to tell if encounters are progressing pleasantly as they should, and how to maintain proper social boundaries. However, no child is entirely capable of making such judgments alone. Your child can hold the dog, and point out new people they think it would be fun for the dog to meet. **But a parent should always make the final judgment whether to approach and talk to a person or just pass at a distance.**

Always set a proper example and introduce yourself politely when approaching strangers. Never invade anyone's privacy if they do not encourage your approach or if they seem uncomfortable. Make every meeting short and pleasant and thank people for their time.

Never force the stranger, your children or the puppy past their comfort zone in any manner. (This also applies if in future you want to introduce your puppy to a stranger's dog.) Everyone should be smiling and your puppy should be wagging during a social exchange. If a person seems afraid of your dog, or if the puppy trembles during the meeting, it's time to leave and try again in a different situation where everyone is more comfortable. If your dog seems just a little tired or unsure when the stranger is touching him, you can continue talking, but back off on the petting for the moment until the dog seems more comfortable and confident.

Keep the meetings and greetings fun, and limit them to only one or two a day so you don't overwhelm the puppy. We see many dogs that never travel beyond their backyard for several months at a time paraded out proudly to huge seasonal events sponsored by our local humane society for the purpose of "socializing" them. And it's no surprise that these dogs act like emotional wrecks! If your dog is unusually young and/or cute, he's likely to be fondled excitedly by literally hundreds of humans who don't ask permission *and* also force their dogs on him. This is *not* the same as letting your dog meet one-hundred people and dogs over the course of a year. **Social meetings for a dog are like vitamins- it's healthy to have them every day, but very unhealthy to get a year's supply in *one* day.**

You will want to see that your dog encounters novel stimuli every day of his life and your kids will probably want to help. They will start thinking creatively. "Oh, look, here's a field with cows. Can we stop so that the dog can see them?"; "Our puppy is a Great Dane. Let him see that tiny Chihuahua, since he's never seen one before,"; "Let's bring him into the city with us, so that he can see tall buildings" or "Let's walk him by those housewives with strollers". **The dog becomes versed in different stimuli, different environments and different people and, as long as it's done right, he'll become a much more balanced adult.** Meanwhile your family's horizons will expand as well, and "Diversity Training" will add dimension to everyday outings that might otherwise feel monotonous.

Playground Built with Dog Games
- small changes in the playground can make your dog an asset, rather than a problem, at kid's playtime -

A stressed Samaritan once complained to us that their next door neighbor's young Pit Bull barked all day every day while frantically circling the family's kids as they jumped on their trampoline. Had the owner asked us for help, we could have made a suggestion- since they were going to design their yard with their kids' playtime in mind, why not include the dog as well? With the proper planning, the dog's exuberance could become an asset and he could play *with* the children, rather than constantly making trouble because he wasn't being included.

Those of you who have a new home or a blank backyard have the perfect opportunity for change, since you can design your playground or playset any way you want to. Some children's playground equipment lends itself obviously to dogs. An example is tunnels or mazes. Different sizes suit different breeds, and the same dogs that excel at the tunnel obstacle in agility practice will love a tunnel on the playground. Terrier breeds are an obvious example. (See Tunnel Crawl, Chapter 3.)

A textured surface to climb on is also good for dogs and some dogs will jump over low hurdles, or clamber over steps or blocks. Just like kids, dogs also like to play hide and seek, so playground equipment with little walls and windows will be popular with both. Dogs and kids both love playing with balls and dogs may also enjoy a ball tethered to a rope. Another piece of playground equipment based on a classic agility obstacle is a tire that your dogs can jump through. Get the right size tire swing and it may be perfect for both your dogs and your kids.

Some kids' playsets include a sandbox. Your dog will definitely enjoy digging in sand, especially to uncover a treasured toy. But only allow the dog to use the sandbox if he has good manners!!! You'll want him not to dig so vigorously that he throws sand up at your children, and never to use the sand as a bathroom spot. A designated sandbox is sometimes a good way to keep a dog from digging your flowerbeds. But be forewarned that the sport could also backfire- making your dog a digger when he never before thought of it, so a sandbox should only be used with care, and only with certain dogs.

Another idea to try, but only with extreme caution, is one dealt with in greater detail in Chapter 11, Water Activities. Including a kiddie pool for your dog to play in will add a whole new dimension to his activities, and it's a great idea for most dogs. The only caution comes **if you expect dogs and children to be sharing a pool. This could cause dangerous hygiene problems if the children drank any pool water, and could also cause injury if the dog knocked a child into the water.** On the other hand, under certain conditions, **and with careful supervision by a parent,** a little plastic kiddie pool can be great fun for both child and dog. (Just imagine them bopping around a big inflated beach ball from one to the other on the surface of the water while they are either inside or outside the pool.)

Kids, dogs and playtime are a natural combination and the right design and equipment in your backyard playspace can make watching their play a delight for you, the parent. At the other end of the spectrum is the *wrong* combination of young kids, rambunctious dogs and equipment that becomes dangerous when both are trying to play together. Parents should obviously select the safest equipment. For example, choose a surface underfoot with the most cushioning in case your children fall.

But parents should also take time to consult experts on both kids' playground equipment and dogs' agility equipment and then let an expert help them design a backyard play area that combines the best of both. Of course, even then certain cautions will apply. Once you've learned about dog's agility equipment, you'll see that certain moves suit a dog, and others don't. It's simply not safe to have a dog climbing monkey bars, balancing on a high-flying swing or sliding down a slide. Let your kids know what your dog can and can't do safely, and **an adult must always supervise young children and dogs when they play.**

Kids and dogs can't safely play together at all times. There may be certain playground equipment that you don't want the dog near. An example might be monkey bars. It's not safe for the dog to climb, and he might also knock your child off accidentally. If you still want to buy that piece of playground equipment, then simply fence that particular area off from the dog. He can still keep the kids company in other areas, providing he plays appropriately.

As a parent you should be constantly observing how the kids and dog play together, and then you must trust your own judgment, erring on the side of caution. The right equipment, attention and training by the owner will usually be enough to channel your dog or puppy's behavior in a positive fashion when he plays with your kids.

But if you suspect there's a more serious problem you may have to call in a professional to assess your dog's temperament and behavior. Perhaps your dog is simply not suited to playing with your kids in the backyard play area and playset. Your kids may be tiny and your dog may be big and overexuberant and may not at the moment know how to control himself properly. This does not mean that all big dogs are unsafe with kids. Some are extremely delicate and careful. But you should always have perfect control of a large dog. If you are having trouble, a true behavior expert can get you on the right track and give you suggestions on how to keep your kids safe.

There are cases of dogs of every size going out control. For example, your small or medium dog may knock your children down or play so wildly that he scares them. Playground equipment with protruding edges or unstable footing makes a dangerous fall more likely, so this dog must be barred from the kids' play area at all times, as hard as it may seem at first! It is likely that proper training will bring his behavior into line and that in future he can come back in and share some activities, but never risk it until you are sure!

You must use similar caution if your kids will not play properly with the dog or puppy on the play equipment, or if the dog is a teacup breed or suffers from a physical illness or serious anxiety disorder. In this case, it is the dog that's at risk and the playground should be kept out of his routine for his safety. Use milder activities with this dog. And, just like in the case above, the solution is simple- fence off the play equipment and/or fence off part of the yard that the dog can enjoy while the kids are on the playset. You'll be surprised at how much better your leisure hours feel when you're not constantly worrying.

Too often our customers think they have to endure a situation even when it feels painful to them. Remember that playtime in the backyard should be fun for all. Even if it means spending a few more weeks in the design process, or even doubling your expenditure on equipment, your family deserves a completely custom set-up made for *your* kids and *your* dog.

Junior Grooming Salon
- important for bonding and many other benefits, even save money -

Never underestimate your kids! Making your kids responsible for grooming your dogs is a great way to combine the needs of your dogs and your children and to pass the time productively on sluggish summer or cold winter afternoons. You may not need to pay a professional groomer when you can do it at home in a more relaxing atmosphere than many crowded and noisy shops. All you need to do is to teach your children how to groom the dogs correctly. Some dogs are easy, requiring no more than a simple bath, while others may sport elaborate show cuts. If your kids are interested then they can become expert at any level (provided your dogs are gentle and tolerate grooming well!).

> *When your kids spend time formally grooming the dog, it's healthier than rough or aimless play, and it helps the dog see the children in more of a leadership role.*

Grooming sessions also give kids and dogs a great opportunity to bond. Often kids tend to touch or play with dogs too much, so the dogs begin to stress. And sometimes kids don't present strong enough authority for the dog to respect them. But when your kids spend time formally grooming the dog, it's healthier than rough or aimless play, and it helps the dog see the children in more of a leadership role.

Parents can devote as much time, money and effort to teaching their children to groom dogs as you like. If all you want is for your kids to help bathe the dogs outside on a hot summer day, this is okay. Or, let them have daily access to a brush and let them brush out your shedding pet whenever they want to (as long as the dog won't nip and the kids are gentle). Daily brushing is fun for everyone, and gives Mom a cleaner home.

If your children are truly fascinated by dogs and might someday want to pursue careers involving dogs, you can give them a great head start. The same is true if you are highly interested in dogs yourself. You may want to set aside an area in the home specifically for grooming your dogs (see "A Room of His Own" in Chapter 5). You can also buy professional grade supplies and products (see Catalogs in Resources) and books and videos that you and your kids can study together. The education your kids receive grooming their own dogs will become a valuable skill and it might even influence career choices later on.

But, no matter how comfortable and in-control your kids seem grooming the dogs, an adult should always supervise. Adult supervision is an absolute must during nail clipping or any work involving scissors or sharp tools. And never let your kids groom a dog unless you are absolutely certain that the dog is overall sweet and relaxed, has never bitten or growled at a person, loves being with kids and always enjoys being groomed. (Save problem dogs for competent adults. You will need to slowly and expertly acclimate dogs that show fear or aggression during grooming and you might require professional assistance.)

Even a dog that is usually calm may become nervous or start to struggle during grooming. Depending on the situation, you may be able to ease the dog back into the rest of the session. But, if the dog struggles at all while a child is handling him, let the child stop. Perhaps the child was causing him some discomfort. You could reinstruct and let the child try again. But work together. **Never force a child to deal with a nervous or angry dog alone.**

You and your kids should practice with your dogs from the time they are tiny puppies to accustom them to the types of touch that happen during grooming (see Chapter 3, Puppy Games). You will need some uninterrupted time where you can gently teach the puppy and the child the right ways to touch each other. This will be a great accomplishment for both. When your dog is older and the kids are older, and they make his newly trimmed coat shine like a show dog's, your dog and your children will glow with pride! Why not take photos or videotape the session to show off?

If you have several kids and several dogs, you can make a "Doggie Salon Day" a regular family get-together. You can even invite friends, neighbors or extended family with their dogs. Make sure all dogs have mild temperaments and get along well. Put on some motivational music and put out snacks. (Include some home-baked dog cookies made by the kids. See the following section.) Everybody can bring their favorite bows and dog jewelry and you can switch off the accessories for different doggie looks each week.

Try out different products for dogs or formulate your own, using dog-safe recipes. For example, you could use natural treatments to soothe cracked skin on your dog's feet. Or try calming aromatherapy oils made specifically for dogs (for example, Bach Flower Essences.) Just consult your vet or holistic professional to learn about the best products and treatments. Having spa days like this is also a good alternative for rural families who may not live near an upscale pet salon or boutique to try novel treatments for their dogs.

The salon day can be a time of lots of fun and laughter. Just make sure that everyone's on the same page. Adults should be patient, and willing to learn the proper techniques of grooming. They should also set aside cell phones during the session, because problems requiring adult attention can happen suddenly when you combine kids, dogs and grooming. The kids that participate in salon day can be any age, but just assign tasks according to their abilities. Even a two-year-old can run a brush over a dog's un-matted coat, but **never let young kids anywhere near scissors, clippers, razors or strongly medicated products. Dog and child could both get hurt!**

Preteens that are good with dogs can learn the more difficult skills, but you should supervise as they are learning. And not every child *wants* to groom dogs. You are trying to teach your dog to remain patient and mellow during lengthy grooming sessions, so only involve children in the more intricate aspects of grooming if they are mature and low-key, have a long attention span for their age and truly want to learn the skill!

One note for parents who may have attempted grooming their dog at home only to be frustrated with the results: sometimes the problem is not you or the dog- sometimes the problem is the tools you're using. Some dogs with thick undercoats do best when you start with a "rake" type brush to remove old matted hair. Pulling on them with a regular brush may cause snags and pain, and it still won't do the job. Dogs with very short coats come out shiny after you rub them down with a "mitt", while a regular brush or comb may do no more than scrape their skin. And one of the greatest tools we've seen is a tiny brush and comb intended for toy dogs. You can also use these with dogs of any age or size to work on the most sensitive areas around face, feet or ears. It's safer and more comfortable for the dog and gets better results! We advise that you search around for the absolute best grooming tools for your dog. You'll be glad you did when you see the results. And even if you purchase the most expensive brush, always test first to see if it's comfortable for your dog before you or your children spend an hour using it on him!

Doggie Bakery
- bake your own healthy treats while socializing with your favorite people & dogs -

Ah, this Brave New World! Are you a dog owner who has recently become concerned about the safety and healthiness of your dog's food and treats? Is your dog allergic to certain grains, meats or preservatives? And do you wish to keep his food all-natural while also not impoverishing your family? Perhaps your family frequents an upscale dog boutique where you've seen elaborately decorated hand-baked doggie cookies that are just so adorable that you can't resist. You and your dog may like such all-natural treats, but you may not be prepared to invest two dollars every time you buy a single cookie!

So why not bake gourmet dog treats at home? And why not turn it into a family activity? Get together all interested parties, including kids of all ages, extended family and friends.

Just include at least one adult or mature older teen to supervise any cooking or baking. Everybody bring in their favorite dog recipe book, or download recipes off the Internet. (If you want to be entirely safe, collect the recipes you wish to use and clear them with your veterinarian or ask him to recommend a healthy "cookbook". We have seen wide variation in dog recipes, with some calling for the use of ingredients that others claim make dogs ill. We advise you use simple recipes with ingredients that you know are safe and let your veterinarian make the final decision if you're ever in doubt.)

Once you know what you'll be cooking, take a group shopping trip and then make your kitchen "party central" as you bake up the ingredients. Younger kids will enjoy mixing and icing the cookies, and more mature kids can actually help you in learning more about dog nutrition. Well-behaved dogs can even hang around to act as taste testers when the different recipes are done.

Some dog recipes are much more long-lasting than others, so check the shelf life and recommended storage procedures. Dry "cookie" type treats tend to last relatively long. You could host a baking party once a month, or whenever you have the time. But if the recipes you want to make are very perishable, you could simply gather the family to prepare Fido's meals at a set time each week, perhaps when you're also making a fun dinner for yourselves. Or get together once a week with a girlfriend who's also a natural foods fanatic and catch up on gossip while preparing your dogs' natural food in big batches together. The point is that your dog's care should not be just another chore that takes up time and separates the family while the parents run to a bunch of different stores. Instead, try to make your dog's care part of family life that brings everyone together!

Hand-baked dog treats are also great gifts. So plan to get together with family or a bunch of your dearest friends for a little pre-holiday party where you bake and wrap up elaborate home-baked dog cookies for everyone on your lists!

Different Handlers
- make obedience more challenging while teaching your dog
to respect all family members -

When training obedience, in order to change things up and make activities more challenging, you don't have to necessarily introduce new tasks but you can simply up the ante about how an old task is performed. For example, let's say you are training your dog to sit. The easiest way to achieve success is with one handler in the least distracting setting. Until your dog perfects the command, the same handler would want to work with the dog, so that the dog is not confused.

Once the dog fully perfects the command in a bland non-distracting setting like inside your own home, you will want to increase the difficulty by increasing distractions. You would "proof" the dog by asking him to sit outside, or maybe in the park. Adding people to the scene also makes completing the task more difficult, so you might ask your children to play nearby to act as a distraction. If your dog sits under these circumstances, you know he's really mastered the command.

Now it's time to move on to the next level of difficulty- different handlers. You might think it's easy for your dog to generalize when a different family member than the one he's been practicing with gives him the already familiar obedience command. Actually, this sets up somewhat of a new challenge for your dog because it's a dog's nature to learn situationally.

For the same reason that obeying a command he's heard in the living room will be more difficult for your dog the first time you introduce it in the park, it's also more challenging the first time the command is given by a different handler. This is especially true if the new handler is very different from the dog's original handler; for example a man rather than a woman, or a child rather than an adult. Your dog can and should make the transition to understanding that he should obey the command when given by any family member, even if characteristics like tone of voice or body posture differ.

This is why an owner's job is not done when they teach their dog his obedience commands. Most authorities on training recommend that the primary handler work with the dog alone at first, until the dog performs all the commands reliably. Then it's time to introduce the next family member as handler. Once your dog masters his commands with this person, you can teach him with the next family member. Now, everybody in the household can give commands at unexpected times throughout the day whenever they need to. This keeps your dog sharp, makes life with him easier and brings the dog and the family members together for quality time that's getting rarer and rarer these days.

Adults must keep in mind, however, that not all kids can be expected to receive perfect results when they train the dog. It's canine nature to respond to certain signals that indicate "pack leader" in the dog world and, unfair as it might seem, some canine signals of dominant status include height and deeper voice. So obviously, small children can't compete well in these departments.

There's debate amongst professionals about what age children should start training dogs obedience and, to address the subject adequately, we'd have to devote an entire book. Along with our philosophy of "safety first" we do advise that when young children are with dogs, adults should properly supervise. Obedience practice is no exception. Parents must use their own common sense in all situations involving kids and dogs and always err on the side of caution.

That being said, it's amazing how certain children seem quite precocious with dogs, including some very young children. Even though a particular child is small, he or she may be blessed with a unique talent for working with dogs. Just like this particular child loves dogs, dogs also seem to take the child seriously and respond beautifully with them. And there are plenty of junior handlers showing champions dogs in the ring to prove this!

Parents should assess how much each of their children should work with each of their dogs, and what kind of results can reasonably be expected. Some kids can give commands on their own, and the dog will obey. Others will need a parent standing beside them to help reinforce. Everybody in the family using standard hand signals along with verbal commands can sometimes help provide consistency.

Parents should encourage each child to train the dog to their own ability at their life stage, while supervising and assisting when needed to make sure that the dog follows though on the commands. Mini sessions every single day of the dog's life are ideal. Make sure each session ends on a positive note and always provide plenty of praise- not only for your dog, but for your kids' efforts as well.

Junior Handlers
- the right way for kids to teach obedience at home
(and maybe even compete at dog shows)

This fun activity for your home is actually based on the professional dog show ring, where handlers as young as nine years old are allowed to compete in AKC events, including conformation and obedience. It's quite impressive when you observe the skill and concentration of junior handlers working dogs of every size. No one forces these kids to do it- they dedicate themselves to the demanding sport of dog handling because it is their passion- and their skill and professionalism sometimes exceeds the adults'. These talented kids aren't in it for a paycheck, nor are they jaded players at dog show politics. Perhaps we find it such a delight to watch them because we can see their true joy in working with dogs.

There's some debate amongst dog trainers about how much contact children should have with dogs at a young age. In our personal backgrounds, both authors trained large guarding dogs to AKC standards and beyond without any adult guidance or supervision at elementary school age. Both of us also related to our dogs as comfortably as if we were canine members of their pack. Looking back at this from the perspective of adults who have read many trainers' warnings that young children and dogs should always be separated, we must honestly ask ourselves what to tell our clients. The only answer is that every parent should use good judgment and common sense. First of all, **there is no reason to leave really young children unsupervised with dogs. Since an adult should always be watching young children anyway, there's no reason they shouldn't watch the kids whenever they're with the dog. This ensures safety for everyone and it still gives the children complete freedom to bond with the dog.**

Only you know your dog's temperament. But even the best of dogs can make mistakes. And children should not be left alone in certain situations! Yes, your eight-year old child may train your dog perfect obedience in your backyard and a large dog can obey a tiny child just as easily as it can a full-grown adult. But if your dog weighs ninety pounds and if you send your child out walking him on a busy residential street, what can your child possibly do if a stray dog of equal weight comes barreling at your dog aggressively?

To our minds, this is just an example of parents not thinking and taking a needless and potentially deadly risk that could never be worth it! Yes, by all means **allow your child to handle your dog with all his commands if the child is mature enough emotionally *and* your dog is of completely loving and placid temperament. But you should keep an eye on child and dog in any potentially dangerous situation**, even if it means following them on the walk a few paces behind, but close enough to instantaneously intervene. (Even if your young child becomes one of those talented junior handlers at AKC shows, you or another qualified adult should always be there to look out for the child!)

Many trainers caution that kids can't enforce dominance strongly enough that dogs will listen. And we believe this does apply with dogs that are out of control. **Dogs that show aggression, pull on leash violently, nip owner's hands drawing blood or jump on people roughly need more than everyday obedience training and small children should never be forced to deal with these serious behavior problems.**

It's also true dogs probably won't respect a child's commands as much as they would the parents'. Kids are physically smaller and weaker than adults, they're often timid or inconsistent and the dog may have already been ignoring or bullying them for months. **In cases of problem dogs, parents should never involve the children until the adults have trained the dog to consistently act gentle and obey basic commands.** If you cannot do this efficiently on your own, you should call in a professional. **Not only can a dog with behavior problems injure a child, but he can also make a child feel bad around dogs in general, rather than growing up to feel comfortable with dogs.**

Even if your dog's behavior is okay, it's less confusing to the dog if one family member, usually an adult, teaches him his basic commands first. After this, we believe the other family members must get involved, and the dog must be willing to listen to and respect all members of your family, no matter how young.

The primary handler will train the dog his basic commands to perfection. Now the next handler (perhaps the spouse) practices the commands with the dog. Next the children practice, with the parents present. Each change of handler presents additional difficultly, but the dog should graduate to where he respects commands given by each family member. (See the "Different Handlers" section in this chapter). Teach your kids to use the correct words, tone of voice and body posture to communicate with your dog and to never to bully, shout at, squeeze or grasp the dog harshly. And instruct them to always call an adult if they run into any problem getting the dog to obey a command, rather than getting into a conflict with the dog that they cannot win.

Some kids of four years old will comply perfectly with all of the above. But some kids of twelve years cannot. You must make the judgment of your child's maturity. If the child is not mature enough to follow all the above instructions, then wait until they are older to ask them to in any way command the dog! Until the child is ready, you should still involve them by having them beside you while you run the dog through his obedience commands and when you take him on leashed walks. This way the dog will still associate the child and good behavior.

But let's say your child passionately wants to obedience train dogs. If you notice that your child uses correct methods and your dog obeys and acts gentle, then we believe you should definitely support your child's interest. You can consult books and videos for junior handlers, your child could become involved in junior handling through the AKC (see Resources) and you can find professionally run classes specifically for kids and dogs in many areas.

Some regular group obedience classes will also allow a child to handle the dog, as long as the parent supervises. Just make sure to choose a compassionate instructor; you don't want your child observing an adult trainer using Gestapo-style methods that make the puppies yelp!

In addition to formal practice, kids should also practice obedience with the dog during day-to-day activities. And don't be shy about showing off your kids' accomplishments with the dog. You might want to videotape successful obedience sessions or urge your kids to show off for their grandparents on the weekend. And ask your kids to give you a "wish list" of dog books or equipment that they might like as gifts.

Get a sense for your kid's true level of interest. Some children can happily stop at just learning the proper way of interacting with the dog and they don't want to practice formal obedience every day. Dogs are simply not their biggest interest, and don't need to be, so let them pursue other hobbies.

But other children may have dreams of a dog career beyond your wildest expectations. And this is the time to support them with your time and financial investment. Provide them with books, videos and/or the chance to watch television shows about people in dog careers; take them to dog shows and obedience clubs and competitions and let them watch real-life junior dog handlers.

Dogs do wonderfully with children because children tend to be honest, intense in concentration and filled with hope and belief in the dog. So never laugh it off if your child says he wants to do great things with his dog. Give him a chance to display his talent and you may be surprised! The only rule is that he must be consistent and responsible as a barometer of his true level of interest. So don't push a child who's highly enthusiastic when the pup first comes home but then misses a walk or a feeding because his friends call him out to play.

If your son or daughter desires to train the dog, he or she should also be willing and able to feed it, brush it, clean up from it and diligently study dog information in books. A child truly impassioned about handling dogs will be fired up to care for your dog and to learn more. If your child is, then you should support his ambitions. Don't hesitate to boast about your child to your friends, for one day you may see *your* child competing internationally!

Assess a Dog
- appeals to kids' natural curiosity. Adults should also learn this important skill -

How much can you learn about a dog in two minutes? As home dog trainers specializing in complex cases, we can learn a lot just from laying hands on a dog. The way a dog smells, the way he holds his ears, the way he pants or even the texture of his fur tell a lot. Some signs and symptoms are vital to your dog's health and others tell you about his mood, his personality and how he'll react.

We assess stranger's dogs in this manner all the time, often in physically dangerous situations. And veterinarians, of course, are expert at assessing a dog rapidly and accurately in order to save his life or safeguard his health. **In a true physical or behavioral crisis, owners should turn to professionals to assess their dog. Adults should always supervise their kids around dogs, especially if there is any chance that the dog is ill or may act snappy, and only allow kids to practice assessing healthy, friendly dogs.**

But as long as your dog is healthy and emotionally well-balanced, all the family members should learn the skill of assessing, and practice it on a regular basis. Not only is the activity challenging and educational for children, but it also helps to set a baseline to know if there is ever a problem.

A good time to assess your dog is after he's exercised and is feeling mellow. You can examine the dog on the floor, on a table or on your lap, depending on his size and what you, he and the children are most comfortable with. And bring some treats to dole out periodically as your dog tolerates the exam in good spirits.

Start with the dog's coat. Explain to your children what coat texture is healthy and normal for his breed. Tell them signs to look out for when they are petting the dog. If something ever deviates from normal, like dry or excessively shedding hair, or any type of sore, they should immediately tell you. The more your kids know about your dog's normal state, the easier it will be for them to report something. Your informed kids may even notice a problem before you do, since they may be the ones down on the floor petting the dog all day, while you're busy with adult chores.

Appropriate to their ages, you can teach kids a little bit about skin conditions, allergies and pests and let them know how these problems are treated. Maybe one of your dogs is old, and one is young. You can show the kids physical and behavioral differences between the older dog and the puppy, or between the different breeds of dogs in your home. Kids can learn about topics ranging from the healthy color of a dog's tongue, a normal heartbeat and temperature and why playing certain games, or squeezing in certain spots, can irritate or anger a dog.

Kids love knowledge and the more they know about dogs, the more involved they'll become, and the more fun they'll have. Once kids understand how dogs are wired, they are also likely to provide better husbandry, offering the dog the type of attention it really needs. Kids are fascinated by dogs. Instead of just playing in rowdy fashion, your child can spend hours quietly assessing your dog, and the activity is productive for everyone. You will likely have no problem convincing your kids to learn the skill of assessment. Kids tend to like new knowledge that's a little tough to master- it's usually their nature to want to learn more.

Adults may be a little harder to persuade. In some families, one spouse has a lot of experience with dogs, while the other has never owned a dog before. In this case, the best thing to do is to make assessment time a fun family bonding time for both adults, the children and the dog. You can even include a grandparent who's highly knowledgeable about dogs. The most knowledgeable of the adults can demonstrate assessment on the dog, starting at the head and moving to the tail. And then other family members can take their turns and ask questions as you reward your dog with lots of treats and praise for standing patiently.

When you assess your dog, you should have a good library of dog books to consult, including veterinary manuals at varying levels of complexity and detailed books on dog breeds and behavior. And you may be surprised when your kids start reading the more complex books on their own! You can also practice assessing dogs with groups of adults, like your breed meet-up group or any small social group whose members share a passion for dogs.

Assessment following illness or injury should be left to professionals. Families should take a little time, at least once a week, to give each of their healthy dogs the once-over, and there's no harm in assessing even more often. **But you should immediately contact your veterinarian if your casual assessment reveals ill health, or any unfamiliar or suspicious symptom relating to health or behavior, including aggression.** Your veterinarian may be able to solve your dog's problem much more easily and affordably because you noticed it early.

Demonstrate Tricks
**-   your kids can give your dog greater purpose & pride
by choosing the best tricks to teach him -**

Kids love to show off their accomplishments. So do dogs. And both kids and dogs would rather spend time productively, accomplishing something they can be proud of, rather than just annoying the parents in the household. Kids are also great dog trainers, as explained in the "Junior Handlers' section above. So why not let the kids and the dogs in the family team up and show the adults what they can do?

Your kids can be as creative as they like in selecting fun tricks they would like to teach the dog. Part of that creativity is selecting the right trick for the right dog. And kids and their parents can use this book as a starting point, perusing different sections to find just the right trick. For example, small kids trying to teach an older St. Bernard to be a "Dancing Dog" (Chapter 5) might bring some smiles to everybody's faces, but not for the reasons intended. This trick might be suited better to the higher energy, eager-to-learn Jack Russell Terrier in the family. And the talented child or teen could surprise Dad by training that St. Bernard to bring him chips, beverage and television remote when the football game is about to start!

If there is a puppy in the family, the children could be in charge of teaching him "Kisses" (Chapter 3). This is a game that will get some appreciative comments when demonstrated and it will also teach your puppy good manners for life. As long as it suits their particular dog's talents and physical abilities, as well as their own, children can teach their dogs the most challenging tricks- including those they've seen on movies and television. Parents will, of course, want to monitor and help their kids at different stages throughout the process, making trick training safe and enjoyable for everybody.

If you are a parent wondering what type of activities would be good for kids over summer break, and especially if you happen to be the parent on your block who always seems to host all the neighborhood kids, then training and demonstrating dog tricks could be a great combination of learning and entertainment. You can make the sessions as simple, or as ambitious, as you like. And let the kids do most of the planning and organizing, which is also part of the fun.

Possibilities are endless. Kids can go as far as designing a flyer announcing when and where the canine trick demonstration will be held. Then everybody can meet in a backyard, community clubhouse or church hall (with permission) and some of the kids can be in charge of setting out snacks for the handlers and the dogs (see "Doggie Bakery"). If your kids are young animal activists they might even decide to raise money at the event and donate it to their favorite canine charity. Or (barring any liability concerns) your local therapy dog organization might even allow a few caring kids or teens to demonstrate their dog tricks for an appreciative audience at the local senior center.

On the other end of the spectrum, teaching and demonstrating tricks can be a private family affair. You might encourage the kids to train the dog, or dogs, one new trick per week and then demonstrate it after Sunday dinner, or during a weekly family games night. And most children would love to prepare a trick or two to show off to out-of-town relatives when they visit.

"Petstar" at Home
- **amp up trick training; compete with family & friends to make it as ambitious as you want!**

Here's a way to take the last entry one step further. Suppose some of the tricks your kids teach your dogs are particularly impressive and creative? Then your kids and dogs will probably really want to show off. Start by watching television shows like *"Petstar"*, in which handlers and dogs compete by demonstrating amazing (and some downright unusual) dog tricks. This can give your kids inspiration and a jumping-off point.

Now, they can set a date to hold their own *"Petstar"* competition at home, and then each child can pick their favorite set of tricks and their favorite dog to work with. As with "Demonstrate, Tricks" above, there are many different ways to enjoy *"Petstar"* at Home.

Your family could set aside a regular night each week or month. Or you could hold the special competition only once at a special event like a family reunion. Just send out an email in advance giving everyone who wants to participate lots of time to prepare.

> *Commands are meant to be executed not just in a show ring, but in the face of real life distractions - kids, other dogs, street noise and the everyday bustle of family life.*

Kids or teens who want to organize a larger event could hold a *"Petstar"* competition at their church or community teen center, day camp, 4-H Youth Fair or a community clubhouse. They could even raise money for charity at a larger *"Petstar"* competition. If your kids are so inclined, this is a great introduction to fundraising.

No matter how small or large you want to make your amateur *"Petstar"* competition, you should make sure that every child, and every dog, has lots of fun and leaves feeling proud. The best way to make sure of this is not to limit yourself to just one winner of the contest. Instead, select winners in several different categories. You might make categories based on the age of the handler (for example, "under five years") or based on the dogs ("puppy", "senior dog", "toy breed") and also based on the nature of the tricks (for example, "zaniest trick", "most beautiful trick", "most athletic" and "multi-dog"). If you hold the competition regularly, you might also want to include a category for "best first-time dog and handler" or even "most improvement".

Adults and kids who are video hobbyists can film the family or community "Petstar" competitions. Then break these films out at holiday gatherings or for friends who didn't get to attend. If your kids and dogs practice and perfect some really great tricks, they can even enter the real *Petstar* competition and you can cheer them on when they're on television!

Test Obedience
- the best ways for family, including kids, to practice obedience so your dog doesn't "forget" -

In "Different Handlers" and "Junior Handlers" we describe how kids can teach dogs obedience commands, including "sit", "down", "heel", "stay" and "come". These and other commands like "watch me", "go to your place", "leave it" and "drop it" are not meant to be trained, perfected and then ignored. Many owners don't understand (and unfortunately lots of dog trainers don't bother to tell them) that the purpose of all these obedience commands is to be used in real life, many times throughout each day.

The commands are meant to be executed not just in a show ring, but in the face of real life distractions- kids, other dogs, street noise and the everyday bustle of family life. Having your dog obey his obedience commands every single time you ask, in the most unexpected of situations helps your dog to experience life with a purpose and to respect you and obey you in general. And obedience is a family affair, so testing your dog's obedience responses is one place where kids can really pitch in and help.

As per the cautions about kids in "Different Handlers" above, an adult should first teach the dog the commands until the dog is completely reliable. The adult will then supervise as each other family member reviews each command with the dog. Not all dogs are ready to be around all age children safely. And since some kids, because of size and age, may not be physically able to use the correct posture or tone of voice to get some dogs to obey, the adults should use careful judgment.

In other words, if your dog listens avidly and complies when your six year-old tells him to "sit", then it will be great practice for the child to give the dog the command at spontaneous times throughout the day to test him and also to increase the dog's respect for the child. In contrast, if your dog acts silly and jumps around when your child attempts to give the command, then it would be counterproductive to let the child give the command on his own. Instead, you can stack the deck in your child's favor by having him give the command as you stand beside him to reinforce it. Practicing this way makes the dog more likely to obey and sets up a pattern of success, until eventually the child can start giving commands on their own.

If your dog refuses to obey the children at all, this would be a good time to have an expert canine behaviorist visit your home and assess the situation. Perhaps it's okay for your kids to use other simpler commands with the dog for now and wait to do the formal obedience until they get a little older. Your dogs might need some more training from the professional just to show basic manners around the kids. In these cases, it's an absolute matter of safety to get this training. Other dogs are sensitive enough that they'll happily and proudly obey commands given by a savvy and confident two-year-old.

But remember that each case is different. You should encourage your kids and teens to frequently test your dog's obedience responses throughout the day, but use caution teaching them how to correct each dog. You may know that when a handler gives commands, they should make sure that the dog follows through, otherwise it teaches the dog a pattern of ignoring. And if you've ever watched an obedience class, you're likely familiar with the image of a handler positioning their dog into a "sit". Physical positioning like this is one way that you could get a dog to follow through with a command, however it's usually the last way we recommend.

Not all handlers are physically capable of positioning. For example, it may be difficult for a small child to position a large dog. The other problem is obvious- it's very easy for the dog to feel discomfort if the handler doesn't execute the move perfectly. If a somewhat awkward child tries to position a puppy, the pup might easily get hurt, and we usually advise against physical positioning for puppies. The same is true for senior dogs and dogs with physical problems. But even a healthy adult dog might snap at the handler if physical positioning hurts him.

A safer alternative for a child handling a dog to get compliance if the dog doesn't obey a command the first time around is for the child to walk the dog around in a little circle and try again. Repeat until the dog gets the command right, and this will help the child to always have the "last word". Another way to increase your dog's compliance is to let the dog know he's likely to get a treat. In some cases it is perfectly safe for a child or teen to physically position a resistant dog into a "sit" or a "down". But it's usually not necessary or advisable. Most parents will feel more comfortable advising their kids to save the physical positioning for when adults are supervising.

Kids must also be advised that everything they do with the dog throughout the day acts as training. If they encourage the dog to leap on them and then they kiss him, this will train the dog to leap on everybody. If they call him over and feed him scraps from the table, he'll learn to raid everybody's food. And if they act wild and crazy with the dog when he's a puppy they will create a crazy adult dog! Make your children cognizant about how each of their actions affects the dog and you'll be surprised how willing and able they will be to do the right things.

Your spouse may be a bigger problem. Once you train your dog obedience, every adult in the family *must* act consistent with him every day and utilizing the standard commands should become second-nature every day for every adult. Your spouse *must* practice obedience with the dog, especially if he's usually tentative around the dog or if the dog tends to take advantage of him!

Dogs are pack animals and they understand life in such a dynamic. If your spouse doesn't practice leading the dog, then the dog will think he should practice leading your spouse. In a dog's eyes, a family cannot be divided. All the workaholic spouses should take a few minutes each day to set down their Palm Pilots, unwind and just practice obedience with the rest of the family and the family dog. They will find this is a lot more satisfying than constantly cleaning up the dog's messes or yelling at the dog. The likelihood is that once your spouse who's not a dog enthusiast spends a few minutes a day giving the commands and watching your dog's smiling face staring up at him and tail happily thumping the floor, he'll be hooked. And next he'll be asking to participate in the family's "Petstar" at Home competitions!

Saki & Maya-
"Ray's little kisses"

Ch. 14- Activities for Owners with Limited Mobility

"No matter your physical condition, with some simple changes you and your dog can live and play together in harmony and joy!"

Also Try These Ideas from Other Chapters for Owners with Limited Mobility:

Puppy Games & Activities: Find the Treat, Which Hand?, Find Mommy, Which Box Has the Fun In It?, Tunnel Crawl, Soccer (dog playing alone), How Do I Get What's In There?, Let's Play Doctor, Shopping Spree, Obedience-minded, Soft Mouth, New Learning Every Day

Mental Games & Activities: Movie Star, Watch Me, Wait, Hold That Position, Move Slow, Doggie Einstein, Ring Toss, Shell Game, Discern Objects by Name, Go To Person by Name

Indoor Games & Activities: Hide & Go Seek, Dancing Dog (Some Moves), A Room of His Own, Doggie Gymnasium (designed to accommodate owner's needs)

Balance & Coordination Activities: Will the Real Dog Stand?, Play the Seal, Walk Like A Man, Frisbee (under certain circumstances), Basketball, Stack

Multi-Dog Games & Activities: Sit On a Bench, What's My Name?, The Long, Long Stay, Under/Over (under certain circumstances)

Continued, next page

Balloons

Play in the Snow

Doggie Day Care

Obed/Agility Clubs

Rehab Together

Try On a Dog

Service Dog

Games on the Floor

Dog on the Table

Chaise Lounge Training

Let the Dog Do the Walking

Dog Stairs

Upstairs/Downstairs

Be Creative

Also Try These Ideas from Other Chapters for Owners with Limited Mobility: (continued)

Problem Dog Games: Catch (possible), Go to Your Place, Take a Bow, Stop Barking On Command, Drop It, Interactive Toys, Wacky Walker (certain circumstances)

Therapeutic & Senior Dog Activities: Massage, Meditation, Stretching, Swim (certain circumstances), Hydrotherapy (certain circumstances), Talking toys, Kong Time, Doggie TV, Bring Me the Puppy

High Energy Activities: Doggie Treadmill, Monkey-in-the-Middle (if capable of throwing)

Water Activities: Kiddie Pool, Continuous Pool, Chase the Hose, Dog's Own Pool

Useful Activities: Find My Keys, Get the Mail, Get My Shoes, Check on the Baby, Check on Grandma, Help Your Special Needs Family Member, Bark for Help, Personal Bodyguard, Lap Dog, Carry My Purse, Ring a Doorbell, Lifesaver

Family Activities: Circle of Love (certain circumstances), Jump Rope (certain circumstances), Playground Built with Dog Games, Different Handlers, Doggie Bakery, Assess a Dog, Demonstrate Tricks, "Petstar" at Home, Test Obedience

Activities for Owners with Limited Mobility-Introduction

"No matter your physical condition, with some simple changes you and your dog can live and play together in harmony and joy!"

Writing this chapter has been particularly dear to us for several reasons. One reason is that this is one area where dog owners seem to get very little advice no matter how desperately they need it. If you are elderly, disabled or physically limited, you may have already sought advice on how to exercise and mentally stimulate your dog through books, group classes or even home dog trainers. Unfortunately, professionals often recommended activities and exercises for your dog that owners with any physical limitations just can't do.

It's an absolute fact that some active breeds of dogs require the equivalent of running full-speed for a half-hour twice a day. And some dog professionals (including the most respected television trainers) recommend twice as much exercise. Meanwhile, dog owners with physical limitations may have difficulty walking half a block from their house! Even dog owners considered "able-bodied", who get around sufficiently in day-to-day life may not have the extra stamina necessary for strenuous exercise with their dog. And owners often feel guilty knowing they cannot do all that's recommended.

Do your physical limitations make you a bad dog owner? We don't think so. In fact, elderly owners and those with physical limitations are usually willing to diligently work with their dog every day, if only they could find some exercises within their abilities. So it's time to be reasonable. Many dog professionals will give you "good advice" that includes walking your large dog two hours a day (in every weather and every neighborhood), _jogging_ with your dog, throwing a ball long distance for fetch and meanwhile taking care of feeding, watering and grooming. They'd also like you to socialize your dog with other dogs!

If you just adopted a highly energetic 80lb dog from your local shelter, the shelter might have scheduled you for the same group obedience class they recommend to everyone else. But most of these classes are highly uncomfortable for frail owners. Many group classes are held in sun-drenched fields in midsummer. And a senior dog owner may be forced to stand on their feet for an hour and jog around in a circle, trying to keep up with other participants who are forty years younger and much more physically fit. Owners with physical limitations may also be asked to perform exercises like bending down and lifting their dog into a lying down pose during class.

Someone who suffers painful arthritis or who is recovering from back surgery simply cannot do this! Yet sadly some dog "professionals" seem to show little compassion for physical challenges. Alternately, the professional may feel sorry for an owner and dog, but simply not know any good dog/owner activities that aren't physically taxing. So they may tell you that you must warehouse your dog at a crowded daycare facility each day rather than finding novel ways to exercise him with love at home.

And a dog owner doesn't have to suffer from extreme illness or disability to be physically limited. Many Americans of all ages are so out-of-shape today that suddenly doing vigorous physical exercise with their dog can be dangerous or painful. And other individuals including asthmatics and pregnant women must be careful about particular movements or exertion in extreme weather. Unfortunately many dog owners feel ashamed to even admit that they have problems, thinking others may look down on them. So they get by as best they can, doing the same old exercises and activities that people in the dog world have been suggesting for the past hundred years. If the owner feels pain, they suffer in silence. Or the dog may suffer without adequate exercise or play because the owner literally doesn't know what to do, or where to turn. As home dog trainers, we walk into many sad situations where an owner has injured themselves trying to walk their dog and has then given up walking completely, leaving the dog with no exercise for years.

> *At five-thirty each evening you likely feel wiped out, just when your dog is most crazed with frustration. But, no matter your physical condition, you can change your lifestyle and workout style so that you and your dog can play together in total harmony and joy!*

The good news is that dogs aren't stupid; they're one of the most flexible and adaptable animals on the planet! Your dog enjoys nothing more than serving and supporting you- as long as he knows what you want of him. For thousands of years dogs have been working beside their owners, taking care of them and protecting them. Only our modern high-tech world has made dogs into wound-up juggernauts ready to spring out at you when you come home from an eight-hour day at your desk job.

Coming home and finding your dog exploding with energy can make attempting a leashed walk with him a daunting chore. And containing your dog all day in a small space makes the problem exponentially worse. At five-thirty each evening you likely feel wiped out, just when your dog is most crazed with frustration. But this is simply an ailment of our out-of-balance world. *And, no matter your physical condition you can change your lifestyle and workout style so that you and your dog can play together in total harmony and joy!*

We believe owners with physical limitations, including elderly owners who live alone, *can* and *should* own dogs. In fact, owning a dog can make you healthier and happier- it's even been scientifically proven that owning a dog can make you live longer.

Some breeds are easier to work with physically, and require less vigorous exercise. And exercise requirements aren't always based on size, so never jump to conclusions without extensive research. For highly experienced owners only, some giant breeds are good possibilities, since they don't require a lot of running. And don't rule out the less well-known breeds. **Studying up until you are truly expert on dog breeds and their characteristics helps you make the best match in terms of activity level. So, if you're bringing home a new dog, study up first to make the best choice.** Double check any information you get about activity level and spend time with multiple dogs of the breed you're interested in.

But don't necessarily be disheartened if you already own a dog with a high energy level. No breed is impossible to work with, and accurately learning your dog's breed characteristics will help you select the best activities for him.

Once you know what your dog needs, read over all of the novel exercise and play suggestions in this chapter and think about how you may incorporate some of these activities in your life. Also try activities from "Indoor Games & Activities", "Mental Games & Activities" and "Problem Dog Games & Activities". This whole book is designed to work for real-life owners rather than superpeople with unlimited energy. Even if your physical condition isn't perfect, even if you don't own a yard or if you're facing extremes of hot and cold weather, you'll find suitable ideas here to engage with your dog.

Remember that not all exercise is physical. The more your dog focuses mentally and the more you work together, the less he'll feel useless or frustrated. Dogs do not demand much, but they do need a purpose in life. Giving your dog structured activity and mental work won't completely substitute for vigorous physical activity, but you'll be surprised how happily tired your dog will be after an indoor game or an indoor obedience session.

With not much energy at and all and with simple, novel equipment you can change your quality of life and make your dog's life a joy. Don't give up on your dog, and don't let anybody give up on you. You'll find suggestions in this chapter for hiring help, and for organizations that can help you train your dog as a service dog. But help can also come in the form of a neighbor, friend or relative. You may be surprised how your dog-related needs may dovetail, and you may be able to work out a perfect plan where you, your new friend and both of your dogs get together so that everybody's needs are met. After all, time with your dog should be *fun* and owning your dog overall should be a *joy*!

Ignore any exercise advice from dog "professionals" that makes you or your dog miserable, and don't worry if you don't do well in group classes or with trainers who use the same program for everyone. And *never* let anybody suggest crating as a long-term solution for you if you cannot control your dog. This "solution" is simply a widespread cop-out by trainers and others in the dog business who are out of ideas. Crating stresses and frustrates your dog, breaks down the bond between you and leaves you with an even bigger problem. Almost any dog can be easily handled if you use the right methods and **there are always better environmental alternatives for control than crating.** Try out new and novel solutions until you find something that works. And trust your dog to show you how well he can work with you.

Give your dog attention, respect and caring. Learn to communicate in your dog's language so that he can understand what you want. In time, your dog can actually make living in the tough physical world an easier thing for you as he learns your specific needs and truly becomes your best friend.

Activities for Owners with Limited Mobility:

Doggie Treadmill (Limited Mobility)
- **Vastly improves quality of life for physically limited owners with high energy dogs if used with care -**

We feature the doggie treadmill as the first entry in this chapter (and we also include it in several other chapters throughout the book) because it's simply one of the best things the average owner can do to exercise their healthy high-energy dog. Yet, surprisingly, very few owners have even heard of the concept!

People may joke that someone should invent a treadmill for dogs, without realizing these really exist. As early as the 1800's dogs were put on treadmills, with their energy used to power lumber mills! Show people have exercised dogs on treadmills for decades. And these days, doggie treadmills are finally becoming a mainstream solution for helping with dogs' daily exercise needs.

For some condo-dwellers or some owners with physical limitations, a treadmill may be the *only* way to keep a high-energy dog and keep him healthy! And there's *no* downside to the treadmill as long as you follow health precautions and use it appropriately.

You'll find information on models of treadmills specifically built for dogs in the "Resources" section. When you inquire about doggie treadmills, you might be a little put off by the price. You might wonder where you will fit such a large piece of equipment in a small apartment or how you can have it delivered. You may wonder if your dog will be able to use it, or if you can supervise correctly. But, even considering these obstacles, many owners really have no choice.

If you've owned your ultra-high energy dog for a while and you can't take him out to run or play, it's not just a problem of neglecting your dog's health and fitness. But total lack of exercise can sometimes turn a dog's behavior destructive. If you're an owner with physical problems like arthritis or a bad back, your dog may be hurting you right now because he's frustrated. A large dog pulling on leash or jumping on a physically frail owner can cause serious injury, and insufficient exercise is often the primary cause of these two behavior problems. Lack of exercise also contributes to anxiety disorders like separation anxiety.

If the cost of trying a doggie treadmill is truly prohibitive, there are several ways you can cope. One is to share the use of the treadmill with a friend or relative. This would also allow you to keep the equipment in whichever home has more room. Another alternative is to use a human treadmill. Working your dog on a human treadmill may be slightly more difficult, since human models are not constructed with protective bars to enclose the dog. You'll have to provide more supervision, but most calm dogs do wonderfully on a human treadmill and you can save considerable expense.

One of the beauties of any treadmill is that you can adjust the speed and length of sessions for your dog's particular exercise needs. **Always start by checking with your veterinarian for how much exercise he recommends and if the treadmill is safe for your dog in particular. For example, exercising a dog with a heart condition unattended on a treadmill has been known to lead to injury or even death!**

Always be reasonable and careful before starting your dog on the treadmill. Never exercise any dog to the point of exhaustion, keep sessions short, keep speed slow and build up demands very gradually as your dog's fitness improves. Bear in mind that ten minutes on a manual doggie treadmill is comparable to about one hour of running outside and ten minutes on an electric powered treadmill is comparable to at least a half hour running outside. **Do not overdo time on a treadmill. A little goes a long way.**

Accustom your dog to the treadmill gradually to get him comfortable using it. Keep your dog on a leash when first training the behavior and supervise carefully. **Always use a harness, rather than a buckle or choke collar, when walking your dog on a treadmill**. Start by having your dog walk on the floor alongside the treadmill while it's running, offering him treats and encouragement. Then have him stand on the machine when it's off and give him treats. Repeat both these steps again and again through several days. When your dog is quite comfortable with the machine, start him walking on the treadmill at an extremely slow speed, urging him forward with treats and praise. If you're physically capable, you can also cheerfully walk in place beside him on the floor.

Be careful! Most dogs will adjust easily to the treadmill. But you must always supervise your dog whenever he is walking or running on it, since he could get spooked or the machinery could conceivably malfunction. This is no different than remaining alert when using a treadmill yourself.

A few dogs may suffer from serious anxieties, or previous bad experiences might make them fear the treadmill. If you think your dog might have such fears, before making the monetary investment in the equipment, introduce him to a human treadmill in a friend's home. If he panics to the point that you fear he will hurt himself on the equipment, you have two choices. You could abandon the treadmill idea entirely and use another alternative for exercise or, if you still wish to pursue the treadmill idea, you could consult a professional trainer who is experienced with the use of the treadmill. Let the trainer assess your dog. If the trainer feels your dog is a good candidate, he or she could get your dog started using the treadmill and you could pick it up from there.

Please note that a reputable trainer will advise you that some dogs' phobias are simply too extreme to exercise them safely on a treadmill. If fear reactions around the equipment persist, even with the professional, it's best to use another method.

Also certain dogs cannot use a treadmill at all because of age or physical infirmity. Many other dogs with physical problems *can* exercise on a treadmill because of the adjustable speed and the fact it can be used indoors away from harsh weather. **But always check with your veterinarian before working any dog on a treadmill.**

Once owners use treadmills successfully with their dogs, we hope you'll pass the word on to acquaintances who may be struggling with dog's behavior problems caused by inadequate exercise. Proper use of doggie treadmills can change quality of life and even improve the health and well-being of dogs on a societal level.

Long Lead
- improves life for every family & dog; highly recommended, but avoid "extend-a-lead" dangers -

A long lead is absolutely one of the best tools that *anybody* can use to exercise their dog, but it's particularly valuable to people with limited physical abilities. Purchase a real nylon leash of 20-30 feet. They cost between $10 and $25 and are available in pet stores, catalogs and discount department stores.

For safety, never use an extendable or retractable lead with a long, cordlike line. Although these are popular and seem convenient, they endanger owners and dogs, as they frequently cause injuries including amputations of human fingers and dog's paws. Thin retractable leads are also dangerous and impractical for owners with limited manual dexterity who might have problems controlling the leash if the dog runs or lunges abruptly. If you wish to use an extendable leash as your long lead, choose a sturdier version that is solid leash, not filament, throughout its length.

The many great uses for a long lead start with letting your dog out for the dreaded late night pee when you're wearing pajamas and don't want to step outside. This is no substitute for a "real" walk which includes exercise and dog/owner bonding. But it makes life easier, especially for women in less than perfect neighborhoods when your puppy must relieve itself at two or three in the morning and the night is rainy.

Always keep your dog in sight when he's out at the end of the thirty-foot lead because of nighttime hazards like snakes, owls, scorpions and feral cats. If you spot a hazard just reel your dog in- a lot easier than calling or chasing him down in a dark wet yard! You can even take several dogs at a time for their last walk of the night using long leads. The lack of feeling restricted seems to help bladders and bowels get moving a lot quicker than if you were standing right by them begging them. And you don't even have to change out of slippers!

For an owner with limited endurance it's also great how the long lead can "magically" enhance your and your dog's experience while at the park. You can encourage your well-trained dog to literally run circles around you for exercise while you simply revolve in one spot, enjoying the fine weather. Or, you can amble along the paths at the speed suited to your physical abilities, while your dog gets to weave back and forth on the long lead, taking thirty steps to each of your steps and sniffing around all he likes.

Other uses for a long lead include practicing the recall or "come" command and practicing other obedience commands at a distance to increase the challenge. A long lead also lets you keep tabs on your puppy without having to walk a lot while he spends hours exploring the backyard. If you don't have a fenced yard, a well-trained dog of any age can stay attached to you on the long line and sniff around for as long as he likes in your unfenced yard or patio area. He'll have a feeling of freedom, while you can rest and relax. (Just pay attention and control the leash so your dog doesn't entangle you!)

Dogs can also play Frisbee and catch while attached to a long lead. Of course a fenced area is a better choice for these games so your dog can run freely but, if you don't have a fenced area, a thirty-foot lead gives your dog a completely different feeling of freedom than a standard six foot one. And it gives your dog some more room to stretch his legs and a little aerobic exercise.

Long leashes are great. But be sure to be a good neighbor. Some parks specify that your dog must remain on a six-foot leash. If the park doesn't insist on this, and you're using a longer lead, be sure to act courteous when passing other park-goers on paths. If you spot other people or dogs or bicyclists approaching, reel your dog in to six feet to put him under stricter control.

Ball Launcher
- makes "Fetch" less tiring for owners; also can be used for doggie "soccer" while owner sits -

A ball launcher is another great little piece of exercise equipment many owners may not know about. These mechanical plastic devices are designed to shoot a tennis-sized ball when you step on the plunger, saving your arm the strain of repeated throwing when playing fetch with your dog. We've seen them in the chain pet stores starting at twenty dollars. Another alternative is a slingshot style ball launcher that releases the ball by pulling back on the device. Or spend more for an automated style that shoots multiple balls.

Depending on whether the dog owner's arms or legs are stronger, you could choose either device. Ball launchers are good for owners with physical limitations and also for elderly owners or children who may have trouble throwing the ball far distances. And some dogs (especially high-energy retrieving breeds) seem to have a seemingly inexhaustible appetite for Fetch, so the device allows their owners to give them the intense workout they need.

Teach your dog a solid retrieve command *before* playing with him with ball launchers. These devices can send balls flying *far*, so you need to be sure your dog will bring the ball back each time if you cannot chase after it. And be careful where you aim the ball launcher. You may need to practice a few times to control the distance. Also use caution that the ball you buy is safe. (See cautions in "Fetch", Chapter 10).

Some owners may also want to try a simpler type of ball launcher, where the ball is cupped in the end of a plastic stick. You can't throw balls as far with these, but we like to recommend them to owners of small dogs or puppies who are confined to a chair or wheelchair. You can release the ball on the floor and use the cup on the end of the stick to move it around, actively playing with your dog without having to stand or bend.

Continuous Pool (Limited Mobility, with Caution)
-   dogs & owners may both benefit from these unique pools, but consider costs & cautions -

See Chapter 11, Water Activities for more details on using a continuous pool for your dog's exercise needs (and see Resources for ordering information.) Because of the expense of installation and other factors, a continuous pool is only an option for certain dogs and owners. But it does have some extreme benefits, so it's worth introducing to let dog owners decide if it might be the right choice for them.

The current in a continuous pool provides much more intense exercise than regular swimming and, if installed indoors, it can be used year- round. It can be used by both dog and owners, and it's one of the most intense workouts available. Having your high-energy dog swim against the current in a continuous pool provides intense workouts that can save owners with physical limitations from tremendous exertion running or playing sports. Swimming is a great choice that gives an intense aerobic workout while protecting a dog or a person's delicate joints. The pool is also great for owners who can't do weight-bearing exercise.

One drawback of a continuous pool is that you must carefully supervise your dog the entire time he swims, and you must help him out of the current when the exercise session is complete. This means you must have physical capacity to hold onto your dog and manipulate him as needed. There's also a possibility the current might panic some dogs, and you might suddenly be faced with your dog's flailing claws. Episodes of panic can be averted if the dog is already a practiced and confident swimmer in a regular pool and is introduced gradually to the continuous pool, starting with the weakest current.

Since use of the continuous pool has these drawbacks, we recommend that owners with weak upper bodies or difficulties standing or balancing ask an assistant to help when they exercise the dog using the current. And always have your dog wear a lifevest with a clip attached to a lead, so you can easily pull him out of the current in emergency.

Only certain owners and dogs will be the right fit for the continuous pool when it comes to budget and swimming ability. **As with any intense exercise, you should first clear with your veterinarian that your dog is physically capable.** But, for certain dogs and owners the continuous pool can provide an Olympic-class workout.

Playdate
- the best way for your dogs to socialize with other dogs outside the family -

The idea of letting your dog play with other dogs for exercise can be either a serious headache or a complete godsend depending on the choices you make. But the worst problems usually occur with strangers' dogs. Planned "playdates" with sweet dogs owned by friends can be a great way to exercise and socialize your already well-balanced and well-behaved dog.

While socialization can be a positive experience, we recommend against off-leash venues open to the public (such as dog parks) where dogs run around and "play" with each other freely. This is especially true if you are elderly or have physical limitations. Imagine trying to pull your bleeding dog out of the jaws of several large attacking animals while their owners stand by passively at the other end of the park, smoking cigarettes. Imagine being laughed at as you cry out for help and told, "Oh, they always play like that; just let them work it out between each other." This happens all too often in dog parks and we're frequently called to owners' homes to rehabilitate traumatized dogs that have been victimized! After their dog is attacked like this, the owner must painstakingly replay the entire socialization process with their dog starting from square one, defeating the whole purpose of the park.

Trying to break up rough "play" while your dog is off leash is not easy and since you never know how many, or what temperament, dogs will show up at a dog park, you can never prepare. As a rule of thumb, it's safest never to set your dog free in public off-leash dog parks, especially those that are very cramped, crowded or known for frequent outbreaks of disease.

Likewise, we don't recommend letting your dog romp, even on-leash, with dogs of strangers that you meet for the first time in any public venue. It's too easy for the dogs to go from rough-and-tumble to seriously biting. The owner might have exaggerated their dog's friendliness or they might not know their dog is aggressive to dogs. Unfortunately, as soon as many owners are confronted with dogs biting and screaming, they freeze. So, even if you have physical limitations, you might get injured jumping in and trying to break the tussling dogs up while the other younger or able-bodied owner stands there seemingly paralyzed. This is just another reason not to trust strangers you meet in parks!

If someone wants their dog to sniff yours and you don't know the person or the dog, we recommend that you just say, "No, absolutely not". It is okay to let the dogs wag at each other from a distance. This is the first step in socialization. You can always graduate to regular meetings in the park or a back yard with this individual to let the two dogs greet and play with each other with physical contact, but get to know owner and dog first. Use the same stringent criteria as if it was a child of a stranger that wanted to play with yours!

The best step is to set up "play dates" for your dog with people you already know, just as you likely already do for your children. Just make sure that the other dog/owner (even if it's your boss or your sister) has the same expectations for the play date that you do. Aim for a set amount of time with everybody watching and supervising and make sure you have a game plan for how to separate the dogs if there is ever a problem.

Next, choose your dog's play date buddies carefully. An ideal match is usually (with notable exceptions) approximately the same size, age and type of dogs (both working breeds, hunting breeds or toys breeds, for example). Opposite sex dogs usually get along better than same sex adult dogs. But before turning dogs free, always make sure everybody's neutered. You don't want the two dogs getting *too* friendly!

Some breeds of dogs tend to be more naturally friendly to other dogs, but temperaments vary widely in individuals, so never jump to conclusions about how your dog will interact with the other dog. The great thing about "play dates" is that you can choose the dogs that possess the best chemistry with yours. When you want your dog to find a new buddy to play with, start with a few trial meetings in neutral territory with both dogs on leash. Study up on dog body language (see books in Resources) and then observe carefully to make sure the two animals are really getting along, not posturing in dominance. (Dog "gestures" and sounds can sometimes seem misleading, so learn the "code".)

For everyday purposes there is no need for your dog to play amongst groups of dogs for him to be adequately socialized. One dog at a time is fine, although your dog can have many individual playmates. While "peer" type dogs make the best everyday playmates, you want your dog to encounter diversity as well, so he'll learn to be civil to all dogs and not become alarmed by the unfamiliar. It's a good idea to introduce your dog to dogs of widely varying ages and sizes. But supervise these encounters more carefully- it's okay if the two dogs just look at each other and relax fully in each other's presence. They don't necessarily have to touch.

Even so called dog-aggressive breeds (such as Akitas, which we've owned) can meet and greet other dogs if they meet them in the careful manner of "play dates". You should not encourage rough and tumble play in these cases, but the dogs can enjoy calmer activities together. If you've socialized your dog adequately as a puppy, even if his breed is genetically predisposed to dog-aggression, you'll probably still be able to let him play with a few favorite playmates when he's an adult. But become expert at dog body-language, and be fair with your friends. Let them know *everything* about your dog's individual temperament and don't try to hide, downplay or recast what his breed was created for.

Never force two dogs to play together. Your best friend's dog may have bad chemistry with yours and there will be nothing you can do about it, while meanwhile a neighbor you know only casually may have a dog that gets along great with yours. So make life easier for yourself and invite over the neighbor with the friendly dog. And don't be afraid of hurting your best friend's feelings. She'll be much more offended if you invite her obnoxious dog over and your dog bites him!

Once you've found some playmates your dog loves, meet up with the dogs and their owners as often as you'd like. (Once a day, once a week or once a month could all be okay.)

Encourage the dogs to exercise together and, if the other owner is physically fit, let him lead the more vigorous games. If neither of you is physically fit, let the dogs lead the games. Give them a big fenced area to romp in. Just keep a close eye on the play and frequently call the dogs back to you to keep things under control. Two simpatico dogs can play in water or with balls or other toys. It's okay if the dogs chase each other at a hundred miles an hour if they seem to be truly having fun. And the playdate is a good time to practice some of the games in this book (especially multi-dog and family).

Dog play dates can be vigorous and can toss around a lot of mud, so they're best scheduled outdoors. But, for hot, rainy or snowy dates, especially if you own small breeds, the dog pals can play together in a playroom, or designated "dog room". After play, spend some relaxation time with dogs and owners together. Practicing tandem obedience, with treats and gentle petting, encourages both dogs' self control. Even a little nap near the other dog can be good.

If you are an older person, or suffer significant physical disability, organized play dates with a friendly dog companion could provide your dog with the exercise he needs, and may make the difference between you keeping the dog and choosing to give him up. You may even find that you bond with the other owner(s) over time.

But don't confuse structured play dates with politely accepting when relatives or neighbors decide to "bring their dogs over to keep yours busy", when you know nothing about the dogs. If your balance is unsteady due to a physical condition, and you open the door to a relative's untrained dog, you could literally be knocked off your feet, breaking bones and requiring surgery. The best way to stand up for yourself is to be proactive in choosing the dogs you *want* to play with your dog, and don't keep an open-door policy.

If you plan and structure playdates in advance, they'll become a pleasure your dog can enjoy throughout its lifetime. Put out feelers in places like your church, your gym, your senior activity center or the clubhouse in your gated community. (But screen the dog owners with extreme caution, since you may be inviting them to your home!) You may be surprised at how many of your peers have dogs just like yours that need an exercise buddy, while the owners feel too shy to inquire. And dog play dates can even mend family fences. If you are from the World War Two generation, and your great niece is Generation X, you and she may not get together that often in today's busy world. But then you may discover that your dogs need each other's company and suddenly you'll be spending lots of time together sharing "shaggy dog stories" over tea while your two dogs chase happily around the yard.

Cat Toy
**-   sparks the interest of small dogs that are gentle chewers;
low cost & low effort for owners -**

We love this game that uses a simple, inexpensive item for an "off-label" task. Just buy a vibrant-looking cat toy of the type attached to a stick and manipulate it as your high-energy puppy or small dog chases the toy around just as a cat would! You can remain comfortably seated while the dog exercises with no strain or your legs and back. And watching little dogs chase cat toys around makes everyone smile!

You can make your own version of a "cat toy" by attaching an indestructible small toy or ball to a long string. Then move it around the room from a sitting or standing position while your dog chases it, rather than having to bend for other types of play.

For safety, stay on constant high alert if using a toy constructed for cats when playing this game with your dog. Cats tend to be more delicate with their toys and they are less likely to hurt themselves. So know your dog's limits before trying this game, and **only use cat toys for adult dogs that play the game for the thrill of the chase, not with the object of tearing up the toy**. When you play the game, always be prepared to react quickly. **Never allow your dog and catch up to, or chew up, a cat toy that might hurt him if swallowed.**

Dog Walker
- helps owners with physical limitations maintain high energy dogs without problems -

As home dog trainers, we sometimes find that owners don't always consider the most straightforward answer in a situation. Sometimes owners believe, wrongly, that a certain solution might be prohibitively costly, when in reality they are paying more for the alternative. One example is the idea of paying for dog walking. The commonly held belief, perhaps held from back when only rich Manhattan socialites hired dog walkers, is that using a dog walker would be far out of the

> *Don't think you need to be wealthy to afford this service that might make the biggest difference in your quality of life with your dog*

financial reach of most regular folk. But this is no longer necessarily true.

Most professional walkers charge in the area of twenty dollars for a half-hour midday walk. If you hire a walker every day, the cost can add up, but walkers will also come less frequently. If you can only afford a professional dog walker once a week, this is better than nothing. Consider taking your dog for short walks daily yourself and then allow your walker to exercise your dog with a longer run, or games in the park.

If your mobility is limited, investing in a dog walker to take care of your dog's most vigorous exercise needs is certainly worth any amount you are able to spend on it.

There are just a few cautions, however. First, of course, make sure that your dog walker is reputable. Investigate their background, their certifications, insurance and references. But, above all, trust your gut feeling. This person will likely be allowed inside your house. Even with the best credentials, if the individual gives you an uneasy sense in your gut, just say no. The same applies if they don't show complete gentleness to your dog(s) or if the dog seems unhappy after walking with them, or unhappy and hesitant the next time they arrive.

Frail elderly dog owners or those with serious visible disabilities should make sure someone else knows the dog walker is present in your home. Having a relative or friend around, especially the first time you interview the dog walker, is also a good idea. A reputable professional will be happy to meet with your support network.

Some owners with limited financial means may choose to hire a neighbor or a friend (perhaps even a high-schooler or a vigorous fellow senior citizen) to exercise their dog. Since there's no real licensure for dog walkers anyway, we see no harm in hiring an acquaintance, especially if it can save you thousands and thousands of dollars over the course of years by doing so. **But be even more careful if you are not hiring an insured/bonded professional!**

Be aware that child labor laws can apply to minors and you may need parental permission if hiring minors of a certain age. If your dog injures a neighbor's child, this could be a terrible tragedy, so make sure any young person you employ really knows how to handle animals, and that your dog is consistently friendly! The same is true for any friend that you hire to exercise your dog. Make sure they really know animals and aren't just agreeing to the job as a favor. And make sure to sort out insurance issues and put a contract on paper before they touch your dog! If you feel too socially awkward discussing insurance and possible lawsuits with a friend, then definitely go the professional route. You cannot afford a mistake- as one dog-related claim could cost millions!

There is one more issue you should check on before you hire someone to exercise your dog. You must make sure that the person you hire is really *exercising* the dog, not just letting the animal out into the backyard to run around and relive its bladder. Letting their dogs outside is all many working people hire their dog walkers to do!

But, if you're an owner with limited physical abilities, you must pay for someone who really wants to go into the outdoors and run, jump and pant to give your dog exercise. You want to pay for someone who is physically vigorous. So, no matter their great intentions, rule out individuals whose physical capabilities are no greater than your own! Next *watch* the candidate exercise your dog and even *spy*, even if it means cruising the neighborhood crouched down in the passenger seat of a friend's car.

This is not immoral. A reputable walker will actually welcome your intrusions! They will love to show off the vigorous games they are playing with your dog. Since some retired or disabled owners may not leave home for a job every day, there is also no need to leave your house vacant for the dog walker. We recommend you stay around and watch them work with your dog as much as possible. You can even join in the games with the walker and your dog, and the dog walker can take over some of the harder tasks, such as chasing after a ball that has gone out of bounds or guiding your dog through an agility course while you help with the commands.

Since the walker you hire will always be doing physical exercise with your dog, it's important they only do it during safe weather conditions. We would advise against keeping a regular appointment. Rather, schedule spur-of-the moment whenever the weather is neither hot, cold or rainy and when the dog walker also has an open spot in their schedule. Walkers desperately need to fill these haphazard open spots, so if you can be flexible, they might even be able to offer you a better price. But do be reasonable. You may be asking for services that are slightly different than what the dog walker is used to providing. If you can find a kind and gentle dog walker who is happy to accommodate your needs, this service is worth paying a little extra.

Borrow a Child (with Caution)
- this solution for exercising high energy dogs has many benefits; just follow cautions -

This is a great idea that can make all the difference in the lives of a dog, a child and a senior or disabled owner. But before "borrowing" a child to exercise your dog, you should first research and be aware of all the potential problems in having a minor child to work with your dog in a paid capacity. This could include violating child labor laws and the lawsuit and guilt that could follow you for a lifetime if the child is ever injured. You face some of the same risks any time you let a child exercise your dog, whether or not you pay him.

In order to stay safe, you must know that your dog is completely friendly and safe around children, and also know that you can trust any child that will be spending time with him. **Always check first with the parents and always supervise carefully! Never ask any child or teenager to work or play with your dog if you know that your dog has bitten people. (And you should never allow a dog like this contact with children in your home!) Asking a child to exercise or care for a dog that you know has bitten people would, and should, be considered deliberate negligence and you would face the legal consequences.**

Obviously a caring dog owner would never think of this. Rather, you'd ask a child to exercise your highly friendly dog if the child has already shown an inclination and the dog and child are already friends. If your dog has a great personality, you may already know a child who loves playing with him. So why not allow this child to exercise your dog as a way to get around your physical limitations and get your dog the physical activity he needs?

Suddenly, when you were despairing that you couldn't continue to own your dog and give him the exercise he needs, you've now found an affordable or no-cost solution! And your generosity with entrusting a child- a niece, nephew or a neighbor- with your dog's exercise and training may change that child's life for the better as well. Working with a dog can build a child's self esteem, and healthy exercise is great for kids. Sadly, some parents simply don't have time to spend with their child to encourage hobbies or activities, but they're desperate for their children to become more involved in productive activities. And some children don't live in a situation where they will ever be able to own a dog, so you- and your dog- can become mentors.

First, get the parents' (written) permission. Then sit down with parents and child to set ground rules for what should happen whenever their child comes to your home to play with or exercise your dog. Despite the fact that you already have a general agreement, the parent should be notified each and every time their child is at your home and informed exactly what their child will be doing. Do not assume anything.

Check each time with the parents so that the parents are always aware of their child's whereabouts (and get written permission for any trips in your car.) Then make sure that you don't ask too much of either child or dog. A five year old child and a three month-old puppy could push around a Nerf ball in your yard, or the child could lure the pup to follow him with a treat while all adults are present. An eight or nine year old could walk your dog on-leash around the boundaries of your large fenced property, with you watching from a window and without the parents present. But don't make the eight year old take your ninety-pound dog out unsupervised on a public street where other loose dogs might rush up to it. No eight-year old should be asked to handle this situation that many adults couldn't!

On the other hand, a seventeen-year-old who drives his or her own SUV and has aspirations of becoming a veterinarian may be able to take your dog for a lengthy run in the State Park or at the beach. He or she could potentially train your dog to professional standards or even exhibit him at dog shows. The benefit to the young person includes a chance to work with a dog when they may not own one of their own or to work with a different breed. Plus you can offer your written recommendation to college or a potential employer detailing how they have helped you with your dog, especially if their assistance has helped you overcome physical barriers.

If you wish, and all legal issues are covered, you can certainly pay the young person, and this could be another benefit. But some families may not wish for you to pay. They just appreciate a productive place for their child to spend time after school and the child appreciates the fun of playing with their favorite dog. And if you're a senior, this is also a chance for two generations to communicate and have fun, sharing the common bond of your dog. Watching your young neighbor and your dog grow up playing together is an example of local community at its best!

Fishing Pole (with Caution)
- keeps your dog on his toes while you sit, but follow cautions, because of serious risks -

This is simply a larger-scale, more vigorous version of "Cat Toy", using a fishing pole with a toy tied onto the line. **NEVER USE A FISHING HOOK**. If you're not sure if your dog will relinquish the toy or if you think he might rapidly twist himself in fishing line, try a more careful version using a cane pole, stick or slim café curtain rod with a string attached and keep it close where you can control it. At the other end, attach a small intriguing toy by **tying** it on. **Caution: Never use hooks when playing with your dog. And never teach a dog this game if there is EVER any chance he may be exposed to the fishing experience in the real world, because he WILL chase after poles that may have hooks embedded in bait!**

If you're sure: 1) your dog will never meet a real fisherman and 2) your dog is relatively small, delicate with his toys and careful about not getting entangled and 3) if you have enough mobility/dexterity to rescue him in case he did get entangled, then go ahead and play with your dog with a real fishing pole out in your back yard. You can make the small toy at the end of the line "jump around" through grass and bushes, then reel the toy in quickly and then cast far out again and again, until your dog is tired. Or use a pole with string attaching the toy in the similar fashion to make your dog chase after- but never catch- the toy. This is also a great game to build confidence in shy, nervous or timid small dogs and to build spunk in lower energy small dogs. It is not recommended for large, high prey drive dogs that may catch the toy before you can reel it in.

Bubbles
- pleasant, cheap and easy activity for dogs that love to chase things -

If your dog likes chasing children's toy bubbles, then this game simply can't be beat for an owner with limited mobility. Equipment costs less than fifty cents, you can play inside or outside, the bubbles look gorgeous and your dog's antics will make you laugh, lifting the spirits of even an owner with major health problems. Instructions are easy- blow bubbles at whatever pace you like, inciting your dog to jump up and burst them- either by bopping them with his nose or by biting.

The game is great for puppies and small dogs. Even big dogs can do it. But play only with patient dogs, not dogs that jump on people, or you will only encourage the behavior. It's safe to play with senior dogs or dogs with limited mobility as long as you don't make the dogs jump high to reach the bubbles. And don't mind if your dog "talks" a little in his excitement as you blow bubbles. This is just a sign that he's having fun.

Although bubble mixture is intended to be safe for kids, it is made of soap. So don't play constantly or let your dog swallow too many bubbles. Ingesting too many bubbles could give your dog diarrhea. And never let him find where you keep the bottle or drink all the mixture.

Balloons
- while some dogs fear filled balloons, others love bouncing them around -

Not every dog will take to this game, but some love it! The sport also has visual appeal that is almost mesmerizing. We once watched the game being played in a park with the venerable St. Augustine, Florida Lighthouse in the background. It was dusk and a young woman led a white boxer mix into the center of a jade green field. She blew up colorful balloons one by one and her dog sprang in the air, hitting each balloon with his nose and keeping them up in the air as long as possible. He chased the balloons along the ground also, nudging them with his nose until they were back up in the air. And he sometimes kept more than one balloon up in the air at a time.

The dog did break the occasional balloon, and some dogs are very afraid of that popping noise. (We sometimes even recommend balloons as a deterrent to couch-jumping when owners aren't home.) The other possible problem with playing this game is that some dogs shouldn't jump high, as it could injure their bones or joints, especially if they are young, elderly or have existing problems. But, if your vet has cleared your dog for other jumping games and if your dog wouldn't be easily startled by a bursting balloon, he may really enjoy the balloon game.

This game is also lots of fun at parties. Several dogs can play and your kids can join in. And once your happy dog realizes that the sound of a popping balloon is no more than a momentary pause in the fun, he'll be less likely to be spooky around other sudden noises. "Balloons" is great high energy game to play with your dog, without you having to do a lot of running around.

Play In Snow
- can intensify exercise benefits & take strain off the owner, just follow cautions -

You've probably noticed that dogs love to play in snow. The good thing about snow is that it's also a great equalizer for an owner who doesn't have a lot of stamina. You may remember from back when you were a kid how difficult it was to run, jump or play in snow for any length of time. (And if you're anything like us, you certainly haven't done it since you were a kid!) But a little snow play is a great outlet for a healthy dog.

Snow dramatically increases the effort needed to run (fifteen minutes of vigorous exercise in snow could equal an hour on flat terrain) and it also stimulates a dog's senses. Have you ever watched your dog chase after falling snowflakes, dig in snow while barking at it in a silly fashion or snap at the top layer of snow and then sneeze and shake his head, as if playing the clown? A little play in snow is *fun*. There's no reason you can't watch from your deck while your dog (or dogs) burn up days' worth of energy and frustration playing in the snow.

Follow reasonable safety precautions when exercising dogs in snow. Some breeds of dogs were specifically bred to live and work in the snow. (If you own one of these breeds, you probably already know it.) Many other breeds have good or decent tolerance for snow and cold. (Research your breed's origin and you may be surprised.) But some breeds can hardly tolerate cold at all! **Before exercising a dog in snow, you must be sure that his breed has good tolerance for winter weather.**

Dampness can make cold more dangerous. And even long-coated breeds can be sensitive to cold and damp if they have spent their whole life indoors with their family. In addition, since running in deep snow is such vigorous aerobic exercise, dogs that are out of shape or have health problems will be immediately strained.

Before exercising your dog in snow, you must ask your veterinarian how your dog will tolerate it. And then exercise your dog reasonably. Never leave your dog outside alone for long periods in snow and cold. His snow exercise sessions should last about as long a person of equivalent physical conditioning (for ex: couch potato, athlete, etc.) might feel comfortable staying outdoors wearing a coat in the same temperature.

Regardless of temperature, never put your dog out in a blizzard or in drifting snow. Just like you could get lost, so could he, especially at night and especially if he is tiny. Small dogs can actually vanish from sight and die in extremely deep snow, and an owner could collapse frantically searching for the dog in such conditions! Avoid problems by not letting dogs out alone in the dark when it's very cold or snowy. Nor should you let the dog out alone when snow and wind obscure visibility. During real blizzard conditions, the safest solution is to remain indoors yourself while allowing your dog out on a long lead just long enough to relieve himself. You can make up for his exercise when conditions moderate.

Whenever the temperature drops below freezing, follow the precautions for extreme temperatures described in "Ice Pup" in Ch. 15. And dry your dog off thoroughly any time he plays in snow! If you follow reasonable precautions, and choose a depth of snow appropriate to your dog's size and athletic condition, you can use the natural resistance of snow as a clever way to shave time off his winter workouts, so you don't have to run around at all. And there are lots of mild days each winter when your healthy, thick-coated dog will thank you for letting him play outside.

Doggie Day Care (Caution)
- **describes the benefits of daycare if you haven't considered it;**
for additional cautions, see Ch. 15 -

If you have physical limitations, or even if you're an apartment dweller with no outdoor space for your dog to run around, someone may suggest that you drop your dog off at "doggie day care", "play care" or "day camp" on a regular basis just so he can exercise. They may also suggest a doggie day care facility as a place where your dog can socialize with other dogs, especially if your physical limitations keep you from taking your dog out much in public.

We must mention the option of doggie day care (cageless boarding facilities, where non-aggressive dogs spend most of their time playing with other dogs in a group setting) since it *can* provide a way for your dog to get regular exercise if you physically cannot provide it. But you must be extremely careful when choosing this option. Doggie day care is not inexpensive. And there are many serious potential physical and emotional risks for your dog if you make the wrong choice in facility.

Please read the full precautions on doggie day care in the "Dangerous Daycare" Section in Chapter 15. Owners that choose to bring their dog to doggie day care should exercise extreme caution. **Trust your own gut instinct and never choose a facility just because it's the most popular in town or because people you meet speak well of it.** Expect doggie day care facilities to spend a lot on great public relations, advertising and decoration of the lobby. So don't be swayed by any of this glitz; it often portrays facilities as much more comfortable for dogs than they really are.

What's more important is that the facility is uncrowded and fully staffed by individuals who are actually with the dogs full-time (don't count staff in the office).You should also get a specific hour-by-hour schedule of what your dog's day will be like at the day care facility, and this should include structured exercise and play continuously supervised by staff members.

You must avoid a sad irony. The only reason a physically compromised owner might bring their dog to day care is for exercise, and yet there is a possibility he will get less exercise there than if he was at home! Make it exactly clear how much supervised exercise you want your dog to receive and make the center understand that you are willing to pay an additional premium for what your dog needs.

Insist on physically checking out the outdoor exercise yard. At home, you may conscientiously wait for sunset in summer to exercise your heat-intolerant dog, while meanwhile at day care they will leave him out playing in full sun in 100 degrees for hours at a time. Or the yard at the center may be one quarter the size of your fenced yard at home, yet crowded with thirty rowdy dogs tramping through their own waste!

And most daycares facilities don't walk your dog on leash unless you specifically pay for this service! If you are elderly or disabled, having someone else take care of leashed walks may be the service you need most, so do whatever is necessary to get it in writing. There are other avenues to get the same services for your dog, but if you're determined to use a doggie day care center, stand firm on your exact desires for your dog's exercise. Meet with the center's owner or manager, looking for a service-oriented individual who won't act impatient when asked to work up a plan for the exact services you need.

For example, ask if you can come by when most other customers are gone for the evening, just to have a staff member vigorously exercise your dog. A few facilities in your town may turn you away, but another may happily offer the service at a reasonable price.

Obedience/Agility Clubs
- don't ignore this fun social option; it's a great fit for some owners and dogs -

Just because you may have physical challenges or limitations, you don't need to think of yourself as helpless when it comes to dogs. If you ever doubt this, then spend some time watching professional handlers with severe physical challenges handling their dogs magnificently in dog shows. A dog is not bothered by his owner's physical limitations. Instead he responds to the power you *do* possess, and he's able to work with you and modify his performance according to your needs.

Joining an obedience or agility club (see Resources for American Kennel Club or AKC) helps you focus on all the positive things you *can* do with your dog and these activities can bring dog and owner a welcome sense of achievement. Obedience, agility and the many other organized dog activities provide great exercise and structure for your dog, and working around humans and dogs in the club provides great socialization. Club members will likely be supportive of your abilities- and understanding about any physical limitations. And dog lovers will enjoy networking with others who share their enthusiasm.

In the club setting handlers that are more experienced will be happy to give you tips on how to best train obedience and agility even with physical challenges. And friends you make in the club may volunteer to run your dog through the course for you when you are having a not-so-great day. The more you participate in obedience and agility with your dog, the more you'll learn that excellence in these sports depends more on a handlers' skill and communication with their dog than on their stamina. And the sporting camaraderie you'll enjoy in an obedience club is also a lot of fun- not only for your dog, but for you as well.

Rehab Together
**- with the right program, you and your dog can work together
to both overcome challenges -**

There's a great variety of different physical limitations and conditions, and one amazing thing about the human (and dog!) body is its ability to heal. When you bring home a dog, you may not be the first person to discover that your health improves! One obvious reason is that if you regularly exercise your dog, the exercise may improve your health as well. Getting up and out of the house, playing, laughing and just relating to another creature can boost your immunity and encourage your body to heal itself. And multiple studies have linked the presence of animals to improved healing for nursing home and hospital patients.

If you'd like to exercise with your dog for rehabilitation first check with your doctor to find out which activities will most benefit your condition, and then start out slow. Most dogs will fall into place perfectly, and they'll be happy to engage in the rehab activity of your choice. Many breeds (see "Service Dog", in this section) are supersensitive to their owner's needs, and they may help you along as you participate in your chosen rehab activity. Some dogs will even guard you if your exercise takes you outside on public streets and you are afraid your age or disability might make you seem vulnerable to crime.

Please note that, unfortunately some dogs- perhaps due to lack of early care or socialization- **do not** have the same intuitive understanding of your physical limitations. So, first be absolutely sure about your pet's judgment, restraint and ability to control himself around distractions such as other dogs before you exercise with him for your rehabilitation. If your dog behaves so vigorous and uncontrolled that you are in physical fear, obviously you cannot take him along as part of your rehab until you consult a professional dog trainer.

And, just as you should realize that it's never too late for you to recover from an illness or injury, you should also realize that there's always hope for recovery if your dog has physical challenges. A nice leisurely walk is great for a senior dog and senior owner together and there are exercises and games to suit any combination of dog/owner limitations. Just like you would ask your doctor, make sure to ask your dog's veterinarian what exercises are best to improve his physical condition.

And don't be afraid to foster a dog (See "Try on a Dog", this chapter) or adopt a dog at this time in your life. If you choose a dog whose exercise needs are low, time you spend together in affection, play and mild physical activity can benefit both of you. Speak to a well qualified expert at your local shelter (a veterinarian or a considerate behavior specialist with an advanced degree as opposed to someone whose opinions are personal, but not scientific.) If you suffer from physical challenges, an expert like this who has plenty of time (as opposed to a regular shelter employee) is best qualified to help you select the right senior or special needs dog whose needs best meld with yours. You can adopt from a shelter, but a safer alternative for an owner with health problems is to contact a breed rescue society. They will put a great deal of time and effort into matching you with the perfect dog and, before you adopt, they will likely allow you to foster the dog so you will know exactly how you work together.

Try On a Dog
- often ignored, the fostering option saves dogs & can be a good fit for dog lovers with limitations -

This is a great idea with absolutely no downside, but unfortunately an option many people with physical limitations may not be aware of. Why not foster a dog from your local shelter or breed rescue society? So many dog owners become literally heartbroken when their age or physical disability makes it hard for them to care for a dog, especially of the breed they were used to. They may even feel useless or hopeless, to the point where we have heard some seniors say, "I am afraid I may not live long enough to care for this dog for all of his life…"

This is one of the saddest things we have heard, especially since we understand how strong the owner's desire is to help a dog, yet how conflicted they feel if they have no family to care for the dog if they pass away or go into a nursing home. Some people's physical condition may vary. Their health may worsen as they fear, or a new treatment may restore them to full functioning, but the person may worry about committing to a dog when they are not sure.

This is why **fostering is perfect. The experts at a rescue society can help you select a dog that is appropriate for your abilities combined with your limitations.** Make sure to be totally honest. Rescues are usually staffed by caring people who will be concerned with your needs. Once they know about your home and your lifestyle, they can send you home with a little (or big) bundle of fun whose life would be in jeopardy if it weren't for your generous help.

The rescue may only need your help for a short amount of time. For example, foster parents often care for small puppies only until they are old enough to adopt out to permanent homes. And, while you're fostering, the rescue may be able to give you some assistance. (For example, if your health limits driving, another volunteer might be able to pick up dog food or drive your foster dog to vet's appointments.) If, at any point, fostering the dog becomes too much for your health, you can ask the rescue to take the dog back for the time being and then host it, or another dog, sometime in the future when your situation improves.

If you have health problems or physical limitations, fostering can let you know how easy or challenging it is to care for a dog at this specific time in your life. If caring for and exercising this dog is too much for you, you can allow him to be adopted by another home as planned. On the other hand, you may find that you and the particular dog are a perfect fit and you can comfortably provide him all the care he needs. Then you can ask to become his adoptive parent; you already know this is the perfect dog for you.

Fostering a series of dogs gives you the opportunity to live with many different breeds and find the exact dog that best meets your current abilities. Plus, it is a highly generous way to give back to dogs, providing help when it's most needed!

Fostering a dog is a great idea with absolutely no downside

"Service" Dog
- some dogs can be trained (by you or formally) to help you regain independence & overcome challenges -

If you have physical limitations, but are not fully disabled, you may not think of yourself using a service dog, and your condition may not qualify you for a free professionally trained service dog. But in recent years the uses for service dogs have expanded dramatically. Examples include, but are not limited to, dogs that help their owners with multiple sclerosis, hearing problems, diabetes, epilepsy and even anxiety disorders.

A dog can help an owner keep balanced while walking, alert an owner to a coming seizure or help an owner who cannot bend to retrieve items off the floors. Breeds of dogs being used for service dogs are increasing every day, and there are many organizations that can give you information about training a service dog. Organizations that advocate for specific illnesses (for example, multiple sclerosis or diabetes) could assist you in reimbursement issues if you want to own a service dog, or you can check websites like The International Association of Assistance Dog Partners (www.iaadp.org), Assistance Dogs International (www.assistancedogsinternational.com), The Assistance Dog Trainer's Network (www.thedogsite.org/new) and Delta Society (www.deltasociety.org). Also see the Resources section.

If you have a disorder that severely impairs your functioning and is expected to last, purchasing a trained service dog might be the best choice of dog for you and you might require that level of help.

But, **if you already own a well-behaved dog that seems concerned with your well-being, you may be able to train your dog to help you on your own.** To what degree the dog can help you depends on many factors including his aptitude and physical condition and your ability to train him. But whether, your dog is a shivery Chinese Crested or a lumbering

St. Bernard there are likely many ways you can teach him to help you. (See "Help Your Special Needs Family Member, Chapter 12.)

Since your pet is a dog, helping you with real tasks around the house should give him a purpose in life and should channel some frustrated playful energy. Even a six-month old puppy isn't too young to learn to help his owner with simple tasks like picking up the keys if you have trouble bending or alerting you to a ringing telephone or doorbell if you are hard of hearing.

You can train your current canine service activities by reading up on training methods or following a DVD (See Resources) or you could bring in a professional specializing in service dog training to get your dog started. Service Dog Organizations, your senior citizens agency or advocacy groups for the disabled might steer you in the direction of a qualified person who will donate time to train your dog.

Safety Note: In everyday situations, your dog may surprise you with his helpfulness but, to be safe, do not depend upon your dog as your only resource in life-or-death situations unless he is formally trained and tested.

Games on the Floor
- often easier than bending, especially when training or playing with small dogs -

This is a fairly simple idea, although owners often have problems with it, due to social issues of "propriety". But we strongly suggest that more adult dog owners get comfortable getting down on the floor to play with their dogs! As home dog trainers we often notice that the very people who might benefit most from not having to bend as much are also the last to part with propriety. And they often own toy breeds dogs where interaction requires frequent bending.

Holding your small breed dog up in your arms or lap all the time is not a suitable solution. All dogs require time on their own two feet. But we notice that bending over repeatedly to teach a small dog tricks or obedience commands such as "sit" or "down" can be painful. And not just elderly and disabled are "creaky". Back pain can afflict anyone who's out of shape!

For ladies who like to wear dresses and heels, we suggest changing into a tracksuit or pajamas, throwing a large yoga pillow on the floor and getting down there for your lengthy play or training sessions, especially for small dogs. This advice is only if your problem involves only repeated bending. Never get down on the floor if you feel you can't get up. And, in fact, you should never attempt to do anything suggested by a trainer, video, class or book if you personally feel it would hurt your body. There are always alternatives.

For example, you can try a low chaise, ottoman or bench, often the perfect height for interacting with and training your dog. Or sit on the edge of a surface like a porch or a stair.

This position allows you to twist around on a level with your dog, but with your legs extended comfortably.

You could also utilize a gradual incline in your yard, where you can be seated comfortably and your small dog can run up to you. For reasons of physical ease, some owners may also wish to train or play with their tiny dogs on their king-sized bed. But only attempt this if your dog is emotionally healthy and is trained to only come up on the bed when invited.

You may have heard that dogs learn a lot about dominance and who is the "leader of the pack" by relative height. That's why dogs with dominance issues should not be positioned higher than their owners (such as on the owner's pillow). However, if your large dog is well-trained, gentle and emotionally healthy, there's no harm being down on the floor with him, even if he does momentarily hold the higher position. Just make sure that, if you have physical injuries or limitations, your dog will interact with you gently.

You should teach your dog to always use gentle physical touch with his owners from the time he is a puppy, and then a little play with you down on the floor on occasion will only reinforce that gentleness. A hundred and fifty pound dog can be just as safe to cuddle with their elderly or disabled owner as a fifteen-pound dog. But neither is safe if you do not absolutely know your dog and don't feel in complete control of his actions solely through your verbal commands!

Having a physically stronger family member around to control the dog is one idea, but a far superior idea is consulting with a professional. Every owner, whatever their limitations, should always feel a hundred percent comfortable getting up close and personal with their dog. Standing up high will definitely put an end to a rowdy play session, and may return you to the "power position", but having verbal control of your dog, even when you're down on the floor, is even better!

Dog on the Table
- another way to train small dogs without constant bending -

Similar to the last entry, this training trick simply gives you easier access to your small dog when teaching some commands, particularly the "down" command. First, gradually introduce your dog to surfaces off the floor to make sure he won't be nervous. Then find a wide solid surface that won't wobble. (An example would be a picnic table, which also has a ready-made seat for you.) Lift your dog onto the table, keep him on leash and train him the desired command(s) using treats, or use the table to more easily groom him or to rehearse for calm visits to the veterinarian.

Placing your dog on any kind of platform or a step above you works on the same principle. It's a great way to save the owner's back from strain when working with smaller dogs.

Just make sure to carefully monitor your dog, especially if he tends to be "hoppy". To be safe, attach his leash to a harness, rather than a collar, if you think there's even a remote chance of the dog jumping and you having to catch him mid-air. To make sure this doesn't ever happen, train your dog to stay calm on a table, starting when he's a puppy. But until you're confident he stays totally calm on a table, stick with raised surfaces at lower heights for your practice sessions.

Chaise Lounge Training
saves your back and makes training & interacting outdoors more pleasurable-

Just like the last entries, this suggestion is based on the fact that not every owner is physically capable of bending enough to train or play with their dog. A low seat is the easiest answer. And, if you're outdoors, a sturdy chaise lounge happens to be the perfect height. If you're in a fenced yard, you can sit on the chaise at any time you want to practice recalls (the "come" command), "sits" or "downs". Also use the chaise to give you and your dog a breather. After a fairly vigorous play or exercise session, your dog can sit by you as you sit on the chaise and you can administer gentle petting or massage.

The chaise lounge can help guests meet your little dog without back strain. Some nervous little dogs feel a little intimidated when they first meet strangers who seem to "loom" over them. The solution is for your guest to get down lower and wait for the dog to approach them. But crouching too long to wait might not be so comfortable for your guest. So, why not suggest instead that they take a seat on the chaise? Now, your dog's tentative approach becomes a pleasure!

Let Your Dog do the Walking
-this idea helps both small dogs and owners with aching arms or backs
- and it's only logical!

This one is not only a back-saving idea, but a sanity saver as well. Constantly carrying your small breed dog (up to thirty pounds) and never allowing him to walk on his own four feet can actually damage his self-esteem and cause bad behavior. In contrast, the time walking beside his owner helps your little dog bond with you as dogs like to, just like dogs following their pack leader in the wild.

Remember that many small breeds, for example many terriers, are bred to do challenging physical work like chasing and hunting vermin. By nature, they are independent animals. And, while they wish to please you, they savor walking on their own four feet. Carry your dog less and walk him more, and see how his behavior improves. His health may improve as well as he gets needed exercise.

Walks with your dog, without all the lifting, may become a greater pleasure for you as well. Some elderly owners, or those with physical limitations, get in the habit of constantly lifting and carrying dogs that weigh as much as thirty pounds. If the dog then becomes nervous about walking on its own, or if he becomes out-of-shape and overweight, the habit can become self-perpetuating. Unfortunately, constant carrying of a dog could really hurt an owner with a weak back.

Consult with your doctor and your dog's veterinarian for the ideal amount you should be walking the dog, and how much the dog should be walking. If you've created a long-time habit that your dog is finding hard to break and your dog refuses to walk on his own two feet, read up on animal behavior training for solutions involving step-by-step desensitization. If your dog has developed real fears about walking, you may have to consult a professional. Sometimes a change of environment is all that's needed.

Whatever you do, don't let your walk-phobic dog encounter many fearful stimuli when you first try walking with him after he's been out of the game for years. Instead, proceed with baby steps. Try to keep him away from other dogs at first. But never act nervous yourself. If something unexpected appears on the walk, you don't have to scoop him up, unless he's in real imminent danger of death. This will only reinforce fears. But neither should you let every strange dog sniff him or let every person on the street pet him. Just calmly steer him away to a quieter area for his first walks on his own paws.

And, especially if your dog's a puppy, do not expose him to the feces of other dogs. Some condo owners find the biggest concentration of "mess" right outside their buildings. Even if your dog's vaccinated, his system might not be able to handle the abrupt onslaught of potentially contagious disease and parasites if he's spent his entire life on carpet or on the silk duvet cover on your bed. Just walk him a little distance away from the building on concrete and then, where it is safe, allow your little guy, perhaps for the first time in years, to sniff the grass!

Dog Stairs (Limited Mobility)
- protects owners and dogs from injury; a necessity, especially if you own a high vehicle-

Read all about the benefits of "Doggie Stairs" for disabled dogs in Chapter 9, Therapeutic and Senior Activities. Even if your dog isn't disabled, consider buying these stairs for yourself if constant bending and lifting your dog hurts you physically! Doggie stairs give a million-dollar benefit for an investment of thirty dollars or less. They are designed to give your dog easy access to high places like furniture or your SUV without you having to lift him, and you can buy different sizes to accommodate every dog.

Even constantly lifting a toy dog can become a serious strain for someone with lower back pain. And imagine those poor individuals with weak backs who find themselves having to lift their giant breed dogs into their SUV's! You might think this could never happen because you have a brawny relative who always lifts the dog(s) whenever needed. But think of what would happen in an emergency if you had to rush your large dog to the veterinarian and that relative wasn't home. **It's a good idea for every pet owner to buy doggie stairs, if only for emergency use.** Then train your dog to become comfortable using them by encouraging him with treats and lots of praise. After a few practice sessions, using the stairs will become second nature.

Most doggie stairs fold up or stow away easily. So keep them ready at all times in your vehicle or garage, and why not demonstrate them to your friends? Note that, if you prefer, you can buy ramps that serve a similar purpose. Look for both stairs and ramps online and in many pet stores.

Upstairs/Downstairs (Use with Extreme Caution)
**-   carefully weigh benefits vs. serious physical risks of this form
of indoor exercise before proceeding-**

If you're a dog owner with problems walking, climbing stairs between floors many times throughout the day likely tires you out. But the same stairs can provide a valuable source of exercise for your dog!

This exercise may work well in some households, but it can be extremely dangerous in other situations. Use extreme caution and consult with your veterinarian before exercising your dog on stairs. You must make sure your dog will not injure you (see cautions at the end of this segment.) **And you must also make sure your dog can safely walk up and down stairs without falling, injuring himself or creating future hip problems.**

Walking up and down stairs can cause pain or serious injury for some puppies, tiny breeds, elderly dogs and some dogs with injuries or chronic conditions! Running on stairs or even too much climbing stairs when your dog is developing can also contribute to hip problems in giant-breed pups. If you own such a dog, and you have stairs in your home, the likelihood is that you already know about the problem. But, no matter what the breed is, it's best to check with your veterinarian to make sure he or she thinks climbing stairs as exercise is okay for your particular dog.

_If_ your dog is healthy and is able to vigorously walk or run up and down stairs with no ill effects, then climbing stairs _can_ be a valuable addition to his daily menu of exercise, especially when the weather prohibits going outside. It can take also some stress off of you when it comes to vigorous running or playing.

The biggest problem with getting the dog to exercise himself running up and down stairs is that dogs love to be with their pack. Therefore, if you tend to come downstairs in the morning and then avoid the dreaded stairs for the rest of the day, your dog probably will too. He'll lie by your feet, getting no exercise, when he could get some exercise going up the stairs occasionally.

The first step is never to discourage your dog from walking upstairs. In fact, you shouldn't discourage him from moving around the house in general if you want him to stay healthy, well balanced and in good physical condition. Yes, you could close off one room upstairs if there's something in there that your dog could really hurt himself with, or if you have one room where you keep highly valuable antiques or work projects. It's also reasonable to gate off your nursery while your baby is napping- one place even a well-trained dog should not enter unsupervised.

But we don't recommend gating off stairs to your entire second floor just because you worry your dog will mess up your décor. Your dog is a family member. He should be trained to respect your possessions and, in turn you should respect him. Invest whatever is necessary to train your dog to safely wander the house. Giving the dog the run of the entire house is *not* immediately practical for young puppies, rescue dogs you've just adopted with unknown background, or a dog with a history of hurting himself. But all dogs can be trained. It's your responsibility as your dog's "parent" to train your dog so he can be free, safely, in any part of your home and can move around the house as much as possible during the day. (See Obedience-minded in Chapter 3, Puppy Games.)

One way to encourage climbing stairs is to leave some of your dog's toys upstairs in a toybox. He will be sure to bring them down one at a time during the day. Another good idea is to practice your recall, or "come" command, with another family member somewhere at the head of the stairs and you at the foot. Your dog will rush up when your family member calls him and he'll get a treat from the family member; then he'll rush back down when you call him and he'll get a treat from you. Do some repetitions with treats, and alternate just offering praise. Practice just a few times and your dog will be exhausted. He'll also be more likely to come when you call.

You could also experiment with "Fetch" on the stairs. Softly toss a cushiony toy up to the top and let your dog retrieve it at a fast walk or a jog, but not running. Be careful that your dog's gentle and light on his feet with this one! Some dogs could get overexuberant and could hurt themselves on the stairs. If the dog gets to this point, you would have to suspend the activity, perhaps for good, so try to work him at a moderate pace.

You should also surprise your dog by calling him to you at various times every day when he's downstairs and you're up and he should happily come running! Or send him upstairs during the day to get items for you. (See chapter 13, Useful Activities.) As long as your dog knows the object's name, he could retrieve your purse or the cordless phone. He could even bring you a water bottle if you're upstairs and not feeling well enough to climb down for a drink. So utilize the full extent of your dog's capabilities!

Observe two serious cautions whenever working on stairs, especially if you have physical limitations. First, be cautious with your dog. Running stairs can be completely exhausting and it can stress a dog's joints. (To avoid future damage, large breed puppies or any dog with hip weakness should never run on stairs.) Only practice on carpeted stairs. And never use stairs for a primary source of a dog's exercise. Just use them sparingly to give your dog a bit of motion each day, particularly when the weather is terrible or you are feeling physically unwell.

And use extreme caution whenever you are on the stairs with your dog. Disabled or elderly owners may have difficulties with balance. So can children, expectant mothers and any family member trying to navigate the stairs at nighttime. Your dog must be trained proper etiquette on stairs from the time he is a small puppy. Train your dog to always give people a wide berth on the stairs. He should walk slowly and carefully if you are anywhere near the stairs and he should never, ever push past you! If your dog ever attempts to charge past you on the stairs, even once, this is extremely dangerous!

Address this serious behavior problem immediately, even if it means hiring a professional trainer. In the meantime do not practice stair exercise with a dog that has ever pushed a human on stairs. Even after the problem is resolved through training, you will never want to encourage this dog to run on stairs, ever again.

Exercise on stairs is ONLY intended for dogs who consistently give their owners room on the stairs. If your dog doesn't respect people on the stairs, you might have to keep the stairway gated for your safety, since one collision on the stairs be deadly! And only consider starting stair exercise once your dog is full grown and has already shown a long history of polite behavior on stairs. You do not want to train a puppy to run on stairs until you are completely sure that the knowledge won't get him into trouble as an adult!

Be Creative
-one of the best ways to make your lifestyle with your dog a perfect fit;
no matter who might laugh -

It's a funny thing about people, especially Americans. We often care too much about what our neighbors or our peers think of us.

For example, Emma grew up in the wintry climate of upstate New York, shivering through her teenage years wearing flimsy jackets to school just because they were considered fashionable. In her late twenties, when she simply couldn't endure the cold of one more winter day, she bought a different type of coat at a discount store. This shapeless coat was as thick as blanket and bright red, Emma's least becoming color and it featured a cinch-up hood. One of Emma's coworkers insultingly nicknamed the coat the "Little Red Riding Hood Coat". And it did look awful. But it was the first time, physically, that Emma ever felt she was winning the battle against the harsh winters! Even though no one liked the coat's appearance, it functioned well. The next winter Emma completely solved the problem by moving to California, and then to Florida, guaranteeing no more cold weather, ever!

If you are a dog owner with physical limitations, we deeply urge you to consider the story of the red coat and to put function ahead of looks or public opinion every time when working with your dogs! **Being adaptable and creative may save your health, and meanwhile preserve your dog's quality of life. It may even allow you to keep a dog when you otherwise couldn't.** Try new products, like strange-looking "talking", or "bumbling" toys that jump around on your floor, try agility equipment inside the home or use a Gentle Leader Easy Walk Harness, a Wacky Walker rubber lead or a gentle head-halter for walks.

Be the first in your neighborhood to hire a professional service to clean up your yard each week, or to build a designated sandbox for your dog. Give your dog his own room, or build special tables, ottomans or benches so you don't have to bend when you feed, groom or play with your dog. Dance with your dogs. Buy them a treadmill, or teach them to use yours. Teach them to splash in a kiddie pool. Use stairs or ramps to help your dog into your car. Or let your dog help you with some simple daily chores. Just do whatever works best for you and your dog, even if you've never seen or heard of anybody else doing it!

Browse specialized catalogs or Internet sites intended for dog professionals (see Resources) and even flip through farm equipment catalogs in order to try new innovations. Some of the best items are designed for veterinarians and groomers and we guarantee you'll be awed by the variety of ingenious products available. Another fun way to find the latest products is to visit trade shows usually frequented by pet shop owners. You just might find that product that will entirely change your quality of life. So who cares what the neighbors think?

Saki & Sammy "Thinking about what they can do to be creative."

Ch. 15- Dangerous Games You Should Never Play With Your Dog!

Dangerous Games- Introduction

What if you found out that you created your worst problems with your dog by games and activities you've been practicing for fun? Concerned families may be comfortable watching their dogs bloom by learning new activities like the ones in this book. But these same owners often become upset when we challenge one or more of their "family heirlooms" -traditionally popular games and activities handed down through the generations. Some of these activities so clearly teach dogs bad habits that when an owner analyzes what they've been doing logically, they may quite feel foolish.

You may have learned some of the "Dangerous Games" that follow from coworkers, fishing buddies or the girls at the country club. Some bad activities masquerade as catering to your dog, but once you stop, you'll notice your dog immediately seems happier and more balanced.

(continued)

Introduction (continued)
In some cases, family members try to blame each other. Mom may accuse Dad of playing too roughly with the dog while Dad points out how Mom spoils her. Children, more comfortable shedding old patterns that don't work, frequently are the ones who point out how both parents must change. Often problems with dogs are rooted in longstanding habits. For example, folks who grew up in the forties without air conditioning may not fancy being called a "bad parent" because they house their dog outdoors. Yet even traditionally-minded owners are usually willing to observe their dog's vital signs and overall demeanor and then select the best activities accordingly. Once they notice how their dog thrives, they're frequently happy to upgrade the dog's lifestyle!

Surprisingly, the biggest problems causing serious damage to dogs today seem to be fueled by trendy ideas, media propaganda and merchandizing disguised as fact. The media and purveyors of products and services like to target unrealistic fancies while downplaying far-reaching problems that "genteel" dog lovers find too painful to face. Meanwhile, these well-meaning dog lovers may be misled into supporting some unscrupulous non-profits that feed off "political correctness" while warehousing dogs in deplorable conditions, subject to no oversight.

Savvy dog owners must remember to be healthy cynics. It's in your dog's best interest if you don't take every glossy article, brochure or television feature as gospel. And carefully weigh potential risks to your dog's health and safety before buying into every popular dog venue, business or massive community event, product or diet. Also be leery of second-hand wisdom pushed on new dog owners by friends, coworkers, dog trainers, kennel owners, groomers and neighbors who have "grown up with dogs". This is the same kind of cocktail- party hype that ensnared many in the real-estate bubble! If your dog suffers physical or behavioral problems when you try out the latest trend, then it just may not be good for him-or for you. So think, research and trust your gut.

(continued)

Ruffle My Ruff

Rude Neighbor

Dog-in-the-Box

> **(Intro. Continued)** All of us, including the authors, have probably practiced some of the bad games and activities in this chapter. But dogs can be as wonderfully resilient as they are forgiving. Start substituting some of the healthy activities throughout the book for the "dangerous games" described in the following chapter. You'll see improvement in your dog's behavior, plus you'll immediately start having more fun.
> And isn't the best way to judge whether you want to play a game more than once how good it makes your dog- and your family- feel?

Dangerous Games:

Weekend Warrior (Owner)

This entry gives owners an opportunity to laugh at ourselves. The sad, but true, fact is that if your dog is an out-of-shape "couch potato" you may be, too. More than sixty percent of Americans are overweight. Our lifestyles are hectic and, for many of us, the best way to unwind at the end of a stressful day is to stretch out in front of the TV, perhaps with our overweight dog snoring on the couch beside us.

And then we may suddenly resolve to change the lifestyle- all on one weekend!

Another problem scenario occurs when an inactive owner impulsively adopts an active young dog hoping the dog will *force* them to exercise, even though their fitness is so poor they have to literally drag themselves off the couch. Because they're concerned with the dog's well-being, this out-of-shape owner suddenly jumps into one afternoon of extreme physical activity- and they collapse!

The episode of exhaustion or injury brought on by one day's marathon exercise session like this may disable this owner from exercising again for months. It may disable them from *working* for months, and it sometimes turns them off on the idea of exercising their dog entirely.

To avoid these problems, **we urge any owner who's not an athlete to first check with their physician before embarking upon any exercise program with their dog.** It's great to get in shape, but owners should consider their own health limitations before deciding what type of exercise is best.

There are safe exercise choices for everybody and an out-of-shape owner can build up the intensity and time of activity gradually to increase their own fitness, as well as their dog's. This section is called "Weekend Warrior" for a reason. You should make sure to do some form of physical activity each weekday, so you don't suddenly do huge bursts on the weekend, possibly injuring or exhausting yourself as well as your dog.

And, while you can eventually build up your muscles, it's very hard to build tolerance to heat. It's just not safe to exercise in extreme hot weather, for dogs or for owners. **And, if you're afraid of being embarrassed in front of your friends if you hesitate to exercise in heat, think how embarrassed you'll feel when a crowd gathers to stare at you, on your back, stricken with heat stroke after deciding to take your pet jogging in a hundred degrees!**

Weekend Warrior (Dog)

You desperately want to be a good owner, so as soon as you first realize your dog is dangerously overweight and/or out of shape, you determine immediately to do something about it. Since his problem is so bad, you want to do a lot right away and you immediately hit the highway with him to go for a long jog! The problem is, most dogs have come very far from their ancestral roots- wolves that live as natural athletes.

Your couch-potato dog may not even make it a block down the road on what might be his first jog in years- or possibly his last jog ever. **Start out too ambitiously, and your dog's first experience with vigorous exercise could prove to be his last**. At the very least, an overly ambitious start could lead to exhaustion or sprains or strains, which will discourage your dog from willingly participating in the exercise in the future and may make you avoid exercising him again for fear of hurting him.

It's essential to start some exercise program for your dog. But make sure to start out slowly, or exercise could do more harm than good. **The first step with any fitness program is to first let your veterinarian clear your dog for activity and recommend which activities are best.**

Your vet may advise you to gradually increase the intensity of something like daily walks that your dog already does safely to slowly build his conditioning. For example, you could increase the duration of walks a few minutes each day or increase the distance by a block or so. You could also gradually increase the pace for short periods or introduce a small incline, gradually building to a larger incline. Take a photo of your pet at the beginning of the training program and do a weigh-in, as well as doing a short write-up about his health and behavior. Then compare results a few months later. You'll be amazed at the overall changes, even though increases in intensity were miniscule each day.

To stay safe during exercise, always make sure to monitor your dog's demeanor and vital signs to make sure he's comfortable with each level of activity. Keep it playful and easy. Unless your dog is a working "professional athlete", most owners can give their dog a good aerobic workout and get him into great condition without ever having to bring him to the point of actual exhaustion.

Tug-of-War

Dog trainers differ in their opinion of whether it's ever advisable to play tug-of-war style games with your dog, but we've seen too many cases of this game contributing to unmanageability and aggression to ever recommend it. Tug-of-war style games tend to cause problems because fighting for possession of toys mirrors fighting over parts of a kill in the wolf world. And, in the wolf world, the animal that ends up with possession of the kill wins- this is just another way that hierarchy in the pack is determined.

> *If you ask us for the final word on playing tug-of-war, here it is: It's easiest to avoid the game entirely, along with the dominance and mouthing/biting problems it can sometimes create.*

This also explains why the game of tug of war is so appealing to dogs- because it's instinctively wired into them. **Has your dog ever become overexited while playing tug of war with you, perhaps even growling? Has he ever played so strongly that he will not allow you to take the toy away at the end of the game? Has he ever frightened you with his intensity at these times?** If your dog also shows other behaviors where he tests your dominance, such as pushing his way onto the furniture or refusing to obey commands he already knows, his experiences winning the games of tug- of-war are probably making things worse.

To be on the safe side we generally advise customers *not* to ever play tug-of-war with any dog, including young puppies, because of the dominant behavior it encourages. (A notable exception is extremely timid or fearful dogs, where a professional may recommend the game to build confidence.) But, in general, it's safest for the average family to simply avoid tug toys, tug-of-war games and the future dominance problems they can create.

Hot Dog

Here in South Florida, where summer heat indexes can reach one-hundred and fifteen degrees, one of the biggest dangers we warn our clients about is overheating dogs during exercise.

Dogs can overheat easily, so **you should never exercise your dog in extremely high temperatures, combined with sunshine and/or high humidity. Young, old and infirm dogs, dogs unaccustomed to heat, long-coated breeds, giant breeds and breeds with short muzzles are especially vulnerable. But the combination of vigorous exertion with extreme heat, high humidity and sunshine is dangerous, and can prove deadly, for any dog.**

Heat stroke (hyperthermia) can easily kill your dog, so always check weather conditions before heading out to exercise. Understand that it's a dog's nature to want to please you when you exercise together. And dogs can act surprisingly stoic when facing physical discomfort, so you may not always know when your dog starts feeling too hot. Unfortunately, many owners don't notice that their dog is overheated until he's already suffering heat stroke. The best thing an owner can do is to protect your dog so heat exhaustion or heat stroke never happens, but it's also important to know the symptoms in a crisis so you can provide first aid and get immediate veterinary treatment.

Symptoms of heatstroke include: high body temperature (above 104 degrees); excessive panting or salivating; difficulty breathing; increased heart rate and respiration, reddened mucous membranes including the gums (or extremely pale mucus membranes if the dog has gone into shock), diarrhea (which can be bloody); vomiting; seizures, collapse and coma.

To provide first aid: Immediately get the dog out of direct heat and sun (seek out air conditioning or shade) and start cooling him with cool water (use a bath, a hose, or cool water-soaked towels.) You should cool the dog until his temperature goes back down to 104 degrees while rushing him to a veterinary hospital. **Even if your dog's symptoms subside, you must have him treated immediately by to a veterinarian, because heat stroke can cause long-lasting, possibly fatal consequences which may not show up for hours or days after the incident.** Damage from an episode of heat stroke can include: kidney failure, problems with blood clotting, destruction of the digestive tract lining, neurological problems including seizures and swelling of the brain, abnormal heart rhythms and respiratory arrest.

The best course of action is always prevention and the only way to observe your dog's tolerance to heat is to observe your dog! Therefore, no dog should be left outside alone for extended periods during extremely hot weather. Dogs should always be provided shade and fresh water or, better yet, keep your dogs indoors in the air conditioning most of the time during the hottest summer days.

It is true that dogs are descended from wild canines that spend all their time outdoors. But unfortunately, the fact that we have raised our dogs indoors for many generations makes them less tolerant to heat. Some breeds are even less heat-tolerant because of specific physical characteristics, like pushed-in faces, that we've bred for aesthetics rather than function. The paving in megacities worsens problems by creating a treeless, oven-like environment with no means of natural cooling.

Another problem is that if an owner is outside with the dog cheering him on to exercise, the dog is unlikely to take a break to cool himself as his wild cousins would- by digging a hole in the cool earth to take a long midday siesta. If your dog were a wolf, he would be sleeping. But, since his beloved owner is playing, your dog wants to be having fun with you. And he probably won't stop for a rest break on his own, even if he's dangerously overheated, so it's your responsibility to keep his exercise moderate and offer him frequent breaks.

Always alternate time in the sun with time in shade, and try to schedule your most vigorous exercise for off-peak hours when the sun is weaker. Also avoid high humidity and days with pollution warnings. On the hottest summer days, try short leisurely walks during the cooler morning and evening hours (as long as humidity is tolerable and your dog is protected against mosquito-borne heartworm). Also try exercises and activities out of the hot sun. (For suggestions see: Chapter 4, Mental Games & Activities; Chapter 5, Indoor Games & Activities; Chapter 11, Water Games and Chapter 14, Therapeutic & Senior Activities for suggestions). Frequently practicing obedience commands indoors also keeps your dog sharp and helps prevent restlessness and boredom when the weather is most extreme.

Exercising your dog when it's too hot can make an owner sick as well! (See the "Weekend Warrior" section above.) If you start feeling ill, or start feeling pain, then it's time to stop exercising. And if your pet shows excessive panting, salivation or noticeably elevated heart rate or breathing, it's time to stop exercising. Provide for a shady rest place during midday activities and always provide adequate water for yourself and your dog! The best plan of all is to avoid working out at all in high temperatures and heat indices. Later, when the sun drops, a breeze kicks in and the heat index drops to the low eighties would be a safer time to head outside! (See the Books section in Resources, and search the Internet for more information on First Aid for heat illnesses.)

Bite Me

Puppies love to do everything with their little teeth; it's how they explore the world. And many owners find it so adorable when their very young puppy playfully chews on them that they encourage the behavior, teasing their puppy with their hands to make it bite on them in play. But owners need to realize that biting games should only be played if you really want your dog to bite you for the rest of his life, even when he weighs one hundred pounds!

Playing the game of "Bite Me" with your puppy could prove very dangerous, especially if you have children, because he won't understand that he shouldn't bite humans when he's full grown. And at that time, even biting completely in play, the dog can easily injure a child or a vulnerable adult or senior.

As an alternative to teaching their puppies to bite in play owners should teach their puppies "bite inhibition", described in the "Soft Mouth" in Chapter 3, Puppy Games. Dogs use their mouths for many purposes, just like humans use their hands. Teaching your dog bite inhibition makes him understand the power he has in his mouth, and how to use his mouth gently, rather than using it too roughly on the people he loves.

Another alternative to teaching your dog to bite you in play is to teach him to give you kisses instead. Find detailed instructions in the "Kisses" section in Chapter 8, Problem Dog Games.

Pro Wrestling

This bad game teaches your dog to roughhouse with you and to act overexcited in the home whenever he sees you. Dogs can only understand consistency, so don't expect your dog to understand why it's okay to leap on their owner or struggle with their owner when the owner wants to play, but not at other times. And teaching your dog to roughhouse with the adults of the family may also make him roughhouse and hurt children or guests. Remember also that dogs, and especially puppies, are not indestructible and gentle interactions are necessary to build a trusting dog/owner relationship. If, every time an owner sees his puppy, he grabs him and throws him down, the puppy may come to fear the owner. The dog may become timid with people in general, he might develop aggressive behaviors towards people or he may even be seriously injured if the owner wrestles too violently!

> *Expect your dog to repeat all the games you played with him when he was little when he's full grown. If you roughhouse with him when he's a puppy, he'll likely want to roughhouse with you when he's older- and you may not be able to stop it.*

Wardrobe Malfunction

This game isn't all bad; but lately the practice has gone so far out of control that some owners are actually hurting their small dogs!

First, we should say that the only correct reason to "dress" your dog is for function, not for fashion. Proper clothing *can* protect dogs in harsh physical conditions, including cold and strong sun, so it should not be ruled out entirely.

This is particularly true for frail, tiny, thin, elderly or very young dogs, hairless or thin-coated dogs or those with albino coloration. Functional warm clothing includes sweaters, hats, caps, raincoats, insulated coats in every weight and booties that protect a dog's sensitive foot pads from ice, frostbite, rock salt or sharp rocks. Thin light-reflective clothing helps in searing summer sun, as do visors, sunglasses and rubber-soled footwear for hot beach sand and pavement. Other helpful accessories include lifevests for water exercise and backpacks made to tote a dog's water supply when hiking.

As home trainers we heartily recommend anything that makes quality of life better for owners and dogs together, and clothes are often the perfect equipment to make outdoor activity smoother, safer and more fun. Years ago, if we recommended dog clothing for and husbandry most owners would have thought we were eccentric, yet today the concept is socially accepted.

The problem now is the opposite, because most of the dogs wearing clothing today *don't* benefit- and sometimes they suffer. Owners sometimes come to expect tiny breeds to constantly make the scene decked out in designer duds, forgetting that Toy Dogs are dogs first, not actually toys.

Toy breeds should never be treated as stuffed animals. They are proud living creatures with strong instincts, strong muscles, strong senses and strong feelings relating to loyalty and the pack structure. As with larger breeds, their strength of character makes these dogs love their owners powerfully. And, caring about dogs, we shouldn't abuse their love by denying smaller breeds the ability to live as active animals free to play, explore, use their senses and exercise their powerful curiosity

Small dogs have the right to walk and move around freely just as big dogs do. Their health demands it. Each breed has its own exercise needs, and these needs vary widely amongst small dogs. **But it's highly unhealthy for a dog of any breed to remain still all the time or never see the outside world. Prolonged restriction of freedom and activity can make a dog frustrated and snappy. It can dull a dog's senses and make the animal apathetic. And it can also make the dog hesitant and fearful of a world he is never allowed to explore.**

There are times when it's safer and more comfortable if you carry your tiny dog or let him repose in a carrier. Examples might include crossing a city street at rush hour during inclement weather, or letting a tiny dog rest during a street fair when the sun is beating down and ten strange people at a time are trying to paw him. But we can't understand why many owners never set small dogs down to walk on their own four feet on balmy spring days in their own quiet neighborhoods.

It's also a shame that owners commonly dress up and treat as "toys" hearty breeds like strong-spirited Shih tzus. Even curious and strong-minded Jack Russell Terriers, originally bred to hunt, and with exercise needs off the scale, are often squeezed into dresses and forced to act like baby dolls just because of their relatively small size. And the dogs dressed up most of all, naturally brave and feisty Chihuahuas, are also the most commonly misunderstood and the most likely to develop serious behavior problems, notably aggression.

The good news is that if you are really just dressing your Chihuahua in a little sweater to keep the chill off, this makes sense, since these dogs are very cold-sensitive. But if dressing him up also means that you plan to clutch the naturally gutsy, courageous and sometimes even warlike dog to your chest for its every waking moment, this is a recipe for trouble! Even tiny lap dogs, Chihuahuas especially, need time to run around and be dogs! Preventing a dog from having freedom to walk beside you on leash, or to follow you in the home, can mess with its natural pack instincts. And if your tiny dog is constantly clutched in your hands with too many people constantly petting him and leaving no natural escape route, the dog could become fearful, snappy or even seriously aggressive.

Also, you should never force your dog into clothing that hurts! Children are often culprits, moving their toy dog's limbs too roughly whenever they dress it, and forgetting that it's not a doll. And even though these items are sold online and in expensive pet boutiques, you should use caution with heavy earrings or necklaces that could choke your dog.

As long as you don't choose the clothing that hurts, we can't say there's physical harm in dressing your dog in clothing so pricey most people would have to take a second mortgage on their home! But remember that dogs don't go by designer labels. A shivering little breed with little hair may really appreciate a snuggly sweater on a winter's day. But you should always choose dogs' clothes for function first and fashion second, if at all.

Popular trends have driven some people to think that dogs actually *like* expensive fashion. If your small breed dog seems to like clothes, it may be that the clothes are comfortable. More likely, though, your little dog likes your attention and loves to see his owner smile, and any tolerance or pleasure he shows around the clothing is motivated by his love for you.

We can't force you not indulge yourself by dressing your dog up on occasion. But please realize that this is *only* a treat for you and *not* for your dog. When owners boast that they spend a fortune on their dogs, it's great if they're talking about splurges on gourmet food, comfortable dog beds or innovative new toys. However, sequined princess dresses, Harley Davidson leathers and literal diamond collars don't count! These are expensive treats designed for *you* to get attention from friends, and they don't actually benefit your dog. It is scary to think that some otherwise logical owners don't understand this...

We've encountered cases where owners spent thousands on expensive clothing and trinkets for their little dogs and then they delayed veterinary care for their dogs, claiming they couldn't afford it. This way of thinking is not only cruel, but horribly ironic!

If you *can* however comfortably afford thousands for veterinary care and high quality food and you can still afford designer dog clothing, there's nothing wrong with it. In fact there is an upside to the recent trend of owners who dress up their dogs, feed expensive gourmet food and constantly fuss over their dogs' care. Regardless if it's considered politically correct to say it, we have noticed that most "cosmopolitan" dog owners tend be responsible and enlightened about dogs and more amenable to modern theories like gentle training and holistic health care.

There's no intrinsic reason for this and great dog owners come from every walk of life. But, statistically, the lifestyle that includes regularly shopping in upscale dog boutiques tends to be incompatible with brutal abuses like tethering dogs out in hot sun, withholding veterinary care, fighting dogs for profit or abandoning them to run the streets to breed indiscriminately.

Of course, there are always cases of wealthy owners abusing dogs behind the doors of mansions. But, statistically, the more interest an owner shows in providing their dog top tier care and husbandry, and the more investment they are willing to make in him, the more interested they seem to be in the well-being of dogs in general. And we hope that many of these owners are reading this chapter. Because, instead of just buying expensive clothes for dogs, we hope these highly involved dog owners will devote more time and resources to help change policy and to educate the community in order to help dogs less fortunate then theirs!

We also hope that the newly popular notions of lavishing care on dogs will trickle down to the general public, becoming a bit more rational. Perhaps then "gourmet food", safe of preservatives and poisons, will simply become the norm and will also become more accessible and affordable to everyone.

As the community becomes more enlightened, we look forward to seeing more equality amongst dogs, starting with tiny high-spirited dogs running in the grass outside their mansions, filling their quivering noses with natural scents. These dogs will get to romp to their hearts' content rather than suffering being constantly squeezed into thousand-dollar evening dresses. And their owners will show the sensitivity to pick them up to cuddle only after the dogs have gotten in a little healthy cardio. And perhaps, as things become even more equalized, we'll someday glimpse an old junkyard dog taking comfort in a simple yet sturdy Wal-Mart jacket as he works through the night on a cold Detroit winter!

Roughhouse With Kids

Children's play tends to get a little wild at times and, if an adult doesn't stop them, they will happily encourage the family dog to join in. But kids playing too roughly can injure a puppy, senior or small breed dog. Even worse, a large breed puppy encouraged to play rough with children when he's young may someday injure children by playing too rough when he's bigger.

It is absolutely the adults' responsibility to supervise dogs and kids playing at all times! Explain and demonstrate to your children how proper handling keeps dogs calm while handling a dog too roughly can bring out snappiness. **And make sure that your kids don't**

learn to run up to strange dogs and start roughhousing. Even if your family dog has a mild temperament and tolerates the behavior, another strange dog the children encounter outside the home may not respond so well, and the results could be tragic.

Kiddie Toys

You should provide your dog with his own safe toys. And you must consistently make it clear that these are the only items he can chew on. In the canine world toys are a major hot button for possessiveness, dominance and even aggression. And you can't expect your dog to leave children's precious new possessions alone if you encourage him to chew up the kids' old toys. Stuffed animals are one of the very worst items owners teach their puppies to chew on. Very, very often we see owners offering their dogs their kids' old stuffed animals to play with and, the next day, the dog starts a bad habit of tearing up all the kids' *new* stuffed animals, plus every upholstered item in the home! If you have kids, and they have stuffed animals, it's also a good idea not to get your puppy used to playing with the stuffed dog toys sold in pet stores.

Encouraging your dog to pull toys away from your children (as in "Tug-of-War", above) is an even more dangerous game and it can make more susceptible dogs learn to bite people. We advise avoiding tug-of-war games or tug-style toys entirely. Be especially careful and never let your dog get into a game of tug involving children's toys or household items. **And never let a small child get into a violent tugging situation with a dog, even in play. Although this happens frequently in many households, it can create aggression in susceptible dogs.**

Also note that, at the conclusion of any game, everyone in your household should be able to safely take the dog's toys away from him without a struggle. The dog should never end up with the toy at the end of a play session, so the adults should practice gently but firmly taking toys away when your dog is a pup in order to teach him good manners for life. This is also the time for the adults to carefully supervise that the kids are able to safely take possessions away from the puppy. **But teach your children never to take anything from any dog without adults supervising!** Adults must exert authority and leadership at these times, so that the dog understands the children are constantly under the adult's protection and care. While you will instruct your children not to take things from dogs, you also want a dog that will be trustworthy even if your children, or a strange child forgets and attempts to take something.

A young puppy's habits can still be changed and this is why it's so important to practice when he's young. If, however, a dog over six months ever growls when you try to take a toy from him, this has become a serious situation! Before trying to intervene on your own, you should consult an expert behaviorist. **And teach children to call you immediately for help rather than attempting to struggle over possession of a toy with a dog of any age. A**

child cannot, and should not, ever be expected to enforce leadership on an unruly dog. It is the parents' responsibility to train the dog beforehand and control the environment adequately so that a young child is never forced to defend his possessions.

Old Shoe

We all too frequently see owners offering puppies items like old shoes to chew on. And then these owners ask us why, a few months later, the dog has begun destroying all their *new* shoes. **Owners must understand that a dog really cannot distinguish an old shoe ready to be discarded from the five-thousand dollar designer shoes you bought specially to wear to a red-carpet gala!** So make it easy on your dog from the start. Make it clear to your puppy which toys are his and never hand over human shoes, socks or anything you wouldn't want him to play with on his own.

Cat Toy (Live)

Some cats and dogs can be great friends. For example, a mature male Collie Emma grew up took it on himself to gently help nurture a litter of kittens the mother couldn't care for. In turn, those cats grew up loving dogs. Cats and dogs should always be properly socialized together from an early age, and they *can* play safe and gentle games together throughout their lives. If the games ever get rough, though, or if either animal seems angry or distressed, it's the owner's responsibility to tone it down. Both pets can get seriously injured or your dog may try the same kind of inappropriate play with your neighbors' less friendly cats, with terrible results.

Violence between cats and dogs shouldn't be tolerated. It's not okay for the cat that was your loving pet for years to have to live out the rest of his life separated from his family hiding under a bed or crouched on a high shelf because, on impulse, you adopted an adult dog that wants to kill him!

Even more heartbreaking is when a family laughs at conflicts between dog and cat, saying things like, "Oh, our cat can take care of himself". It's true that a cat grabbed by a dog may fight like a tiger. But there's nothing funny about this. A panicked cat's flailing claws may seriously injure the dog that outweighs him by seventy pounds. Then the cat may simply slip away deeper into the bowels of the house to nurse his own injuries, not to be seen again for a week after the conflict. Or he may vanish from the home forever.

It's true that cats, more than dogs, are independent animals. But owners have to remember that the creature they're sentencing to live the rest of his life as no more than prey for an aggressive dog was once your loving pet. **Owners who defend their ill-conceived plan in adopting a cat-aggressive dog by saying that it's natural for all dogs to follow their prey drive should visit a home where**

Yes, it's sometimes possible to teach a new dog to stop chasing your cat. But it's heartbreaking to watch owners ignore the problem or treat it lightly. Breeds of dogs with high prey drive will more likely chase or injure cats, and so will dogs that were not fully socialized with cats when they were young puppies. Bringing an adult dog with unknown background into a home with cats is risky- you should only consider it if you've first observed the dog to be completely gentle, calm and loving with every cat, in every situation. And a large dog, or even a large puppy, that vigorously "plays" with your cats can also do serious damage. This type of "play" session sometimes ends with one or both of the animals seriously injured.

dogs and cats get along beautifully. Once you've spent some time around this kind of harmony, you must admit that **there is no reason for a well-raised dog and cat to ever live in conflict.** Even if there are some problems, with reasonable effort you may be able to train the animals to get along on your own or you can hire a professional to do it. But if this does not work, a caring owner should consider the kindest and smartest alternative- finding one of the animals' a different home.

Dog Toy (Live)

This brutal "game" is the same as "Cat Toy" above, only it's played with one large prey-driven dog, and a little white, black or brown piece of canine fluff that he wants to chase down and tear apart. Instead of perceiving the animal he shares a home with as your loyal toy breed dog that's lived happily with you for years, certain dog-aggressive larger dogs may just see an endlessly amusing little prey animal. The problem becomes worse if the dog discovers he can chase this distressed animal around with no intervention from the owners, who stand around cracking open beers and having a good laugh as their little dog desperately attempts to defend himself!

This same toy dog, when he was the only dog in the home, likely was a loving, balanced and well-mannered companion that never bit or growled. But, facing constant attacks by the larger dog, the toy dog may either learn to skitter away in fear or he may become preemptively aggressive, growling and leaping several feet up in the air to take a bloody nip out of the bigger dog's nose seemingly out of nowhere. Unfortunately, because the little dog's fury looks so silly, the owners may giggle as the big dog screams in pain. They may even boast, "See, our little dog is a tough guy; he can really take care of himself!"

We've seen this terrible "game" start two ways. Some families already own an unfriendly big dog that they never bothered to socialize to small dogs when he was a puppy. And then they buy a toy dog or puppy on impulse.

Other families, who already own a small dog, suddenly take pity on a large dog they come across facing euthanasia at the pound, or advertised on Craigslist. The former owners may be so desperate to rid themselves of a dog that they'll lie to the new owners, promising he'll act friendly to their small dog. Unfortunately, owners trying to unload a dog may boast that he's great with dogs, cats or children when he's never experienced them or even when he's tried to attack them. **To be safe, you must introduce your existing dog to the new dog on neutral territory and make sure they get along great before you bring the new dog home.** If the dogs *don't* get along wonderfully *or* if the former owner refuses to let you try this, then the deal should be off!

Suddenly bringing home a large dog of unknown background to live with a small dog is dangerous. And small dogs with unknown backgrounds can also act aggressive and inappropriate with other dogs. As in the "Cat Toy" section above, **it does not make you a caring owner if you rescue a dog from the pound only to force him to live out the rest of his life in a basement or garage because he keeps trying to kill the animals you already have at home.**

It's also cruel to rescue the big dog, but leave your cherished small dog confined to a crate for the rest of his life just because he looks like prey to the big one. Violence in the home isn't acceptable amongst humans and families shouldn't consider it acceptable amongst dogs. Consider the fact that owners and kids can also get hurt constantly trying to break up fights!

Owners who think aggressive behavior is just the nature of dogs should visit a balanced multi-dog family to watch all the dogs getting along in harmony, and they should strive for no less! If the dog-on-dog aggression in your home is serious, and if you cannot train the dogs on your own, you can hire an expert behaviorist who will use gentle methods specific to your situation. There are also a small number of cases where even expert treatment cannot resolve the problem, and the best solution can be to find one of the dogs a new home.

Dangerous Dog Parks

In this section, if we wanted to do what is currently considered "politically correct" we could have advised you on how to use your local dog park considerately and safely to get your dog his exercise and socialization. But, instead, before you take your dog to a dog park, we must warn you of possible dangers that you should weigh against the benefits. The first thing dog owners should notice in regard to their dogs' health is that most of these parks are unsupervised, so the only enforcement on vaccinations may be a small sign that only conscientious owners bother to read. And dogs *do* contract disease and parasites in these parks, although it's not widely publicized.

But the biggest concern you may have is whether other dogs will be aggressive to you and/or your dog. And, unfortunately, this is a legitimate concern! Dog parks are public parks, so anyone could show up. The only thing stopping a surly recent parolee from loosing two aggressive ninety-pound dogs in the park is a small sign telling him not to do it. Then imagine trying to pull your beloved standard poodle, covered in blood, out of those dogs' jaws! The attack can happen in an instant and the likelihood that a strange owner will back you up if their dog is inappropriate with yours is almost zero.

And dogs don't have to be big to be aggressive. We once watched an owner of a dog-aggressive Shih Tzu laugh in helpless embarrassment as her dog attacked two larger, but much more passive, dogs that futilely tried to escape. Ironically, this otherwise pleasant and attractively dressed woman had taken a day off just to bring her demon dog to the dog park to "cure" his hatred of dogs! **In fact many owners set their aggressive dogs loose in dog parks because of this same strange philosophy and many "dog professionals" urge them to do it.** In contrast, we believe that if you suspect your dog is not totally friendly and may hurt other dogs, it's your responsibility to society *not to* just throw him in with a strange pack to try to make him better!

Modern metropolitan/suburban dwellers have serious problems finding a good place for their dogs to run free. But most public dog parks, especially at crowded hours, are not a solution! A safer alternative is to find a private fenced area for your dog to run, even if you have to get creative by making lots of calls to private parties and then paying dearly for the privilege. Even if you can't find a place where your dog can exercise alone off leash, there are many wonderfully safe public parks where your dog can exercise with you while he's leashed. (Or use a long lead, up to thirty feet, to give him more room to run, if the venue permits.)

To socialize your dog or puppy, we recommend you avoid public dog parks and instead arrange "play dates" or parties with nice dogs owned by reliable friends. Or, if all other conditions are right, you can enroll your dog in a group obedience or agility class that you first check out thoroughly. We recommend you first "spy on" a session of the class on your own, rather than taking the trainers' word that all the dogs there are friendly. Unfortunately, a significant number of obedience instructors, in search of higher profits, deliberately neglect to screen dogs adequately. And you certainly don't want to pay for a class, only to get the same kind of surprise you might at the dog park!

Road Warrior

We urge owners to frequently take their dogs off property for exercise in novel venues like parks, but *never* transport your dog to fun and games unsecured in your car with his head hanging out the window or in the bed of a pickup truck. (This practice is illegal in some communities.) And don't undo the good of a healthy exercise session by then leaving your dog alone in a hot car, even for a minute. This can be even more deadly if your dog just completed exercising, because his body temperature will be elevated.

Ice Pup

As a rule of thumb, dogs tolerate cold conditions much better than heat. But extreme cold can be dangerous, especially for short-haired or hairless breeds, young pups, elderly dogs and any dog that has spent its whole life inside in overheated conditions. **If you plan to exercise your dog in the cold or snow, first ask your veterinarian what length of time and what temperatures will be safe.**

Then use common sense. Choose milder winter days for extended periods of exercise beyond your dog's daily walks. Make sessions short, come in from the cold frequently and always dry your dog off thoroughly. Be cautious of rock salt and try doggie coats, booties and sweaters for the more cold-vulnerable breeds. Most dogs are quite hearty and thrive on the opportunity to play in the snow, but exceptions include hairless and toy breeds (like Chinese Cresteds) and dogs with medical conditions. Even brief exposure to winter weather can be dangerous for these dogs, so always consult with your veterinarian first.

"Shake"

Many people don't know it, but this popular parlor trick encourages your dog to paw and eventually to jump on people! In fact, many problem jumpers we're called to treat have owners who taught them this "game" and who now must undo the damage. The truth is, teaching your dog this behavior isn't fair. Even though "giving paw" or "shaking" has been a favorite through the generations, it's easy to live without this game once you realize the problems you can avert.

You shouldn't encourage your dog to lift his paws to push at or jump at you, but you should teach your young puppy to accept you holding and squeezing his paws without protest. When you reward your pup with treats and praise for tolerating touch on his sensitive paws, it makes him trust humans and prepares him for veterinary exams and regular nail clipping throughout his life.

Sink or Swim

A traumatic introduction to water could make your dog afraid for life. Instead, teach him to love water and it could be a lifelong part of his exercise routine.

Dogs *can* drown regardless of what some down-home experts may tell you. Just like children, dogs should always be taught to swim gradually, never left in a pool unsupervised and not made to swim in overly rough, cold or polluted water or water that might conceal hidden hazards. And your backyard pool should contain accessible steps so that if your dog ever accidentally falls in, he can get out on his own.

The best idea is to fence your pool if you own dogs just as you would for toddlers. Barring that, always provide some supervision when dogs are around the pool. And large or rowdy dogs shouldn't play wildly around a pool, because they can easily cause an accident for your family and guests. The day you host a party on your pool deck is not the safest time to bring your dog in to swim. And never let your kids or guests taunt or terrify a dog that is in the water, or push his head under. If you do this, your dog may develop a phobia of water and never want to swim again. Luckily, the reverse can also be true. With lots of love and patience, even a dog that is afraid of water can be taught to swim. (See: "Kiddie Pool" in Chapter 11, Water Games).

Garage Playroom

There's a good chance that your garage may contain spilled antifreeze, which most owners already know is lethal if ingested by your dog. But many other chemicals commonly kept in the garage are also poisonous to your dog, including fire ant killer, herbicides, glue, solvents, paints, gasoline, varnishes, household cleaners and many others. And, even if you remove all the chemicals, they may still leave dangerous spills that dogs can lick.

People also tend to leave sharp tools exposed in their garages, next to tiny bins of nails, hooks and fishing tackle. And of every room in modern homes, the garage tends to be the one space left with no heat, ventilation or air conditioning. So why do so many suburban owners house their dogs and young puppies in their garages? We strongly advise against this! To avoid potential disaster, forget about the garage for housing your dog, giving time-outs or playing with your dog and instead select an equivalent space in a safe, climate-controlled spare room inside the house.

Dangerous Landscape

Fresh, wet chemicals on your lawn can poison your pet and most owners are aware of this. But becoming a dog owner means you should also research the overall safety of any chemical you'll be using on your yard. Especially if your kids roll in around the grass with your dog, we think the best option is to go "green". These days, more landscape companies offer natural alternatives to dangerous herbicides and pesticides that were all-too-popular in residential settings just a few years ago.

New owners can also save money, and potential grief, by checking that none of your landscape plants are poisonous to dogs. (Check online, with your veterinarian and in Resources.) Before you're sure of a new dog's behavior, don't invest in elaborate landscape projects. Some dogs tend to dig holes or damage landscaping when first adjusting to a new environment. Puppies usually grow out of this behavior and even neurotic dogs can be cured with positive training, but you can save yourself stress by waiting to install expensive landscaping until your dog fully settles in.

And while you're hiring someone to take care of your yard, why not hire someone to clean it also? Many owners allow dogs to take care of all their bowel movements in their backyards. Of course, you *should* be walking your dog several times daily for dog/owner bonding, socializing, exercise and obedience. But, for the millions of owners who still let their dogs relieve themselves in the back yards of their beautiful homes, within days the filth accumulates horrifically.

Dog waste festering in the hot sun is more than an annoyance. It can infect or re-infect your dog(s) with parasites; it can easily infect your *children* with parasites such as worms or protozoa and it makes the yard completely useless for play, exercise and obedience involving owners and dog. Imagine playing many of the games in this book if your yard is a minefield of dog waste!

Your yard should be kept as a functional space to work with your dog every day. And solutions are easy. Just go to your favorite pet store, catalog or Internet site and choose one of the many products for cleaning up dog waste (see Resources). Products range from long-handled scoops to a dog "septic system".

An even more trend-forward solution is to hire someone to regularly clean and disinfect the yard. Companies specializing in dog waste removal are springing up around the country in response to the needs of a changing society. Their prices are surprisingly affordable, many are bonded professionals and they can schedule regular visits as often as you need. If you do hire someone, you should of course use the same care as you would with any service person you allow onto your property. Your regular dog walker might even be persuaded to perform the service for a fee, or they can steer you in the direction of someone who can. But whatever method you choose, high tech or low tech, high or low priced, keeping your yard clean of waste is one of the best (and most often overlooked) things you can do for your family and your pet.

Bad Bones

Most people already know that **cooked chicken bones can cause internal hemorrhaging and kill your dog.** But other types of bones, and even popular rawhides and other treats can be dangerous as well. Simple plain rubber is usually a safe material for chew toys if your dog chews vigorously or select a toy labeled "indestructible". If you're unsure of what toys are safest for your particular dog, you should check with your veterinarian. If you do choose to let your dog chew on rawhide or bones, supervise carefully. Supervise even more carefully when multiple dogs are involved. Since these natural treats resemble a wolf's "kills", they can cause fighting amongst your dogs. We advise against presenting bones to multiple dogs, especially if you are unsure of any of the dogs' backgrounds.

Tether

Many communities have laws against tethering dogs because it can be a dangerous, even deadly practice. A dog can literally hang or choke himself if a chain or rope is connected in the wrong position, or the wrong equipment is used. Dogs can also suffer from the elements- heat and cold- when left tethered outside for hours.

And dogs tethered out alone for long periods with no socialization can eventually become vicious; in fact, some owners intentionally "train" their pit bulls to fight in this manner.

While the average owner would not tether their dog in such a manner, accidents can happen surprisingly fast and dogs do not have the capacity to untangle themselves. Leave your dog playing unattended tied up on a rope or chain, and you might later find him hanging. Leave your dog tethered in shade, and you may come back to find him panting in sun with his chain wrapped around a bush. If you don't have a fenced yard and you want your dog to play outside, safer solutions could be a playpen for puppies or a fenced kennel or run area for larger dogs. Or try a cable specifically designed to allow your dog to run back and forth without tangling. And, if you ever must tie your dog out briefly for any purpose on a regular rope or chain, make sure to carefully supervise!

Backyard Hunting

Frequently, dogs that spend a lot of time unsupervised in their owners' back yards get into the bad habit of chasing and killing small animals like lizards, birds and squirrels. And for some reason owners often encourage this behavior. Of course, it's natural for your dog to want to obey his instinctive prey drive and chase animals, but a wise owner discourages this behavior, along with controlling their dog's behavior in every way so that he is a good citizen.

With the notable exception of true working settings, the experience of killing small animals will have a devastating effect on your dog's personality and your ability to control him. Each time the dog kills something, it will intensify his already intense prey drive, and later this aggression could possibly extend to domestic animals and then even people. If you've encouraged your dog to act violently, chasing and killing animals, there's always a chance that this dog could escape your property and injure your neighbor's pets, or even their children. Sadly, this situation happens frequently.

There's also real danger to your dog if he kills and eats animals in your yard, or while out on walks. In our part of the country, "Bufo" or "Cane" toads are poisonous and many Florida dogs die from consuming them. Animals like squirrels, raccoons, possums or even stray cats can carry rabies, pests and other diseases and can seriously injure your dog if they get into a tussle. Scorpions, poisonous snakes, large poisonous spiders and alligators are present with surprising frequency in suburban backyards here in South Florida. And other parts of the country have their own hazards as development steals more and more wild habitat.

So watch your dog; teach him to come back to you when you call, even if he's in pursuit, and teach him to obey the "leave it!" command. Fence off canals, clear brush and always check for hazards before letting the dog out. Install a floodlight and/or use a long lead when sending your dog out for his last pee of the evening so you can keep him in sight. Never leave him out unattended for long periods and **never encourage hunting behavior in a non-working dog.**

Sic 'Em

This "game" is a more macabre version of "Hunting in the Backyard", and although there's no scientific evidence of a gender bias, we have seen more males teach their dogs to "play" Sic 'Em than we've seen females. The problem starts if there is something annoying in your neighbor's yard that continuously irks a particular family member. This could be squirrels, unsupervised cats that continuously use your yard as a litterbox or even a neighbor's shrill little Pomeranian that barks at Dad every time he comes out to read the Sports' section or fire up the grill.

Dad may have put up with these nuisance animals for years, but now he brings home a new dog, usually a hunting breed, and the dog likes to give chase, baying loudly and seemingly intent on killing the nuisance animal if he catches it. You would think that Dad would attempt to stop the dog. But instead, some guys have been known to urge their dog, out of the corner of their mouths to, "Sic 'em!" This may seem like harmless fun, and it may even leave your guests laughing the first time your dog nails the squirrel, cat or Pomeranian and gets a mouthful of fur, leaving the other creature fleeing for its life, fussing and hissing.

But the next step is that the dog *will* eventually kill something if his owner encourages his already strong prey drive in this irresponsible fashion. Today it may be a squirrel that he attacks, but tomorrow he may go after your neighbor's cat or even your neighbor. Teaching your dog this terrible "game" is not a good way to make friends in the neighborhood!

> *Owners are often shocked at their dog's power and speed. If you say "Sic 'em" just joking around and then attempt to pull your dog off whatever he is trying to kill, you may find it impossible!*

Jump Up

Owners may find it cute to encourage their puppy to run up to them when they come home from work, crashing into them with all his weight. But they should realize that whatever you teach your dog to do when he is a 5 lb pup, he will also do when he is 100 or 150 pounds! At that time the joke will be on you when your year-old dog knocks you off your feet every day when you walk in the door and you are powerless to stop it.

Your grandparents, children and guests may also get hurt by the poor dog that doesn't know that what you taught him was fun when he was only 10 or 20 pounds can get him sent to the pound when he's bigger. And just like with good behaviors, each time you encourage your puppy to jump on you when he's young will make the behavior more deeply ingrained and difficult to change when he's older.

Wake Daddy

Many people find it funny to tell their dog to lick the face of a sleeping family member to wake them. But, without intending to cause harm, a dog can easily step on a person or scratch them in the face or eyes. Or the rudely awakened person may swat at the dog so hard they fling him across the room and hurt him!

Having a dog jump into bed and demand attention from an owner in the morning is dominant behavior that should never be encouraged, and it's a contributing factor in many serious behavior problems including aggression. If your dog is well-behaved enough not to attempt this on his own, a truly caring owner will not teach him to do it.

"Beg"

Even if your family enjoys this, your guests probably won't. And, because of the way canines think and react, "begging" at the table tends to lead to dominance, and then disobedient, behavior. This is one dangerous game that most owners have likely been cautioned about, but it seems so adorable when your dog gazes up at you yearningly when you're eating that you just may want to share, especially if you live alone. Some single owners crave their dog's "company" so badly at the dinner table that they may even encourage him to sit up on a chair!

But no matter how cute your dog seems at mealtimes you, as a human, must be wise. Mealtime represents a primal situation for canines, with high potential for fears and violence, so it's essential that the humans eat first and set boundaries in order for their dog to understand his rightful place in the pack.

Even if your dog doesn't display outwardly dominant behavior like jumping on the table or stealing food from your children, being allowed to beg at the table can hurt him psychologically. Dogs that are allowed to do this often defy their owners in other areas of life, constantly pulling on leash or even snapping when the owner tries to take their toys away. Other dogs may react with neurotic eating behaviors like "I'll Only Eat If" described in Chapter 2, Games Dogs Play on Their Owners. Believe it or not, your dog will *not* take offense if you eat without him, and the best place for him to be when the family is eating is out of the dining room!

Dangerous Day Care

Is taking your dog to a professional "doggie daycare" facility five days a week a good way to exercise him when you can't be home? Or do these facilities expose your dog to so many physical and psychological dangers that it should be avoided? To be fair, we have included day care as a positive option in Chapter 14, Activities for Owners with Limited Mobility. But we also include it in this chapter because of very real dangers.

Theoretically, the idea of supervised day care to ease your dog's loneliness and inactivity while you work long hours has merit. Daycare could be a great alternative to your dog spending his days alone and bored if all facilities offered: 1) Sufficient educated and caring staff people actively supervising a small number of dogs; 2) Vast outdoor, and/or equivalent indoor spaces for dogs to run, as opposed to tiny, overcrowded prison-style yards or rooms; 3) Protection from dangerous overexertion in heat and full sun; 5) Leashed walks, rather than dogs being forced to soil the rooms where they rest or the tiny yard where they play; 5) Sensitive or timid dogs offered protection from bullying by overdominant dogs, so your delicate pooch would never come home from a "fun" day at "day camp" with permanent scarring and expensive vet bills.

In the real world many popular daycares don't live up to all these ideals, even though they may distribute charming advertising and collect pricey fees. **Some facilities boast that, on busy days, they host over a hundred large dogs** and they show off photos of enormous "packs" like this playing together! But a hundred large dogs does not represent a party!

Unfortunately anyone who's worked in one of these facilities (like Ray) knows this isn't safe. While dogs are pack animals, they're *not* meant to socialize in vast numbers, with different animals coming and going each day. If you carefully watch dogs' body language in overcrowded areas at some day cares you will discover that some of the dogs are unhappy, agitated, fearful or physically and emotionally "burnt". Meanwhile, other dogs constantly threaten, bully or push for dominance- even though, to the untrained eye, they might just appear extremely playful.

The problem is worse because **many owners bring their dog to daycare because the dog has serious behavior problems.** At home these owners may keep their problem dog crated constantly, feeling unable to interact with him or control him at all. They then invest a sizable sum at the daycare facility (as much as $600 each month) so that the unmanageable dog "blows off enough steam" to fall asleep, completely exhausted, when he comes home at the end of the day. Despite the cost, which may represent a large portion of their income, and continue for the rest of the dog's life, having this monster "dead to the world" is worth it to these owners!

So what do these hyperkinetic "monster" dogs do in daycare to exhaust them enough that all they do is sleep when they get home? The answer is that all day at daycare they incessantly chase smaller or more timid dogs- bullying, pestering and sometimes terrifying or injuring them!

Meanwhile, at some facilities, a single minimum-wage staff person in "back" may be left alone to supervise and care for thirty or more dogs, with no help from the sleek sales expert(s) up front busy soliciting new business. The daycare staff "in back" are usually decent people who genuinely care about dogs. But one person cannot clean up waste from thirty dogs, break up serious fights and still find time to intervene every time a dog gets bullied. And underpaid staff, depending on the job for their next bus token or their kids' next meal, are often afraid to complain when management overbooks the facility (common on weekends and holidays). Even when it's not deliberate, inexperienced daycare owners or managers can feel overwhelmed and agree to take extra dogs, hoping no serious problems occur.

Managers sometimes know that certain dogs that are "regulars" at their daycare act aggressive to other dogs around toys and food. But the facility may have to pay rent and/or pay back a start-up loan, and these cases may be their bread and butter. Or a starry-eyed owner or manager may hope that constant play with the group will eventually transform a domineering or hyperkinetic dog.

If *your* dog is large, boisterous and insensitive, then he might do fine in daycare with no ill effects. But if your dog is small, slight, timid, young, old or medically compromised or if he already has great house manners and a soft disposition, we recommend you keep him out of most daycare facilities to preserve his physical and emotional well being!

As a better alternative, for an equivalent price, you can easily hire a professional dog walker to come to your home and provide exercise and company for your dog.

Or ask a trusted friend or neighbor, ideally one with a large fenced yard, to provide "family-style" daycare for a small fee while you work. If your acquaintance owns well-behaved dogs that your dog already knows and likes, these dogs will be healthier playmates than thirty to a hundred dogs owned by strangers!

Socialization is good for dogs, but it's not necessary for your dog to exercise or play freely with dogs owned by strangers. It's true that puppies should occasionally meet strange dogs to build confidence and forestall future nervousness or reactivity/aggression. But the more the *owner* knows about the dogs, the better.

We like to recommend carefully arranged and supervised "play dates". (See "Playdate" Chapter 14, Games for Owners with Limited Mobility) rather than allowing your dog to play freely with strangers' dogs in off-leash dog parks, dog beaches or doggie daycare. Even though our recommendation goes against current "politically correct" ideology, it's our responsibility to advise our customers, and our readers, of what is safest. And, unfortunately, there's a great record of misery after visits to such places, including injuries, contagious disease and lasting psychological damage to dogs.

We are animal lovers, too and all we can do is urge the well-meaning folks who create these venues to also ensure that they are one-hundred percent safe, all the time. After all, this is the world of the millennium and you would not want your treasured dog to be injured or infected with disease, pests or parasites. One well-known and well-respected trainer literally stated in her book that some degree of injury, ie: *facial scarring* in such publicly shared dog facilities is acceptable. This is where we part ways in ideology!

If you absolutely must use doggie daycare with no alternative of a friend, relative or dog walker to provide care, then first investigate the daycare facility from the viewpoint that your dog's life depends on it. **Even in a disappointing industry, there are some superior and safe facilities available, which actually provide all the benefits to dogs that they advertise. A good doggie daycare facility will offer:** 1) Small staff to dog ratio (ideally at least one staff person to ten dogs, not including front office staff); 2) Hospital-level cleanliness, an emergency vet on-staff or on-call 24-hours a day and staff present in the facility 24-hours a day if dogs stay overnight; 3) Dogs exercised and housed in the smallest groups possible and never allowed to mingle in a huge pack. Over ten or twelve dogs loose together has no positive value and becomes increasingly dangerous. Insist on seeing the big dogs, and not just the small dogs, when you first tour; 4) Dogs **rigorously** screened for temperament and health. Even though many facilities claim to turn dogs away, you want real evidence that your facility actually does this. 5) Even if your facility meets the above criteria, double check that it also includes spacious areas for your dog to exercise (including shade to escape hot summer sun). Exercise areas should be significantly larger than your yard at home, or taking your dog to the facility for daycare may not be worth it.

Once you find a truly extraordinary facility that meets all the criteria above, next make sure your dog is the one in the pack getting all the best privileges- even if this means paying extra for special services. You can often request a private suite, private walks or extra exercise. And any service you need that's not listed on the facility's menu may be available for a sufficient tip! Since daycare is pricey no matter what, we also recommend that you consider upgrading to a top-tier "luxury" or "upscale" facility if there are any good ones in your area. Of course, just because a facility is labeled upscale won't make it the best choice if there's a less crowded and more caring family-run daycare next door. And your dog doesn't need "spa" services, "big-screen TV's" or flavored bottled water. The best real perks that progressive facilities offer include: the cleanest, largest and plushest private sleeping accommodations, plentiful highly qualified staff interacting with a small number of dogs, and a veterinarian on staff.

Boxing

The little game of boxing at each other with hands and paws seems to be a favorite for many people to play with their puppies. The problem is that when these pups mature, the same owners who taught the dog the game often have to give him up when he hits them in the stomach or scratches them in the face. Suddenly, being hit by the adult dog's paws is no longer fun for the owner. Of all the breeds, this "game" of Boxing seems to bring the worst results if your dog is a Boxer. It's bred into Boxers' genetics to use their paws for everything (and they were even given their name because of how they use their paws when fighting). If you teach a boxer the "boxing" game when he's a young impressionable pup, and then you try to recondition his behavior as an adult, it will be extremely tough. Not only will you be working against the habit you created, but you'll also be fighting instinct and genetics. Instead, it's much easier to teach your boxer, or any puppy, *not* to flail at you with his paws when he's little, and then you'll never encounter the problem when he's an adult.

Boo!

You don't really want your dog afraid of you, do you? Yet many people find it funny to sneak up and scare their puppy. Sometimes they will notice that their dog spooks at a certain item, such as a Halloween mask. These owners will make the fear worse by putting on the mask, jumping around the dog and then laughing when he panics. Other owners may make a hissing sound or sneak up on the dog when he is sleeping to scare him.

> *Pleasantly exposing a puppy to new stimuli builds confidence and improves behavior for life; terrifying him produces the opposite effect.*

It's sad that some of these owners may have the mistaken belief they are "toughening up" the dog and improving his mental health by surprising him with the new stimuli. In reality they could be setting the stage for dangerously neurotic behavior. Or later in life the dog might encounter the stimulus and feel so afraid that he strikes out!

There *is* some merit to accustoming your young puppy to being wakened from sleep or to encountering novel stimuli. Puppies are naturally shy and must be acquainted with the world. And exposing puppies to novel stimuli when they are young is necessary to forming proper character- as long as the puppies are kept emotionally comfortable throughout the process. The idea is to show a puppy that the new stimulus *won't* hurt him, not to use the new thing to terrify him! It's also good to teach your puppy that it's okay if you suddenly waken him from sleep. But always greet him with a nice stimulus, such as a treat, a word of praise or a gentle pat when you do it. This will help raise a stable dog.

Poor Baby

This is an easy mistake to make if you own a fearful dog, because you naturally want to use your words and your touch to comfort him when he's feeling afraid. But unfortunately, showing obvious worry about your pet can reinforce his anxious behavior. If your dog whines, cries or shies away from people or if he panics at loud noises or thunderstorms, it's very easy for a well-intentioned owner to cuddle the dog to them, petting feverishly and repeating in a high cooing voice, "Oh, poor baby! Are you afraid? Oh you poor little thing!"

The problem is that all this worried comforting will only make your fearful dog sense that *you* are uncomfortable. Your dog looks to you for guidance, and if he sees that his owner feels nervous he'll believe the thing he fears is, indeed, extremely dangerous. The attention he gets from your petting and cooing will also make him want to repeat the fearful actions again.

Dogs can hurt themselves as a result of fear and panic and terrified dogs that perceive themselves cornered may strike out. Fears and phobias also tend to intensify over time, so it's important you work with your dog correctly. There are good books available on the subject (see Books in Resources) and, if your dog's fear (or fear-related aggression) is severe, you should also consult a professional.

Here's some simple advice on how to act more level-headed and not go overboard on the comforting behaviors. Look in a mirror and observe how you're petting your dog when he's acting fearful. You will probably be able to notice your own tension. You want to change the way you pet your dog to use slow calming strokes, rather than quick nervous ones.

And don't touch your dog at all if he's acting really panicked. Allow him his space. Speak in a low calm voice, not a high excited one. If your dog exhibits an action you don't want repeated, such as barking at a visitor in a shrill tone and then ducking behind your legs, ignore him. Walk away and don't encourage the behavior. Next, praise and pet him as soon as he shows the slightest sign of acting calmer and more appropriate. Then withhold attention if the unwanted behaviors appear again.

If your dog shows fearful behavior, such as panting and whining during thunderstorms, you must act calm and centered yourself. Present a picture of calm leadership and control and act as though you are having fun during the storm. Above all, don't let your dog's fear make you act upset. Curing serious canine fears is complex and may require long-term behavior modification. But one simple thing you can be sure of is that if your dog's fears send you into obvious panic, this will make things worse!

Small Dogs- Big Problems

For toy dogs that may remain as small as puppies all of their lives, you must avoid certain activities that can hurt your dog. You must also avoid games, activities and practices that can make your dog aggressive to humans. Before you dismiss this concept, thinking small dogs are harmless, you should understand how many serious bites come from small dogs and how often the victims are children.

Adults should supervise young children whenever they play with any dog, including small breeds. And the frailest small breeds aren't appropriate for young children who can't play gently. Improper handling can cause injury and/or continual anguish to a tiny dog. This stress can in turn create emotional/behavioral problems including aggression.

Always treat teacup-sized dogs gently. Never shake, throw or play roughly with a small dog, even if he "seems to like it" and **never use force to train a tiny dog.** A choke collar correction of the same force you could use safely with a larger dog could kill your tiny dog or seriously injure his esophagus, neck or back! Also be careful with the training equipment you use- items like choke and prong collars are not really designed for tiny dogs and can be an impeccable recall when he's young, so he'll always come back immediately when you call, and always pay attention to your surroundings when you are out with him.

The next caution might seem even more ridiculous, but it's another serious danger. **Until you are used to being around such a tiny creature, make sure you do not lie on or step on your small dog. Toy dogs, especially puppies, are often hurt or killed when their owners step on them, and owners are frequently seriously injured tripping over toy dogs!**

Big Dogs- Big Problems

Owners encounter two different types of problems when they decide to own an unusually large dog: 1) risks that endanger the dog and, 2) risks that endanger people.

You should never bring home a large breed dog just because you saw one on television or just because you like how the breed looks- this is a truly explosive recipe for disaster. Nor is it enough to meet just one dog of the breed- for example, if a neighbor owns one. Customers we see every day can attest that choosing the wrong dog can cause pain and stress for the next fifteen years, or devastating guilt if you decide to give the dog up because you cannot handle him. **To spare yourself years of problems, before buying or adopting a dog you should first spend time with an adult of his breed, ideally in your own home. This is especially true for the giant breeds.**

Giant working breeds require an experienced, knowledgeable owner and the average family cannot accurately envision living with a dog of that size until he's actually in their home. It's not enough to view a picture of a dog on the Internet, nor to watch a dog in a movie or hear about the breed from a friend. Instead you should meet one, touch one and, if possible, spend time around a whole pack of them at a qualified breeder's. And always listen to breeders' cautions. Reputable breeders will caution potential owners extensively, and they are often the best source of information about their breed of dog.

If you want to adopt a pup that is likely to grow extremely large from a shelter and he's a mixed-breed, first try spending some time with a full-grown dog of the largest breed in his mix. A rescue society can give your family a chance to foster dogs of that breed and size for a short time before you decide if you want to adopt for good. If you immediately recoil at the idea of waiting at all, or find yourself painfully impatient, you should probably look deeply at the source of your impatience. Impulse will only harm you when selecting a dog.

It seems like a cliché, but we get many calls from families who bought their big dog as a puppy, at approximately four-months-old and already fifty pounds. And, for some reason, they were sure that this would be the pup's full-grown adult size as well. When the dog got too large,

No matter how popular, big dogs are not for every family.

dangerous for them. And be very careful about any trainer or handler you allow to work with your tiny dog. Rough methods are not appropriate!

Tiny dogs can easily injure themselves jumping off furniture or out of cars, and they can be very easily dehydrated or chilled. They really do require special care and are only recommended for already experienced owners. First buy from a reputable breeder who can educate you more and always consult with a veterinarian who is also expert and experienced in toy breed care.

Remember that fancy clothes and carriers sold in boutiques don't count as husbandry for your dog. It's okay if you play with these trinkets, but they're no substitute for a safe environment, and the best veterinary care and training. You must remember that your small dog is a **dog**.

Never smother him with stimuli and attention to the point that the petting becomes painful. Train him to respect humans, and give a little breathing space. **Do not laugh off behaviors like snapping or growling just because your dog is small.** Instead, use gentle training methods to deter these behaviors so that they do not escalate.

Never, ever let larger dogs (or even cats) play roughly with your tiny dog. Not only will this keep your small dog safe, but it will prevent him from getting snappy in defense. Have the two pets meet away from your home on several occasions and make sure they get along perfectly. And also study up extensively on the proper methods of adjusting pets to each other before bringing the new dog home. Some dogs and cats can never safely coexist with a toy dog, and others do surprisingly well. So supervise constantly at first and never assume anything.

One of the saddest spectacles we see is owners who bring home a rowdy large dog and allow it to play roughly with their toy breed. Then, when the toy dog starts snapping and growling they say proudly, "See, isn't the little guy feisty! Look how he stands up for himself!" In reality, the little dog is becoming fear-aggressive, feeling he must strike out at the big dog first. A tiny dog snapping at a big dog may *look* funny to certain people. And we've watched whole families sitting back on their couches laughing uncontrollably while their little dog leaped at the big dog in a furious frenzy. But the truth is, every time this happens both dogs are being hurt and both their personalities will suffer in future. In future these dogs may someday strike out at other dogs or even people. The owners have two choices- either take control of both dogs and teach them to get along properly, or consider re homing one of the dogs. No animal should feel it has to act aggressive just to defend itself!

Don't lose your small dog in your house! This happens frequently, and it kills dogs. Tiny dogs trapped in tight spaces can suffer suffocation, heat illness/dehydration or they can get seriously injured when their owner tries to pull them out. If a small dog is a resident of your home, you should carefully "dog proof", always keeping his size in mind. Your toy dogs can also easily get lost forever in shrubbery, woods or the banks of canals and ponds if you leave them off leash to relieve themselves at night. Tiny dogs are attractive meals for animals like owls, hawks and alligators and other predatory wildlife. So teach your toy do they felt they had to get rid of it.

Everybody should be informed that breeds like English Mastiffs can routinely grow to over two hundred pounds. Some people find this size exciting because it gets them attention when they walk their dog down the street. But an owner must be fair to a dog and know that they'll be able to take care of it. Will a dog this size fit in your vehicle? Will he have room to move around your home without knocking things over? Will every member of the family feel confident walking him? And how will your landlord and or your neighbors feel when they see him?

Just size alone does not make a breed unmanageable. But many homes are literally not big enough to accommodate such big dogs, and certain games owners choose to play when the giant dog is a puppy can badly compound the problem. Rough games, and jumping games that are cute when the puppy is relatively small can wreck your house when the dog is full grown- and he will have a hard time understanding if what you ask has suddenly changed.

Owners who don't take time to constantly practice walking gently with on leash with their large dog when he's a puppy will likely pay an unendurable price later on. If you don't practice, walks can become constant combat for dog and owner. This can cause serious discomfort to both dog and owner throughout the dog's lifetime.

These problems don't just occur with giant breeds like Mastiffs, Newfoundlands and Great Danes but also with relatively large dogs like German Shepherds and Labrador Retrievers. **Never play with your large-breed puppy by making him jump on you or any family member!** When he grows up, a big dog can seriously injure a child or elderly person by jumping. But your dog will have trouble understanding what's wrong with the behavior if you encouraged it when he was a pup.

You must make sure that you do not do anything that will teach a large dog to bite. **So never play games with a large-breed puppy where he chews on humans, or treats humans in any way like prey.** Never let children tease giant breed puppies or dogs by shoving their heads inside the dog's mouth to impress their friends. **And never teach your large-breed puppy to play games where he chases after humans- especially kids.**

Teaching your dog these "games" could lead him to hurt family members or guests when he's bigger, with no immediate way for you to turn off his rowdiness. And if a giant dog bites a child, even if injury is minor, the chance is good that you will be sued and/or your dog will be euthanized.

We've all encountered scary news items about dog attacks. The fact is that many complex factors cause aggression, and some individual dogs have greater tendencies to show aggression to humans based on genetics, health and upbringing. Lack of proper socialization and training by negligent breeders or former owners can also contribute to aggression, so these factors must be ruled out before making a diagnosis.

But sometimes bad behavior can be cured as easily as replacing bad habits with healthy ones. And one easy change to make is to stop playing the wrong kind of "games" that teach a dog aggressive behavior is okay. Rough games, biting games or chasing games played with humans and any game where a puppy is hurt or terrified tend to encourage violent tendencies later on!

Even if he has no violent intentions, but just wants to play the same rough games he was taught as a puppy, your large dog could chase down and playfully mouth a child in the neighborhood. The animal you know as a two-hundred-pound overgrown puppy can appear horribly menacing to your neighbors and, because of his size, they may resort to radical measures if they think he needs controlled for their safety. (Calling the police, attempting to hurt the dog, and shunning/harassing the owners are common reactions, and some disputes between neighbors become quite ugly.)

The alternative to starting a neighborhood feud is to teach your pup great manners when he's young and he'll grow up to become a neighborhood ambassador for the giant dog breed cause!

And don't forget, giant dogs can be delicate. Lots of people know that many medium dogs (for example, Pit Bulls) and smaller large breed dogs (for example, German Shepherds and Vizslas) need an incredible amount of vigorous exercise. But it does not follow that the largest breeds need the most exercise! In fact **some giant breeds, such as English Mastiffs, have very low exercise requirements. And some large breeds have extremely bad heat tolerance, ruling out exercise in many conditions and forcing owners to get creative.**

To be safe, know the breed characteristics exactly before exercising your large dog and preferably before buying or adopting! Large dogs, and giant dogs especially, are prone to hip dysplasia because of their weight. **Vigorous weight-bearing exercise and lots of jumping can stress large-breed puppies' hip joints and prevent them from developing correctly. And the terrible results won't bear fruit until several years later when it may be too late.** Limit stressful exercise and jumping for large and giant breed pups up to two years- and consult your expert breeder and/or a veterinarian who specializes in large breeds for recommended exercise. Also consult with your vet about how much and what brand to feed for your puppy's individual needs.

Just because giant breeds look sturdy and are often game for any activity their owner enjoys, this doesn't mean they can't be hurt. Follow all the exercise precautions throughout this book and never try stunts like loading up all your kids on your large dog's back to play "horsey"! Even though your dog may tolerate it, there are less damaging ways to channel his unique energies. Read Chapter 12, Useful Games, for some ideas.

Ruffle My Ruff

We wonder why some dog owners find this particular kind of play so delightful, especially when their dog weighs over a hundred pounds, looks like a bear and gets easily agitated! These owners will roughly caress or "ruffle" the dog's ruff or jowls or the sides of the dog's body so hard that they almost send sparks flying and they won't stop even if the dog cringes or squeals. Nor will they stop or even slow down if the dog begins panting, snapping or leaping around uncontrollably.

When they've created a dog that literally bounces off walls whenever they come home, they still wait for that one second of quiet and then they lean down and attempt to show affection by ruffling the ruff really hard again. And when they call us to try to solve their dog's behavior problems, they will often roughly "pet" their dog in front of us for the entire assessment. The first thing we sometimes tell people is that the way they are petting their dog is causing some of his problems. The truth is that if you *want* an uncontrollably excited dog, then manically ruffling up his ruff is a good idea. Otherwise, it's best to pet your dog on the sides of his face or simply stroke or grasp the ruff gently. Just this one change in how you show your dog affection may lead to a visible improvement in calmness.

> *The authors' favorite game*
> *NOT to play with dogs!*

Rude Neighbor

Throughout the book we constantly tell you that the one thing you can do to guarantee misery and lots of behavior problems in your dog is not to exercise him. So, wouldn't it be great if you could simply give him the best exercise of all- running free out in the wide world, on beaches, in parks and even on that vacant farmland you spotted on one of your rare country drives? Well, it might be great for *you*, but not every member of your community will love your unleashed dog's intrusion.

Even if your dog is well mannered, your neighbors may be afraid of dogs or they may want to enjoy a romantic picnic without an uninvited dog nosing around their food or jumping on their children. And your neighbors pay taxes to enjoy their parks and public areas without dogs running free! Keeping dogs leashed is simply the law in a great majority of public places.

For logistical problems with exercising a dog without lots of space, throughout the book we've offered suggestions including: lots of mental stimulation, using a long lead, agility trials or renting the use of land. But we can't give a simple answer for the greater philosophical problem of craving freedom for your dog to run. We do advise you to respect the law, respect your neighbors and don't rush off to try the off-leash exercises described in this book unless you have a securely (and legally) contained space to practice. Like you, many of your neighbors probably miss the forests and the fields and the "old" America where an owner and his dog could run free for a half hour and never see another soul around! But, for the moment, it's best if we all respect each other's feelings and find the most peaceful ways for our dogs and families to get along in our modern communities.

Dog-In-the-Box

This activity is both popular and dangerous, yet unfortunately many dog "professionals" advise owners to do it, often against the owners' gut instincts. We are talking about the practice of crating dogs for life.

Some owners interact with their dog as a family member and have never used crates. But excessive crating is becoming a dangerous trend that's spreading. Today, a majority of dog owners seem to be using crates for housetraining, and many continue crating for the remainder of their dog's lives!

The theory behind "crate-training" a puppy is to keep him in a small wire cage so he will follow natural canine instincts and not soil his den. For this reason, the floor space must be kept small- just large enough for the dog to turn around. Families often lock a puppy in a crate as early as 8:00 or 9:00 pm in the evening and then they don't let him out until 7:00 the next morning. After a quick potty break in the yard, the dog is returned to the crate and the owner leaves for work for eight, nine or ten hours. Some pups don't see freedom again until five-thirty that evening.

To make matters worse, in order to protect their homes from puppy behaviors such as chewing, many owners with hectic lives put the puppy back in the crate the moment he misbehaves in any way. For example, dogs are often returned to a cage during dinnertime, or during the hours the family watches television. And many owners continue crating the dog like this FOR THE REST OF HIS LIFE.

We are often called to nice suburban homes where we discover otherwise kindhearted owners crating adult dogs for years FOR EIGHTEEN HOURS A DAY or more without realizing the number of hours! We have even seen adult dogs crated for TWENTY-ONE TO TWENTY-THREE HOURS a day without owners realizing it is excessive. These are often the same owners who call us because their dog's behavior is completely out of control.

The fact is, excessive crating deprives your dog of the chance to ever learn proper house manners or socialization. It creates dogs that rush out of their crates like wild animals- hyperactive, nervous and unable to connect emotionally with humans. We must then rehabilitate these dogs, reintroducing them to family life and the world. And ironically, crating is not even the best solution for housetraining!

When you choose to bring a puppy home, you *are* responsible for keeping him out of trouble, monitoring his housetraining and making sure he doesn't hurt himself. And it's a good idea to confine your pup to a safe area without hazards while you are away. We feel a good solution is a blank room with some bedding and unbreakable toys (see "A Room of His

Own" in Chapter 5, Indoor Games). But you shouldn't leave young puppies alone too many hours at a time, and you need to spend time with adult dogs, as well. Dogs are pack animals and extended separations from their family can be psychologically damaging, especially if the dog is left with nothing to stimulate his senses.

We blame much of the problem on the so-called dog professionals who push crating as a panacea, rather than advising owners on how to interact and communicate with dogs. Once you buy a crate and peers and professionals you trust reassure you that it's a good thing to use it, it's easy to start crating constantly whenever you're busy and don't want to deal with your dog. Suddenly the crate becomes the go-to solution. If the dog barks, crate him. If guests are coming, crate him. If you don't want to be disturbed talking on the phone, crate him.

We've visited lovely homes owned by our training customers where there's no sign of a dog in any of the vast common areas. This is because the dog or puppy sits in a crate behind closed doors in a stuffy utility room, garage or sun porch where it's all too easy for the family to forget him, even on weekends!

These owners are not monsters. Instead, they may be the family next door, who feel they truly love their dog and want the best. When we explain to customers why we're against crating dogs, many confess they had reservations about it also. They tell us their initial instinct was that locking an intelligent being in a cage for "training" was cruel, but they took the word of a friend, neighbor or professional who pressured them to do it and then it simply became habit.

Your dog CAN live in your home as a polite and productive member of the family and very many families achieve this without crating. After reading this book, you know of the many ways a dog can help his owner- from carrying the groceries to protecting the home if an armed intruder breaks in. The key is to train your dog with consistency from a young age and always give him positive and productive activities to do. A well trained dog by your side for all the years of his life can bring you a thousand times more joy than he could have if you left him locked up in a box!

Bella Says, "Dogs Hate Crates, Shouldn't You!"

Resources

Dog Breed Information: AKC.org or dogbreedinfo.com
Pet Waste Removal Products and Companies: find one in your area at pooper-scooper.com/scoopers.html
Service Dog Training: sdog.danawheels.net, deltasociety.org
Hydotherapy: find info at ahealthyme.com/topic/doghypotherapy
Agility Equipment Find at dogagilityusa.com
Doggie Backpack: check out futurepets.com backpacks for dogs under 10lb up to 250lb
Doggie Stairs: find at petedge.com or local pet sore
Tellington Touch Massage: tellingtontouch.com
Water Rescue Dummy: find at dummiesunlimited.com
Agility Clubs, Obedience Clubs, Rally Clubs look at local training clubs or AKC.org
Canine Good Citizen: look on amazon.com for books or AKC.org for information
Freestyle: worldcaninefreestyle.org
Skyhoundz: skyhound.com
Continuous Pools: endlesspools.com
Custom Pools: dogpools.com
Dog Treadmills look at petedge.com or pawwws.com
Automatic Ball Launcher: Find one at buygodoggo.com
Dog Lifejacket at doglifejacket.com
Interactive Toys (Buster Cube, Tug a Jug, Talking Toys): petedge.com
Wacky Walk'r: wackywalk'r.com
Pet Poison Control Hotline: 888-323-8870
Poisonous Plant Info: dogpatch.org/doginfo/plants.html

Books: Many books on dog topics can be found at dogwise.com or amazon.com
Books we believe may be helpful include:
Meditation: James Jacobson- *How to Meditate with Your Dog*
Massage: see Massagethedog.com to order
First Aid: Cynthia Copeland- *Complete Book of First Aid for Dogs*
Fears, Desensitization & Related Products: Nicole Wilde- *Help for Your Fearful Dog*
Therapy Dog Training: Kathy Diamond Davis- *Therapy Dogs*
Agility: Margaret H. Bonham- *Introduction to Dog Agility*

Index of Activities

About the Authors:

Ray and Emma Lincoln, husband and wife, and owners of Awesome Dog Professional Training based in Southeast Florida, specialize in canine psychology and helping dogs with complex problems in families' homes. Philosophically Ray and Emma champion the healthy dog/owner bond, which may be our last real link with nature in our modern world. Emma has written for newspapers and magazines and has completed several novels of Florida suspense. Ray's specialties include animal behaviorism, Eastern philosophy and fine art photography. Ray and Emma travel extensively, exploring unique beaches and rural communities, and they've loved nature and animals all their lives. They were compelled to start their own dog training business after discovering widespread misinformation and victimization of dogs and their human families by the dog industry. Even as the industry exploded, many families couldn't find science-based diagnosis or careful and compassionate behavioral treatment for their dogs in trouble. So Awesome Dog began specializing in highly involved cases including fears and lifelong emotional damage. Ray & Emma enjoy helping dogs one-on-one, and their larger mission is to empower dog owners on a societal level through their books and presentations.

****

Awesome Dog travels the Southeast to present dog behavior seminars for private groups, pet professionals and community policy-makers. Topics include training, husbandry, choosing the right dog and bite-prevention. Or we can create a customized seminar, DVD or audiotape for your needs or travel to homes where our particular services are needed.

Make life better for dogs! Through our experience, the authors believe excessive crating, including home crating, is THE single biggest abuse destroying quality of life for dogs and their families today, despite effective alternatives. No matter where you live, feel free to call the authors at Awesome Dog Professional Training. We will provide general advice free to any dog owner, professional or policy-maker sincere about releasing dogs from cages!

Also look for our next book, a shocking science-based expose on the damage caused by excessive crating. Please follow our website awesomedogtraining.com or awesomedogtraining.net for release date and ordering information.

Order a copy of Awesome Dog Professional Training's books for a friend.

Ways to order: Use the form below, buy at Amazon.com or order by credit card at awesomedogtraining.com. Check our website for news on new books or if you ever need Awesome Dog's help in your home.

Mail form to: Awesome Dog, P.O. Box 1157, Roseland, FL 32957

The Cure for Useless Dog Syndrome: Activities/Games/Learning for Every Dog, Every Owner, Every Day $20.00

#copies   price   total

*The Cure*_____/ _____/ _____.

Subtotal _____.
Tax adds 6% in FL_____.
S/H add $3.99 per item _____.
Total _____.

Name
Address   **Email**
City, State, Zip
We will need email to send confirmation of shipment of order.
Payment options: Enclose your check or you can charge on a credit card through PayPal at awesomedogtraining.com.

Order a copy of Awesome Dog Professional Training's books for a friend.

Ways to order: Use the form below; buy at Amazon.com or order by credit card at awesomedogtraining.com. Check our website for news on new books or if you ever need Awesome Dog's help in your home.

Mail form to: Awesome Dog, P.O. Box 1157, Roseland, FL 32957

The Cure for Useless Dog Syndrome: Activities/Games/Learning for Every Dog, Every Owner, Every Day $20.00

#copies   price   total

*The Cure*_____/ _____/ _____.

Subtotal _____.
Tax adds 6% in FL_____.
S/H add $3.99 per item _____.
Total _____.

Name
Address   **Email**
City, State, Zip
We will need email to send confirmation of shipment of order.
Payment options: Enclose your check or you can charge on a credit card through PayPal at awesomedogtraining.com

CPSIA information can be obtained at www.ICGtesting.com
Printed in the USA
LVOW11s0510240713

344261LV00006B/131/P